SPEED CAPITAL

SPORT AND SOCIETY

Series Editors
Aram Goudsouzian
Jaime Schultz

Founding Editors
Benjamin G. Rader
Randy Roberts

A list of books in the series appears at the end of this book.

SPEED CAPITAL

INDIANAPOLIS AUTO RACING
AND THE
MAKING OF MODERN AMERICA

BRIAN M. INGRASSIA

UNIVERSITY OF
ILLINOIS PRESS
Urbana, Chicago, and Springfield

Parts of chapter 5 previously appeared in Brian M.
Ingrassia, "A 'Splendid Flying Field' in Indianapolis:
Aviation and Speedway Spectacles in the Great War
Era," *Middle West Review* 8, no. 1 (Fall 2021): 109–32.

Library of Congress Cataloging-in-Publication Data
Names: Ingrassia, Brian M., author.
Title: Speed capital : Indianapolis auto racing and the
    making of modern America / Brian M. Ingrassia.
Description: Urbana : University of Illinois Press,
    2024. | Series: Sport and society | Includes
    bibliographical references and index.
Identifiers: LCCN 2023029699 (print) | LCCN
    2023029700 (ebook) | ISBN 9780252045554
    (cloth) | ISBN 9780252087660 (paperback) |
    ISBN 9780252055218 (ebook)
Subjects: LCSH: Indianapolis Motor Speedway
    (Speedway, Ind.)—History. | Fisher, Carl G. (Carl
    Graham), 1874–1939. | Automobile racing—
    Indiana—Indianapolis—History.
Classification: LCC GV1033.5.I55 I54 2024 (print) | LCC
    GV1033.5.I55 (ebook) | DDC 796.7209772/52—dc23/
    eng/20230721
LC record available at https://lccn.loc.gov/2023029699
LC ebook record available at https://lccn.loc.gov/
    2023029700

Dedicated to the memory of
Kathryn J. Oberdeck (1958–2022)
Scholar, teacher, and mentor

CONTENTS

ACKNOWLEDGMENTS

It seems ironic that a book about annihilation of space and time took so much of both to complete. I would like to thank some folks who helped me along the way, from the first time I saw the Indianapolis Motor Speedway in person to this project's completion years later.

Much of the work for this book was done at West Texas A&M University, where I am fortunate to be surrounded by dedicated colleagues: I thank Chelsea Ball, Tim Bowman, Bruce Brasington, Elizabeth Clark, Paul Clark, Courtney Crowley, Kris Drumheller, Marty Kuhlman, Byron Pearson, Matt Reardon, Wade Shaffer, Jean Stuntz, and Bryan Vizzini. I also thank our students, especially members of urban history graduate seminar: Katey Denney, Patrick Diepen, Eliana Flores, Edie Heuss, Kirbi Kelley-Diaz, and Jose Martinez. The many folks at West Texas, past and present, who enjoy discussing culture and its meanings include Daniel Bloom, Ryan Brooks, David Craig, Deana Craighead, Renea Dauntes, Tim Foster, Nick Gerlich, Matthew and Ana Harrison, Daniel Helbert, Kimberly Hieb, Alex Hunt, Jenny Inzerillo, Eric Meljac, Laura Mueller, Jenni Opalinski, John Pleming, Bonnie Roos, Steve Severn, the late Charles Townsend, and Amy Von Lintel. Ashley Pinkham once asked me why I was writing about her hometown, and I hope this book answers that question; I thank her for her support and friendship. Institutional funding for research was provided by a West Texas Foundation grant and a Faculty Development and Scholarly/Creative

Activities (FDSCA) grant from Sybil B. Harrington College of Fine Arts and Humanities (FAH); I thank Jessica Mallard for her leadership of FAH.

Before coming to West Texas in 2015, I spent seven years in non-tenure-track positions at Georgia State and Middle Tennessee State Universities, where I began writing this book. I thank MTSU colleagues and friends, especially Jeremy Aber, Andrew Baker, Emily Baran, James Beeby, Clay Cooper, Michael Fletcher, Derek Frisby, the late Louis Haas, Amy Harris-Aber, Mary Hoffschwelle, Rebekka King, Tim Langille, Aliou Ly, Kris McCusker, Becky McIntyre, Susan Myers-Shirk, Mike Paulauskas, Ashley Riley Sousa, Suzanne Sutherland, and Van West. Jeremy Aber was kind enough to make the excellent maps for this book. Michael Fletcher helped with my move to Amarillo in 2015, and he continues to be a great friend—as well as a fine historic preservationist and rock-and-roll drummer. At GSU, where I did some of the early research, colleagues included Casey Cater, Robin Conner, Alex Sayf Cummings, Larry Grubbs, Scott Matthews, Mike O'Connor, David Sehat, Lauren MacIvor Thompson, Wendy Hamand Venet, Kate Wilson, and Larry Youngs, as well as the late Denis Gainty and Cliff Kuhn. I thank Larry Grubbs for hosting me on my visits to Atlanta and for always asking incisive questions.

In Champaign, Illinois, where this project spent its first few months, I had a wonderful group of friends whom I cannot thank enough for making graduate school a pleasure. They include Will Cooley, Paul Droubie, Dave Hageman, Steve Hageman, Debbie Hughes, Mike and Kate Pedrotty, Karen Phoenix, Paul Ruth, Beth Savage, Greg and Miha Wood, and Kerry Wynn. I especially thank Matt Jennings (and Susan and the boys) and Jason Tebbe (and Lori Perez and the girls) for their close friendship and for always making me welcome in their homes in Georgia and New Jersey—homes filled with love and music and great conversations about history.

Frank Bellizzi, Bonnie Roos, and Jason Tebbe read and commented on early drafts of the manuscript. Thank you. I also thank the University of Illinois Press, especially editors Danny Nasset, Tad Ringo, and Mariah Mendes Schaefer, series editors Aram Goudsouzian and Jaime Schultz, and reviewers David Lucsko and Michael Fein, who provided helpful comments and suggestions.

Librarians, archivists, and museum professionals are essential for the historical enterprise. I thank the staffs of libraries at West Texas A&M, MTSU, GSU, and the University of Illinois, especially Steve Ely, Laura Marshall, and Carolyn Ottoson at WTAMU. I also thank the staff of the HistoryMiami Research Center, especially Dawn Hugh and Jeremy Salloum, as well as the staff of the Indiana Historical Society, especially Regan Steimel. At the Indianapolis Motor Speedway Museum, Roxie Dunbar and Jason Vansickle shared their extensive knowledge of Carl Fisher and the track. At the speedway itself, Joe Skibinski cheerfully provided access to the Indianapolis Motor Speedway Photo Archive. My cousin Donald Barclay, library scholar extraordinaire, provided some essential last-minute tips.

Many scholars offered input that made this book better. There are too many wonderful folks at the North American Society for Sport History (NASSH) to name here, but I will mention Zach Bigalke, Jen Guiliano, Dan Nathan, PearlAnn Reichwein, Steve Riess, Maureen Smith, and Bob Trumpbour, who provided helpful feedback on pieces about Indianapolis. A 2021 NASSH workshop on sport and intellectual history helped fine-tune some ideas; special thanks to Amira Rose Davis, Mark Dyreson, Robert Greene, Andrew McGregor, Natalia Mehlman Petrzela, Seth Tannenbaum, Samantha White, and Michael Wood. Scholars in the Midwestern History Association, including Justin Clark, Jon Lauck, and Jeff Wells, also provided helpful feedback. Likewise, I thank members of the Society for US Intellectual History (S-USIH), especially Lora Burnett, Janine Giordano Drake, Ray Haberski, Andrew Hartman, Tim Lacy, Paul Murphy, and Andrea Turpin. The Society for Historians of the Gilded Age and Progressive Era (SHGAPE) provides an excellent home for early-1900s US history; Alan Lessoff, in particular, offered feedback and encouragement throughout this project's long lifespan. I also thank Greg and Miha Wood and the fine folks at Frostburg State University in Maryland for hosting me for a talk in 2022; it was a wonderful visit and gave me a new perspective on this story.

The longer I work as a historian, the more I realize the importance of the teachers who make what we do possible. At the University of Illinois, Kathy Oberdeck trained me to think critically about culture and its relationship with the built environment, and I was so looking forward to her being able to read this book, which I started researching before defending my dissertation in 2008. But, just as the manuscript was submitted in 2022, Kathy announced she was terminally ill and passed away not long afterward. Cancer sucks. I am still grappling with that loss, as are all of us who benefited from Kathy's knowledge, wisdom, and humanity. This book is dedicated to her. An incomplete list of excellent teachers at Illinois who influenced this project would also include Jim Barrett, Adrian Burgos, Antoinette Burton, Max Edelson, Kristin Hoganson, Fred Hoxie, Mark Micale, and Dave Roediger. My US history professor and mentor at Eureka College, Junius Rodriguez, can take a great deal of credit for inspiring me to think about history's geographical contexts. Loren Logsdon, a beloved Eureka College English professor and noted scholar of the Midwest, succumbed to COVID in 2020; I think he would have enjoyed this story of Indianapolis.

New friends and acquaintances accrue during a long project, but so do losses. Since I began work on this book, I lost my father, Marty Ingrassia, and several aunts and uncles: Lucy Ingrassia, Wally Ranney, Marianne Clinch, Mary Barclay, and Larry Buchanan. In 2018, we lost the legendarily funny and creative Jeremy Loberg, a high school friend and onetime fixture of Peoria's punk scene. I miss these folks dearly. My first trip to the speedway in 2002 was courtesy of the late Ralph and Linda Griffith; I thank Linsey Griffith and Ken Doughman for continuing to welcome me into their home, whenever I am traveling for research or just stopping by. Similarly, Torrie and Chris Buchanan hosted me during a conference trip to Springfield in 2016. As usual, I am delighted to thank my extended family, but especially my mother, Betty Ingrassia, and my brother, Mark Ingrassia, who have always supported my desire to be a historian and read and write books and travel to (and live in) places maybe just a little too far from central Illinois. And finally, I thank Jenni Opalinski, who lent her keen aesthetic sense and creativity while I was rounding up the illustrations and, importantly, provided much inspiration.

INTRODUCTION
BRICK DESCRIPTION
Speedway as Cultural Text

On August 19, 1909, the *Chicago Tribune* reported the impending opening of a racetrack on the edge of Indiana's capital city. "Tonight the largest and most representative field of space-annihilating racing machines ever brought together in a single carnival of speed is, figuratively speaking, panting and puffing, eager to start in the grim contest with Father Time at noon tomorrow." Describing the setting for this epic showdown between modern machines, space, and time, the writer called the 2.5-mile speedway a "marvel" and agreed with those who billed it as the "greatest race course in the world."[1] The big motor sport facility was not yet paved with brick—that was still a couple months away—and the first 500-mile sweepstakes race would not be run until nearly two years later. Yet readers in Chicago and other cities were already aware of something revolutionary happening in Indianapolis. The track, built by a group of enthusiasts led by auto-parts mogul Carl Graham Fisher, promised to demonstrate modern technologies that annihilated space and battled time in an entertaining manner. The new motor-sport venue was a model for transportation innovation that also provided a veritable speed carnival in an era when Americans were learning how to consume a stunning array of popular amusements.

As it turned out, the speedway was deadly. Although the first events held there in June 1909 were relatively sedate balloon contests, the inaugural races in August were another story, as several racers died in one notorious

Program for August 20, 1909, races at the new Indianapolis Motor Speedway. (IMS Photo Archive)

weekend. Despite the carnage, Fisher and his colleagues soldiered on, reportedly spending another $180,000 to pave the speedway with more than three million vitrified bricks. If they were in for millions of pennies, they were in for millions of pounds of paving blocks. Fatalities declined yet never quite went away. The 1933 race, in fact, was among the deadliest, and thirty-nine total had died there by 1940. Nevertheless, the track was quickly cemented in popular lore as a place for fast cars and big crowds. The massive brick oval was a site for all manner of risk-taking: gambling on speed and economic growth, as well as on the ability of the (white, male) human body and mind to pilot ever-faster vehicles.

Auto racing emerged at a time when the United States was an industrializing and urbanizing society where *here* and *there* could be farther apart yet had to be closer together. Motor sport reflected transformations in spatial and temporal relations, a cultural ritual where men made visible the promises of technology and infrastructure, testing their own ability to withstand the liberating yet deadly implications of modernity. A primary site for this activity was Indianapolis, a city that seemed to be every place or no place, depending on one's perspective. The metropolis was founded in the early 1800s on unnavigable water, and so Hoosiers[2] sought novel infrastructures to connect their capital to places far from Indiana's glaciated plains. The same transportation technologies that carried grain or manufactured goods, though, also moved tourists or sports fans and even provided entertainment. This was the context in which Carl Fisher, with James Allison, Arthur Newby, and Frank Wheeler, built a tar-and-gravel speedway in spring 1909 before paving it with brick later that year. Although most accounts portray the oval's first events, the aforementioned balloon contests, as publicity stunts, they are more accurately viewed as spectacles demonstrating space-eliding technologies.[3] Auto races were not the only attraction, but speed was more legible in two dimensions than in three, and so contests between wheels ultimately became more easily commodified than those between wings.

The Brickyard, a trademarked name derived from a once-state-of-the-art pavement, is a key site for understanding complex relationships between technology, mobility, and popular culture. To examine these relationships, we may look to anthropologist Clifford Geertz. Using a method called "thick description," Geertz showed how men in mid-1900s Bali asserted community loyalties through cockfights, betting on trained roosters, fluffing their feathers to coax a few more moments out of surrogate combatants. Speaking of the Balinese cockfight, Geertz said that "societies, like lives, contain their own interpretations," which are discerned by analyzing cultural rituals' layered meanings.[4] One might playfully style a study of racing as *brick description*, a way to explore the contexts of a track where men in fast cars tried to outdo each other and, in the process, gained fame or died or—perhaps worst of all—faded into obscurity. After all, races were never just about drivers or cars. They were about the bricks that paved racing ovals and city streets. They were about consumers who studied maps in newspapers, seeking routes from Chicago (or New York or Omaha or Terre Haute) to Indianapolis for Memorial Day races—and then watched cars speed at nearly unthinkable velocities on a properly paved surface. Readers learned about good roads in the same columns where they were reminded to buy tickets for upcoming races. People remade relationships to modern space in spectacular ways, and, as urban space expanded, motor technology helped them circumvent natural disasters or labor strikes. All the while, though with decreasing frequency, aviation continued to be part of the show, a vestigial history still visible in the track's winged-tire logo. The speedway was a place where people learned to be comfortable with, even entertained by, the rise of what geographers call "machine space."[5] The famous oval represented advances in mobility, as well as changes in how Americans spent their spare time. Progress and popular culture intertwined.

As auto racing emerged, cities retooled for automobility. Although the City Beautiful movement remade urban centers for aesthetics and public spirit, by 1910, not long after Henry Ford introduced his famous Model T, planners shifted to the City Practical. Municipalities paved streets, elevated rails, and sprawled into former hinterlands. In Indianapolis, a city originally platted as a government center with radial arteries extending from its center, people with cars transformed the countryside into suburbia. In 1912, Carl Fisher even established the auto-themed suburb of Speedway City in Indiana before initiating the east-west Lincoln Highway and north-south Dixie Highway. Near its southern terminus, the Dixie Highway entered Miami, where, after 1913, Fisher built the seaside resort of Miami Beach. This town, located on a former mangrove-choked sandbar, focused on comfortable living—at least for well-off white Americans, including transplants from the Midwest. Along the way, novel ideas about speed, space, time, distance, work, and leisure were paved in brick, poured in concrete, and

Carl Fisher's transportation empire: United States map with Lincoln and Dixie Highways and selected cities. (Jeremy Aber, Middle Tennessee State University)

written indelibly on urban and rural landscapes. Fisher was an industrialist, pop-culture impresario, real-estate mogul, and welfare capitalist who may have had as great an impact on spatial mobility as Henry Ford. But if Ford constructed a vertically integrated *production* empire, Fisher built a vertically integrated *consumption* empire. By the time he sold the speedway to World War I flying ace Eddie Rickenbacker in 1927, Fisher was building the elite development on Long Island that would bankrupt him. He had moved beyond racing, but not the ideas it represented. Fisher annihilated space so that he and other men could redevelop it in tune with modern desires. Later track owners transformed the Indianapolis Motor Speedway from an obsolescent place for demonstrating spectacular infrastructure advances into a site of nostalgia and cultural commodification, thus anticipating a late-twentieth-century economy based more on consumption than on production.[6]

Fisher, Ford, and other auto moguls created "a technological ecosystem, an intricate set of interconnected inventions, institutions, and behaviors" that "defined the American way of life."[7] These men who made motor sport rarely left a substantial body of writing reflecting sustained thought, yet they might be seen as *organic intellectuals*, everyday thinkers who work "to sustain a conception of the world or to modify it" and thus "bring into being new modes of thought." By reading speedways as cultural texts, scholars can flesh out the motives of those who used technologies of mobility and public assembly to create commodified transportation spectacles that fit modern America's expanding urban fabric while also making automobility's potential legible to a multitude of paying spectators. At the most funda- mental level, this is a story of how capital shaped American life. Karl Marx once argued that capitalism is based on intertwined processes of produc- tion, distribution, and consumption, of which annihilation of space is a key component. To make profits and build economies of scale, capitalists broke down spatial and temporal boundaries. Racing was the process by which space annihilation was commodified and transformed into an exchange value suitable for an emerging pop-culture marketplace.[8]

If space, as philosopher Henri Lefebvre argued, is a social construct, then speedway racing was a site for cultural production and reproduction of modern space and time, where a significant but not inclusive cross sec- tion of early-twentieth-century Americans witnessed the possibilities of hard pavement and fast cars. Speedways hosted public gatherings in which spectators paid to view progress in technologies of mobility that offered the potential to commodify an even wider array of pastimes. Americans enjoyed car-focused sport while they also learned to drive to suburban sporting facilities. Indianapolis auto racing quickly became a commercial spectacle, but by the 1930s its significance began narrowing into nostalgia for its own legendary story. In the era of Eddie Rickenbacker and Tony Hul- man, the Indianapolis Motor Speedway became a site for invented traditions immortalizing a brick oval as an iconic place.[9] While the pre–World War I track focused on elision of *geographic* space, the postwar track increasingly stressed elision of *temporal* space, doing so by bringing people closer to imagined sporting pasts.

Racing was not an elite sport limited to the wealthy, but it was accessible mainly to middle- or upper-class spectators who could afford a ticket and transportation to what was then a suburban speedway. Indianapolis resi- dents might ride a streetcar to the oval, but many of the tens of thousands of spectators who filled the grandstands on race day had to have the means to drive and park a private automobile and locate safe lodging along the way. Mobility was essential for spectatorship as well as participation. Not surprisingly, the sport was limited to white men. Around 1910, racers drew a color line barring African American drivers such as Jack Johnson, who wanted to race at the speedway but was excluded because of his skin color. Carl Fisher may have wanted Johnson because of the boxer's marketing potential, but other drivers worked to maintain racing as a white man's job. In later years, talented Black drivers like Indiana's Charlie Wiggins never got the chance to race. Motor sport's color line resembled those drawn earlier in horse racing and baseball, and later in pro football. In fact, the first African American to qualify for the Indy 500 was Willy T. Ribbs in 1991, a full eighty years after the first 500-mile race. Sport's exclusion of nonwhite racers was emblematic of the segregation of American life. Indeed, Fisher and other developers were equally adept at creating racially exclusive suburban spaces, especially subdivisions with restrictive covenants designed to keep out people of color.

Although gender was rarely discussed openly in early racing, masculinity looms over this narrative like a cloud of toxic exhaust fumes. Scholar Steve Marston argues that early racers and writers coded racing as masculine.[10] In fact, observers frequently proclaimed motor sport was limited to those with strength, stamina, and "nerve"—a combination of "brain and brawn."[11] The sport was physically demanding, but it was also mentally draining, and when women tried to compete they were denied, supposedly because they had neither the proper physique nor enough mental control. No woman qualified for a 500-mile race until Janet Guthrie in 1977, and even then she faced taunts and jeers despite years of dues paying.[12] Women were excluded from racing, yet newspaper accounts increasingly recorded their presence as spectators or aspiring racers. As in cockfights, men gathered around a spectacle to boast of prowess in coaxing performance from machines, bolstering their own egos and moneymaking potential in the process. Even when racing men died in the races, apologists portrayed the tragedies as rituals necessary for progress in developing modern technologies of transportation, paternalism, and nationalism.

By understanding racing as a central node of Carl Fisher's automotive empire, scholars can better perceive sport's importance within the modern built environment. Of course, one may debate whether auto racing is properly considered sport, yet the historical record clearly shows that people in the past saw it as a type of sport or game. Indeed, while we often associate the word *sport* with athletics, the term itself once denoted men's (illicit) pastimes, especially those on which they gambled. In short, scholars should take motor sport seriously: five hundred miles might be seen as a unit of achievement akin to four quarters, nine innings, or 26.2 miles, and companies like Marmon or Stutz—or Chevrolet and Honda, to use more recent examples—were sporting brands akin to Spalding or Nike. Historian Rayvon Fouché argues that a *technoscientific* revolution has changed sport in recent years, as state-of-the-art equipment became essential for many athletic activities. Racing, in fact, may be the quintessential technoscientific sport, in which achievement is based on technology as much as on physique. Racing places stressful demands on the human body and nervous system, and the idea that it was not real sport was not broached until the 1930s, at a time when racing had become so deadly that observers justified it as a practical activity for developing motor technologies. In general, though, racing is sport because it is a type of unscripted drama, lacking predetermined outcomes, carried out by skilled bodies within parameters (rules) allowing individuals to profit from the unpredictability of the final result.[13]

It is difficult to prove or disprove whether Indianapolis's speedway was built as a place to test and develop automotive technology, yet we can see that Carl Fisher and his compatriots saw racing as sensational spectacle. Indeed, Fisher explicitly stated in 1906 that he desired to build a track where drivers could develop racecars—not standard passenger cars. Claims that the track was a scientific laboratory and that deadly races were necessary for progress seem like post hoc justifications, even though the track and its famous races did have the effect of developing and popularizing innovative automotive and paving technologies. Like later hot-rod enthusiasts who built racing machines able to perform at high speeds on roads or rural drag strips, early-twentieth-century racers blended technological innovation with sensational enjoyment. Speedway impresarios and drivers crafted a pop-culture spectacle that, in turn, shaped modern mobility.[14]

Racing's early years represent a story of the turn-of-the-century Progressive Era, a time when Americans, inspired by overseas influences, banded together to craft and implement reforms that might solve problems stemming from urbanization and industrialization. Reformers even tried to eliminate corruption from consumer goods, including spectator sports.[15] Others reshaped the urban fabric by promoting modes of transportation for traversing cities and the rural spaces between. Speedways existed in a liminal space where infrastructure improvements met pop-culture spectacle.

As Indianapolis developed into a regional metropolis, racing impresarios used the Hoosier State's simultaneously central and peripheral location to transform it into a site for profitable cultural spectacle. The city became America's motor-sports center in part because many people drove from other cities, especially Chicago and Detroit, to consume races. But over time, the lower Great Lakes region went from being an industrial pioneer to a place ossified in its manufacturing role. In this context, it is no surprise that a fabled speedway in Indiana eventually became a site for nostalgia as much as for technological innovation.[16]

The automobile is a paradoxical Progressive Era technology: cars improved individual mobility and tied the nation together, but they also helped weaken a progressive public spirit.[17] Autos undermined powerful railroads and the traction companies that operated streetcars, yet also could limit the impact of organized labor and the progressive reforms that prioritized free public spaces over commodified ones. Some people thought cars might allow each (white) man to live like a king on a quasi-rural estate on the edge of town where he and his family could breathe fresh air, but these machines also ended up causing pollution and diffusing residential and commercial space. Fossil-fueled vehicles allowed people, residences, and businesses to spread farther from city centers than ever before. Cars took up space, and the more space they took up, the farther outward they pushed machine-centered settlement. Because motor vehicles needed streets, highways, parking lots, and garages, they themselves became agents of spatial change. While cars may have been a way to escape railroads' dominance, they also led to a new kind of path dependency.

Scholars of automobility, the complex relationship between people and cars, note modern society's ambivalence toward automobiles; they also show just how greatly modern society is based on spatial institutions created by motor vehicles. To quote historian Christopher Wells, the United States is a "car country," with an environment inextricably based on autos and related infrastructure. Engineers, politicians, and businessmen covered a significant portion of the nation with asphalt or concrete, transformed public spaces into vehicular thoroughfares, and in turn built the modern state. A generation of excellent research on cars and the good roads movement, however, has done little to show connections between popular culture and spatial reform. In fact, we now know that some highway proponents saw races as a way to promote better roads. Without roads, few spectators could have traveled to Indianapolis by car, and without races, it may have been harder for them to learn about the possibilities of good roads.[18]

Indianapolis created motor spectacle at the same time that its residents transformed their city into an automotive metropolis. While scholars often invoke *autopia*, a near-utopian (or perhaps dystopian) society built on car-friendly structures, that term is limiting. After all, "Autopia" originated in the 1950s as the name of an attraction at Disneyland.[19] To fully understand automobility, scholars should refocus attention on the nation's industrial core. In doing so, we might find the origins of auto addictions not in California's autopia but in Indiana's speedway city—the world's speed capital. Sometimes called the Circle City, after a central loop where streetcars once converged, Indianapolis is now better known for an oval track on its edge, a sports venue that bestowed its name on the suburban enclave where it is located. What better place to understand how Americans learned to embrace cars and automotive dependency?

Scholars have examined Carl Fisher's role as a builder of transcontinental highways and leisure spaces, even exploring the speedway as a place representing changes in the built environment.[20] Yet historians too often ignore Indianapolis in favor of its big-shoulders cousin Chicago, hard-luck neighbor Detroit, or touristy offspring Miami. By contrast, this book reads over the shoulders of early-twentieth-century Americans to construct a detailed yet critical narrative of Indianapolis auto racing while also exploring the era's motor mentalities. It echoes scholarly arguments about sport's role in shaping urban space and making modern cities legible.[21] This study provides a template for understanding motor sport, yet it is not a definitive history of racing; scholars need additional analysis of drivers, tracks, owners, and fans. After all, speedways in Atlanta, Chicago, Los Angeles, and other cities were part of the built environment or, in some cases, the "unbuilt environment": places imagined yet never actually constructed.[22]

Nine chronological chapters highlight aspects of speedway history, using Indianapolis and its famous races to illustrate how Americans embraced car culture. Chapter 1 shows how nineteenth-century Indiana built canals, roads, and rails to become a seemingly central place eventually known as the "Crossroads of America." Chapter 2 analyzes early events held at the speedway, including aviation contests, illustrating the many ways modern machines could annihilate space. Chapter 3 shows how early 500-mile races—so-called speed carnivals—entertained crowds while exhibiting possibilities of motors and pavement. Chapter 4 examines the peak of the Progressive Era, when cities reconfigured themselves for cars and pioneered the automotive metropolis. Chapter 5 analyzes the Hoosier speedway's role in World War I, when it returned to its role as a site for aerial experimentation and Fisher imagined it as the center of a national aviation network. Chapter 6 shows how media turned racing into an essential, even legendary, part of the so-called Golden Age of Sports at the same time Fisher worked to make Miami Beach into America's tropical playground. Chapter 7 details how Detroit auto executive and World War I flying ace Eddie Rickenbacker bought the facility and perhaps saved it from demolition in 1927, but then doubled down on pop-culture spectacle in an era when the track's practical utility for exhibiting space annihilation waned. Chapter 8 examines the oval's struggles to survive the Depression, when the speedway invented new traditions and assumed legendary status. Chapter 9, which doubles as an epilogue, shows how the speedway fell into disrepair during World War II and was nearly bulldozed. Instead, Terre Haute businessman Tony Hulman bought the oval at the urging of Wilbur Shaw, three-time winner of the 500-mile race, and completed the facility's transformation into a global icon and site of lucrative sport nostalgia.

Racing, once a so-called Sport of Titans, is a modern spectacle based on technologies that allowed humans to pilot (to use an early-twentieth-century term) machines at seemingly superhuman speeds. Drivers compressed journeys normally consuming massive amounts of time and space into an enclosed track hosting races witnessed by multitudes of paying spectators, many of whom had driven there using a version of the technology on display. Like vaudeville, motor sport effectively "offered modernity as a commodity."[23] Indy-style auto racing is a relic of a time when auto tycoons roamed the earth and some invested fortunes in a spectacle demonstrating the potential of motor vehicles, paved roads, and suburban real estate, helping to reinvent spatial and temporal relations. For a transformative figure such as Carl Fisher—who combined aspects of P. T. Barnum and Henry Ford in a persistent quest for entertainment and consumption—the modern ritual of auto racing connected city dwellers to far-off areas and taught them how to leave former times, places, and mindsets behind forever.[24] We now turn to the oval's nineteenth-century prehistory, an era vastly different yet strangely similar to our own.

1

CROSSROADS OF AMERICA

Inventing Indianapolis

Since 1909, the Indianapolis Motor Speedway has loomed large on the edge of the capital city of a state proclaiming itself as the "Crossroads of America." The Indiana legislature formally adopted this motto in 1937,[1] one year after the speedway's banked turns were rebuilt, the Borg-Warner Trophy debuted, and the 500-mile champion first drank milk in victory lane. In the twenty-first century, the slogan is emblazoned on highway signs and a 2002 commemorative quarter-dollar (which of course features a race car). It is no surprise that a self-proclaimed central transportation hub also hosts the world's most famous motor race. To know the story of how Indiana became America's purported crossroads is to know speedway racing and its history. In the century preceding the speedway's founding and the inauguration of its iconic races, Hoosiers sought infrastructures linking their capital city to the rest of the world and, in effect, paring the amount of time needed to reach other places. A landlocked city—virtually invented amid nineteenth-century attempts to move people, goods, and capital over spaces appropriated from indigenous peoples—subsequently transformed mobility into entertaining spectacle.

Initially, Indiana was a place where Shawnee, Miami, Delaware, Potawatomi, and other Native American groups lived. Within the context of US political history, the area began as part of the Northwest Territory, a region ceded by Great Britain in the 1783 Treaty of Paris. Before the US

Constitution was ratified, the Confederation Congress passed laws distinguishing the Northwest Territory from other western lands. The 1785 Land Ordinance initiated survey and sale of lands beyond the Ohio River, and a committee led by Thomas Jefferson thought the territory might be carved into as many as ten states with grandiloquent names like *Illinoia*, *Metropotamia*, and *Sylvania*. Those names were never realized, but Jefferson's vision foreshadowed the area's settlement. Surveyors carved lands into townships and 640-acre (one-square-mile) sections, or fractions thereof, for sale to settlers. Americans anticipated incredible future economic development within the region's lands. The 1787 Northwest Ordinance funded public education, introduced a mechanism by which territories could become states, and at least nominally outlawed slavery. The Northwest Ordinance also specified that the number of states carved from the territory would be between three and five, not Jefferson's ten. Ohio gained statehood early on, in 1803, most of the remaining land was renamed Indiana Territory, and eventually the region begat four additional states: Indiana (1816), Illinois (1818), Michigan (1837), and Wisconsin (1848). By the early 1900s, people in these relatively large, rural, and industrializing states would embrace automobility.[2]

Lines marching across the map belied the resistance of indigenous peoples as Native Americans tried to hold onto their lands. Settlers wrested the first chunk of present-day Indiana from Native Americans in the 1795 Treaty of Greenville, signed one year after the Battle of Fallen Timbers, which established southern Ohio and a sliver of present-day Indiana as a space for white settlement. Predictably, the government broke this treaty, so people continued moving north and west, seeking farmlands and river access. Territorial governor William Henry Harrison, a future US president, used trickery, alcohol, and violence to take millions of acres of present-day Indiana and Illinois. His efforts culminated in the 1811 Battle of Tippecanoe, fought near present-day Lafayette, Indiana, in which US forces overwhelmed those of Tenskwatawa, the Prophet, brother of Shawnee warrior Tecumseh. Harrison's victory did not immediately eliminate indigenous influence in the Wabash Valley, yet it did foreshadow Native American losses during the War of 1812, after which American empire continued moving westward, especially in frontier river cities such as Cincinnati, Louisville, and St. Louis.[3]

As native peoples were forced out, settlers from Kentucky, Virginia, and Ohio moved into the region now known as the Midwest. One person who took part in this migration was Carl Fisher's grandfather, Jacob Fisher, an

Crossroads of America: Indiana map with selected rivers, cities, and nineteenth-century roads. (Jeremy Aber, Middle Tennessee State University)

Ohio settler and 1812 veteran who worked as a land surveyor and then as a real-estate developer in Indiana. Such settlers, argues historian Nicole Etcheson, created a midwestern identity based on free-labor ideology and regional exceptionalism. Initially, administrative functions were housed in southern Indiana, with Vincennes, near the mouth of the White River, serving as the territorial capital. But in 1813 the capital moved to Corydon, near the Ohio River. By the time of statehood, Indiana's population center was still moving northward as newer migrants arrived and settled lands more recently taken from Native Americans.[4]

Many residents hoped to establish a government seat nearer Indiana's center, and Congress donated four square miles for the new capital. In 1820, a commission appointed by the Indiana General Assembly selected a site near the confluence of Fall Creek and the White River, located on what commissioner Joseph Bartholomew, a Tippecanoe veteran, called "high, dry, rich and well timbered" land with "durable streams for mills and other machinery." Bartholomew and his colleagues mistakenly believed the river was navigable there, and for the time being others remained similarly unaware. When the legislature named the new city Indianapolis, some scoffed. A Vincennes newspaper called the moniker "ridiculous"; it could not be found in any of the world's "libraries, museums, [or] patent-offices." The name was "like nothing in heaven nor on earth." It was "not a name for man, woman, or child; for empire, city, mountain or morass." The writer may have had an ax to grind, coming as he did from the spurned capital of Vincennes, yet he had a point: in both name and placement, Indianapolis seemed artificial. Transportation technologies and infrastructures would be necessary to connect this place to far-off points.[5]

Indianapolis's designer was Scottish-born Alexander Ralston, who worked with Pierre L'Enfant on the District of Columbia survey in the 1790s and was influenced by L'Enfant's design for Washington. Indiana asked Ralston to create a four-square-mile plan, but he doubted the city would grow that large, and so he limited his design to one 640-acre section. The resulting "Mile Square" featured a grid and radial arterials stretching outward, allowing future expansion. A central circle, originally designated for the governor's mansion, inspired the nickname "Circle City," and west of Circle Street lay a block reserved for the statehouse. About two hundred settlers quickly moved to the site and built cabins that disregarded Ralston's plan; some dwellings placed on planned streets later had to be removed to accommodate rational growth. Finally, in 1825, state government relocated to the new capital. Accounts said the road from Corydon to Indianapolis was nearly "impassable"—it took ten days to cover about one hundred sixty miles. Indianapolis was small, with fewer than eight hundred residents in 1826, but eventually it grew larger and became better known for the oval racetrack on its edge than the circular plaza at its center.[6]

Indianapolis's original "Mile Square," 1821, platted by Alexander Ralston, who also worked on Pierre L'Enfant's survey for the District of Columbia. Note Pogue's Run, southeast of downtown, which was later covered during the 1910s Progressive Era. (Indiana Historical Society)

Although centrally located, Indianapolis was a poor candidate for what geographers call a central place, a focal-point city for a regional system of settlements. Central-place theory dates from the 1930s, but the German geographer who created it based his ideas on the 1820s writings of Johann Heinrich von Thünen. Indianapolis's planners were surely unfamiliar with this thinker, yet they dealt with similar issues. In 1826, writes historian

William Cronon, von Thünen "imagined a completely isolated world" where "a single city sat in the midst of an endless and uniformly fertile plain," a site for concentric zones of economic activity radiating outward from commerce to agriculture to hunting, with real-estate and transportation costs being a key factor in land usage.[7] If Chicago used transportation and credit networks to become an urban center exploiting resources in outlying hinterlands, Indianapolis developed an intermediary role, serving as Indiana's metropolis while also existing at the periphery of other cities' hinterlands, especially those of Chicago, Cincinnati, Detroit, and Louisville. Soon, motorists traveled to spectacular races at a track built on former farmland, watching the same technology that brought them there.

In the 1830s, Hoosiers discovered that only shallow-draught flatboats could access their capital most of the year. They would either have to create artificial waterways or rely on overland transportation. Early routes included the National (Cumberland) Road, supporters of which included Kentucky's Henry Clay, later founder of the Whig Party and a promoter of internal improvements. Construction began in Cumberland, Maryland, in 1811, and five years later Congress appropriated $100,000 to extend it westward. The National Road's eastern portion reached Wheeling, (West) Virginia, before stretching into Ohio and Indiana. It was supposed to pass thirty miles south of Indianapolis, but Hoosiers convinced the federal government to route it through the new capital. Construction in Indianapolis began in the late 1820s, with all-white labor crews grading the roadway and building bridges. The road eventually extended to Illinois's capital city, Vandalia, although work halted as a result of the Panic of 1837. The route promoted mobility and commerce, linking Indiana towns from Richmond in the east to Terre Haute in the west. Hoosiers soon witnessed a stream of migrants heading westward.[8] The city also saw a wave of Germanic immigration around 1848, when settlers brought Friedrich Ludwig Jahn's Turner (gymnastics) movement and established *Turnvereine*, or Turner societies. Although Indiana's 1851 constitution barred African Americans, migrants developed a thriving Black community in Indianapolis centered on Indiana Avenue, which became a social and business hub, including Madam C. J. Walker's famous beauty products company.[9]

Indianapolis was a crossroads city, with an important north-south highway being the Michigan Road, stretching from the Ohio River to Lake Michigan. Construction began in the late 1820s after the Potawatomi ceded lands north of the Wabash. The road's northern terminus was Michigan City, at the mouth of Trail Creek, Indiana's largest tributary to the big lake. Despite surveyors' claims, Michigan City was not a good place for a port. It was built on sandy soil with dunes created by winds whipping off the lake. Because the water was shallow there, goods had to be unloaded from ships and taken ashore in smaller boats, and sand bars frequently blocked the harbor. Michigan City never realized promoters' dreams of opening Indiana to the Great Lakes, yet the Michigan Road did fuel growth of cities like Indianapolis and South Bend. By the 1870s, two of the speedway's founders would be born and raised in towns situated along the road.[10]

It was not long before canals seemed like landlocked cities' saviors, combining water transportation's low expense with roads' siting convenience. New York State started building the Erie Canal on July 4, 1817, with thousands of Dutch American and Irish American immigrant laborers working eight years to build a 363-mile canal from the Hudson River to Lake Erie. Though some dubbed it a folly, the Erie Canal was anything but; it realized enough revenue to pay for itself even before construction was complete. New Yorkers pitted artifice against nature, and artifice won—with profitable results. Commerce flowed over the canal while tourists used the artificial waterway to travel to far-off leisure spots such as Niagara Falls and Saratoga Springs. Soon, other Great Lakes states rushed to build similar waterways. A 308-mile canal connected Lake Erie to the Ohio, while a 96-mile canal connected Lake Michigan to the Illinois River. The Great Lakes region effectively became a hinterland of New York. Indiana was at a disadvantage, with fewer than sixty miles of sandy lakefront, yet Congress granted the state land for a canal between the Wabash and Maumee Rivers in 1824, and three years later it authorized a grant to subsidize the Wabash and Erie Canal, connecting the Great Lakes to the Ohio River.[11]

This mad dash for infrastructure had some devastating results for state finances. In 1836, Indiana passed the infamous Mammoth Internal Improvements Act, allowing it to borrow $10 million to finance internal improvements. Proposed projects included a network of canals crisscrossing the state, including an extension of the Wabash and Erie Canal that would link to the Central Canal at Indianapolis. The law also funded a planned railroad from Madison to Lafayette and a macadam (crushed and impacted rock) road from New Albany to Vincennes. But the Panic of 1837 plunged the state into insolvency, and work ground to a halt after 1839. None of the projects was ever finished, although partial segments of roads, railroads, and canals were completed—including a still-extant section of the Central Canal. But the state could not pay even the interest on its debt, let alone the principal, and so its credit plummeted in the far-off financial centers of New York and London. Indiana's capital remained on unnavigable water, with its residents awaiting new ways to annihilate space.[12]

Canals, it turned out, were a transitional technology, harbingers of steel rails and steam locomotives. As historian Carol Sheriff writes, "If the Erie Canal compressed distance and time, the railroads annihilated them, or so it appeared to the amazed observer." America's first railroads were built in the late 1820s, and people quickly realized rails would be canals' rivals, not their tributaries. Railroads were cheaper and easier to build and did not freeze, while locomotives were faster than canal boats, with a length not limited by locks or dams. On July 4, 1828—eleventh anniversary of the Erie Canal groundbreaking—construction began on the Baltimore and Ohio (B&O) Railroad. By 1830, trains provided entertaining jaunts for tourists, and although water transportation remained common for heavy freight, railroads siphoned away lighter freight and passengers.[13] As historian David Nye writes, "The slow unwinding view seen from a wagon or a horse was transformed into a sliding world that seemed to move by while the passenger sat immobile."[14] Hoosiers wanted connections. An Indianapolis newspaper said rail would give farmers a way to get produce to market, and it would also provide the nation with a "guarantee of perpetual union."[15] Internal improvements "promised not only to bind together divergent interests in the economic sphere, but also to draw distant geographic areas closer together."[16] They also later became a foundation for novel cultural spectacles.

Railroads grew quickly in places where flatness fostered locomotion, and they served as pathways reorienting global commodity exchange—especially the movement of grains from rural production sites to urban consumption sites. In 1840, America's rail mileage equaled its canal mileage, but by 1850 railroads outstripped canals, 8,879 miles to 3,698. Indiana possessed only twenty miles of track in 1840, but it had more than two hundred by 1850.[17] The Midwest was soon dotted with rail hubs, with the biggest being Chicago, established in the 1830s at a point between the Great Lakes and Mississippi watersheds. Railroads extended Chicago's hinterland, making it a gateway city linking the Great West to the Atlantic.

Indianapolis also received a boost, if a smaller one. When the Madison and Indianapolis Railroad linked the city to the Ohio River in 1847, the newly chartered municipality was transformed from a muddy town into a bustling city. According to a hyperbolic account in the *Indiana State Journal*, rails brought commerce to Indianapolis for the first time. Now, "the rattling of the cars and the whistle of the locomotive" would never subside. The city's population jumped from fewer than three thousand in 1840 to more than eight thousand in 1850. By the start of the Civil War, it was Indiana's biggest city, with more than eighteen thousand residents.[18] Railroad growth was impressive, but by the 1910s a different kind of track would make the growing Hoosier metropolis world-famous.

Indianapolis was well sited for roads and rails, perched as it was on level, mostly dry land between the hilly Ohio Valley and the glacial marshes near the Great Lakes. Like Chicago, Indiana's capital occupied an intermediary spot between watersheds, straddling the place where water drained either to the Ohio or to the Great Lakes. The Lower Midwest's dense rail network diverted trade to this central focal point, and, by the 1850s, boosters planned more routes, including railroads running to northern and southern Ohio and central Illinois. Although local residents bought railroad stock, much investment capital came from East Coast or European investors. Rails "brought new settlers, broke down rural isolation, transformed villages into cities, brought far-reaching changes in agriculture and everyday life, and hastened the beginnings of mining and industry." A rural state was now tied to national and international networks.[19]

Railroads changed temporal and spatial relationships. As scholar Wolfgang Schivelbusch writes, locomotives made it seem as though "space was both diminished *and* expanded." Reduction of time spent in transit elongated the amount of space reached in a given amount of time. Railroads connected outlying areas to cities, shrinking perceived distances along linear routes. In Chicago's case, rails linked city and countryside, enabling financiers and industrialists to transform grain, trees, and animals grown in far-off hinterlands into commodities. The concept of space being annihilated originated in Karl Marx's nineteenth-century theory of capital, yet the colorful term emerged independently in early-1900s newspaper coverage.[20] Railroads shrank time and space so that all points seemed closer to the Hoosier State's artificial metropole, which now seemed to grow nearer to Chicago, Detroit, and New York. By the 1910s, trains and cars would bring thousands of motor-sport spectators from these urban centers to Indianapolis.

Plank roads were another short-lived way to connect landlocked cities. Canada built North America's first timber roads in 1834, and New York State built the first US wooden turnpike twelve years later. Like the Erie Canal, this board highway sparked a craze, especially in areas with cheap lumber. Farmers saw plank roads as an inexpensive way to move produce. By 1851, Indiana chartered more than thirty roadbuilding companies that planked hundreds of miles of roadways, including portions of the National Road. But low population density led to light and unprofitable traffic, and wooden pavers decayed quickly, leading to high maintenance costs. The fad passed.[21] Something similar happened in early-twentieth-century motor sport, when fast, board-paved tracks briefly gained popularity but were abandoned after they rapidly deteriorated.

Whether traveling on wood, dirt, or iron, Americans were on the move. Indiana grew by a third in the 1850s, even though those cities most important to its economy remained outside its borders. Yet centrifugal forces threatening to tear Indiana apart also had a centripetal effect: Indianapolis developed into a crossroads metropolis. In 1852, the *New York Times* noted that despite an attractive, leafy skyline, the city featured unimpressive buildings; it had "scarcely a public building that would pass muster in a first-rate New-York village." But it had potential. Indianapolis's banks had decent buildings, a hotel was planned, business was booming, and a "spacious dépôt" would soon unite the city's numerous rail lines.[22] Trains entering the "centre of Hoosierdom" carried "people and products from different points of the compass," tying the city to the Great Lakes, the Mississippi and Ohio Rivers, and the Atlantic Ocean. Soon, rails would foster a "moving panorama" all the way to New York. As Indianapolis became a regional metropolis, far-off markets hailed new lines that might shorten distances between Gotham and the West.[23]

Indianapolis grew enmeshed in a commercial nexus, with rails siphoning capital from the countryside and distributing it to far-off cities. Some called Indiana the "Railroad State." In the 1850s, it was nearly unthinkable to plan a railroad in Indiana that did *not* pass through the city.[24] The capital was "no longer a rugged, scattered village—but a young, vigorous and healthful city with a bright future before it."[25] Midcentury financial panics slowed growth, yet Indianapolis's real-estate market saw a modest boom. By 1855, eight railroad lines entered the new union station. Boosterish newspapers cherished growth statistics, claiming publicity would make capital flow to the city "as the rivers do to the ocean." With roads made of metal, who needed water? Financial institutions gravitated to Indianapolis while hotels made it a convention site. Indiana's capital became an economic and cultural hub, a veritable central city for the American West, a status to which other cities, including St. Louis and Kansas City, also aspired.[26]

The Civil War hastened railroad growth. Trains moved soldiers, supplies, and news, and most battles were fought near rails, especially important junctions like Atlanta and Nashville. In 1862, congressional Republicans passed laws using western lands—again, taken from Native Americans—to subsidize commercial and industrial development. One such law, the Pacific Railway Act, supported by a majority of Indiana's House delegation, granted land to fund a transcontinental railroad. The law represented an old infrastructural dream: connecting the Atlantic and Pacific Oceans. Growth continued. In 1870, Indianapolis had about forty-eight thousand residents, roughly two and a half times its 1860 total, and by 1880, Indiana's four thousand plus track miles reached nearly all of its ninety-two counties. After 1870, rails connected Indianapolis to Peoria, more than two hundred miles west, via the smaller Illinois cities of Danville, Bloomington, and Pekin, cutting distance from Cincinnati to Omaha by sixty miles. By connecting to the Illinois Central at Champaign, the route linked the Midwest's rich farmlands to East Coast markets and coastal ports. Indianapolis was no longer isolated.[27]

Hoosiers, like other Americans, embraced popular culture, with sport becoming a visible way to contest urban rivalries. By the late 1860s, the Circle City boasted a baseball team that, while technically amateur, featured semipro athletes employed in make-work jobs. National holidays were times for sport. In 1867, two years before Cincinnati's Red Stockings toured the continent, beating nearly all comers, the Indianapolis Young Men's Christian Association (YMCA) held a baseball game on July 4. Soon, the city hosted teams such as the Blues (formed 1876) and Hoosiers (1884), the latter of which briefly played in baseball's National League in the late 1880s. By 1904, the Indianapolis Indians were a member of the minor-league American Association. In latter decades, holidays, especially Thanksgiving and Memorial Day, grew into important days for college football games and auto races. Whether it was appropriate to play sports on such holidays, however, would be hotly contested, and in the 1920s a debate over Memorial Day competitions nearly ended the city's fabled speedway races.[28]

Late-1800s Indianapolis was a central economic point. A *New York Times* correspondent said the city sat "in the direct line of east and west communication," "situated to receive and distribute business from and to all parts of the country." Each day, scores of mail trains and a thousand freight cars passed through a city with an estimated population of sixty-five thousand.[29] As a rail hub, Indianapolis was prone to labor disputes. The Great Railroad Strike of 1877 began when B&O workers walked off the job in Maryland and West Virginia to protest wage cuts, and they were quickly joined by sympathy strikers. The strike spread quickly, affecting nearly the entire nation, and cities were immobilized. Initially, many Americans were sympathetic, but soon public sentiment turned and some middle-class men formed antistrike militias. One Indianapolis militia member was Benjamin Harrison, a Civil War general who later, like his grandfather, was elected president. Harrison and his compatriots confronted mostly nonviolent strikers who diverted rail traffic to disrupt capital.[30] This labor action—not the last time strikers targeted Circle City rails—demonstrated widespread resentment of corporations, especially railroads controlled by distant brokers. A multitude of Americans pushed back against capital, seeking new technologies or organizations to circumvent seemingly all-powerful railways.

In 1888, Indianapolis replaced its 1853 union station with a grand Romanesque structure, the nation's biggest and most attractive rail depot, which hosted two hundred trains a day by the end of the century. Yet even as rails became a central part of American life, some people sought to escape this path dependency. They were aided by new industries that thrived in Indiana, partly from the state's brief but intense natural gas boom. In 1886, prospectors struck gas in Ohio and then Indiana, and towns lit huge *flambeaux* to show off the seemingly inexhaustible supply of gas. East-central Indiana quickly became known as the Gas Belt, with small towns like Muncie growing into midsize industrial centers. Indianapolis was outside the gas field yet consumed much of the abundant fossil fuel. Manufacturing increased nearly 40 percent in the 1890s and the number of factories rose to more than nine hundred by 1900, with Indiana becoming one of America's most industrialized states. But careless usage and unmetered sale of gas, worsened by Chicago's insatiable demand, resulted in the boom's demise by 1901. Some factories folded, while others located alternate supplies of natural gas or retooled for coal.[31]

Indianapolis's Union Station, completed 1888. This building's predecessor, completed in 1853, was the world's first union station. (Library of Congress)

The 1900 census counted more than 2.5 million Hoosiers, with more than 169,000 in Indianapolis, where an extensive streetcar system carried residents to and from the central business district. Streetcars transformed urban life. Although earlier transit experiments took place in the Midwest, America's first practical electric streetcars debuted in Richmond, Virginia, in 1888. By the mid-1890s, Chicago had the globe's most extensive system. Indianapolis's electric trolleys debuted in 1890, when Windy City investors founded the Citizens' Street Railroad Company. Indianapolis's major lines formed a loop in the city center, merging at the circle that Ralston had once designated for the governor's mansion. Streetcars made city blocks surrounding the downtown circle perfect for offices or retail stores seeking locations near concentrated foot traffic.[32]

Streetcars presaged development of residential suburbs or entertainment zones in the hinterland areas von Thünen had once envisaged for agriculture. Transit companies often built lines to points beyond the edge of town and then constructed amusement parks or resort hotels. Such attractions spurred future growth and kept riders paying fares on evenings and weekends, turning nonwork hours into profitable times for transit companies. Since trolleys traveled faster than horsecars, about twenty miles per hour, more distance to the city center did not mean more transit time. Residents had once been restricted to so-called walking cities, spread no more than two miles from city centers, but now they could move five or six miles out. Indianapolis, like other cities, developed streetcar suburbs, including Irvington, Brightwood, and Woodruff Place. These municipalities, incorporated from 1870 to 1876, predated electric trolleys, but electric transit enhanced post-1890 expansion. Elite Woodruff Place was only a mile and a half from the city center, but Brightwood was three miles out and Irvington four. Eventually, automotive suburbs emerged, including the supposedly horseless town of Speedway City.[33]

Cities dependent on streetcars were subject to transit strikes. Perhaps the most famous was the 1886 New York streetcar strike, which fueled the mayoral campaign of economist Henry George (who came in second, ahead of Theodore Roosevelt). Almost six years later, in January 1892, the Brotherhood of Car Drivers, Motormen, and Conductors walked off the job in central Indiana, in large part because the Indianapolis Citizens Street Railway (ICSR) rescinded workers' riding privileges. After more than a week without service, the union and ICSR agreed to arbitration. Disagreements over work hours and wages were not resolved, though, so the union struck again in February and a judge placed the company in receivership. By March, ICSR regained control, with few substantial gains for workers. In July, American streetcar workers met in Indianapolis to form the Amalgamated Association of Street Railway Employees of America. It would be another twenty years before the city's streetcars were again disrupted, at a time when residents increasingly turned to individual modes of mobility—especially automobiles.[34]

New technologies made it so distances between urban points grew as transit time shrank. Suburban expansion decreased population density, with Indianapolis averaging slightly more than one family per residential building in 1890. More densely populated cities, by contrast, averaged around eight families per structure; New York City had 18.5.

As Indianapolis diffused, it built an iconic focal point that in later years attracted many of the same visitors who attended auto races. The Indiana Soldiers and Sailors Monument was conceived as a Civil War memorial supported by the Grand Army of the Republic (GAR). President Benjamin Harrison dedicated the cornerstone on August 22, 1889, at the site of Ralston's old Governors Circle, or, as it came to be known, Monument Circle. Sport was part of the program that day, with Indianapolis's National League baseball team playing a doubleheader against Cleveland. After a dozen years of construction—including delays caused by diversion of materials to Chicago's 1893 World's Columbian Exposition—it was unveiled in May 1902. The 281-foot-high limestone obelisk, designed by Prussian architect Bruno Schmitz, cost nearly $600,000. The dedication attracted a crowd of fifty thousand, which heard former US secretary of state John W. Foster deliver a nationalistic oration.[35]

The Soldiers and Sailors Monument foreshadowed the turn-of-the-century City Beautiful movement. Urban planners such as Charles Mulford Robinson advocated using public art and trees, along with grand plazas or civic centers, to enhance urban aesthetics and public spirit. For its part, Indianapolis formed a parks commission in 1895 and consulted with landscape architect John Olmsted, adopted son of Frederick Law Olmsted, to create a system of parks, bridges, and boulevards. After 1899, Indianapolis built spans over the White River and Fall Creek, including the Emrichsville Bridge at Sixteenth Street, an ornate stone structure that carried traffic from the city to Riverside Park and, by 1909, to the speedway. Olmsted's plan was challenged in court, yet the city's spatial reinvention continued. In the 1910s, Indianapolis built auto parkways designed by landscape architect George Kessler, best known for his work in Dallas and other western cities.[36]

Indianapolis, the nation's twenty-first-largest city by 1900, carved out an economic niche as a hub for interurban railways, electric lines running between cities. Patrons liked interurbans because they were quieter, cleaner, and cheaper than steam railways, and made more frequent stops. Indiana's interurban network began in the rapidly industrializing Gas Belt, and the

Soldiers and Sailors Monument, dedicated in 1902 and pictured here in 1924. (Library of Congress)

first cars reached Indianapolis by 1900. The city built its large Traction Terminal by 1904, and soon a web of tracks connected it to other midwestern cities. By 1920, Indianapolis found itself at the center of one of North America's largest interurban networks.[37]

Bicycles were another innovative conveyance, and bicyclists were America's first good roads proponents. Two-wheelers first appeared in the 1860s and spurred formation of the League of American Wheelmen (LAW), which worked to convince Americans that roads were economic devices demanding investment—not natural features to be taken for granted. Good roads that did not become messy sloughs in wet weather helped people, especially farmers, evade the so-called "mud tax," a contrived figure showing that freight costs were higher on poor roads.[38] Indianapolis even held America's first pavement convention, sponsored by the Commercial Club (later the Chamber of Commerce), in 1890. About twelve thousand people from dozens of cities attended the exposition at Tomlinson Hall, a brick convention center built the same year as the new Union Station. They viewed exhibits about street paving while industry representatives touted various "products including brick, clay, crushed stone, and Indiana limestone blocks." The following year, the mileage of Indianapolis's paved streets had almost tripled. Later, by 1909, the speedway would turn to vitrified paving bricks to provide a safer racing surface.[39]

Cycling received a boost with the 1880s development of the safety bicycle, a machine equipped with improved brakes, pneumatic tires, and chain-gear-driven wheels of equal size. Americans saw a bicycle craze the following decade, with many riding bikes for pleasure or for commuting. Proponents portrayed the devices as having nearly utopian implications: bicycles could prevent neurasthenia (nervous exhaustion) by soothing nerves; they could help doctors save lives by making house calls; and they could reduce the spread of disease by eliminating animal-waste pollution on city streets. Whether or not bicycles actually fulfilled the progressive dreams of the City Beautiful, there is no doubt that they did alter mobility. Many women now ventured out in public on their own for the first time, and bicycles effectively shrank cities' perceived size. Advocates who touted bikes' ability to annihilate space even compared their liberating characteristics to flight. "In the days before mechanized aviation," writes historian Evan Friss, bicycles "enchanted Americans."[40]

Bikes even spawned a new spectator sport. Boston and Chicago held bicycle races, and by 1895 more than five hundred cycling clubs had formed throughout America. Racing became an urban phenomenon for women as well as men. In Indianapolis, industrialist Arthur Newby, a founder of the local Zig-Zag Cycling Club, built a bicycle velodrome, a quarter-mile pine-board track with banked curves, located at Central Avenue and Thirty-Second Street. The $23,000 track's grandstands and bleachers seated more than eight thousand. It opened on July 4, 1898, and hosted races until 1903. By the turn of the century, at least eight Indiana cities produced more than $3 million worth of bicycles or parts. Blessed as it was with miles of level, well-paved streets, Indianapolis even hosted LAW's national meet at Tomlinson Hall in 1898. About two-thirds of the attendees came from Indianapolis, while others traveled from as far away as Philadelphia; some biked from Chicago or Richmond, Indiana. The city welcomed convention-eers—including women "by the score"—with an elaborate reception hosted by Republican governor James Mount. Bicycle races, with cash prizes, were held at the Newby Oval. Eleven years later, Newby and his fellow speed enthusiasts would host motor races at a bigger and, eventually, more leg-endary facility.[41]

The bicycle craze subsided about the same time Indiana's gas boom went bust, but America's mania for mobility did not disappear. The urbanizing Midwest was a place of technological innovation. In Dayton, Ohio, two bi-cycle mechanics, brothers named Wilbur and Orville Wright, experimented with heavier-than-air flight, relocating to a flat strip of windy beach at Kitty Hawk, North Carolina, where on December 17, 1903, Orville flew a rickety biplane for twelve seconds, traversing one hundred twenty feet. Longer flights followed. Initially, at least, the significance of the Wrights' invention was unclear; some people thought they had flown a dirigible or a blimp. It was not until the brothers publicly demonstrated their innovative craft in New York in 1908 that the remarkable achievement became evident. As historian Robert Wohl writes, the miracle of flight grew from seemingly mundane origins: "What . . . was a flying machine except a powered bicycle that moved through the air by means of wings?"[42]

Another product to which Midwesterners contributed was the auto-mobile, a machine that first emerged in Europe in the 1890s, around the same time engineer Elwood Haynes imagined a horseless carriage as he traversed Indiana's massive Gas Belt. Haynes subsequently contracted with two mechanically inclined brothers, Elmer and Edgar Apperson, to build such a machine. He and the Appersons eventually went separate ways, but all continued making motorcars into the 1920s. Eventually, a number of Indiana cities, including Evansville and Richmond, built their fortunes on autos; farther north, in South Bend, Studebaker made cars until the mid-twentieth century. Hoosier auto manufacturing, though, centered on Indianapolis. Waverly, initially a bicycle company, made electric cars, while Howard Marmon, owner of a milling-machinery firm, started building gasoline-engine cars in 1904. Cole Motor Car began as a wagon manufacturer. Standard Wheel originated in Terre Haute before moving to Indianapolis in 1905; later it moved to Toledo, Ohio, changed its name to Willys-Overland, and developed the Jeep. By 1909, Indiana ranked fourth nationally in value of cars produced. Eventually, it grew difficult for Indiana cities, lacking inexpensive water transportation, to maintain production on a scale similar to Detroit's, but the industrial base provided by rails and natural gas made the state a major parts supplier. In Muncie, Warner Gear manufactured transmissions; in Anderson, Remy Electric made generators and magnetos. Kokomo produced tires, while two Indianapolis firms, Marvel and Wheeler-Schebler, built carburetors. The head of the latter company was Iowa native Frank Wheeler, who moved to Indiana around 1900 and later helped bankroll a new motor speedway, where many Indiana parts firms ultimately sponsored prizes for early speedway races.[43]

Automobiles, which did not depend on fixed tracks or linear routes, annihilated space more effectively than railroads. The time was ripe for entrepreneurs to feed America's appetite for mobility. Henry Ford (born 1863) developed an internal-combustion engine while working for a subsidiary of Thomas Edison's and then became instrumental in transforming Detroit into America's Motor City. But while Ford gained a reputation for his ability to streamline manufacturing processes—resulting in the efficient Model T, the so-called universal car—his Indianapolis counterpart, Carl Graham Fisher, was more attuned to the ways cars and pavement could entertain. Fisher was born January 12, 1874, in Greensburg, Indiana, along the Michigan Road. After his parents separated, Carl moved with his mother and siblings to Indianapolis around 1880. His eyesight was poor and he dropped out of school around the age of twelve, but he read voraciously and was clever and intellectually curious; later in life, he developed several patents. Although young Carl participated in few organized sports, he loved daredevil stunts. Biographer Mark Foster says Fisher "possessed a remarkable ability to combine work and play" and "was mesmerized by speed in any form." A card-carrying LAW member, he even built his own bicycle with a massive, nine-foot-tall front wheel. In 1890 the sixteen-year-old Fisher, along with Arthur Newby and about a dozen other bike enthusiasts, formed the Zig-Zag Cycling Club. These young men shunned newfangled safety bicycles, preferring the more challenging *ordinaries*, with big front wheels, which they rode all over the city and even on gravel roads. According to one account, the club had about 150 members before disbanding in the

Hoosier Barnum: Carl Graham Fisher, 1909. (Library of Congress)

mid-1890s. Other members who later became prominent in Indiana's auto industry included James Allison and Howard and Walter Marmon. Foster surmises Fisher's experience navigating muddy roads as a cyclist sparked his later desire "to promote transcontinental highways."[44]

Fisher rode the rails as a news butcher, selling newspapers and such to passengers. One colorful anecdote says he made an apron concealing a picture of a nude woman, which he then flashed to bored passengers. He usually made the sale. Enterprising and with a keen sense of humor, by the age of seventeen Fisher and his two brothers opened a downtown repair shop catering to fellow LAW members. Before long, they were also selling bicycles. By the time Fisher was nineteen, the shop distributed Pope-Toledo brand bicycles, thanks in part to an 1893 stunt in which he released hundreds of balloons, crafted by his friend George Bumbaugh; finders of fifty balloons with lucky numbers attached received free bikes. Fifteen years later, in 1908, Fisher used a big gas balloon to carry an Ohio-made Stoddard-Dayton car—stripped down, with no engine—aloft over Indianapolis. Reportedly, this stunt attracted the attention of twenty-one-year-old Jane Watts (she later claimed she was only fourteen at the time), who soon married Fisher. Jane later said that although some people were annoyed by Carl's escapades, they realized he added to the Circle

City's reputation. Carl Fisher was fascinated by the idea of traversing large amounts of space. Around 1908, he planned a transatlantic balloon flight that never happened, but soon his thriving shop sold motorcycles and cars. By 1909, he and several partners, including Newby and Allison, formed the Empire Motor Car Company, which briefly manufactured modest automobiles at a former bicycle factory on Indianapolis's north side. A would-be motor tycoon, Fisher was well connected in Indianapolis and beyond. He befriended prominent racer Barney Oldfield, as well as Booth Tarkington, who later won the 1919 Pulitzer Prize for *The Magnificent Ambersons*, a novel about a once-wealthy family trying to revive its fortunes in a sprawling heartland metropolis. As might be expected, Fisher was among the first Hoosiers to own an automobile. He purchased a small French-made motorized tricycle in 1898. Two years later, he and Oldfield attended a New York auto show; both men bought cars and drove them back to Indiana.[45]

Carl Fisher, like Henry Ford, was a racer. Historian Steven Watts says Ford turned to racing after his first two motor companies failed, because he "saw the need for public attention that would revive interest" in his products. Victory helped make him a celebrity. In October 1902, Barney Oldfield won the Manufacturer's Challenge Cup race at Grosse Pointe, Michigan, driving a car Ford had built. Oldfield later said the victory launched his own career, as well as that of Ford Motor Company.[46] Fisher may have seen motor sport in a similar light. By 1902, he and Oldfield, with Louis Chevrolet and others, raced on tracks throughout the Midwest. In a tragic event at a county fair in Zanesville, Ohio, in September 1903, Fisher's three-thousand-pound car burst a tire and plunged off the track, plowing into a crowd of spectators. He and his riding mechanic, Dayton bicycle racer Earl Kiser, were both injured, along with five bystanders. One victim, a Civil War veteran and GAR member named John Goodwin, suffered a crushed leg and internal injuries, and died several days later. Although Fisher claimed he would quit racing, he was not done with speed. Two years later, he planned to enter a car in the 1905 Vanderbilt Cup race, but the vehicle was too heavy, so he got creative. Workers drilled holes in the frame and axles and replaced the drive shaft with chains. Still, it was rejected, and Fisher responded by rebuking the race's organizers in a newspaper ad. This car did, however, compete at the Indiana state fairgrounds that year, averaging a then-astounding 59.21 miles per hour.[47] Fisher's inability to contend for the Vanderbilt Cup may

Prest-O-Lite Factory on Sixteenth Street in Speedway City, pictured here in 1913. (Bass Photo Co. Collection, Indiana Historical Society)

have prompted his desire to build a speedway where, by the late twentieth century, museum visitors could view that ancient, hole-filled racecar.

Fisher was doing well as a bicycle and car salesman, but he and James Allison made their fortune when they formed Prest-O-Lite Company, America's first headlamp manufacturer, in 1904. Allison was born in southern Michigan in 1872, and his family moved to South Bend in 1874, about the same time Fisher was born fewer than two hundred miles south along the Michigan Road. The Allisons, who owned a coupon-manufacturing company, relocated again to Indianapolis in 1880, a few years before the gas boom and about the same time Carl's family came to the city. Prest-O-Lite was a significant firm. Before headlights, nighttime driving was difficult, with kerosene lanterns or other lamps undependable for drivers motoring in the dark. Fisher was intrigued when inventor Fred Avery approached him with an apparatus that produced a bright light with compressed carbide gas. He and Allison purchased the rights after spending a few days figuring out how the device worked. Filling the tanks was a dangerous endeavor, though, and several factory buildings exploded. In one particularly bad explosion in June 1908, several Prest-O-Lite employees and occupants of nearby buildings were injured. These disasters, including the fatal collapse of a concrete building that was under construction in 1911, caused by contractor error, brought a significant amount of negative press. Fisher and Allison soon moved the Prest-O-Lite factory to Indianapolis's far western edge, near the motor speedway they had built two years earlier, and then later sold the business to Union Carbide. The national firm was especially interested in Prest-O-Lite's factory buildings and its efficient distribution networks. Despite the company's bumpy existence, after selling the business, Fisher gained a fortune in the form of Union Carbide shares worth approximately $5.6 million in early-1900s dollars, which he subsequently used to bankroll real-estate developments and transportation-based spectacles.[48]

By the early twentieth century, Indianapolis was America's legendary crossroads. The 1910 census placed its population over 230,000, making it the nation's twenty-second-largest city. Although the gas boom was over, Indiana had a firm industrial base and 2.7 million people, making it the nation's ninth-largest state. The White River was still not navigable and the canals had never quite panned out, but Indiana's strategically located capital was now a transportation hub. When Fisher, Allison, Newby, and Wheeler decided to build a motor speedway in 1909, they drew upon the city's industrial foundation and location at the heart of North American transportation networks to create the world's premier site for automotive spectacle.

2

AMERICA'S BROOKLANDS

Annihilating Space at the Speedway

Indianapolis may have been a thriving rail hub and manufacturing center by 1909, but it was not yet the world's racing capital. When Hoosier industrialists announced construction of a new motor speedway there, Americans seeking a reference point called it the Brooklands of America, referring to England's premier auto racing and aviation site, built in 1907. Indiana's oval, though, soon became the global baseline in the modern quest for speed. It demonstrated a multitude of ways humans could annihilate space on the ground and in the air, as well as the means by which racetrack impresarios could make money from the spectacles.

The speedway was an undertaking of Carl Fisher, James Allison, Arthur Newby, and Frank Wheeler, men firmly rooted in Indianapolis's auto industry. Fisher and Allison had started Prest-O-Lite, and Allison later headed an engine firm; Newby founded National Motor Vehicle, while Wheeler led Wheeler-Schebler Carburetor. Indianapolis banker Stoughton Fletcher was going to be involved, too, but he withdrew support at the urging of his bank. The remaining four investors contributed finances and vision, but Fisher was the guiding force. After all, in 1906 he had published a short piece in *Motor Age* magazine proclaiming a need for better raceways. One-mile dirt tracks were dangerous, said Fisher, and road races were inadequate because they gave spectators "little enjoyment" by providing only "fleeting glimpses" of drivers. Americans had to build better tracks. An enclosed oval would

Founders of American mobility: left to right, Henry Ford, Arthur Newby, Frank Wheeler, Carl Fisher, and James Allison, circa 1909. (IMS Photo Archive)

allow manufacturers to "test their cars continuously at high speeds" so that they could win international races against Europeans. He advocated a five-mile course "with proper grandstands." Such a track, he said, could pay for itself after just a few events.[1]

According to an unsubstantiated 1961 account, when Fisher's car broke down along the National Road while returning from Dayton in 1908, real-estate agent Lemon H. "Lem" Trotter challenged his friend to move ahead with plans for a racetrack. A separate account says Fisher and his fellow speed enthusiasts were "seated around a camp fire at the Indiana state fair grounds, smok[ing] cigars and watch[ing] a twenty-four hour [*sic*] race on the dirt horse track" when they joked about building a track in a cornfield. In reality, developments on the other side of the Atlantic may have been a deciding factor. In 1905, Fisher had traveled to France as relief driver for road races, but he disliked the twisting mountain course and lost interest once he realized novice Americans could not beat experienced Europeans. Two years later, he traveled to England, where he saw construction of Brooklands, the brainchild of industrialist Hugh Locke King who, after watching races in Italy in 1905, feared British manufacturing was falling behind. The 2.767-mile track was built by fifteen hundred laborers at a cost of £150,000 and started hosting aviation and auto contests in June 1907. Fisher decided to build a similar facility in Indiana.[2]

Spectatorship was key. Scholar Annie Gilbert Coleman has observed that circular movement "made the race a spectacle because it concentrated speed in one place," while historian Daniel Simone notes that oval tracks require less maintenance than linear courses, made it easier to reach injured drivers, and facilitated ticket sales. As Fisher explained, straightaways might be faster, but enclosed ovals allowed greater visibility. As of 1913, Brooklands had not hosted a crowd of more than six thousand, yet Indianapolis accommodated tens of thousands of spectators.[3] The Hoosier oval signified a new way to commodify speed, and it also represented shifting terminologies of space. In the 1800s, Frederick Law Olmsted had coined the term *parkway* for a limited access, tree-lined roadway and, after the turn of the century, planner Charles Mulford Robinson argued that parkways gave city dwellers access to recreational greenspaces. Soon, though, parkways became sites for speed. In Buffalo, drivers raced on an Olmsted-designed parkway, while in Detroit, people called Olmsted's Grand Boulevard "the Speedway" long before cars defined that city. In the 1890s, New Yorkers built the Harlem River Speedway while Bostonians built the Charles River Speedway. Historian Clay McShane says developers justified these new speedways by claiming they offered "recreation" for spectators who "could sit along the bluffs and watch the many informal races below." In turn, the meaning of *speedway* would soon migrate from park-lined roads to enclosed tracks with grandstands.[4]

Fisher, Allison, Newby, and Wheeler considered building their speedway at French Lick, a southern Indiana mineral-springs resort town, but supposedly they could not find enough level ground there. It did not help that French Lick had few rail connections to major cities. They instead chose a site four miles west of Indianapolis's city center and about a hundred miles closer to Chicago. Aided by Lem Trotter, the investors purchased several tracts of land. Although local residents called the area the Pressley Farm, once owned by a John Pressley, the group actually bought eighty acres (a half-quarter of Section 31, Township 16, Marion County), for $24,000 from Kevi Munter, plus two hundred forty acres (three half-quarters of Sections 29, 30, and 32) for $48,000 from Daniel Chenoweth. These tracts were located near Haughville, west of Riverside Park, on the Crawfordsville Road, an extension of Sixteenth Street. The men capitalized the venture at $250,000, and in January newspapers reported that the site would be America's own Brooklands. The main grandstand would seat thirty-five thousand, with twenty more fifty-seat stands and more than four hundred reflected arc lights around the perimeter. People could reach the track by train, streetcar, or auto, with parking for fifteen hundred cars. Incorporation papers were filed on February 8, 1909, and construction began one week later. Newspapers reported that the banked curves might facilitate speeds of as high as one hundred miles per hour, and winding through the infield would be a twenty-five-foot-wide course to simulate road races at speeds up to sixty miles per hour (though this interior track was not built until nearly a century later). Indiana secretary of state Fred Sims certified the speedway's incorporation on March 20, 1909.[5]

Fisher initially wanted a three-mile oval, but once engineer Park Andrews pointed out such a big track would leave virtually no room for grandstands, he decided on a 2.5-mile circuit. Working in spring, an army of workers employed by railroad contractor C. C. King Brothers used "scrapers, scoops, rollers," mules, and tractors to grade the site. King Brothers' winning bid was for $14,750, but the reported total cost of construction was between $220,000 and $400,000.[6] After grading, the track was paved with crushed rock and 235,000 gallons of "asphaltum oil." This macadam track became one of America's biggest sports venues the same year steel-reinforced-concrete baseball stadiums opened in Philadelphia (Shibe Park) and Pittsburgh (Forbes Field) and just one year after the St. Louis Browns converted Sportsman's Park into baseball's first steel structure. As spectators flocked to Indianapolis to watch construction, racer Lewis Strang predicted records set at Brooklands would soon be shattered there. Meanwhile, carmakers such as Ransom E. Olds visited the track and requested to use it for testing. According to a 1940s account, Fisher watched the speedway's construction from a balloon tethered nearby.[7]

Part of the new grandstand toppled in a May storm, but Fisher said everything would be ready for balloon meets in June. When driving the track for the first time, he said his "fondest dreams" were coming true.[8] An American Motor Car Manufacturers' Association official said it was perfect "for aeronautical and motor sports."[9] The speedway opened on June 5, 1909, with a distance balloon contest sponsored by the Aero Club of America

(ACA) and an endurance contest sponsored by Fisher's recently founded Indiana Aero Club (IAC). One writer calls the craft hot-air balloons, but they were actually filled with natural gas or coal gas, not heated air. Nine balloons participated in contests for elaborate medals or trophies.[10] Each balloon was sponsored by a city: Chicago, Cleveland, Indianapolis, New York, or St. Louis. Pilots included Fisher, Albert Bond Lambert (namesake of St. Louis's airport), and New Yorker A. Holland Forbes, and timekeeper and starter was Charles Glidden, a Boston telephone magnate who traveled the world by car in the early 1900s and organized American Automobile Association (AAA) endurance contests often referred to as Glidden Tours. Annihilating space was key. One ACA official said elsewhere that the group hoped to make aviation "as familiar as automobiling."[11]

Thousands arrived by train or car and Indiana National Guardsmen stood by as crews inflated each "great sky chariot" using a six-inch gas line stretching four miles from downtown.[12] Balloons began launching at 3:45 p.m. Spectators included Governor Thomas Marshall, a good-roads proponent who later served as Woodrow Wilson's vice president, who got stuck in traffic heading to the track but still was able to watch the balloons lift skyward. Each basket was equipped with three days' worth of provisions, as well as

The balloons *Chicago, Indiana,* and *Hoosier* (left to right) preparing for the June 1909 contests at the speedway. (Library of Congress)

life preservers and carrier pigeons. The US Weather Bureau's Henry Hersey even supplied balloonists with maps and information about high-altitude weather. After all, they were in for a long ride. A scientist at Harvard's Blue Hill Meteorological Observatory said a balloon might reach Nova Scotia. Some thought one might break a distance record of 1,200 miles, while others feared balloons would fly over the Great Lakes—a dangerous area even in good weather—or get lost over the Canadian wilderness.[13]

Such predictions proved wildly inaccurate. Winds pushed the balloons southward while more than three thousand spectators sat in the grandstands and another forty thousand watched from outside. No one, of course, saw the whole contest. Competitive ballooning was made possible through timepieces, telegraphs, and telephones. Readers in far-off places, including New York, Chicago, Atlanta, and Los Angeles, read about the balloons' progress. By June 6, some ACA balloons were still aloft, as far south as Alabama, but all three IAC balloons had touched down: *Ohio* landed fifty miles south of Indianapolis, while *Chicago* came down in Kentucky and *Indianapolis* landed in Tennessee. By June 7, both St. Louis balloons, along with *Hoosier*, had landed in Tennessee, while Forbes's *New York*, which remained aloft over thirty-six hours, landed at Corinth, Mississippi, some three hundred seventy-five miles from Indianapolis. Not all went as far. *Cleveland*, in the air for less than three hours, landed forty miles away at Columbus, Indiana. Meanwhile, it was unclear whether *Indiana* was still eligible for the endurance prize, since Fisher's balloon had appeared to touch ground and was ultimately disqualified. In any case, the only way Fisher could have broken a distance record set by German balloonists the previous year would have been to venture far out over the Gulf of Mexico.[14]

Balloonists were literally taken out of their comfort zones. Forbes recorded intense heat at low altitudes, followed by bone-chilling cold at higher ones. John Berry noted that while passing over Chattanooga at ten thousand feet it was thirty-nine degrees Fahrenheit, the most frigid June weather he had ever encountered. Over Alabama, Berry "lost the current" and dropped ballast in an attempt to gain altitude. He finally landed near Fort Payne and took a train back to Indiana. Some balloonists flew over places that did not welcome them. When Forbes and Clifford Harmon descended to nine hundred feet to let out ballast near a village north of Birmingham, a man reportedly shouted, "Come down here, d[am]n you, or I will bring you down." He fired a rifle three times, and one shot penetrated the basket. Lambert and Fisher also reported shots over Indiana and Tennessee. When Fisher finally landed west of Nashville, a farmer ran through his fields with a rifle. Once he realized Fisher was a human being (it is unclear what else he might have been), the farmer put his gun down. Some rural dwellers may have worried about spooked livestock, or they may have been former Confederates who recalled the Union's Civil War–era Balloon Corps.[15]

It is tempting to dismiss the 1909 balloon contests as publicity stunts. Balloons were slow, and these events were held six years after Orville and Wilbur Wright pioneered heavier-than-air flight at Kitty Hawk. Lighter-than-air craft never exhibited great utility for transporting passengers or freight. Yet such arguments are teleological. Early coverage of the Wrights was spotty and the brothers were notoriously secretive, and so what they had accomplished was not quite clear in 1909. Americans were only starting to realize aircrafts' potential, and balloons still seemed an innovative technology promising to loosen spatial fetters.[16] German engineers experimented using balloons to help lift trains over mountains, and some people thought lighter-than-air craft might facilitate Arctic exploration. Flyers and motorists shared the same goal: linking distant places and annihilating space. A "sky pilot" simply traveled less-well-marked "air roads."[17]

Two months later, the speedway saw its first motor races. On August 10, 1909, a Federation of American Motorcyclists endurance run left Cleveland for a two-day, 362-mile journey ending with motorcycle races at the speedway. The track had not been properly oiled, because of construction delays, so the races saw many injuries. Albert Gibney was thrown from his cycle at sixty miles per hour, while Jake De Rosier was hurt when his front tire flew off and his body skidded across the track; J. S. Tormey was injured in a separate accident. Cyclists were unhappy with the rough and dangerous surface, and the events were cut short.[18] The next week, the oval held its first auto races. Bob Burman, Louis Chevrolet, Ralph De Palma, Barney Oldfield, and other drivers raced cars made in Indiana (Apperson, Marion, Marmon, National), Michigan (Buick, Chalmers-Detroit, Jackson, Lozier), Ohio (Stoddard-Dayton), Massachusetts (Knox), Pennsylvania (Chadwick), Germany (Benz), and Italy (Fiat). Times were measured by a device, accurate to one-hundredth of a second, made by Warner Instrument of Beloit, Wisconsin. Motor companies, including Overland and National, furnished prizes. The Prest-O-Lite trophy cost $1,500, while the 8.5-foot-tall Wheeler-Schebler Trophy, made of $5,000 worth of sterling silver, was crafted by New York's Tiffany and Company.[19]

Cars line up to race, 1909. (IMS Photo Archive)

Motor enthusiasts flocked to America's new motor mecca, with thousands who came by car temporarily turning the infield into the world's biggest parking lot. The Chicago Motor Club and Chicago Automobile Trade Association inaugurated a tradition of race-weekend pilgrimages, with about two hundred Chicagoans riding in fifty cars that departed from a Michigan Avenue hotel at 6:00 a.m. This "Hoosier Glidden" [Tour] was led by writer and former auto dealer Charles Root, who drove an Indianapolis-made National that served as a confetti car, marking the trail with bits of paper, a pathfinding method then common in long-distance tours. Tourists planned to lunch at noon in Lafayette, Indiana, and arrive at Indianapolis by 6:30 p.m. Averaging seventeen miles per hour, the motorists traveled a route that would eventually be spanned by much better roads. Just a few months earlier, in fact, a developer in an Indiana Gas Belt town had proposed a $1.5-million tollway between Indianapolis and Chicago.[20]

Once in Indianapolis, many travelers stayed at the Claypool Hotel, a 450-room facility completed in 1903 near Monument Circle that was a center for commerce, tourism, and political gatherings. According to scholar A. K. Sandoval-Strausz, hotels were "engines of modernity"; like roads and rails, they broke down spatial boundaries and circulated capital. The Claypool

The 450-room Claypool Hotel at the northwest corner of Illinois and Washington Streets, downtown Indianapolis, 1904. (Library of Congress)

enabled people to travel to a central location in a city where they paid to watch an entertaining type of the same sort of automotive space annihilation that had brought them there. Yet automobility eventually sowed the seeds of hotels' demise, as roadside motor courts and motels became the choice of midcentury travelers. The Claypool later closed and was demolished in the 1960s, at a time when many visitors to the famous track and its museum lodged at motels in or near the speedway.[21]

The 1909 races were dangerous. Clifford Littrell, a riding mechanic (also called a mechanician) for Stoddard-Dayton's racers, fell off a car as it exited a downtown Indianapolis garage on its way to the speedway and was run over; he later died at Methodist Hospital. Despite this tragedy, excitement for the races was tangible. Days before the race, Bob Burman drove Betty Blythe, a writer for the *Indianapolis Star*, over the track at a reported sixty miles per hour. Blythe said it felt like traveling "on the crest of a gale."[22] This was the same time when the *Chicago Tribune* said "space-annihilating racing machines" were "panting and puffing, eager to start in the grim contest with Father Time." The revolutionary race was made legible by a big scoreboard near the grandstand. A press box with telegraphs and photographic facilities allowed journalists to disseminate accounts and images of the race. By the mid-1910s, in fact, enthusiasts in Southern California would follow Indianapolis races via telegraph, with updates posted at car dealerships and even a local speedway.[23]

In one short race on August 19, spectators saw Barney Oldfield drive his Benz in the fastest mile ever in 43.2 seconds (83.33 miles per hour), but the crowd of fifteen thousand may have gotten more than they bargained for in the two-hundred-fifty-mile Prest-O-Lite race. As the event became "a monotonous grind" after fifty-seven laps, tragedy struck. Canadian-born driver William (Wilfred) Bourque and riding mechanic Harry Holcomb trailed Swiss-born Louis Chevrolet when the two appeared to divert their gaze during a turn when the crowd cheered. Their Knox skidded, hit an uncovered drain on the track's edge, and flipped into a fence. Bourque fractured both legs and his skull, perishing on impact; Holcomb broke his arm and skull, dying on the way to the hospital. Competing driver Albert Denison was "hysterical" upon learning of the deaths, and when Chevrolet viewed the bodies he "staggered to a chair," unable to stand "the physical and emotional strain." Referee Lewis Speare ordered the drain covered and the track oiled, but Knox withdrew its remaining racers. After the race got back underway, Lewis Strang's engine caught fire and then Chevrolet dropped out. Finally, Burman's Buick crossed the finish line.[24]

Tragedy did not keep people away; in fact, it may have attracted even bigger crowds. Twenty thousand spectators saw new records set on August 20. Strang won the one-hundred-mile race, finishing in 1:32:48.5 (64.65 miles per hour), slightly slower than Chevrolet's first hundred in the two-hundred-fifty-mile race. The next day, Oldfield won the twenty-five-mile race for the Remy Grand Brassard, sponsored by Remy Electric, which gave the victor fifty dollars, a silver armband, and a seventy-five-dollar weekly stipend as long as he maintained the title using Remy products. But that day's big attraction was the three-hundred-mile Wheeler-Schebler race, which was cut short after two hundred thirty-five miles. Charlie Merz was speeding across a bridge over the creek on the track's edge when a tire blew; his National flipped and plunged into a group of spectators. Three died: Claude Kellum, Merz's mechanic; James West, a local butcher; and Omer

Jolliffe, a farmer from Trafalgar, Indiana. Miraculously, Merz was not hurt, but fifteen minutes later Bruce Keene's Marmon smashed into the same bridge and he sustained head and neck injuries; riding mechanic Robert Schiller fractured his skull yet survived. Referee F. B. Stevens immediately ended the race. "Owing to the physical condition of the contestants, who had been subjected to the strain of a three days' race meet under trying climatic conditions," he "deemed it to be to the best interests of the entrants and spectators to abandon the race." No prizes were awarded, although Stevens did recommend issuing engraved participation certificates. Merz, whom some accused of driving longer than his tires (or nerves) could handle, said the race would be his last.[25] One auto dealer, shaken by what he saw, said speeds of a mile per minute were "fast enough for any sane man."[26]

Five died at the oval that tragic weekend, not counting Clifford Littrell or six-year-old Elmer Grampton, who was crushed by a carful of spectators heading to the race. Although Fisher claimed the track was in good shape, not everyone agreed. A National Guard officer observed that friction from tires softened the tar, causing rocks to rise to the surface. Marion County coroner John Blackwell concluded the grounds must not have been ready, which explained why a hospital was built there. Fisher conceded the speedway was not yet complete, in the broadest sense, but defended the builders by saying the track would *never* be finished; they would always be working to improve it. The deaths, he insisted, were accidents. Blackwell disagreed and held Fisher responsible. One AAA official thought the crashes were caused by driver exhaustion and said the association would not sanction long-distance events unless track conditions improved.[27]

Motor sport's impending demise seemed certain. Some manufacturers stopped racing, saying the industry suffered a blow with every injury, and some auto clubs also protested. But others said it must continue. Americans seemed to be infected by a "speed microbe"; if racing were stopped, irresponsible "speed annihilators" might cause mayhem on any roadway.[28] Racing was "a necessary escape for a certain flow of animal spirits and energy" for Americans, who "must have such a blow-off or find their outlet in evil ways." Like boxing, football, or baseball, motor sport seemed to be one of modern society's cultural "safety valves." It must be reformed, or it might be outlawed.[29] One fan alluded to social Darwinism, declaring, "Give us Speedway races and dangers met and overcome that we may grow. Give us thousands who gaze, enthralled, and then go forth stronger, better equipped for life's battles."[30] Others insisted the deadly sport should be abolished. Racing was "barbarous," an "amusement congenial only to savages." A "civilized" society could not tolerate an ostensible "sport" so frequently ending in death.[31]

Public outcry prompted action. Grandstands on the first turn were moved and concrete walls were built to protect pit crews. The track surface, which clearly could not withstand long-distance racing, also had to be replaced. Initial reports said the oval might be repaved with wooden blocks or a bitulithic asphalt similar to that used on Chicago's boulevards. The speedway even commissioned chemical analyses of more than a dozen samples of potential paving compounds, but most proved too soft or too hard.[32] Instead, it chose brick. A call for bids said bricks would be laid on a compacted bed of sand, with joints grouted multiple times with precise mixtures of Portland cement and sand. Work had to be done by skilled masons using correct practices and tools. No pieces smaller than a half-brick (cut at right angles) would be used, with the surface rolled multiple times by a heavy roller. Bricks had to be perfectly flat, with no depressions greater than one-quarter of an inch, as indicated by a straightedge at least four feet long spread out horizontally over the track.[33]

Many of the bricks came from the Wabash Clay Company. In mid-September, Fisher visited its factory in Veedersburg, Indiana, to inspect its products, including its street-paving bricks called Culver Blocks. The company estimated 3.1 million bricks, at thirteen dollars per thousand blocks (or $13,000 per million), were needed to pave the track. The blocks, warranted to be free of flaws including cracks or excessive lime, carried a five-year guarantee if properly unloaded from railcars and installed according to guidelines of the National Paving Brick Manufacturers' Association. The company saw usage of its pavers on the track as an advertisement and offered a fifty-cent discount per thousand bricks ($500 per million) if all advertisements for the track, through 1910, specified the speedway was paved with Culver Blocks. The company also expressed interest in placing a thousand-square-foot billboard at the speedway. It is unclear whether such marketing opportunities were pursued, especially since bricks from manufacturers based in Crawfordsville, Terre Haute, and other Indiana towns were also used.[34]

Sports venues are built with available materials and labor. The same way Harvard Stadium (1903) was built with innovative reinforced-concrete and Pittsburgh's Forbes Field (1909) used large quantities of steel milled in that city, Indianapolis's speedway relied on bricks and skilled bricklayers. In September, Meredith Construction Company of Indianapolis advertised for "expert brick setters" to begin the repaving, while Wabash Clay hired hundreds of extra workers to make the bricks. The 3.2 million vitrified paving blocks arrived via railcar over two weeks. Contractors were from as far away as Paris, Illinois, and St. Louis, Missouri. The work cost about $180,000, bringing total expenditures on the track to a reported $700,000.[35]

The Indianapolis Motor Speedway was now the world's only brick-paved track, and it seemed to foreshadow the future of transportation. *Good Roads Magazine* wrote that speedways, while "intended primarily for the sport of racing," gave highway engineers a chance "to study the effect of traffic composed entirely of motor driven vehicles." A properly built track provided "data regarding the relative merits of various wearing surfaces intended to withstand the action of motor vehicles." Brick promised a safer, faster, all-weather surface.[36] After inspecting the oval, a Toronto civil engineer said Indianapolis should have brick streets as well paved as the speedway, and the Circle City's own engineer agreed. Logan W. Page, head of the federal Office of Public Roads, predicted Indianapolis might prove brick to be more durable than macadam. Other cities could monitor the "experiment" to learn whether bricks would withstand heavy use by motor cars. The United Brick Association of America even watched installation of the final bricks when convening in Indianapolis.[37] Jane Fisher, who married Carl around this time, called the track "a brick-lined test tube, designed to test the stamina of American machines and men."[38]

Manufacturers used the new speedway for promotion, claiming their products were able to withstand racing's strenuous demands. A Jackson advertisement touted the company's success in the Wheeler-Schebler race yet assured consumers that it sold "safe, reliable, economical and serviceable cars."[39] Buick boasted that its products' "strength" and "stamina" demonstrated "indestructible soundness." The company even encouraged readers to clip and paste advertisements into scrapbooks, to remember the astounding racing feats.[40] Marmon ads claimed the company's cars withstood "tremendous strain" at "mile-a-minute" velocities. "Do you know of any other fast car that can stand up to punishment like that?" Studebaker touted one model for shattering records at Indianapolis, while Firestone, Michelin, Monogram Oil, and Remy Magneto also invoked races to promote products. Historian Jackson Lears observes that early-twentieth-century advertisers demonstrated a P. T. Barnum-like sensationalism, and so it seems appropriate that they used racing to market cars. With performance-grade machines, Americans might fulfill dreams of space annihilation.[41] Was the track built to test auto technology, or did manufacturers take advantage of famous races to push sales of consumer goods? It was hard to tell, but the latter seems most likely.

As news of the races spread, cities grew inspired. New Yorkers read that a "motordrome" would be constructed in New Jersey's Meadowlands, while the Chicago Motor Club admired proposals for a $250,000 track, and Detroit promoters planned a $500,000 speedway and aviation facility on a four-hundred-acre site near the horse track at Grosse Pointe. Among the first cities to build a speedway was Atlanta, landlocked transportation hub of the Southeast. The Atlanta Automobile Association, with support from Coca-Cola tycoon Asa Candler Sr., bought a three-hundred-acre tract and spent $400,000 on a two-mile speedway seating forty thousand. Designers sculpted long straightaways and banked curves, anticipating speeds up to one hundred twenty miles per hour. This state-of-the-art oval, which promoters claimed was better than the one in Indianapolis, opened nine miles south of downtown in late 1909, during Automobile Week, when Atlanta hosted the South's first-ever meeting of the National Association of Automobile Manufacturers. Thousands saw Chevrolet, Oldfield, and Strang break records there. For a moment, Atlanta ruled racing. But with few major cities within easy driving distance, Atlanta's speedway was abandoned by 1913 and eventually became the site of the world's busiest airport.[42]

Indianapolis did not stand still. Besides laying bricks, workers added box seats, bleachers, and pedestrian bridges, as well as an aerodrome (aviation field) in the infield. Although several events had to be postponed—including a twenty-four-hour endurance race and an exhibition in which one company planned to drive a car a thousand miles per day for ten days—aviation meets were still held. After all, Fisher said aerial sport might eventually surpass auto racing.[43] Aviator Glenn Curtiss, a New Yorker who had recently broken a world airspeed record in France, said the brick surface would make the speedway the world's best. Curtiss promised to return once the work was done, but in the meantime, he advised aspiring flyers to use gliders to learn the mechanics of flight. Fisher's friend George Bumbaugh, a balloonist in Springfield, Illinois, announced plans to pilot a dirigible from the oval to downtown Indianapolis.[44]

Flyer Joseph Curzon, who visited the speedway several times in 1909, deemed it America's "best enclosed plot" for aeronautics. Curzon planned to build airplanes and start an aviation school there, predicting a day when people would spend spare time learning to fly. Flying offered "comfort and relaxation" in the face of modern stresses. "To drift off through space, with all the world with its hard knocks and bumps, both in reality and figuratively, far below you, is to feel that you are really living." While some thought sports could alleviate the turn-of-the-century malady of neurasthenia, or nervous exhaustion, others thought flying might do the trick.[45] Curzon planned Indianapolis's first heavier-than-air flight in late 1909, but the weather did not cooperate. His wife, who hoped to join him on the trip, said "nervous and hysterical women" might not be able to fly, but "brave women" like herself would have no problem. She thought women would "soon be flying in their own air ships just as they now do [drive] in their own automobiles."[46] Possibilities for female space annihilation were already tangible by 1909, yet it would be sixty-eight years before a woman raced in Indiana's most famous event.

Repaving was completed before Christmas, and Governor Marshall presided over the December 17 rededication ceremony. The final brick was supposedly a gold-plated silver paver embossed with *Indianapolis Motor Speedway*, but the vandal who later chiseled it out discovered it was actually made of a melted-down carburetor. Racing, it seemed, was modern-day alchemy. The purported $500 brick was laid in front of the main grandstand and guarded around the clock until the mortar set, when drivers immediately put the track to the test. Frigid temperatures cut short the first day of racing, but the electric timer recorded impressive performances: Lewis Strang covered a mile in 40.61 seconds, a new track record; Walter Christie drove a quarter-mile in 8.78 seconds, or 102.51 miles per hour, and then Strang covered the same distance in 8.05 seconds, or 111.80 miles per hour. These speeds were the fastest ever recorded in America, and nearly as fast as the concrete track at Brooklands. Attempting to race in such cold weather, though, seemed foolhardy to some. One critic thought the speedway just wanted to retake records from Atlanta, and he was probably right. He claimed even unscrupulous gamblers or gamecock handlers would consider racing in such cold midwestern winter to be "unsportsmanlike."[47]

Indiana's brick oval symbolized modern progress. In 1910, said the *Indianapolis Sun*, the city's factories employed five thousand workers producing twenty-five thousand cars worth $35 million. Thousands of freight cars shipped seven autos per hour. Rapid automobility liberated "men from the limitations of time and space." Echoing common early-1900s tropes about cars' nearly endless benefits, the newspaper said doctors making house calls now had greater ability to save lives. Motoring itself was intrinsically therapeutic: a car's "swift motion" negated summer heat, making a brief drive more advantageous than "a few weeks in the mountains or at the seashore." A man could propel his "family through the air rapidly, cooling the blood, charging the lungs with oxygen" and relieve his own stress by seeing "the beautiful country at [his] leisure." Cars even promised to bring rural dwellers and urbanites together.[48] Hoosiers believed the speedway put Indianapolis in the vanguard of cities and exhibited its world-class aspirations. A Claypool Hotel official overheard a Chicagoan say that "he would give a million dollars if that Speedway were set down within twenty miles of Chicago." A New Yorker said "nothing in the world" compared to it.[49] The oval was a point of municipal pride. A sign on the grounds read "Help Make Indianapolis the Greatest Automobile City in the World!"[50] Racing official Fred Wagner claimed that while Detroit might build more cars, Indianapolis's products were "better represented in the racing and contest fields."[51]

Other cities might build tracks, it seemed, but none could match Indianapolis. The *Sun* said the speedway was the world's best "place for great spectacles of all kinds, for aviation contest[s], for balloon races and sporting events of international importance." Maybe it would even host the Olympics someday. The oval was "a place for big things" in a world of big things, at a time when Americans started seeing sport as part of their national identity.[52] One small-town paper said Fisher would make the track a "camping ground for all nations of the globe." Other cities had hosted grand events, like Chicago's 1893 World's Columbian Exposition or St. Louis's 1904 Lewis and Clark Centennial Exposition and Third Olympiad. Indianapolis, too, might host big, international attractions.[53] The speedway connected the Circle City "with every point in the world where there is civilization enough to demand the world's news dispatches." Hoosiers boasted that East Coast papers now reported on their state's auto races, not just its folksy literary heritage. The track's fame "carried further than anything else that ever originated in Indianapolis." The speedway itself produced fifty thousand copies of a souvenir booklet that portrayed Indianapolis as one of the nation's best and most accessible cities.[54]

Other cities did, in fact, try to imitate Indianapolis. In 1910, Frederick Moskovics of Indiana-based Remy Electric announced a circular, one-mile wooden course in Playa del Rey, a beachfront community near Los Angeles. The banked track, seventy-five feet wide and elevated twenty-five feet on the outer edges, had a pine surface topped with a "powdery, absorbent crushed shell preparation"; engineers reportedly praised the surface, claiming rubber tires generated less heat on wood. Bleachers accommodated seventeen thousand spectators while boxes seated three thousand, and the track was lit with arc lights at twenty-five-foot intervals; motorists and pedestrians accessed the infield via three concrete tunnels. The track opened in April 1910 and, ultimately, about two dozen similar board tracks were built in the Midwest and West during that decade.[55] Meanwhile, Chicagoans grew impatient. A Windy City speedway would presumably be better than the Hoosier track, since they had learned from Indiana's costly experiment. In fact, maybe Chicago could simply convert an existing track. Barney Oldfield's manager, W. H. Pickens, set his sights on the old Hawthorne track, built in Cicero, Illinois, in 1891, but which had closed in 1905 when Chicago outlawed horse racing. Pickens hoped to build a wooden saucer like the one at Playa del Rey. Beating Indianapolis at its own game, though, was easier said than done. Ray Harroun said he still preferred Indianapolis over Atlanta or Los Angeles and predicted records set in California would fall at Indianapolis in 1910.[56]

The speedway announced AAA-sanctioned events for 1910, including Memorial Day, Independence Day, and Labor Day, holidays that had become days of leisure and recreation. Historian Matthew Dennis writes that after Memorial Day (or Decoration Day) commemorations became common in the 1870s, there was no clear consensus on the holiday's meaning. Veterans' groups wanted it to be a time of solemn remembrance, but working-class Americans made it a time for sport, including horse and bicycle races. Memorial Day and Labor Day became what were called St. Monday holidays, long weekends celebrating summer's beginning and end. By the 1900s, Memorial Day in Indiana became nearly synonymous with racing, but it was controversial. Disputes first arose in 1910, when Governor Marshall declared National Guardsmen working security at the track could not wear uniforms because veterans considered Memorial Day "sacred." Fisher evaded the edict by ordering militia-style uniforms from New York. Such controversies eventually got worse, nearly ending speedway races in the 1920s.[57]

On Memorial Day 1910, "space-destroying machines" contested in three days of racing: a one-hundred-mile race for the Prest-O-Lite trophy on Friday;

Action at the track, 1910. (IMS Photo Archive)

the marquee two-hundred-mile Wheeler-Schebler event on Saturday; and several races on Monday, including a fifty-mile Remy-sponsored event. None was over two hundred miles, which then seemed to be humans' endurance limit. Chicagoans made trips of similar length, either by train or car, to watch the races. The way to Indiana had what were then considered good roads, but it was not an easy drive; the trip required significant planning and at least a full day of driving. The *Chicago Tribune* outlined the route in detail, alerting motorists to detours. Dolton, Illinois, was installing a sewer system, and so its torn-up streets had to be bypassed; at Thayer, Indiana, meanwhile, a bridge over the Kankakee River was out of commission.[58] Despite such obstacles, thousands of spectators filled Indianapolis. On Friday, the crowd saw Circle City native Thomas Kincade finish first in a locally made National in the Prest-O-Lite race. Kincade won the silver trophy in a time of 1:23:43, which beat Louis Chevrolet's Atlanta record by twenty-five seconds. Johnny Aitken also set a new US record in a ten-mile race.[59] On Saturday, Ray Harroun won the two-hundred-mile Wheeler-Schebler race in a Marmon in 2:46:31, beating Chevrolet's Atlanta time by seventeen seconds. On Monday, fifty-five thousand spectators viewed shorter events. The bricks were about ten miles per hour faster than the old surface, and they were also safer. There were crashes, but none was fatal. The speedway cleared about $100,000 in 1910.[60]

Although racing was becoming the speedway's dominant sport, flying continued to be a major attraction, with some boosters saying aeronautical events showed Indianapolis was a progressive city that had come a long way since its early days as a stagecoach stop on the National Road. In early 1910, speedway official E. A. Moross traveled to Europe to attract international aviators, and in June the track hosted a weeklong meet that included exhibitions by Orville Wright and the brothers' protégés who trained at their flying school in Alabama. (Fisher paid the Wrights a reported $95,000 to exhibit non-Wright machines as well.) One flyer was Dayton's Walter Brookins, who ascended to a world-record height of 4,384.5 feet, as calculated by Albert Lambert. In one ascent, fifteen thousand spectators watched his biplane swing around in circles—apparently out of control—before regaining his bearings. Brookins also raced a lap in an Overland Wind Wagon, a propeller-driven land vehicle, beating his nearest competitor by twenty-five yards. Crowds were dazzled as the line between aviation and spectacle blurred. Jane Fisher later said the Wright brothers resembled "a comedy team in a vaudeville show."[61] Another writer called aviation the "King of Sports."[62]

In September, nine balloonists participated in a national qualifying event preceding an international competition in St. Louis. Fisher's *Indiana II* landed more than three hundred fifty miles away at Pittsburgh, while *America II* and *Buckeye* made it to Virginia. A St. Louis balloon landed in West Virginia, while *New York* touched down east of Cincinnati, traveling just over two hundred

National aviation meet at the speedway, June 1910. (Library of Congress)

miles but staying in the air longer than the other balloons. Although it may have been evident to some that balloons were not as easy to control as airplanes, lighter-than-air craft were part of a shift in thinking about three-dimensional space. As American cities grew congested in the late 1800s, visionaries imagined horseless cities and envisioned what scholar Jeremiah Axelrod calls the vertical city, with elevated sidewalks and roadways, subterranean railroads, and airships tethered high above streets. It was becoming clear that vertical space could be as useful as horizontal space.[63]

On Independence Day weekend 1910, Indianapolis's speedway hosted record-breaking events. Louis Chevrolet cut the previous record on the five-mile race by more than a minute, while Kansas City's Eddie Hearne won a ten-mile free-for-all race for a trophy known as the Speedway helmet. On July 4, thousands of spectators watched fourteen cars race for the Cobe Cup, sponsored by Chicago Automobile Club (CAC) president Ira Cobe. The Cobe Cup had been run as a road race in 1909 in northwestern Indiana, and suburban Elgin bid to host it in 1910. But CAC feared road races did not hold as much interest, and so the organization held the Cobe Cup as a two-hundred-mile speedway event in 1910, when Indiana native Joe Dawson drove his Marmon to victory. Chicago motorists again trekked to Indianapolis for these races. Later, in September, Hearne won a one-hundred-mile Labor Day race, earning $1,000 and retaining the helmet—with its fifty-dollar weekly pay—he had first won in July.[64]

Aspiring racer and champion boxer, Jack Johnson, at the wheel of his ninety-horsepower Thomas Flyer, seated next to an unidentified man. (Library of Congress)

In the Jim Crow era, of course, Americans did not all have equal access to space annihilation. When spectators arrived for Labor Day races in 1910, they did *not* see one of the world's most famous athletes. Heavyweight champion Jack Johnson was a masterful Black boxer unafraid to flaunt his wealth or drive fast cars, angering those who disdained his challenges to white supremacy or his unwillingness to fit notions of Black respectability. As historian Mia Bay writes, "Johnson received tickets for speeding, reckless driving, obstructing traffic, and other moving violations wherever he drove, which discouraged him not at all." He saw his aspiring racing career—and speeding more generally—as a form of "advertising."[65]

On July 4, 1910, the same day as the Cobe Cup, Johnson defeated Jim Jeffries, the "Great White Hope," in a highly publicized boxing match in Reno, Nevada. White rage in response to Black pride prompted race riots (sometimes better termed race massacres) throughout America, causing dozens of injuries and at least eight deaths. Newspapers soon reported that Johnson—who had visited the track the previous November, while preparing for Reno, and stated his intent to race—was offered $10,000 to drive at Indianapolis. In early 1910, Johnson was quoted as saying, "For a long time I have been anxious to compete with some of the best drivers in the world, and I believe this race will afford me the opportunity." But after Reno, white drivers threatened a boycott. Louis Chevrolet proclaimed, "There are no negro [sic] automobile race drivers at the present time, and if I understand correctly, there is a ban against it. I am not willing to allow my name to be used in the same race program as that of Jack Johnson, and if the Indianapolis motor speedway management cannot confine itself to automobile racing without bringing a negro barn-storming pugilist, I believe it is time for the white drivers to quit the game on that track." Meanwhile, Bob Burman echoed Chevrolet's implication of a racist gentleman's agreement. He declared that "white men who make a business of automobile racing" should "censure" the speedway. White racers also insulted Johnson's intelligence, claiming he did not understand how cars worked—despite the fact he had previously raced as a riding mechanic. In response, Johnson offered to give a mere driving exhibition at Indianapolis, but that was still too much. He was banned. Racers and officials drew motor sport's color line the same way athletes and officials in other sports, including baseball and horse racing, drew theirs in the late 1800s and early 1900s.[66] It is no surprise, however, that white boxers did not receive similar treatment. Newspapers even pictured Jim Jeffries—the so-called Great White Hope himself—seated in a Stoddard-Dayton at Indianapolis in November 1909, surrounded by Fisher, Allison, and others. Jeffries was one of the first men to drive a ceremonial lap on the newly paved brick speedway.[67]

As racing became a white man's game, more cities tried to get in on the action. By 1910, Denver announced plans for a speedway, while Cheyenne, Wyoming, hosted races at Frontier Park. Farther south, on the High Plains, a speedway near an amusement park in Amarillo, Texas, replaced a previous track sited around a playa lake. Closer to Indiana, it looked like a one-mile board motordrome might be built on a former horse track near Louisville, while Philadelphia promoters announced plans for a brick track in New Jersey seating more than fifty thousand. In October, a manager of the Indianapolis races visited New York to explore sites for a $3 million "speedway and general athletic grounds" with "aviation field," motor-testing facilities, and an "exposition building" for trade shows and conventions. This five-hundred-acre facility might even bid for the Olympics. Like other tracks planned for cities with expensive real estate, though, the New York speedway did not come to fruition. Indianapolis remained the racing world's focal point.[68]

Fisher, who had grand ambitions, announced a five-hundred-mile International Sweepstakes Race in May 1911 for cars with engines displacing less than six hundred cubic inches and able to sustain seventy-five-mile-per-hour speeds; some even speculated steam cars might compete in the race. Entry blanks specifying a $500 entrance fee went out eight months in advance. The purse was initially set at $25,000, plus an additional $25,000 in prizes sponsored by manufacturers. Most readers may not have realized they were witnessing the birth of a world-famous speed ritual, but at least one writer anticipated the "greatest season in the annals of the sport."[69] Perhaps with deadly 1909 races in mind, or in response to the controversial 1910 Vanderbilt Cup, officials outlined numerous precautions. Police and militiamen would supervise entrances to the speedway, guard parking lots, and surveil the facility's perimeter. No one could cross the track during the race. "Speedway guards" would use telephones to report problems, while mounted police would direct auto traffic. Crowd-control measures may have been as innovative as the pavement. Five months before the big race, the American Road Builders' Association met in Indianapolis, and attendees toured the speedway, proclaiming it an example of scientific "roadway engineering." In 1911, the bricks were still a state-of-the-art driving surface.[70]

Indianapolis's speedway demonstrated innovative technologies for breaking down spatial and temporal barriers. America's early-twentieth-century dream was to lubricate wheels of commerce while uniting people within sprawling economic, political, and social webs. Yet cars and popular culture created new kinds of public spaces. The speedway demonstrated the seemingly limitless potential of mobility technologies, but it was a privately controlled space primarily for making money. It was no public park. Fisher and his associates privatized the parkway concept and in the process launched a spectacle that became one of the world's most famous sporting events. The brick oval at the heart of Fisher's automotive empire turned space annihilation into popular spectacle and ultimately made Indianapolis the capital of international motor sport.

could develop *racing* cars. He desired profitable spectacles that would beget more spectacles. Fisher was more Barnum than Ford. From day one, the speedway's grandstands equaled the era's biggest professional and collegiate sports venues and offered a comparable type of consumerism. In 1909, for instance, the speedway corporation signed a contract with concessionaire Paul Franklin to sell sandwiches, peanuts, popcorn, ice-cream cones, and Cracker Jack, as well as coffee, tea, soft drinks, lemonade, milk, and buttermilk. The contract even included guidelines for liquor sales. Speedway patrons could also purchase programs, pennants, postcards, seat cushions, chewing gum, and tobacco products. The track's cut for each item ranged from 10 percent for programs to 60 percent for popcorn.[2]

The first International Sweepstakes Race attracted the most spectators of any sporting event in American history at that time, with a hundred thousand expected to watch a "magnificent field" of "motor Titans"; on an international scale, such a large crowd was exceeded only by a 1907 race in Germany. The track itself, with forty-one buildings on 328 acres, may have been even more impressive than the event. Grandstands seated forty thousand while the grounds accommodated up to two hundred thousand people and ten thousand cars. Trains, autos, and interurbans brought tens of thousands of spectators, with the Indianapolis Terminal and Traction Company carrying five thousand passengers per hour; taxis carried another thousand per hour. Indianapolis's Union Station saw as many as 180,000 pass through on race day. By comparison, America's largest baseball stadium in 1911, New York's Polo Grounds, then seated about thirty-four thousand; Philadelphia's Shibe Park (1909) and Chicago's Comiskey Park (1910) each accommodated fewer than thirty thousand. The Yale Bowl was not built until 1914, and so when the speedway debuted, America's biggest college football venue was still Harvard Stadium in Boston, which then held around forty thousand. The 500-mile race may have been motor sport's biggest spectacle yet, but its date was already controversial. Historian Nicholas Saccho notes that as early as 1911, churches and veterans organizations opposed Memorial Day sports. At one point, officials said they would move the race to July 4, a somewhat less sacred holiday, yet stuck with Memorial Day.[3]

The Hoosier track functioned like an amusement park, but one that attracted spectators from other metropolises to the edge of a less-populated, centrally located one. Indianapolis was establishing itself as a centrally located city for pop-culture amusements focused on speed. Indeed, many spectators came from Chicago, demonstrating that Indianapolis was part of the Windy City's cultural hinterland—along with the parks, forests, and semirural resorts of the Upper Midwest, which Chicagoans visited with increasing frequency by the early 1900s. Auto races also echoed turn-of-the-century world's fairs, in which the pop-culture attractions of the midway outdrew the ostensibly civilized, urban-style spaces at the heart of the fairs.[4]

Because getting to Indianapolis's motor midway was still somewhat of an ordeal, as many as 40 percent of the five thousand Chicagoans who trekked to the first 500-mile race traveled by rail. A Big Four Railway special train carried more than two hundred fifty passengers, while the Pennsylvania Railroad carried Chicago Athletic Association members on a round trip. The fare was twelve dollars, a considerable sum, indicating that many who attended that first big race were middle- or upper-class individuals able to afford a days-long jaunt to watch motor sport. For those planning to drive, the Chicago Automobile Club (CAC), the Chicago Motor Club (CMC), and the Chicago Motorcycle Club made elaborate plans for a five-day trip. Cars flying CAC banners headed to Lafayette, Indiana, on Saturday, where they were met by representatives of the Indianapolis Auto Trade Association. On Sunday they traveled to Indianapolis, planned an excursion afterward outside the city on Monday, watched the race on Tuesday, and then returned to Chicago on Wednesday. In an era before reliable road atlases, motorists needed guidance. In 1911, the CMC sponsored a confetti car, while pilot cars, including a Wisconsin-made Rambler, guided drivers, many of whom used a CMC pamphlet with detailed directions. The Hoosiers marked roads leading into Indianapolis with metal disks placed four per mile. Charles Root, editor of *Motor Age*, warned Windy City tourists to watch for potholes near Virgie, Indiana, where he had recently almost wrecked his car. Likewise, he recommended bypassing a poor bridge over the Kankakee River near Shelby, Indiana. The journey was not easy, and it was not cheap. Motorists expected to spend twenty-five to fifty dollars for a typical trip.[5]

At the time, many improved roads were simply paved with impacted clay, a method then promoted by the federal Office of Public Roads (predecessor to the Federal Highway Administration). Such roads, though, did not always hold up well in bad weather. In 1911, late-May showers prompted many motorists to take the train instead, but some still went by car, believing well-made Hoosier highways would be serviceable. For motorists coming from Chicago, rain turned the stretch to Roby, Indiana, into a virtual swamp, but once the tourists made it past the meatpacking town of Hammond, Hoosier roads were reportedly in good shape. It "was almost a boulevard jaunt." Motorists needed eight or nine hours to reach Indianapolis, where they saw innovative traffic-control methods, including a one-way traffic loop that limited congestion near the speedway. This was around the same time New York City's William Phelps Eno promoted reforms such as stop signs, traffic circles, and crosswalks in an influential pamphlet titled *Street Traffic Regulation* (1909).[6]

Trains brought people from New York, Texas, and California, and enthusiasts motored from Cincinnati, Cleveland, Dayton, Louisville, Milwaukee, Pittsburgh, St. Louis, St. Paul, and other cities. Driving to Indianapolis, though, was not necessarily safer than competing there. One elderly man arrived in town with a makeshift splint on his arm and a patch obscuring the damaged remnants of one eye. With his car stuck in a ditch five miles outside the city, the man calmly asked where he could find a surgeon; he planned to watch the race with his remaining eye. The speedway was already a must-see attraction. Before long, ticket requests came from every US state plus Canada, Cuba, Mexico, Panama, and Europe. Groups such as the American Chemical Society even toured the track. With so many people descending on a city of 240,000 residents (compared to Chicago's 2.2 million or Detroit's 500,000), hotels were cramped and the speedway created a bureau to locate rooms in private homes. Initially, it sought eight hundred rooms, but it ultimately had to find more than two thousand. Guests checked in at the speedway before being directed to lodgings throughout the city.[7]

The oval fostered celebrity because spectators could see cars pass by multiple times and could even glimpse drivers' faces. People wanted to see "gasoline-driven space annihilators" up close.[8] The big race was the first in a national program of seventeen major races and fifty-three other events in cities such as Philadelphia, Detroit, and Savannah. Racing was "high-class sport" with "business-like management" run by armies of clerks.[9] It resembled vaudeville and baseball, both of which were developing into profitable interstate entertainment circuits. In April 1911, Detroit Tigers outfielder Ty Cobb visited the track. The speedster did not break any records at Indianapolis, but he did drive fast during an exhibition lap. Meanwhile, theatrical metaphors abounded in press coverage. Reed Parker said the race was "down stage" of other events, while John DeLong wrote that

Early-twentieth-century racing celebrity Berna Eli "Barney" Oldfield, circa 1910s. (Library of Congress, George Grantham Bain Collection)

racing's "stars" stood "in the wings awaiting their cue," ready "to lift the curtain" on the "big outdoor stage" for "motordom's biggest show." It was like Broadway.[10] In 1912, observers called the race a "curtain raiser" for events in Milwaukee, Los Angeles, and other cities.[11] In 1916, the *Chicago Tribune* ran a series of driver biographies titled "Dramatis Personae of the Speed Spectacle," which resembled the detailed profiles featured in official race-day programs.[12]

In the days leading up to the race, a motley crowd filled the lobby of the Claypool Hotel, where grease-stained drivers interacted with fashionable patrons, while attractions elsewhere kept the throngs entertained. Washington Park, grounds of minor-league baseball's Indianapolis Indians, hosted nighttime boxing matches illuminated by electric lights. Such fights became a race-week tradition, even though boxing was a risky proposition at a time when progressives linked pugilism to gambling and some states or cities outlawed matches, especially those violating the color line. By 1913, Indianapolis allowed only one match per year, the night before the 500-mile race. In 1915, Jack Johnson was scheduled to fight, but Mayor Joseph Bell canceled the bout, saying boxing had "degenerated into fake prize fights." Surely, Johnson's skin color factored into the decision.[13] The AAA even barred Barney Oldfield from racing after he competed against Johnson at Brighton Beach, near Coney Island; an indignant Oldfield announced his retirement yet continued publishing ghostwritten attacks on racing. Soon, Oldfield was reinstated and raced again by 1914. Johnson, meanwhile, never got a chance to compete on the track. In some cases, drivers got into trouble simply for fraternizing with any boxers—not just Black ones.[14]

Speedways used crowd control measures common in other pop-culture venues. Tickets were numbered, as in theaters, and spectators were told to take precautions against petty theft. Indianapolis police captain William Holtz advised hotel guests to lock doors and keep a tight grip on wallets. In 1911, a man from Guadalajara, Mexico, had $500 stolen at the speedway, while others lost smaller amounts. A thief took a diamond pin from a Plymouth, Indiana, man's shirt as he ordered lemonades from a vendor, while two local women were allegedly accosted at Michigan Street and Toledo by a "[N]egro purse snatcher." Because the signature event attracted America's finest pickpockets and confidence men, in 1912 police brought Pinkerton detectives in from other nearby cities, such as Chicago, Cincinnati, and Louisville.[15]

The big crowd was almost as dangerous as the races. Oldfield, who claimed the bricks were damaged over the winter, grimly predicted the race would have a terrible end. Oldfield was not the only one expressing such concerns. The mother of racer Walter Jones implored officials to disqualify her son so he would not race on the potentially deadly track. Although the bricks were safer than the old tar-and-gravel pavement, such fears were not unfounded. In one practice run, a driver and his riding mechanic were thrown over the wall, with the latter badly bruised and lacerated. But even if "speed kings" had to face the dangerous reality of crashes, said one observer, they were ready. Racers, more than other men, seemed immune to fear.[16]

Why was such dangerous sport so popular? Or, put another way, "What is it anyway in the heart of man that makes him mad for speed?" One writer claimed humans had always loved speed, yet now Americans used modern technology to fuel this innate obsession. Strenuous races "put an unusual strain upon nerve and muscle," with drivers "skimming the rim of death" on each turn. What would high speeds do to human bodies and minds? What would happen when the race turned into "hard punishment," when strength waned and a driver tired? What would happen "when his nerves begin to show signs of shattering and there is nothing but the unending, painful grind"? Racing at seventy-five miles per hour required "great strength" plus "equally abnormal quickness of brain—action, sense of sight, and a muscle control" that made "it possible to 'throw' a car with a burst tire, to dodge another swerving machine or to do one of a thousand things which ha[d] to be done" in case of emergency. The spectacle was a dangerous game—a "man's game" contested by he-men with nerves of steel. If an engine stalled and the driver had "to crank his heart out" to ignite the engine, the "nervous fear" that he might not be able to start it could "wear him out" even before physical exhaustion set in. Seven "hours of driving at the highest tension" could "tear the strength, nerves, and ambitions of the most determined [driver] into shreds."[17]

Motor sport existed at the place where desire for modern amusements intersected with fear of technology's capacity to destroy bodies and minds. But enthusiasts thought experienced men could withstand the strain. Sportswriter and former gridiron star Walter Eckersall said drivers stayed at "top notch mental tension" throughout a race, which, like a football game, might be "won by clever head work."[18] Johnny Jenkins was a former boxer known for his "nerve and skill," while Ralph De Palma had "wonderful skill and more wonderful nerve."[19] This was an era when medical researchers explicitly compared football players to soldiers and sailors, speculating aloud whether men's bodies could withstand modern warfare's nervous strain, and similar analogies surfaced in racing. De Palma compared seasoned drivers to military men, who did not get "nervous." A "driver's brain" was engaged throughout the race, monitoring speed, engine, tires, and other drivers. One account even compared racers to shells fired from a howitzer on a dreadnought-type battleship. Cars were not quite as fast as artillery shells, but they still placed incredible strain on humans who had not yet figured out their physiological limits at high speeds. Although some observers feared a 500-mile race was too long, most racers said they were not intimidated. Ralph Mulford even thought a one-thousand-mile race would be possible at Indianapolis. To make motor sport safer, drivers began receiving physical exams in 1914.[20]

Racing was risky business, but risk meant profit. One account estimated 1911 wagers at $10,000, with bets typically placed on cars, rather than drivers. Some gamblers bet on average speed, while some callous individuals wagered on deaths or injuries. Auto-racing gambling, said one observer, might even shock horse-race fiends. Drivers could be superstitious. Old-field kept a prayer book in his pocket during races while Strang wore an "heirloom" ring; David Bruce-Brown refused to race without first kissing his mother. Most drivers tried to avoid racing in unlucky, accident-prone vehicles.[21] Speedway officials tried to negate their liability through insurance, an increasingly common strategy in the lucrative world of sports. In 1911, the track applied to Lloyds of London for a policy that cost $10,000 and offered $100,000 of protection in the event of rain—possibly the first-ever insurance policy for a motor race. Insurance companies would underwrite nearly any calculable risk in an era of statistics, probabilities, and government-backed weather predictions. While actuaries weighed the probability of precipitation, the track made contingency plans, even receiving AAA permission to postpone the race until June 3, if necessary. Rain did interfere with some travel plans, but it did not cause cancelation or postponement of the 1911 race.[22]

Drivers held differing opinions on how to prepare for the event, with some saying racers had to condition themselves "like ball players and other athletes."[23] Indiana native Joe Dawson trained like a prizefighter, with punching bags and medicine balls. Chicago's Louis Disbrow said gymnastics provided no benefit; drivers had to prepare by "taking a daily course of hard knocks over the county roads in a racing car at a fairly good rate of speed." His practice runs were as long as five hundred miles. Some drivers even traveled to remote farmhouses while training so as to soothe their nerves, a pregame routine also employed in turn-of-the-century intercollegiate football. Some racers stayed at farms within five miles of the track, while others went as far as ten miles away. Some took advantage of rural comforts. One driver bathed in a creek after daily practice and hiked to the farmhouse for a hearty dinner before retiring early to bed.[24] And, as people discovered the dangers of mixing alcohol and internal-combustion engines, some insisted on banning booze. Indianapolis residents invoked fear of drunk driving when they opposed a liquor license for a saloon located on the speedway grounds, and Ralph De Palma warned that any driver could succumb to drink's fatal effects.[25]

Who were these drivers who readied themselves to perform at top speeds before tens of thousands of spectators? Some were former taxi or demonstration drivers, such as De Palma, Louis Chevrolet, and Bob Burman.

Most were native-born Americans, but others originated overseas. Vienna native Joe Jagersberger ("The Flying Dutchman") once worked as a Mercedes driver in Paris, while Swiss-born Chevrolet came to Indianapolis via Detroit. Drivers often saw themselves as workers who had to protect their livelihoods from younger, less-experienced upstarts.[26] Racing was dangerous and expensive. The first 500-mile race featured machines worth a combined $225,000; thousands more were spent on tires, gas, and oil, plus shipping the vehicles. Prizes in 1911 were significant yet not outlandish: $10,000 for first place, $5,000 for second, and $3,000 for third. Auto-parts companies sponsoring awards included Splitdorf Magneto, Rayfield Carburetor, Wheeler-Schebler Carburetor, Monogram Oil, Bosch Magneto, Red Head Spark Plug, Dorian Rim, and Connecticut Shock Absorber. The lines between entertaining spectacle and technological improvement blurred on the Hoosier track.[27]

White men were considered capable of racing cars at deadly speeds, but women were excluded. Philadelphia's Vivian Prescott, a movie actress, stated her intent to compete at Indianapolis in 1913. According to the *Chicago Tribune*, Prescott was a "society girl" who once took an unauthorized spin "disguised as a mechanician." (Like Jack Johnson, perhaps she knew more about cars than men gave her credit for.) Paraphrasing track manager Theodore "Pop" Myers, the writer asserted, "The speedway would never dream of allowing a woman to compete in an event as grueling as the five century grind." It was too dangerous.[28] In 1914, Leotia Northam, a Los Angeles "sportswoman," planned "to enter all the important meets of the season" as an owner, but first she had to form a corporation. AAA rules declared any "entrant" had to be a "man" or "organization"—and since Northam was not a man, she had to be an organization. Driving, of course, was out of the question. Fisher had clear opinions on the subject: "If at any time a woman should be injured in connection with his races he would close the track." His stance echoed *Muller v. Oregon*, the 1908 Supreme Court ruling allowing states to limit work hours to protect female bodies. Racers drew a gender line, not just a color line, to protect white male earnings and reputations while shielding potentially maternal bodies.[29]

At 9:55 a.m. on Tuesday, May 30, 1911, starter Fred Wagner set off a series of bombs exploding 250 feet in the air; then, at 10:00 a.m., Fisher started driving the pace car at forty-six miles per hour. Once Fisher crossed the line, Wagner detonated a firework in the shape of a US flag to signal the start.

Six hours, forty-two minutes, and eight seconds later, Ray Harroun—ears packed with cotton to reduce noise and nervous tension—finished first in an Indianapolis-made Marmon Wasp equipped with an innovative rearview mirror that allowed him to ride alone, with no mechanic. Ralph Mulford was second in a Detroit-made Lozier, and David Bruce-Brown finished third in an Italian-made Fiat. The race was deadly. A wheel flew off Arthur Greiner's Indiana-made Amplex, throwing both the driver and his mechanic, Sam Dickson. Greiner only broke his arm, but Dickson hit the wall and died on impact. In another crash, driver Harry Knight and four others were injured. Crashes "kept the immense crowd in a state of fearful expectancy." To make matters worse, eighty thousand spectators were not easily controlled. After Greiner's crash, a mob of fans "swarmed across the infield," so that guards "had to club their guns to clear a space for the surgeons when the ambulance arrived."[30] Harroun, the victor, immediately retired. "This is my last race," he said; "It is too dangerous."[31] Two years later, he reiterated that the "strain" was "too great to be borne by flesh and blood." It was "too strenuous." He never raced again.[32]

To others, racing seemed like a superior sport. Cars sped wheel-to-wheel, crossing the line at virtually the same time, unlike in aviation contests, in which it was hard to tell who was leading. Two-dimensional races were easier to regulate, measure, and view than three-dimensional events. The International Sweepstakes Race was a carefully recorded spectacle. A throng of officials, reporters, and timers used complex "timing, scoring, checking, and announcing" methods. Charles Warner's electric horograph, only two of which existed by 1915, captured precise times every four laps, while four adding machines recorded cars passing over a wire stretched across the track. Scoreboards were operated by men who received constant updates from telephones around the oval. The race was also captured in sound: two Dictaphones recorded it on one hundred twenty phonographic records so it could "be preserved in proper sequence" and heard "by future generations." Such an amazing event had to be recorded for posterity, yet modern technology only went so far. After Bruce-Brown protested his third-place finish, officials realized one of the devices recording the number of laps completed had been out of commission for part of the race.[33]

Racing was (usually) a precise sport, but the risks made it appealing. Barney Oldfield said his was a "fast age" when an "athlete . . . willing to sacrifice his bones and gore on the altar of a highly-seasoned sport" attracted

Infield scoreboard, 1911. (IMS Photo Archive)

notice.[34] Some fans may even have bought tickets to see whether anyone died. Protests and criticisms of the sport ensued. Sam Dickson's father said the track should be closed: racing dozens of cars at high speeds on a single track practically guaranteed deadly crashes. The Indianapolis Ministerial Association denounced racing as a moral crime, while a Baptist preacher compared the races to uncivilized spectacles: "We denounce cock fights, bull fights, and such sports of the southern republics," he thundered, "but until we put a stop to these race exhibitions we dare not lift a voice of protest against these others. When a man goes on a racetrack he is taking his life in his hands—he is flirting with death."[35] Race cars, said one critic, were "devil wagons."[36] To another, such a long race was "human sacrifice."[37]

Yet some simply wanted change, and they echoed football reformers who, rather than outlawing that sport during its early-twentieth-century crisis years, created the National Collegiate Athletic Association (NCAA) and altered rules to make it safer and subject to scrutiny. In 1911, a drivers' association suggested precautions, such as limiting the number of qualified entrants for races so cars would be more spaced out. Some observers expected the AAA to ban dirt-track races, while preserving paved tracks. Carmaker Lozier said it would prioritize safety by competing only on speedways such as those at Indianapolis, Atlanta, and Los Angeles, or on road-race courses like Elgin's and Savannah's, where spectators were separated from drivers. Fred Wagner said that for any sport to be "legitimate," it had to be "on the level" and "above suspicion." Reforms would make the sport safer for American consumers.[38]

Why did people seek reform, rather than abolition? Perhaps the thrills outweighed the dangers. Also, unlike college football, motor sport rarely threatened elite young men's bodies or minds; few early racers emerged from the elite classes or attended college. Calls for reform also invoked racing's potential for spurring technological advances, an idea most frequently touted after deadly races. Harvey Firestone claimed long races exposed design flaws and pushed companies to make better products. Motor tycoons repeated the same argument horse-racing proponents used: it improved stock. Walter Marmon asserted, "Exponents of . . . horse racing have always advanced the view that the premier purpose of racing was the development of the pedigreed thoroughbred, thus improving the breed of horses, and applying the same principle to automobiles, the highest development of the racing car is the manufacturer's stock touring car."[39] In 1912, Fisher claimed he had built the oval to provide carmakers with a way "to test their product[s] at any speed they desired" so they could fix problems and exhibit improvements.[40] It is unclear whether this aim was actually Fisher's main goal in 1909, or if he just wanted to conduct a spectacle. Yet it is certain that, over time, technological progress became a common, even convenient, justification for racing fatalities. In 1912, automakers displayed new car models at the Claypool Hotel during race week, and printed ads extolled racing's practical benefits. Arthur Newby's National Motor Vehicle said the sport was "part of the manufacturing process," with the track complementing the company's factories. Two hundred laps around the brick oval concentrated wear and tear, demonstrating "reliability, power, and longevity" to consumers. Other companies, though, disengaged from motor sport. Michelin said too many people opposed the spectacle, which no longer seemed quite so valuable for developing tires.[41]

Indianapolis's speedway may or may not have been built to test *auto* technology, yet it certainly demonstrated possibilities of *paving* technology. By 1912, the track's two-and-a-half-year-old brick surface was holding up well, even though the stresses to which it was subjected had increased. Brick's value as a paving material was becoming apparent. The same newspaper readers who learned of the Hoosier track's durability could glance at the next column over to learn about an "exhibition of diversified clay products" at the Chicago Coliseum, with "model brick pavement, street, curb, and sidewalk" displays. A "model street" was located in the convention hall's annex, while the central exhibit area held "street sections" provided by the National Paving Brick Manufacturers' Association. Right before the second 500-mile race, the Association of American Portland Cement Manufacturers met at Chicago's Hotel La Salle and discussed the idea of city-to-city highways. Delegates even trekked from Chicago to Detroit to examine Wayne County's new concrete roadways, which were America's first and, at that time, finest.[42]

As the quest for durable, safe roads became a crusade, the speedway introduced state-of-the-art innovations, unveiling new concrete retaining walls and a tunnel under the track. This viaduct, drained by gasoline-powered pumps, allowed cars and pedestrians to cross safely into or out of the infield. Fisher said the project, budgeted at $2,000, ended up costing $10,000 after workers hit quicksand. Such experiences are expensive yet valuable. Fisher said knowledge gained over two years could have saved him $150,000.[43] In later years, grade separations similar to those built at the speedway improved transportation and enhanced safety in American cities, and the experience gained while building the speedway may have aided Fisher's development of Speedway City, Miami Beach, Montauk Point, and the Lincoln and Dixie Highways.

By the 1910s, motorists took up the cause of pressuring governments to build better streets and highways, a movement originally launched by bicyclists in the late 1800s. In March 1912, Chicago's Sherman House Hotel hosted a good roads conference, with attendees including Edmund James, president of the University of Illinois and chairman of the state's highway commission. Such dignitaries discussed the best route for a potential highway crossing the state from Lake Michigan to the Mississippi River, and the *Chicago Tribune* clearly expected people interested in the goings-on at the conference also to be interested in races, since it reminded readers in the same article that, if they hoped to attend the upcoming 500-mile race, they should book rooms immediately; more reservations had already been made at the Claypool than during the previous year. Officials now anticipated visitors from all forty-eight states.[44]

Racing went hand-in-hand with the Good Roads Movement. In 1912, the Indiana Good Roads Association teamed up with the Hoosier Motor Club (HMC) to launch a postcard barrage articulating the groups' joint platform:

taxes on cars to fund roads, efficient route classification, nonpolitical road building and maintenance, and cash payment of road taxes. Some Hoosiers worried they were falling behind other states, but one observer said that Indiana's fine paved roads reflected well on the state. Federal funding was also becoming a possibility for roadbuilding. Theodore Roosevelt's Progressive (Bull Moose) Party included a good-roads plank in its 1912 platform, and Carl Fisher ran for Marion County commissioner on the Progressive ticket, stressing the need for better roads. That year, moreover, Congress debated a memorial for Abraham Lincoln: would it be a road between Gettysburg and Washington, DC, or a Greek-style shrine in the federal district? The Lincoln Memorial ended up taking the form of a stately temple, but soon Fisher began his crusade for a highway ultimately named for Lincoln.[45]

Meanwhile, racing's future was uncertain. Atlanta's speedway fell on hard times and closed, and it seemed there might not be enough entrants for Indianapolis's second 500-mile race. Nevertheless, the speedway issued rules that whittled down the number of entrants while demanding higher performance, which combined to make racing a more exacting sport. Cars had to weigh at least 2,000 pounds (down from 2,300 in 1911) and qualify by running a lap at seventy-five miles per hour. Each car had to carry a riding mechanic. The AAA limited the number of contestants to three per four hundred track-feet, meaning Indianapolis would no longer see more than thirty-three qualified entrants, except for a few years in the 1930s. Disregarding veterans' organizations who protested Memorial Day races, Fisher pondered a one-thousand-mile race for 1913. After all, the spectacle promoted Indianapolis as one of the world's great car cities.[46] In the weeks leading up to the race, Indianapolis's downtown buildings were decked out in "flags and the colors of the automobile clubs and associations." Trains brought people from other cities, while motor clubs as far away as Colorado arranged driving tours. Thousands of out-of-towners packed the city, with rooms reportedly going for as much as four hundred dollars per night.[47]

Most of the 1912 race was not very exciting—one wit suggested bringing "a deck of cards, a novel, or an entertaining friend"—yet the ending was spectacular. For most of the event, Ralph De Palma's Mercedes led the pack, but then Joe Dawson's National began gaining as De Palma's engine developed an oil leak and started making terrible sounds. Bored spectators "threw down their newspapers and magazines and began to take notice." Suspense grew: "The minutes were centuries, [and] people who had grown blasé, during the long hours of monotonous grinding, stood up and yelled."

Joe Dawson crossing the line, 1912. (Library of Congress, George Grantham Bain Collection)

About seventy thousand still remained when Dawson finished in a record time of 6:21:06 (78.72 miles per hour). The crowd was ecstatic: a hometown boy had won in an Indiana-made car.[48] Yet De Palma, who lost in the most incredible way possible, exhibited a tenacious sportsmanship that made him a crowd favorite for years to come. His engine died as Dawson passed, so he and his mechanic got out and pushed. After crossing the line, the tired and frustrated De Palma leaned against his car and requested "a sandwich and some lemonade"—perhaps the first (but not the last) media-reported demand for consumables at the end of a big race. Film of the dramatic loss soon became a vaudeville staple.[49] Racer Eddie Rickenbacker later recalled De Palma had "failed in a wonderful way" and the crowd loved it. Meanwhile, victory boosted Dawson's career. Besides about $26,000 in prize money and a bonus from National, he received offers to race at fairs and dirt tracks across America.[50]

The speedway immediately announced another big race for 1913, hoping for more international drivers—which, in turn, would mean even more publicity and spectators. Fisher announced plans to replace the main, wooden, grandstand with one made of steel—this in the same year Boston's Fenway Park and Detroit's Navin Field (Tiger Stadium) opened. New York investors,

Ralph De Palma and riding mechanic Rupert Jeffkins push their way toward the finish line, 1912. (Library of Congress, George Grantham Bain Collection)

meanwhile, announced plans for a "scientifically banked" brick track seating two hundred thousand at New Jersey's Meadowlands. Surrounded by fences and illuminated at night, the Meadowlands facility could host "aviation meets, baseball, football, field and track athletics, circuses, wild west shows," and motorcycle races. This project was abandoned, though, once it became clear that draining the land and building the foundations would cost at least $1.5 million. Developers then shifted attention to a former airfield near Garden City, Long Island, but this plan also fell through. New Yorkers insisted they should not have to go all the way to Indiana to watch races, but it was becoming clear that land near the Big Apple was too expensive. Chicago, meanwhile, was probably too close to Indiana's famous oval, yet the Windy City kept trying, with businessmen traveling to Indianapolis to figure out how their city might embrace the profitable spectacle. Investors in Germany even planned a speedway to rival the Hoosier raceway.[51]

Racing made legible the potential of cars and pavement, but if space between distant points could be annihilated by motors and bricks, then cities and suburbs might be rebuilt for a type of living based on automobility. According to one late-1920s account, Carl Fisher sat in his office during the speedway's early years, weaving grand visions of a horseless city. "Airplanes are in their infancy," he pontificated, "but you will live to see them [as] familiar travelers across the sky. Anybody with even the dullest foresight can visualize the passing of the horse as a factor in transportation." Fisher then explained his vision for a suburb next to the speedway:

> Make it an industrial city devoted to motorization of all traffic. Put it down as a rule of the municipality that all horses be barred from its confines. Do everything by motor. Electricity and gasoline would be the motive powers employed. Every business house, industrial plant and home would have the most modern equipment. The homes would be homes, not shacks that so frequently come to infest an industrial center. We haven't thought of a name yet, but it probably would be Speedway City.[52]

Fisher may not have said these exact words, yet they likely represented his way of thinking, and they certainly did reflect the basic shape of Speedway City's eventual development.

In 1912, Fisher and James Allison teamed up with real-estate agent Lem Trotter—the same person who helped them purchase the rural land on which they had built the speedway three years earlier—and by 1913 they formed Speedway Realty Company. Trotter, a novice urban planner, platted a working-class residential development that took Ebenezer Howard's 1898 idea for clusters of industrial garden cities and updated it for the automotive age, a layout similar to what Los Angeles urban planners would construct in the 1920s. No horses or "barns or watering troughs" would be allowed, and virtually all houses would be built with garages. Speedway City, as it was in fact originally named, was planned around machine space. Its main industry, besides racing, was auto-parts manufacturing, especially headlamps, batteries, and engines, with Prest-O-Lite consolidating several factories into a new complex. Speedway City was a modern place. By June 1912, workers began digging wells and excavating foundations. Major structures in the town would be fireproof, with tile roofs and reinforced-concrete walls. Wide streets—lined with houses, parks, and playgrounds—were named for auto pioneers like Ransom E. Olds and Henry Ford. Fisher and Allison hoped to attract skilled, hardworking men, heads of motor-age families who might become permanent residents of "a shining novelty in American municipalities."[53]

Speedway City echoed other early-1900s industrial towns. A few years earlier, U.S. Steel planned a gigantic mill town at the edge of metropolitan

Chicago, near Lake Michigan's southern tip. Gary, Indiana, represented the rising importance of the urban periphery as "an indispensable part of proper city functioning." It was a satellite city such as those about which Chicago social scientist Graham Taylor wrote in the 1910s. Gary was utopian only insofar as it fulfilled the dreams of capitalists and accountants, but it symbolized a shift of essential urban functions to the metropolis's sprawling edges. Speedway City also anticipated by a decade the suburb of Dearborn, Michigan, sited near Ford's massive River Rouge plant. Industrialists like Henry Ford presumed that better quality of life prevented radicalism, so they engaged in welfare work, eventually known as welfare capitalism, in part by building pleasant towns that compensated workers beyond mere wages. Scholar Andrea Tone shows that welfare capitalism first emerged in Progressive Era companies, such as Dayton's National Cash Register, which provided workers with health care, housing, and leisure. Playgrounds, company-sponsored sports teams, and theater productions were part of the compensation package. To industrialists, these tightly controlled and orchestrated benefits seemed better than the cheap amusements many working-class people embraced.[54] Industrial towns also offered the wages of whiteness as an essential benefit. By the mid-1900s, Speedway (as it was then known) had hardly any Black residents and was rumored to ban them in its city charter. Indeed, it may have functioned as a sundown town, from which African Americans were barred by statute or by custom.[55]

Speedway's track and industrial town were the nucleus of Fisher's quest to remake space for efficiency, profit, and leisure. In September 1912, during a banquet at Das Deutsche Haus, an ornate Turner hall on Massachusetts Avenue near downtown Indianapolis, Fisher unveiled his next undertaking: a transcontinental highway from New York to San Francisco. He and other motor moguls, including Allison, pledged hundreds of thousands of dollars, while newspapers, chambers of commerce, HMC, and former Indianapolis mayor Charles Bookwalter all endorsed plans for the eventual Lincoln Highway. Construction was expected to be finished by 1915, in time to facilitate trips to San Francisco's Panama-Pacific International Exposition. The road's estimated cost of around $25 million would be financed by contributions from auto interests, and individuals could join the association at rates of five, one hundred, or one thousand dollars. Fisher expected interlocal competition—a "natural rivalry among counties"—to drive fundraising for this "ocean to ocean highway." He shunned government aid, insisting private interests could plan and build the road.[56] Federal officials endorsed the idea, if not the details. Federal road official Logan Page calculated the road would cost almost $60 million, more than twice Fisher's estimate, yet he thought the proposal would arouse "public sentiment to the necessity of co-operative plans" for highways.[57]

The Lincoln Highway, initially known as the Coast-to-Coast Rock Highway, was "an idea whose time had come." The number of cars registered throughout the United States had climbed into the hundreds of thousands by 1912, and motorists grew bolder as cars improved. But they needed roads, and Fisher was among the first to offer a viable plan for a transcontinental route.[58] He saw the automobile as humanity's crowning achievement: "Of all the cunning devices of the human brain, nothing has ever equaled it in its capacity to serve the need, the convenience, and the pleasure of mankind." The highway could foster unity, education, and prosperity, while also prompting tourists to spend money in America, rather than in Europe.[59] If the Lincoln Highway was a patriotic undertaking, there was little doubt that it also promoted the auto industry. Fisher entered a Marmon in a twenty-two-car tour that left Indianapolis in July 1913 for a five-week, 2,453-mile sojourn to the Pacific Coast variously publicized as a pathfinding tour for the Lincoln Highway or as a promotional tour for Indiana-made cars. Jane Fisher, who met up with Carl at Lake Tahoe on the tour's far-western leg, described the trip as one in which cars "were dragged from mud pits" in Iowa and "hauled out of sand drifts in Nevada and Utah." Crossing rivers and mountains was not easy. Despite the difficulties, or perhaps because of them, others joined Fisher in dreaming of better roads. By 1913, some congressmen advocated federal funding of highways, at a time when the federal Office of Public Roads was already gathering information about potential routes.[60]

Allison claimed that when Fisher first approached him with his plan for the Lincoln Highway, he thought his business partner "was crazy, it seemed [like] such a dopey scheme." But Fisher eventually convinced him it was a good idea. Even more important, he convinced Henry B. Joy, the respected head of Detroit's Packard Motor Car. At this point, Henry Ford, who preferred to sell as many durable Model T cars as possible so the government would eventually use tax dollars to build highways, had already rejected Fisher's repeated overtures, but Joy got behind the plan, offering $150,000. Joy helped site the route and also suggested finding a better name than Coast-to-Coast Rock Highway, prompting Fisher to come up with its eventual and legendary name, the Lincoln Highway. The Detroit industrialist imposed a discipline his Indianapolis counterpart lacked. Fisher had virtually promised the governors of Kansas and Colorado the highway would go through their states, even when it was unclear whether that was the best route; soon he considered a complex web of roads like that which eventually comprised the north-south Dixie Highway. As in racing, Fisher thought the best way to promote highways was through competition—in this case, between counties and states. But once Joy took over the Lincoln Highway Association, he declared an efficient route from Chicago through Iowa, Nebraska, and Wyoming, crossing the Rockies at a lower elevation than any Colorado route. "Directness," writes historian Drake Hokanson, "was all that mattered to Joy."[61]

Fisher—who demurred when people wanted to call the new road the Fisher Highway or proposed a statue of him along the route—could be modest, yet he was never one to put off a new project until the previous one was complete. Soon he promoted *another* transcontinental road. HMC first broached the idea of a north-south road from Michigan to Florida in 1914, and early coverage referred to this "Hoosierland to Dixie" route as a Lincoln Highway "tributary."[62] Always motivated by the idea of moving people and dollars, Fisher hoped to boost development in Florida, where he was starting to hack a community out of a mangrove thicket on a Miami sandbar. This time, his project had help from key political figures. Indiana's Democratic governor Samuel Ralston met with governors of potential Dixie Highway states in Chattanooga, a transportation hub located where the Tennessee River cut through the Appalachians. For the next decade construction proceeded, county by county, until a web of roads stretched from Sault Ste. Marie, Michigan, through Chicago, Indianapolis, Nashville, and Atlanta. The route traded on national history, passing through Lincoln's Kentucky birthplace (about one hundred fifty miles from the Indiana town where Fisher was born precisely sixty-five years later), as well as sites of significant Civil War battles, including Murfreesboro, Tennessee. Historian Tammy Ingram writes that, while "plans for the Lincoln Highway lingered for years and other marked trails never made it past the proposal stage, the Dixie Highway evolved into a viable route within a few short months." Yet it was still mostly an inconsistent network of local roads, the best possible scenario in an era before federal funding or coherent planning. As Illinois and Indiana squabbled over the Chicago-to-Indianapolis route, Fisher, who sided with the Hoosiers, entertained good-roads proponents at the speedway in October 1915. That same month, highway promoters, including Fisher, Bookwalter, HMC's William Gilbreath, and writer Kin Hubbard, drove a Michigan-made Reo from Indianapolis to Miami. Technically, the highway was opened at a ceremony in Martinsville, Indiana, in September 1916, but work was not really done. By 1917, Fisher lobbied the Indiana State Highway Commission to improve a 143-mile section between Indianapolis and South Bend, along the right-of-way of the old Michigan Road.[63]

Transcontinental routes such as the Lincoln and Dixie Highways—which intersected near downtown South Bend—provided a template for the federal highway systems that tied the nation together first in the 1920s and then again after 1956. But many Americans had already witnessed automobility's possibilities in spectacular races that combined progress in motor and paving technologies with sensational popular culture. Modern mobility was displayed for the ticket-buying public, thousands of whom drove to Indianapolis's big brick track. Speedway impresarios orchestrated veritable speed carnivals that ended up altering cities as well as the spaces between. Carl Fisher centered his motor empire on a heartland city that was growing into an automotive metropolis. By the mid-1910s, in fact, Indiana's capital worked to rebuild itself in the image of the modern machines celebrated annually at its famous speedway.

4

AUTOMOTIVE METROPOLIS

Reinventing Indianapolis

As the speedway became famous, Indianapolis's built environment underwent profound transformations. In spring 1913, when a major flood devastated the Ohio River Valley, motor vehicles proved instrumental for recovery. Later that year, strikes shut down public transit and prompted residents to seek alternative forms of mobility, and then in November, voters elected a mayor who seemed poised to lead the Circle City in its transformation into an automotive metropolis. Meanwhile, as other cities tried to copy Fisher's famous speedway, construction continued on the Lincoln and Dixie Highways, as well as Speedway City and Miami Beach.

First came the flood. On Easter Sunday 1913, heavy rains started falling in the Ohio Valley. Over the next five days, up to twelve inches of precipitation inundated Ohio and Indiana, causing millions of dollars of damage and killing at least seven hundred people. The White River crested nearly twenty feet above flood stage and levees failed. About twenty-five people died in Indianapolis while seven thousand families were displaced from their homes. Water rose high enough by Tuesday to disrupt streetcars and fire service; residents fled to higher ground, perched on rooftops, or sheltered in churches and hotels. By nightfall, ten feet of water covered parts of downtown. Floodwaters washed away telegraph and telephone lines, as well as railroad and streetcar tracks. As locomotive and interurban service was interrupted, police commandeered boats to aid rescue efforts. The swollen

Great Flood of 1913 at Riverside Park, Indianapolis. (Library of Congress)

White River swept away the Washington Street Bridge and damaged other spans. Finally, by Wednesday, the floodwaters receded and cleanup began.[1]

The Great Flood of 1913 illustrated the value of machines. Motorboats, unlike canoes, could navigate raging floodwaters, while local auto dealers and manufacturers loaned vehicles to help people reach hospitals or shelters. Cars and trucks moved first responders around the perimeter of flooded areas, and they also helped rebuild storm-damaged roads. Two cars equipped with drags made of split logs covered with steel could do the work of several teams of horses. This new take on an old design was a sensation, with farmers and good-roads proponents writing to its builder, local engine manufacturer George Weidely, for information. (The next year the federal Office of Public Roads issued a pamphlet promoting a similar device as an effective means of maintaining dirt roads.) Scholar Kevin Rozario argues that natural disasters can prompt reconstruction if they come at the right time, and in this case, Indiana's flood coincided with a push for good roads. In wake of the flood, the Hoosier Motor Club launched a road-improvement campaign, placing white bands on telegraph poles to mark state routes and railroad crossings.[2]

The speedway, located on relatively high ground, remained accessible after the flood. With so many spectators traveling to the track, one wag even called Indianapolis a suburb of Detroit. But getting there took a lot of planning. The *New York Times* told drivers coming from New York and New England to go through Albany and Buffalo to Erie, Pennsylvania; then, from Cleveland, they could head to Toledo before turning southward to Columbus. This route had many clay roads, however, so in wet weather drivers should take sturdier roads through Akron. At Columbus, motorists could go west on the old National Road, or detour through Dayton. Mid-Atlantic tourists, however, might head west across Pennsylvania before crossing the Ohio at Wheeling, West Virginia. Drivers were told to use caution, since floodwaters had knocked out many roads and bridges. And once in Indiana, they had to monitor their speeds. A few days before the event, racers Ray Gilhooley and Joseph Byrne were arrested for driving too fast on Indianapolis city streets—a blazing thirty miles per hour. Police Chief Martin Hyland and Mayor Lewis Shank used a city squad car to chase them down. Upon arriving in town, motorists navigated a tidy loop that kept traffic flowing in one direction to and from the track.[3]

In 1913, fifteen thousand spectators showed up for trials and more than one hundred thousand attended the race, the first to feature a pagoda-style control tower. Racing was an international sensation. French carmaker Peugeot entered two cars, while England's Sunbeam entered one that had motored at Brooklands. Italy's Isotta entered three cars, while Germany's Mercedes entered two. Continental drivers included Frenchmen Jules Goux and Albert Guyot, Italians Paolo Zuccarelli and Vincenzo Trucco, and the Belgian Théodore Pillette. The track even provided an interpreter. American drivers included Louis Chevrolet, Ralph De Palma, and Johnny Jenkins.[4] Two British engineering societies, visiting America for a Society of Automotive Engineers meeting, filled a section of the grandstands. Their interest had been primed by races at Brooklands.[5]

The third 500-mile race featured new rules, including piston displacement limited to 450 cubic inches (down from 600). Jules Goux's Peugeot finished first in 6:41:43.45, averaging 76.59 miles per hour. The Frenchman won the Remy Grand Brassard for leading at two hundred miles, as well as the Prest-O-Lite Trophy (at three hundred miles) and Wheeler-Schebler Cup (at four hundred miles). Goux earned about $40,000 that day, more than in his entire career up to that point, and was the first non-US driver to win. There were injuries in 1913, but no fatalities. Michigan's Jack Tower broke his leg, while riding mechanic Lee Dunning suffered broken ribs and a punctured lung. The big crowd got plenty of excitement, and soon the speedway announced new stands would raise permanent seating to sixty thousand.[6]

Some of 1913's most striking results may have been seen on roads leading to Indiana. In Illinois, Governor Edward Dunne, a progressive Democrat, lamented that only 10 percent of Illinois's 95,000 miles of roadway was improved, in comparison to 20 percent in Kentucky, 28 percent in Ohio, and 38 percent in Indiana. Bad roads, warned Dunne, harmed schoolchildren, voters, and farmers. This complaint was a common Progressive Era trope: inadequate highways impaired Americans' ability to gather or conduct business. Dunne proposed a car tax to fund roads and, like other governors in the Midwest and South, advocated using convict labor to build them. Such advocacy came at a time when good roads garnered state and national attention. In March 1913, seven hundred delegates from forty-six states met in Washington, DC, for the second annual Federal Aid Good Roads Convention, where they heard from Democratic President Woodrow Wilson, passed a resolution favoring highways linking state capitals, and asked Congress to form a roads committee. Kentucky Democrat Alben Barkley (later Harry Truman's vice president) said highways would make Americans prosperous and happy, while in Missouri, Judge J. M. Lowe, an advocate of the National Old Trails Ocean to Ocean Road, thought a $210 million expenditure could result in a nation "gridironed" with roads. The AAA's Laurens Enos said better roads would especially improve conditions in the western states, where there were few transportation options. By the 1920s, the nation's first interstate highway network, with its distinctive white-and-black shields, would become reality.[7]

Meanwhile, public transit was disrupted in Indianapolis. On October 31, 1913, workers walked out after the Indianapolis Terminal and Traction Company (ITTC) refused to recognize the Amalgamated Association of Street and Electric Railway Employees of America. Workers demanded union recognition, better wages, reasonable work schedules, a grievance procedure, and arbitration. Transit and mail delivery came to a halt. ITTC imported hundreds of strikebreakers from Chicago, while Mayor Shank asked Marion County's sheriff to deputize two hundred men to run streetcars. The sheriff refused, though, and dozens of policemen declined to protect strikebreakers. Although the union denounced violence, large crowds that may have included strikers threw bricks and rocks at the scabs. ITTC struggled to get trolleys moving. A week into the strike, Governor Samuel Ralston sent in thousands of National Guardsmen. ITTC hoped to put soldiers on trolleys, but five thousand strikers, including hundreds of members of the International Ladies Garment Workers Union (ILGWU), marched on the capitol to pressure Ralston to remove the troops. ITTC finally agreed to arbitration, and on November 9, streetcar service resumed.[8] During the weeklong strike, four people were killed and more than a thousand were injured. Most workers were reinstated, but not all, and Chief Hyland resigned in wake of what was called a police mutiny. The strike was not the city's last labor stoppage of 1913. Three weeks later, Teamsters Local 240 struck for higher wages, with the ILGWU again offering support. Mounted police dispersed strikers from the central business district, yet commerce remained at a standstill. As historian James Barrett notes, teamsters had unique power to disrupt urban life. Wholesalers and retailers could not move goods, while garbage went uncollected. Shank, who faced impeachment because of his inability to mediate the dispute, resigned a month before his term ended, and Harry Wallace took over as mayor. Wallace prohibited gatherings larger than three persons and ordered police to crack down on strikers. Residents of the middle-class suburb of Irvington collected money to fund neighborhood patrols protecting strikebreakers, while motorists established a Commercial Vehicle Protective Association to safeguard automobiles and fund "rewards for the arrest and conviction" of violent strikers. After a week, the strike ended.[9]

Historian Georg Leidenberger argues that, in 1905, a months-long Teamsters' strike in Chicago prompted middle-class residents to adopt individualistic technologies of mobility, and something similar happened in Indianapolis, where people turned to cars or bicycles during the 1913 strikes. A bicycle store told customers that bikes were commuters' "best assurance against strikes." In addition, automobility infiltrated urban life. ITTC initiated auto delivery of mail when the strike kept it from fulfilling its federal distribution contract, and some postal carriers now reached their routes by car. People had to get creative to navigate the city. An ad for a new residential development informed prospective buyers that, if the strike prevented them from taking streetcars to see lots in the residential addition, they should telephone an agent, who could pick them up in a car. The *Indianapolis News* now used trucks instead of streetcars to deliver bundles of newspapers, while scores of cyclists helped the paper gather election returns.[10]

Streetcars, pedestrians, and horse-drawn vehicles crowd the intersection of Illinois and Washington Streets in downtown Indianapolis, 1906. (Bass Photo Co. Collection, Indiana Historical Society)

Meanwhile, access to city streets by anyone or anything besides motor vehicles narrowed. A month after the strikes, the Hoosier Motor Club implored residents to "facilitate progress and prevent accidents." The club encouraged driver caution but placed the burden on nonmotorists. Horse-drawn vehicles should stay to the right, pedestrians should cross only at crosswalks (after making sure to "look both ways"), and children should play only on side streets. This was the new auto-age order of things: "You have the right of way at crossings but not elsewhere." Such advice was the first step in a stigmatizing of pedestrianism that grew common by the 1920s, when streets were transformed from gathering places into vehicular thoroughfares.[11] Police cautioned pedestrians to follow traffic ordinances on race day, since it was dangerous for cars and pedestrians to occupy the same spaces. In a semisensational series on industrial accidents, the *Chicago Tribune* published accounts of those who nearly died at the speedway. In one story, a guard was "patrolling" the track when a race car "thundered by and blew a tire." As he moved to retrieve a piece of the tire, he underestimated the racers' speed and three cars quickly bore down on him; one sent the rubber flying. If he had gone any farther, he would have been hit.[12]

It was a turbulent time in Indianapolis, but it was also a time of reform, with residents primed for reconstruction. A few months after the first 500-mile race in 1911, a group of about two hundred progress-minded residents drove to Chicago and viewed the Windy City's boulevards and suburban Ravinia Park, then being reimagined as a City Beautiful–style cultural space. The next day they returned to Indiana, having made the 450-mile round trip in three days. In the Progressive Era, similar tours were not uncommon, with city leaders monitoring spatial progress in other urban areas, and it is likely that what Hoosiers saw in Chicago helped them imagine ways to rebuild their own city. Their trek took place two years after architect Daniel Burnham issued his famous Plan of Chicago, with its grand civic center, plaza, and radial arteries, and the same year Pittsburgh developed a similar plan. Such plans were rarely fully realized, yet they represented a broad desire to rebuild American cities.[13]

In January 1914, a month after the Teamsters' strike in Indianapolis, a new mayor, Democrat Joseph Bell, took office. Like other progressive mayors, Bell promised to eradicate prostitution and improve infrastructure. He organized a public works department and consolidated the superintendents of streets and the municipal asphalt plant into one street commissioner earning $3,000. This amount was less than the combined $3,600 two previous officials received, but the higher single salary attracted applicants with appropriate expertise for a position supervising more than a million dollars' worth of work per year. After one year in office, Bell claimed city streets were in good shape. Municipal work crews labored nonstop, and now Indianapolis had "better and cleaner streets than . . . any other large city." Even if he oversold his reforms, Bell's efforts were typical of cities that prioritized clean streets and efficient circulation. Urban planners or landscape architects such as Charles Mulford Robinson and George Kessler advised cities to create orderly street gridirons to facilitate traffic flow, or to build beautiful and efficient urban centers with boulevards, parks, civic plazas, levees, and union stations. Although many common traffic control methods first emerged in New York, by 1914 the center of innovation had shifted to the Midwest.[14]

As cities retooled for automobility, progress continued on transcontinental highways. The Lincoln Highway's logo—a capital L between blue and red stripes—adorned utility poles across the continent, while a pamphlet helped guide tourists to San Francisco's Panama-California Exposition. In reality, however, the Lincoln Highway was rough and largely unfinished west of the Mississippi. When writer Emily Post and her son tried to drive to San Francisco in 1915, they encountered nearly impassable sections of roadway, which prompted them to detour through New Mexico and Arizona and finally take a train to California. Nevertheless, AAA president John Wilson said American roadbuilding just needed some federal help to reach maturity. In 1916, Congress passed the Federal Aid Road Act (Bankhead-Shackelford Act), providing $75 million of matching funds to be distributed over five years. The law also spurred states to create highway departments. The Indiana State Highway Commission formed in 1919, after two years of legal disputes, and ultimately built thousands of miles of roads traversing Indiana's ninety-two counties. Governor James Goodrich asked Carl Fisher to serve on a state road commission in 1917, but Fisher demurred, claiming he had shifted his legal residence to Florida.[15]

As Americans debated the merits of highways, racing's prewar popularity peaked. Eleven foreign-made and nineteen American-made cars competed in 1914, with manufacturers on either side of the Atlantic hoping victory would provide access to international markets. Racers included Frenchmen Georges Boillot, Jean Chassagne, Ernest Friderich, Jules Goux, Albert Guyot, and René Thomas and Germans Josef Christiaens and Arthur Duray. International tensions were high. Goux created controversy when he said Bob Burman was not good enough to drive a taxi in Paris; Americans retorted by calling Goux a "poor sportsman." Former champion Joe Dawson insisted, incorrectly, that track familiarity would help Americans win the race.[16] Nationalism was palpable. The flags of Belgium, England, France, Germany, and Italy hung downtown, and, the night before the race, a band struck up *La Marseillaise* at the Claypool while Goux and Boillot—two "sawed off, chunky Frenchmen with stubby mustaches"—bowed to cheering onlookers as bettors placed wagers in a nearby room.[17] The field of racers seemed the best ever to compete in America, and time trials augured the breaking of numerous records. Goux's Peugeot reached 98.3 miles per hour in practice, and the next day Boillot turned an even faster lap. Suspense filled the air: who would finish first? Although many favored Boillot, some observers thought he was better suited for road races. The soon-to-be World War I flying ace supposedly disdained "monotony," preferring instead

a "kaleidoscopic change of scene and pace" to soothe "his nervous disposi-
tion." Experts, therefore, picked Goux.[18]

Spectators still traveled by rail to Indianapolis, but cars were becoming a
primary mode of transportation. Advertisements for Marshall Field's store
encouraged male and female Chicagoans to purchase coats or "Steamer
Rugs and Lap Robes for Traveling and Motoring" before heading to Indianapolis. Hundreds of spectators slept in cars along roads leading to the
speedway, while another ten thousand stayed in nearby towns. To satisfy
Windy City readers, the *Chicago Tribune* rushed twenty-five thousand copies of its morning edition to Indianapolis and reported on the feat as if it
were a race: the 184-mile journey via truck and express train took just four
hours and eleven minutes. Speed was not the only concern for motorists,
some of whom did not have proper tags and therefore ran afoul of registra-
tion mandates in South Bend. Residents distributed pamphlets warning
of overzealous police, and they even considered ousting municipal leaders
responsible for the crackdown.[19]

By 9:00 a.m. on race day, roads were so congested it took two hours to
drive three miles from Monument Circle to the speedway. In stark contrast
to this snaillike progress, the race itself saw a frenetic pace. René Thomas's
French-made Delage won in 6:3:45.99, his 82.47 miles-per-hour average de-
molishing previous records in front of 115,000 spectators, including 60,000
in the recently expanded grandstand. It was a chaotic race. On lap forty-
seven, Ray Gilhooley's Isotta smashed into the wall and flipped over. Joe
Dawson, trying to evade the wreckage, was thrown from his Marmon but
lived. Doctors were unsure Gilhooley would survive, but he did, albeit with
major facial wounds. He soon announced his retirement.[20]

Racing's dangers did not stop other cities from emulating Indianapolis.
Chicagoans considered building a $750,000 brick or concrete speedway
seating a hundred thousand on a five-hundred-acre tract along the Lincoln
Highway. Like their Atlanta counterparts, Windy City boosters claimed
they could build a better track, and, like New Yorkers, speculated the infield
might host aviation or athletic contests. The Chicago speedway was not
built, but Chicagoans did not stop dreaming. Promoter Tom Carey revived
the possibility of turning the old Hawthorne track into a raceway similar
to Playa del Rey. Yet Chicago did not get a major raceway until a two-mile
board track opened in suburban Maywood in 1915. Chicago's mayor-elect
William Hale Thompson called Speedway Park the nation's "biggest sporting

proposition." Its inaugural 500-mile race, delayed by a transit strike, was won by Italian-born British racer Dario Resta, whose Peugeot finished in 5:07:27 (97.6 miles per hour) before more than eighty thousand fans. Soon, promoter Tex Rickard visited Chicago to gather information for a group hoping to build a track in Argentina, while German carmaker Opel announced plans for its own speedway.[21]

Motor sport was gaining national and even international popularity in the early- to mid-1910s. Sioux City, Iowa, a midsized city on the Missouri River, opened a fifty-thousand-seat speedway and hosted a three-hundred-mile Fourth of July Classic, the so-called Mini Indy. One driver attracted by the $25,000 purse was Ohioan Eddie Rickenbacker, who won Sioux City's big race in 1914; the following year, he collaborated with Fisher and Allison to create a racing team. Elsewhere on the Great Plains, Omaha built a track, while Des Moines's speedway—a wooden saucer like Los Angeles's Motordrome—hosted auto races and aviation contests. Despite a local newspaper's boosterish claims that it was the best track ever built, a three-hundred-mile race held at the Des Moines track did result in a fatality.[22] Still, such tracks thrived. In 1915, a one-mile, asphalt-paved Narragansett Park Speedway opened near Providence, Rhode Island. In its first event, Bob Burman set a world record with a 45.73-second mile. In Detroit, a Speedway Country Club planned a multipurpose, three-hundred-thousand-seat facility called "the Concourse of Clubs." Cleveland anticipated construction of a $700,000 speedway, while investors in Kentucky, Ohio, and Indiana reportedly capitalized a speedway near Louisville at $250,000. Philadelphians hoped to build a $2 million, suburban, two-mile brick speedway, seating a hundred thousand, while St. Joseph, Missouri, also planned a $2 million facility. On the West Coast, San Diego, Seattle, and Tacoma built tracks, while San Francisco designed a speedway that was to open by the start of the 1915 Panama-Pacific Exposition. In the Southeast, Birmingham and New Orleans planned speedways, as did Toledo and Cincinnati in Ohio.[23]

New York promoters built a million-dollar, creosoted-pine-board speedway at Brooklyn's old Sheepshead Bay horse track, with an infield that could accommodate golf, football, and an aviation school; some thought it might even host the Olympics one day. The all-purpose sport and cultural grounds, located within an hour's drive of eight million people, reportedly had backing from Wall Street financiers and several figures associated with Indianapolis racing: Carl Fisher, Arthur Newby, and Ralph De Palma.

State-of-the-art grandstands, seating a hundred thousand people, sported entrance tunnels similar to those at the recently completed Yale Bowl in New Haven. Sheepshead Bay was touted as the world's biggest "arena for outdoor sports" and the globe's fastest track. It opened with the three-hundred-fifty-mile Astor Cup race attended by at least sixty thousand spectators. Gil Anderson won in record time, pushing his Stutz to 102.60 miles per hour. Indianapolis, in turn, worked to stay relevant, announcing plans for new retaining walls and a drivers' clubhouse with recreation facilities. New stands brought covered seating to seventy-five thousand, making the speedway's capacity even larger than that of the Yale Bowl.[24]

By August 1915, Fisher severed ties with Sheepshead Bay, turning his attention instead to other projects. In Minnesota, he and Frank Wheeler invested in the Twin City Motor Speedway, which they predictably claimed was better than the one at Indianapolis. Yet construction was rushed and the concrete was rough, and so the track was not as fast as expected and attendance was lackluster. Wheeler suffered huge losses that forced him to sell his Indianapolis Motor Speedway shares to James Allison, who then became majority owner. The ill-fated Minnesota speedway closed in 1917 and later became the site of the Minneapolis-St. Paul airport.[25] This episode was just one time when a former racetrack was converted for aviation. By the 1920s, places that had once turned two-dimensional space annihilation into profitable motor spectacle were transformed into places that profited by turning three-dimensional space annihilation into commercial aviation.

Closer to home, Fisher and Allison continued working on Speedway City. The land initially cost nearly $117,000, but the sale of a factory site to Prest-O-Lite for more than $29,000 defrayed the cost. Globe Real Estate invested substantial amounts of money into roads, sidewalks, and curbs ($20,362.39), water works ($12,952.40), and gas lines ($12,262.52). Real-estate agent Lem Trotter studied drafting in night classes so he could lay out a neat grid and tidy lots to make Fisher's vision into reality. Despite the town's loosely enforced ban against equines, Speedway City may have had more horses than racial minorities. A Speedway Realty Company ad boasted that the community—with its stately trees, electric lights, telephones, and interurban service—would "keep out all undesirable persons and lines of business." The turn of phrase may have been a dog whistle for restrictions barring nonwhite residents.[26]

Meanwhile, Carl Fisher began efforts in Florida that would bring him great fame and wealth. He and his wife first visited Miami in February

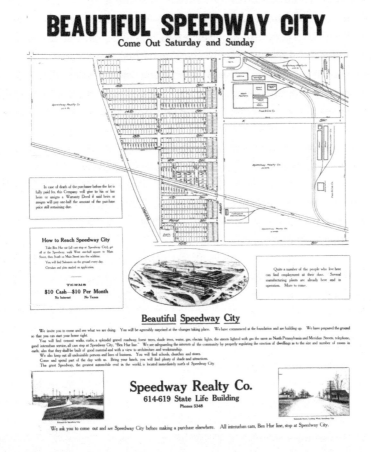

Speedway Realty Co. ad. (Bass Photo Co. Collection, Indiana Historical Society)

1910, after a friend recommended the area and a big storm battered their yacht in the Gulf of Mexico. Carl and Jane were smitten with the area, so they bought a house there. According to some accounts, during a 1913 visit, Fisher was out on his speedboat in Biscayne Bay when he met an elderly agriculturalist named John Collins, who was then building a wooden bridge from Miami to a barrier island where he and his family planned to restore a former coconut and avocado plantation. An intrigued Fisher loaned Collins $50,000. Upon completion, the $150,000 causeway was the world's longest wooden bridge, supported by more than two thousand concrete-and-steel pilings. In return, Fisher received two hundred acres on the island, and he later bought another hundred fifty acres from local landowners. As a visionary who had more ideas than he knew what to do with—as well as extensive infrastructure-building experience—Fisher decided to transform the sandbar, once occupied by Native Americans known as the Tequesta people, into a town for elite vacationers. Jane was not impressed with the mangrove swamps and mosquitoes, yet Carl went ahead, as he usually did, turning Union Carbide capital—funneled from New York to Florida via Indianapolis—into an artificial place. After securing permission from the state and the Army Corps of Engineers, Fisher began reshaping the tropical land. When dense thickets proved too thick for workers to cut in a cost-effective manner, Fisher's friend Al Webb devised a heavy plow, pulled by a caterpillar-style tractor, to hack mangrove stems down several feet above the sand. After building a retaining wall, Fisher used suction dredges to pull millions of cubic feet of sand and muck from the bay floor to fill in the former swamp. Jane later recalled that after the smelly, soupy landfill settled and cured, soil was brought from the Everglades "and spread over that blinding whiteness." It was ready to be remade.[27]

Filling the polo fields, Miami Beach, July 1923. Note suction dredge pipe at right. (Claude Carson Matlack Collection, 131–13, HistoryMiami Museum)

At Miami Beach—which he originally called Alton Beach, after seeing the name on a Chicago and Alton railcar—Fisher eliminated vestiges of natural space to build a profitable, man-made resort. By the 1920s, he spent millions on bulkheads, bridges, roads, streetcar lines, lights, and water mains. Lincoln Road, Miami Beach's eventual shopping mecca, cut an east-west swath across the island. The place was made for consumers. When someone noticed the golf course was too flat, more dirt was brought in from the Everglades to build a hill. As writer Christopher Knowlton observes, "Fisher had created a brand-new, if somewhat artificial, tropical paradise suitable for a subdivision"—a leisure town built largely with nonwhite labor. Fisher even paid Black women and children a pittance to plant Bermuda grass, sprig by sprig, on newly created land. Ecologically, the former sandbar was unrecognizable once Fisher and his crews were done with it. From Indianapolis, he brought in gardener Fred Hoerger, who, according to historian Mark Foster, "scoured catalogs of rare, exotic plants from around the world, searching for species that would thrive in Miami's climate." Specimens included Australian pines, an invasive angiosperm

African American work crew transplanting a coconut palm on the grounds of the Nautilus Hotel, Miami Beach, July 1923. (Claude Carson Matlack Collection, 120–13, HistoryMiami Museum)

that still thrives on Miami Beach. Fisher also worked to eradicate native fauna, killing multitudes of rattlesnakes, raccoons, and rats. After 1919, he built polo fields and imported expensive polo ponies to attract wealthy visitors. Fisher also relocated flamingos from the Bahamas and Africa in an unsuccessful attempt to replace the flocks of colorful birds that had been driven away by the island's engineering and reconstruction. Allison, an avid sport fisherman, built a fancy aquarium that opened on New Year's Day, 1921, but it had closed by 1923. Its animals were either dispersed around the Caribbean or relocated to the Detroit Aquarium.[28]

Incorporated in 1915, Miami Beach was a place for the well-off and privileged, with restrictive covenants often limiting residence to non-Jewish whites. A 1920s ditty about a buyer who could not make payments on his lot lamented, "I know a guy/That I could sell it to,/But he's a Jew—/What'll I do?" Most subdivisions specified "Caucasian Race only," although some allowed servants to reside on properties. Usually, Black construction or service workers had to live in Miami proper. Fisher advertised Miami Beach as an open shop (nonunion) town, an assertion that local labor leaders protested.[29] The town was based on racial and class exclusivity, as well as on Fisher's beliefs about recreation. According to Jane, her husband's "philosophy for a new design for living" saw "play as soul-saving as work or religion." Carl sold Miami Beach "as a paradise for the sports lover, a playland for youth," and a "haven" for the elderly. Florida was becoming a playground for American elites, and while Speedway City may have been a model welfare-capitalism town, where suburban living was part of a worker's compensation package, Miami Beach was different. It was a getaway, a place for the wealthy to consume round-the-clock leisure. Fisher even formed a fishing club and built exclusive swimming pools and golf courses alongside the polo fields.[30] Miami Beach may have pioneered the idea of year-round recreation, but the idea of basing a place around sport was not exclusive to Florida. Soon, Fisher and Allison would consider repurposing Indianapolis's speedway as a one-stop shop for leisure.

As Fisher created a play-focused town near the Dixie Highway's terminus, cities reimagined space to exploit the infrastructural developments then making auto racing, motor touring, and suburban sprawl into reality. In 1915, with support from the Chamber of Commerce (formerly the Commercial Club), Indianapolis laid more than 83,000 square yards of asphalt. Oiled streets reduced dust and improved drainage, augmenting residents' "health and comfort" while also extending the pavement's lifespan.[31] Mayor

Bell proudly proclaimed the city's Board of Public Works had implemented "more public improvements" that year than in the previous century. He credited engineer B. J. T. Jeup with overseeing construction of sewers, sidewalks, and streets. The city also rerouted and covered Pogue's Run, a polluted downtown creek, in a concrete box culvert. Turning the waterway into a covered drain rationalized the city's layout and improved traffic circulation. Now Indianapolis could complete Alexander Ralston's four-square-mile plan by platting right over the stream. Bell insisted the creek's reengineering was a spectacle that had to be seen: "Every citizen of Indianapolis who has not already done so should visit the place where this work is being done, to the end that he may be able to comprehend the magnitude of this undertaking."[32] It may not have been as amazing as turning a sandy island near Miami into a tony resort town, but, in its own way, the covering of Pogue's Run was a modern engineering feat.

Such work represented the larger reinvention of Progressive Era space. Indianapolis had hired George Kessler to improve its parks in 1908, and the noted landscape architect worked with the city off and on until his 1923 death and burial in Crown Hill Cemetery. Kessler reportedly thought any city could make itself more beautiful—and increase property values—as long as the plans fit its natural settings. The same way Denver prioritized mountain views and Kansas City showcased river bluffs, Indianapolis could exploit "broad, open vistas." From 1909 to 1915, around the same time he developed a comprehensive plan for Dallas, Kessler designed seventy-five miles of parkways and green spaces for Indianapolis, with some stretching along Pogue's Run, Eagle Creek, and Fall Creek. Parklands and mobility developed side by side. A boulevard connecting Riverside Park to the city center was situated atop a levee that separated the drive from the White River by a strip of green space, effectively transforming the floodplain into an attractive park. Elsewhere, a parkway along Fall Creek protected low-lying ground from the sort of flooding that struck the Ohio River basin in 1913. Residents appreciated that Kessler was doing for them what he had already done for other cities.[33]

Auto congestion first became a concern in US urban centers around 1915, which was the same time Indianapolis rebuilt itself for efficiency and improved its traffic flow by elevating railroad tracks, a method that Progressive Era cities used for concentrating function while relieving congestion. As with the tunnels at the speedway, motor vehicles passed under tracks that were dangerous if crossed at grade. Besides adding this vertical dimension, the city cultivated safety in other ways. In the mid-1910s, signs funneled streetcar patrons to "safety zones" so vehicles could use the rest of the street. University of Chicago sociologist Charles Zueblin observed that Indianapolis was especially strict in regulating pedestrians. Soon, Detroit and Cleveland adopted similar precautions. At the speedway, meanwhile, a new footbridge allowed pedestrians to cross the track safely. At the same time, an updated hospital and a second access tunnel were also added to the racing facility.[34]

Grade separations effectively counteracted friction between various transportation modes, an idea that traffic expert Miller McClintock later developed in *Street Traffic Control* (1925).[35] To accommodate more cars, Indianapolis improved an additional thirty-five miles of streets in the mid-1910s, but more pavement meant more cleaning. The city now had to sweep hundreds of miles of streets, costing $19,136.41 per year. Streets also had to be illuminated, so ITTC cooperated with a utility company to erect poles carrying trolley wires and streetlamps. Hundreds of attractive "lampposts, each equipped with five tungsten filament bulbs enclosed in diffusing globes" lit downtown Indianapolis. As geographer John Jakle writes, such illumination facilitated nighttime activity and enhanced surveillance. It "was part of a larger process of urban evolution, whereby movement and nighttime visualization were conjoined." Car lighting, too, became standard; by 1916, Indianapolis passed a law regulating headlamp usage.[36]

As traffic increased, thoroughfares had to be enlarged. Indianapolis widened its central north-south artery, Meridian Street, from Sixteenth Street to Fall Creek, even though property owners protested. Formerly, the street was so clogged it could not accommodate enough cars, but afterward traffic flowed more easily. Elsewhere, a wider Indiana Avenue made space for streetcar lines heading to Riverside Park, while another rerouted line relieved Washington Street. Echoing Charles Mulford Robinson, city leaders removed "dangerous off-sets and jogs" by condemning land at awkward intersections, such as Illinois and Sixteenth, thus improving aesthetics as well as "safety and convenience." Bell's administration tried to regulate parking without inconveniencing motorists. The city built a municipal parking garage where city vehicles were stored and maintained. Not yet a horseless city, Indianapolis maintained a stable for police mounts.[37]

The Hoosier capital was becoming a car city in both practical and spectacular terms. Bell's 1915 report was dated May 25, less than a week before the big race and just four days after he canceled a bout that would have featured Jack Johnson. If boxing seemed like a showy spectacle threatening racial order, racing was practically a scientific activity limited to white men. Racers now had to maintain a minimum speed of eighty miles per hour in time trials, and engines had to displace no more than three hundred cubic inches. Despite an international field of racers, in which car colors now reflected national origins—rather than manufacturers, as in the prior year—the fifth annual 500-mile race featured the smallest number of racers to date: twenty-two cars from five countries including England, France, Germany, and Italy, in addition to the United States. Qualifying speeds ranged from 81.8 to 98.9 miles per hour. After rain postponed the race from Saturday to Monday, an estimated crowd of fifty-five thousand watched a memorable race. Ralph De Palma finished in a record 5:33:55.5, pushing his Mercedes at an average clip of 89.84 miles per hour. The speedy Italian American again supplied plenty of drama when his car seemed on the verge of breaking down on mile 498, but this time he finished, and his record endured until 1922. All top three finishers in 1915 had better times than René Thomas's showing the previous year.[38]

As had sports leagues established in the late 1800s and early 1900s, tracks banded together to coordinate motor sport. There may have been some truth to oft-denied stories that Indianapolis planned to split from the AAA. In 1915, officials from the nation's seven biggest speedways met at the Claypool to form the Speedway Association of America (SAA). Later that year, there was an attempt to create a "national commission" to oversee racing, composed of officials from the SAA, the AAA, and the International Motor Contest Association, which oversaw dirt-track races. SAA appeared to be trying to muscle the AAA out of the way. Such organizations, and resulting squabbles over control, were typical of national oversight groups formed in the early-twentieth-century Progressive Era, such as the National Collegiate Athletic Association (NCAA), which effectively assumed oversight of intercollegiate football from older rules-making bodies.[39]

As motor sport bureaucratized, urban life may have seemed more mundane than ever. Indianapolis streets now had clearly visible signage, an improvement that rendered the city legible and navigable. Yet the Circle City still struggled with congestion, and it coped by dispersing a growing population to the metropolitan fringes. Officials rerouted streetcars that formerly converged at Monument Circle, pushing retail activity to outlying areas. They also extended thoroughfares into the city's hinterlands, prompting the spread of "valuable platted city property" all the way to Broad Ripple, a suburban community eight miles north of downtown that housed the White City amusement park, a pleasure park emulating the sensationalism of Chicago's 1893 world's fair midway. With such expansion, said Mayor Bell, Indianapolis had "grown and developed in every direction" beyond the confines of its original Mile Square.[40]

Despite its transformation, not everyone was impressed with Indianapolis. Theodore Dreiser, an Indiana native and a noted author, undertook an auto tour from New York to Indiana, which he chronicled in his 1916 book *A Hoosier Holiday*. Dreiser said that before cars, such a trip could have been made only by rail; autos truly were reshaping the world. Travel was now cheaper, quicker, and more pleasurable than in the era of locomotion. Cars meant freedom. This new form of mobility, as well as the infrastructure supporting it, seemed most apparent in Buffalo, where Dreiser and his chauffeur (whom he dubbed "Speed") "raced" on "a solid, smooth, red brick boulevard, thirty feet wide and twelve miles long" as if "it were a bowling alley." The United States seemed to be on its way to creating the world's best roads, especially in the Midwest, where paving bricks captured the regional imagination. Dreiser was critical of the homogenizing effects of railways and welcomed changes wrought by automobiles. Sure, Indianapolis bragged about being one of the world's "principal railroad centers," but who cared? "Once you have seen the others," sneered Dreiser, Indianapolis had "nothing to teach you." He was "tired of the mere trade city devoid of any plan or charm of natural surroundings." Indiana's capital—still in many ways shaped by railroads—was just a dreary and "minor" city with "a few high buildings" trying to mimic the skyscrapers of Chicago and New York. It is unclear, however, whether Dreiser realized that newfangled motor cars might just eventually lead to newer and equally boring—or even destructive—types of urban homogeneity and sprawl.[41]

In an era of epic road trips, long-distance racing may have seemed less than exciting. Although initial reports said the speedway would host a one-thousand-mile race with a $100,000-purse, limited to manufacturers who had already won Indianapolis's big event, the 1916 Memorial Day race was actually shortened to three hundred miles. Fisher, who may have been influenced by the three-hundred-fifty-mile Astor Cup race at Sheepshead Bay, announced, "I am convinced that the shorter race will be more popular with the race-going public." Shorter races were neither so hard on cars nor so boring for fans, many of whom were adapting to utilitarian automobility.[42] The purse was reduced to $30,000 in 1916, and the number of racers declined that year, partly because of World War I, but also because of other factors. Bob Burman died in a race at California's Corona Speedway, while Ralph De Palma was excluded after he tried to extract appearance money from Fisher and then delayed submitting his entry blank until after the deadline. Still, the time trials were exciting. Barney Oldfield set a track record with a lap timed at 1:27.7, or 102.623 miles per hour.[43]

Despite drizzle, tens of thousands converged on the speedway, with Hoosier poet James Whitcomb Riley being one of the first through the gates. Dario Resta won the three-hundred-mile race in a Peugeot in 3:36:10.82, averaging 83.29 miles per hour. Ninety thousand spectators watched Resta take an early lead after Eddie Rickenbacker's Maxwell broke down in the tenth lap. The shorter race seemed less thrilling than earlier "motor derbies," yet there was still danger. Relief driver Jack Le Cain flipped his Delage and nearly died. Tom Rooney's Premier smashed into the wall and turned over twice; he broke a femur and bruised his shoulder. Thrill-seeking spectators had an additional attraction in September 1916, when Indianapolis hosted a one-time Harvest Auto Racing Classic. Its twenty-mile, fifty-mile, and one-hundred-mile races were all won by Indianapolis's own Johnny Aitken, who averaged 89.44 miles per hour in the final event. Another contest scheduled for October, however, was canceled because of rain.[44]

There was some truth to the idea that the speedway was a technological testing ground, although usually few spectators were present for actual tests. In 1914, Marmon tested a reported water-naphthalene fuel substance, dubbed Zoline, at the speedway, and Fisher was one of many who expressed cautious optimism regarding this modern-day alchemy. But Zoline was too good to be true. Some reports said it was too costly to produce on a large scale and froze in cold weather; later accounts, however, said it was the scheme of a Dayton confidence man who simply mixed water and a small amount of gasoline into a concoction barely strong enough to power an engine for a few minutes. For the time being, at least, conventional fuels would persist, as would natural-latex rubber. By 1916, the United States produced huge quantities of tires, while its total number of exported cars, valued at more than $97 million, reached 77,496.[45] Americans used more cars to get from place to place, and their ability to connect points on the map was illustrated in 1916 when Indiana-born vaudeville performer Erwin "Cannonball" Baker, who had competed in the 1909 motorcycle races, drove a Stutz 196.5 miles from Chicago to Indianapolis in an amazing three hours and forty-two minutes, an average of 53.108 miles per hour. By the 1920s, Baker would be well known for record-setting drives. His 1916 run was not exactly a race, yet his time was much faster than the seventeen miles per hour Chicago motorists had averaged just seven years earlier over a comparable route. Racing fans understood the tantalizing resemblance between highways and speedways. One spectator at a 500-mile race held in Chicago in 1915 observed that he had driven 488 miles from Omaha, nearly the same distance as the racers. He was amazed. A train took thirteen hours to cover that mileage, but racers did it in just over five.[46]

As better-engineered cars and roads helped drivers navigate interurban space, the Circle City planned for additional auto-focused growth. One pressing question was where the dead would find their eternal rest in the automotive metropolis. Mayor Bell thought new cemeteries should be placed at least ten miles from the city, so as not to inhibit urban expansion. The ability to traverse space had increased dramatically over time, he said, and so it was no longer necessary to inter bodies near the city center. Warning about potential limits to north-side development, Bell explained that when Crown Hill Cemetery opened in the 1860s, mourners used horse-drawn conveyances. But now, a burial ground ten miles from city limits could be accessed as easily by autos as Crown Hill had been during the Civil War era. The area north of Thirty-Eighth Street should be filled with fine homes, said Bell, not gravesites. He implored Indianapolis not to build an "everlasting obstacle" to expansion. The city's "principal crosstown boulevard . . . should not be made to run through a graveyard." With a growing modern capacity for space annihilation, there was no need for deceased bodies to take up land quite so close to downtown.[47]

Automobiles changed Indianapolis's urban fabric, and Booth Tarkington's Pulitzer Prize–winning 1918 novel, *The Magnificent Ambersons*, illustrated that transformation. The auto-themed novel takes place in booming Midland, a thinly disguised version of Tarkington's native Indianapolis. The speedway does not appear in the story, but Fisher's industry makes a cameo appearance when one character invests in a local headlamp company, clearly a reference to Prest-O-Lite. Whereas protagonist George Amberson likes horses and social stasis, his foil is motor enthusiast Eugene (nearly "Engine"), who speculates that future streets may extend "five or ten times as long as they are now." After all, says Eugene, "It isn't the distance from the centre [*sic*] of a town that counts"; rather, "it's the time it takes to get there." Eugene notices Midland is "already spreading"; although "bicycles and trolleys" had done their part, extensive auto usage would soon "carry city streets clear out to the county line."[48] Tarkington understood changes

Booth Tarkington, 1913. Tarkington wrote the Pulitzer Prize–winning novel *The Magnificent Ambersons* (1918), in which "distances had ceased to matter" in sprawling "Midland," a fictional city based on Indianapolis. (Library of Congress)

in the automotive metropolis—or at least the way many white, middle-class readers *perceived* such changes. Midland expands tremendously throughout *The Magnificent Ambersons*, with houses built farther from a city center that grows poorer, dirtier, and less desirable as it fills with European immigrants and African American migrants moving from the South. Such changes resulted from cars' ability to erase spatial limitations: "And with the coming of the new speed, 'farther out' was now as close to business as the [Amberson] Addition had been in the days of its prosperity." In the brave new world of the automotive metropolis, "Distances had ceased to matter."[49]

In the time of speedway racing's prewar peak during the Progressive Era, Indianapolis reconfigured itself into a sprawling automotive metropolis. Carl Fisher reigned over a spectacle that attracted drivers and spectators from around the world at the same time as he built a working-class development near the speedway and a Florida resort town that embodied new ideas about urban space, recreation, and leisure. By the time America entered World War I in 1917—and the speedway once again became a site for aviation innovation—it seemed as though modern transportation technologies were stretching the city outward more greatly than ever before.

5

FINEST FLYING FIELD IN AMERICA

The Speedway Goes to War

US entry into World War I curtailed motor sport. There were no races at Indianapolis in 1917 or 1918, but that did not mean a lack of wartime activity in Speedway City, which hosted an aviation repair depot and an Italian airplane firm. Carl Fisher, meanwhile, attempted to build a regional aviation network that might cement Indianapolis as a center for three-dimensional space annihilation. But when motor racing returned to the speedway after the war, it was in an augmented form that exposed just how unsuitable the old bricks had become. By 1919, fond recollections of prewar racing infiltrated talk about the races and the track's old pavement, presaging an era when nostalgia became one of the speedway's biggest attractions.

As early as November 1914, it was clear that most racers in combatant nations would not be competing at Indianapolis anytime soon. Europeans hoped to return to the sport, but the question was when. French driver Jules Goux claimed he was in good "spirits" in Alsace yet feared the war's prolongation might interfere with his return to racing. André Boillot, meanwhile, wrote to Johnny Aitken to say the Hoosiers should "prepare the supper for our next winning in the Indianapolis Grand Prix."[1] Boillot survived to race at Indianapolis three times between 1919 and 1921, but his older brother Georges was not so fortunate. A chauffeur for French general Joseph Joffre, Georges became a flyer and was fatally shot down in combat. As millions died on Europe's battlefields, even more drivers were absent. During the war, aviator René Thomas crossed the Atlantic to race at Indianapolis, but Albert Guyot was stuck chauffeuring French military officers, while Jean Porporato drove an Italian ambulance on the Eastern Front.[2]

Early on, the war affected developments in aviation technology, with wartime urgency compressing the time needed for innovations. Speedway general manager Theodore "Pop" Myers claimed airplane engines had advanced by a decade during the war's first eighteen months, and some observers thought manufacturers had to be involved in racing if they wanted to make progress. Fisher even contemplated offering prizes for tests of aviation motors. In one instance, Packard tested an innovative twelve-cylinder engine—perhaps a precursor to the V-12 Liberty engine—in a car driven by Ralph De Palma. Some people thought Detroit should build its own test track to emulate Indianapolis's speedway.[3] Yet despite motor sport's seeming utility, there was no guarantee it would continue. As early as June 1916, Fisher offered the speedway to the Naval Consulting Board, headed by Howard Coffin of Detroit-based Hudson Motor Car, as a site to train military aviators. He also considered moving the 1917 Memorial Day race to a speedway near Cincinnati, partly in response to price gouging at Indianapolis hotels, but also perhaps because he thought the Hoosier track would be otherwise occupied at that time.[4]

By early 1917, it was clear Americans would no longer be observers to war. In January, Germany proclaimed unrestricted U-boat warfare in the Atlantic, and soon the United States learned of Germany's proposed alliance with Mexico via the Zimmermann Telegram. Conflict seemed imminent when, on March 5, President Woodrow Wilson was inaugurated for his second term. Wilson had been narrowly reelected in November 1916 on a platform of keeping America out of war and then gave a speech in January calling for "peace without victory," but by late March he and his advisers chose a different path. On April 2, the president delivered a message to Congress allowing little room for dissent: any "disloyalty" would meet "a firm hand of repression." War was terrible, but victory might make the world safe for democracy. Four days later, Congress heeded the president's call. The United States entered World War I.[5]

The day after Wilson's inauguration in March, James Allison had announced that if the United States declared war, the speedway would not hold its annual race. Motor sport consumed resources needed for war, and so Allison urged Americans to "conserve the rubber, steel, parts and other

Soldiers' farewell parade in Monument Circle, downtown Indianapolis, 1918.
(Library of Congress)

materials used in racing."[6] The race was canceled just a few days after Wilson's Cabinet decided to go to war. The speedway's technical shops would design and build airplane engines, while the track and infield might train aviators. This situation echoed developments at England's Brooklands, which served as a Royal Flying Corps (RFC) facility during the war. Fisher said he regretted the 500-mile race's cancellation, but he thought it was "the best thing to do under the circumstances." Indiana businessmen commended the speedway for its patriotic action.[7]

Americans mobilized resources to defeat the Central Powers by purchasing war bonds, serving in the military, or cultivating victory gardens, with the latter facilitated by Congress's approval of Daylight Savings Time in 1918. Later that year, the Student Army Training Corps (SATC) began training officers at more than five hundred colleges and universities; Indiana hosted at least nineteen SATC chapters, including three in Indianapolis. The federal Committee on Public Information, better known as the Creel Committee, made propaganda pamphlets, posters, and speeches.[8] Industry also mobilized. Packard, Ford, and Nordyke and Marmon designed and produced Liberty engines, lightweight yet powerful V-12 motors for use

primarily in aircraft; by war's end, twenty-four thousand Liberty engines had been built. Companies found creative ways to contribute. Stutz donated seven ambulances to the Indiana National Guard, while Cole Motor Car devised a program in which consumers traded Liberty Bonds for vehicles.[9] Prest-O-Lite manufactured explosives, while Carl Fisher personally donated $10,000 of Union Carbide stock to the YMCA War Fund and offered a speedboat as a submarine-pursuit craft. Jane Fisher led local food conservation efforts. Although some Hoosiers were isolationists, most supported the war. Indianapolis tried to present a unified front and mute ethnic differences with an Americanization Day parade on July 4, 1918.[10] In addition, municipal government built a $75,000 road to Fort Benjamin Harrison, ten miles northeast of downtown; Mayor Bell saw the road's construction as a "patriotic duty." This road echoed prewar infrastructure improvements, which had not come cheap. By 1918, Indianapolis's bond debt totaled nearly $5 million.[11]

Wartime Americans debated whether natural, industrial, and animal resources should be used for sport. Although some thought an exception might be made for horse racing, which supposedly developed cavalry mounts, they saw that other sports, especially those based on modern machinery, could interfere with the war effort. By March 1917, the AAA announced that year's season would have no official championship. Subsequently, some manufacturers quit motor sport. A grand newspaper ad said B. F. Goodrich announced its "retirement," or "graduation," from racing. The self-serving ad claimed the company had learned all it could from competition. The war demanded "new duties and responsibilities," so the firm was now "devoted to making the RIGHT tires for the serious business of war." Goodrich would only return to racing if and when its "experts" decided it had "something *further* to *teach* us."[12]

Motor sport was not entirely dormant, but interest in it declined. Cincinnati's new board speedway, located in suburban Sharonville, Ohio, initially announced it was placing its racing schedule on hold, yet it did stage a two-hundred-fifty-mile race with a $29,000 purse on Memorial Day. The throng of motorists heading to the Queen City, however, was light in comparison to the crowd typically descending on the Circle City. Besides the serious business of war, it was a longer drive. Chicagoans would have to travel about three hundred miles to Cincinnati rather than a mere two hundred to Indianapolis. Motorists who desired an automotive jaunt, said the *Tribune*, might simply drive as far as they pleased over Indiana's good roads before turning back, viewing "wooded countryside and quaint, historic towns."[13] New York's Sheepshead Bay hosted a one-hundred-mile race in 1917, but other tracks shut down altogether. Chicago's Speedway Park offered itself as a training camp, aviation school, or site for Red Cross fund-raising but called off "commercialized sport." Lumber baron Edward Hines purchased Speedway Park in 1917 and donated it to the federal government, which built a veterans' hospital there. Minnesota's Twin City Motor Speedway hosted a Red Cross auto derby before closing in 1917 but, in the 1920s, the land became Wold-Chamberlain Field, an airport named for two World War I aviators.[14]

As early as 1915, Fisher spoke to close associates about aviation's military uses, especially in coastal defense and aerial bombing runs. By 1917, he was named chairman of a subcommittee of the National Advisory Committee for Aeronautics and wrote to the New York–based Society of Automotive Engineers for advice on how to turn the speedway into an aviation field. The group recommended gathering support from local residents and submitting an application to Henry Souther, the US Army's chief signal officer.

Fisher insisted the track was ideal for military aviation, since it already had most of the necessary equipment and personnel. The grounds were surrounded by a ten-foot fence and had more than ten miles of drainage tiles; the field could accommodate landings or takeoffs even after a hard rain. Modern conveniences included lighting and telephones. Fisher conceded the only things missing were hangars, which he said could be built in three weeks. (He lamented that two years earlier a big hangar at the speedway had burned, destroying several aircraft.) And it was easy to reach the track. Fisher boasted, "We have interurbans, railroad, freight platforms, Post Office, fine water and city gas mains." The facility, he claimed, could be ready more quickly and cheaply than any other airfield and would help the nation catch up with European flyers. A six-inch gas line, installed in 1912, could fill fifteen balloons at once. Fisher was confident that if the military furnished three forty-thousand-cubic-foot balloons (at $12,000 each), he could develop a balloon corps.[15]

Fisher fired off a flurry of letters, hoping to convince the government to adopt his plans. A man of big ambitions and hasty action, he was perpetually impatient with bureaucrats. The speedway's board of directors estimated annual maintenance at $30,000, so he submitted an offer for the military to use the facility for that cost. Fisher even offered to pay for "tearing down about five or six miles of fence, rebuilding some buildings, cutting some trees and rolling the sod." The speedway could be the "finest flying field" in America.[16] Someone just had "to cut the red tape from a bundle of five Curtiss [airplanes], six extra engines and 15% of miscellaneous parts."[17] Fisher began arranging for experienced pilots to teach at the speedway; he also sought out instructional materials on tools, maintenance, and equipment, as well as detailed maps of the local area with highways, rivers, and railroads marked. American flyers needed knowledge to defeat the Central Powers. Fisher said an assistant named Kantner had "experience with all sorts of machines," as well as important information about European airplanes that would help American builders. He had "good pictures of all the latest French, Italian, and German motors" installed in aircraft.[18]

Despite Fisher's optimism, military aviators were less sanguine. When Glenn Curtiss and S. D. Waldon of the Aircraft Production Board visited the speedway, they said the government would have to purchase three hundred acres north of the oval to make the site adequate. Chicago-based Signal Corps officials realized the track was not ideal for one of the training fields they hoped to establish in the Midwest. They needed at least 640 acres, and it did not make sense to invest in a temporary facility in a place that experienced harsh weather several months each year. (By World War II, many airfields were sited in warmer locations, especially Texas.) Although the speedway did not become an aviation school, it did serve as a landing field for aviators based in Ohio and Illinois, and Speedway City hosted an aviation repair facility. US and British planes were stationed at the speedway during the war, especially between war-bond drives.[19]

Indianapolis was also a site for airplane design and construction. Speedway City hosted about twenty-five employees of the Pomilio Brothers Corporation, a firm based in Turin, Italy, which had already built aircraft for the Italian army. The collaboration was orchestrated by Nordyke and Marmon and the Chamber of Commerce, along with Allison's engine firm, which provided space for the Pomilios. The federal government contracted to pay the Pomilios about $360,000 to build six fighter planes and six bombers that could accommodate Liberty engines; the dollar amount was later adjusted upward to reflect actual costs. Although aircraft construction carried out at the speedway was not well publicized, it was no secret. The Pomilio Brothers advertised locally for clerks, draftsmen, laborers, and a "colored" chauffeur. The *New York Times* even mentioned their work.[20] While in Indiana, the Pomilios traveled to Dayton to visit the Wright brothers and discussed with Fisher the possibility of building planes capable of transatlantic flight. Aircraft added a third dimension to warfare, circumventing seemingly impenetrable trenches on the Western Front. According to one 1920s retrospective, airplane builders won the conflict in wartime laboratories and aided postwar civilian aviation. After the war, McGraw-Hill published Ottorino Pomilio's *Airplane Design and Construction* (1919), while he and his brothers planned an amphibious seaplane for use "as a sporting model."[21]

As the Pomilios developed aeronautical technology, Fisher worked to build a regional aviation network centered on Indianapolis. When he agreed to chair a subcommittee of the National Advisory Committee for Aeronautics, Fisher was told he would be responsible for planning aviation fields in cooperation with the Civil Aerial Transport Committee. By July, the army's chief signal officer, Major General George Squier, approved his project "of mapping and marking emergency landings for cross country aviation flights." Fisher soon consulted with officials at Dayton's Wilbur

Wright Field.[22] His work made practice flights safer, since novice pilots had clearly demarcated routes to follow with regularly spaced landing fields and repair facilities. Larger, three-hundred-acre fields should be "located within one mile of an interurban or steam railroad, on a hard road, near a center of population of about 5,000." Each field needed access to "telephones, electric lights and good water," as well as hangars and repair shops. Land had to be level and dry, but this was no problem, since many farms in once swampy, glaciated areas of Illinois and Indiana had already installed mile after mile of perforated drainage tiles.[23]

Fisher worked diligently to mark fields radiating from Indiana. Early on, he proposed emergency-landing sites in every county between Indianapolis and Detroit, no more than forty miles apart. Other routes stretched to Dayton, Ohio, and Rantoul, Illinois. By July 1917, Fisher had "secured forty-eight first class landing fields between Indianapolis and Richmond, [Indiana]," near the Ohio border. He corresponded with the National Defense Council's Advisory Board about the best design for markings and, after considering various suggestions, decided to paint barn roofs with signals. The system had to be standardized, said Fisher, since it would "be confusing if a man in New Jersey" devised "a code of signals of his own and if a man in Illinois [had] a different idea."[24] This way, a Texas-trained aviator would understanding markings in Indiana, and one based in Dayton would "recognize a marker he sees in Pennsylvania, day or night."[25] Markings included the field's number (ten to twelve feet high, painted in white and outlined in red), "an arrow pointing to the landing station," and a symbol "to indicate the size of the field or the length of the gliding possibilities."[26] Fisher conceded he had little experience with airplanes, but he was a seasoned balloonist and thought his scheme the best one possible. He equipped a car with extension ladders capable of placing workers with brushes and paint buckets on barn roofs; by July, his crew marked signals from Indianapolis to Ohio. The first roof painted was on the farm of one R. Z. Winsell, north of the speedway. At least eighty farmers along the National Road or the highway to Fort Benjamin Harrison allowed property to be used for landing fields, although three demurred. One was an antiwar Quaker, one was of German ancestry, and one demanded compensation. Army officials planned to use their fields anyway.[27]

Fisher's painting of signals on barns anticipated a postwar moment when, scholar Jason Weems writes, "rooftops . . . became navigational signposts for both local and transcontinental aviators."[28] And, as Fisher marked regional routes for flyers, he began considering even bigger, *national* routes and offered the Lincoln Highway as one possibility. He recommended a system wherein "numbers [for landing fields] be used up to 99, and then start over again," with "suitable markings" at each state border. For some Americans, marking barn roofs for military aviators seemed a harbinger of an era when flying would be part of everyday life. The *Indianapolis Star* said in 1917 that the nation was preparing to spend $640 million to build aircraft and train aviators, and the newspaper predicted Americans would see as much progress in aviation during the next decade as they had seen in automobility during the previous ten years. Bicycles and cars had brought people closer together, and now aircraft might do the same. Painting roofs was just the first step toward a postwar future in which people routinely traversed three-dimensional space.[29]

By late August, Fisher's marking crew reached Dayton. Stations on the east-west route from Ohio to Indiana were sited at regular intervals "along the old National Road," following a nearly straight line between Dayton and Indianapolis. For beginners making their first solo flights, fields were sited close enough "to offer a landing at any time under almost any emergency." Fisher thought that with help from army personnel, he could complete another route connecting Dayton and Detroit. These tasks took time—for example, marking the one-hundred-thirty-mile route to Rantoul consumed five weeks—yet they were essential for building an air corps. Aviators were instructed not to fly over business districts, presumably to minimize noise or to limit crashes in urban areas. When coming into Indianapolis from the east, pilots turned north toward Fort Benjamin Harrison before circling west to the speedway. In 1918, Indiana's Republican senator Harry New flew from the raceway oval to Dayton in a Curtiss biplane, which took just one hour.[30]

To aid aviators flying by night, Fisher established a series of veritable lighthouses on a web of airfields connecting the lower Great Lakes region from Pittsburgh to Rantoul by way of Dayton and Detroit. In Indianapolis, he requested funds to purchase "signal lighting equipment" for nighttime aviation. He wanted the city to be among America's first urban areas illuminated for flyers. The city's board of trade furnished floodlights while the electric company provided power. Each lamp cost $1,200, and the electricity cost several hundred dollars per month. At first, it seemed lights would be put on the capitol dome, but ultimately they were instead placed on the 218-foot Fletcher National Bank building (completed in 1915), since it was easier to install lights on a flat-roofed office tower than on the 255-foot statehouse dome or the 284-foot Soldiers and Sailors Monument. Fisher, who nearly always prioritized private initiative over public funding, was sure he could get similar lights installed in smaller towns at no federal cost.[31]

Fisher thought bigger cities—Dayton, Richmond, and Indianapolis, as well as Danville and Champaign, Illinois—might each "use a cluster of four searchlights, two reds and two white," while smaller towns would "use two white searchlights." They might "contribute the cost of these lights and their maintenance" as a "patriotic" duty. Eaton, Ohio, saw lights as symbolic of its war-effort contributions; the town planned nonstop illumination for several hours each night "as an attraction to the citizens" as well as "a mark of patriotism."[32] Although Fisher's motives, like those of some small towns, may have been patriotic, his methods were firmly rooted in developments already undertaken in Speedway City and Miami Beach. In late 1917, Fisher informed Major William Durand that he would have to leave Indiana temporarily and thus limit his work with the Air Mapping Committee. He had invested a lot of money in the Miami area, where he was constructing "some twenty miles of roads, filling in a thousand acres of land" with "seven million cubic yards of sand," and "building three and one-half miles of sea-wall." He needed to spend two months in Florida supervising the work.[33] Plans to create a modern, leisure-focused city could not wait, even for a global conflict.

Back in the Midwest, lights were placed at fourteen-mile intervals from Dayton to Rantoul, although inclement weather and a limited number of Liberty engines meant only a few flyers used the routes. In September 1917, Fisher reported one hundred thirty-five fields had been marked on a nearly direct line stretching more than two hundred miles from Eaton to Rantoul. At Indianapolis, the speedway built an illumination tower while Prest-O-Lite added a tilted, revolving light atop its factory building. Flyers could now use the field any time of day. Fisher modified his idea for transcontinental routes after realizing that simply placing lights along the Lincoln and Dixie Highways might be easier than creating landing stations alongside them. Now, it seemed, highways might even help aviators annihilate space. Fisher imagined a time when American aviators could elongate routes "in any direction."[34] Extension meant more landing fields, markings, and lights—all of which might endure after the war. In fact, by 1919, Fisher considered leasing the speedway for "an aerial school or a transportation base field."[35]

Before the war was over, space was tight at the speedway, so Fisher offered to lease the government additional land east of the oval, for one dollar per year, and to build more hangars. Even then, there still might not be enough room to accommodate all the aircraft based there. With so many British flyers stationed at the speedway, many planes flying from Ohio or Illinois could not find a place there; even the Pomilios were getting crowded out. According to Fisher, more hangars should be built to store aircraft that would be used in the Fourth Liberty Bond drive. Even if it never became the training field that Fisher had imagined in 1917, the speedway was an important aviation site. After the armistice, a British-made Handley Page bomber based at the track attempted a seven-hundred-mile trip from Indianapolis to Washington, DC.[36]

A hard lesson reinforced at Indianapolis was that flying, like racing, was deadly. In June 1918, as soldiers at the repair depot prepared to play against a local baseball team at Washington Park, an airplane crashed while three thousand spectators watched from the grandstands. Captain E. P. Webb, a personnel officer, was lobbing a baseball to the field from the plane when a streamer connected to the ball got stuck in the plane's propeller and caused the plane to crash. Webb suffered a fractured skull and was killed on impact. The pilot, Major Guy Gearhart, was also gravely injured. Three months later, RFC flyer Captain Joe Hammond died in a crash after returning from selling bonds at Greenfield, Indiana. Fisher was at his house, a mile and a half east of the track, when he saw Hammond's plane coming in for what looked like a hard landing; then he heard the impact. Racer Howdy Wilcox figured the plane must have malfunctioned. Fisher mourned the loss of Hammond, whom he considered a friend, and had the flyer's body interred at his personal mausoleum in Crown Hill Cemetery. Other planes based at Indianapolis met similar fates. In one tour of the Midwest, British ace and instructor Captain James Fitz-Morris died after crashing near Cincinnati. Another plane wrecked near Effingham, Illinois, causing multiple casualties.[37]

AAA officials canceled the 1918 season but soon considered resuming racing when the Speedway Association of America decided to sanction events. Some observers speculated whether, or in what form, motor sport would continue after the war. With Indianapolis perhaps out of the picture, Sheepshead Bay might dominate racing. Meanwhile, drivers such as Dario Resta, Arthur Duray, Louis Chevrolet, and Barney Oldfield announced their intent to resume competition.[38] It was comforting to see these familiar names, and in some cases racing inspired nostalgia. National Motor Vehicle's George Dickson wrote that the "game" was asleep and, "like the princess of the fairy tale, awaiting the awakening kiss of a promised prince—peace." Dickson said his company owned a scrapbook preserving "the story of achievements in road races and hill climbs, on speedways and dirt tracks" by drivers who raced National-made cars before the war. The scrapbook was one of the company's "most cherished possessions," holding "the intrinsic value of a rare old first edition."[39] But the fact that there were no races in 1918 did not mean there was no spectacle. Indianapolis's speedway hosted boxing extravaganzas with aviation exhibitions and musical performances. This was a time when the armed forces saw boxing as an adjunct to military training, and so fighters were men stationed either at the speedway or at Fort Benjamin Harrison. The anxiety that prewar Hoosiers exhibited toward pugilism was not as evident in matches contested between personnel in the racially segregated military.[40]

The world started returning to normalcy, whatever that might mean, after the November 1918 armistice. Manufacturers resumed production and people resumed consumption. B.F. Goodrich, for instance, estimated Americans would spend over a billion dollars on tires alone in the first year after the war. For his part, Fisher said that, if the nation redirected spending to roads, the entire Dixie Highway could be turned into a smooth "boulevard" for the mere cost of one battleship. In 1919, Allied leaders mostly ignored President Wilson's progressive Fourteen Points; instead, the Treaty of Versailles punished Germany for supposedly starting the war, and in the process it may have sown the seeds of another global conflict. Roughly eighteen million died in the war, but even greater carnage resulted from the postwar influenza pandemic that killed about fifty million people worldwide. In the United States, around 675,000 perished from several waves of the deadly flu. In October 1918, multiple cases were reported at the speedway. Thirty-three-year-old Johnny Aitken, the racer who took pole position in 1916's big race and swept the Harvest Auto Racing Classic later that year, died of flu-related pneumonia.[41]

What would happen to speedways that had been pressed into wartime service? Postwar Americans did not seem as interested in motor sport as they had been just two years earlier. At the end of 1918, it was unclear whether racing could be revived, but happy news came in December when Fisher, Allison, and Newby met in Miami and announced the speedway would once again host its marquee event in 1919: a 500-mile race with a $50,000 purse, the first event at that distance since 1915. Soon, Fisher modified plans by announcing the first postwar race would be held on Saturday, May 31, instead of May 30, apparently in response to a recent controversy— which reemerged in dramatic fashion during the 1920s—over Memorial Day racing. Observers anticipated the field of racers would include drivers from Belgium, England, France, and Italy, as well as Americans such as Caleb Bragg and Eddie Rickenbacker.[42]

Aviation captured the global imagination during World War I, and the individuals most responsible for this newfound desire to reach the sky were the ace flyers who gained fame by shooting down enemy aircraft. At first, planes were used mostly for reconnaissance and scouting, but by 1915 aerial combats between flyers equipped with machine guns were common. These so-called dogfights created legends. Historian Robert Wohl contends the war years transformed the pre-1914 aerial sportsman into the post-1915 "airborne knight armed with a machine-gun who jousted in the sky." Aces included French aviator Adolphe Pégoud and German flyer Manfred von Richthofen, the Red Baron, while America's foremost flyer was Eddie Rickenbacker (then usually still spelled "Rickenbacher"), an Ohioan who started the war as General John Pershing's personal chauffeur but soon was promoted to aviator and made headlines by shooting down a reported twenty-six German aircraft. Rickenbacker had raced at Indianapolis between 1912 and 1916, while also competing at Omaha, Sheepshead Bay, and Sioux City.[43]

Speculation about the postwar return of "Rick" was rampant. In late 1918, it seemed certain he would reenter the "racing game," perhaps in an English-made Sunbeam.[44] But in early 1919, uncertainty still reigned: "Will he be an entrant? Will he exhibit to the gathered thousands of his countrymen his prowess as a flyer? Or will he merely be an inconspicuous spectator?" Rickenbacker did not compete in 1919, but he did serve as referee for that year's 500-mile race and rode in the pace car.[45] The day beforehand, Rickenbacker delivered a speech at the Claypool asking Indianapolis to maintain its role in technological progress. The speedway had fostered military aviation during the war, and so now the city should build a commercial aerodrome to capitalize on that foundation. The ace predicted that within a few years, aircraft would be essential to daily life. Rickenbacker said the city, with its long history of motor innovation, "should be among the first to come to the front for the newest addition to the motor world."[46] Seven years later, the speedway's infield almost became the site of Indianapolis's airport, but instead Rickenbacker bought the track and solidified it as a legendary place for motor spectacle.

In 1919, Rickenbacker's ownership of the speedway was still far off, and it was unclear whether racing would regain its former popularity. Privately, Pop Myers confessed that ticket sales were slow. Newspapers ran typical ads and people talked about the race, but ticket orders mostly came from out of town. Enthusiasm seemed to wane elsewhere, too. A Prest-O-Lite salesman conceded the old Minnesota speedway—which itself was just a few years away from being turned into an airport—might be "producing a fine crop of pumpkins" by the following season. With proper ticket pricing and marketing, the old enthusiasm for racing might return, but first the European drivers who had helped create the speedway's international notoriety had to overcome hardships. After the armistice, Louis Chevrolet asked for aid to bring three cars across the Atlantic to race in Indiana, but the speedway rejected his request. For a free-enterprise enthusiast like Fisher, it may have sounded like socialism, a topic scorned in the era of the postwar Red Scare. Pop Myers thought there would be few European drivers in 1919, although he realized the situation could be improved. To attract foreign racers, Myers thought the speedway should promptly announce rules for upcoming races.[47]

The speedway was no longer America's most modern raceway, yet it was still the nation's "motor racing center," a "battleground for the brains and brawn of the mechanical world."[48] Indianapolis even capitalized on aviation enthusiasm by securing participation of French flyer André Boillot, whose famous brother, Georges, had been shot down on the Western Front. André had worked as a prewar demonstration driver for Peugeot and raced often at Brooklands before working for French airplane company Blériot. James Allison thought an aeronautical exhibition featuring Boillot and Rickenbacker was a good idea. Boillot sailed to America in April 1919 for his first 500-mile race and, during qualifying week, gave aerial exhibitions in a Spad airplane similar to one he flew in the war. Rickenbacker endorsed Boillot's abilities, but the American ace did not take part in the exhibitions. On race day, planes flew overhead "and mingled their roar with that of the racing cars being tuned for the long grind."[49]

As racing's sights and sounds returned to Indianapolis, Hoosiers began to realize—or perhaps imagine—their city's special role in automotive spectacle. Other cities had tracks, but there was "only one real Speedway classic." Motorists continued to drive from all over to see the race, and so hotels were packed. Reaching the speedway for the temporarily renamed Liberty Sweepstakes was still not easy, but now the reason was highway construction. In Lafayette, Indiana, one section of the Jackson Highway was rutted and nearly undriveable. Motorists could get detailed directions and avoid such obstacles by writing to the newspaper's automotive department.[50] When spectators arrived in Indianapolis, they saw a surplus of talent competing on the decade-old bricks. One writer said the race could be called the "Allied Liberty Sweepstakes," since entrants represented Belgium, England, France, and Italy, and the United States. Italy's Fiat planned to send three cars, while France's Peugeot anticipated sending one. England's Sunbeam also planned to enter two cars, but it had to withdraw because of miscalculations in engine size. Although the war was over, reminders of conflict remained. Some European drivers, of course, had not survived, and manufacturers now used materials developed during the war, including aviation motors. The spirit of international competition, too, had not disappeared. Some speculated the 1919 race would be won by an American for the first time since 1912. Apparently, for such writers, Italian American racer Ralph De Palma, who won in 1915, did not count as an American.[51]

De Palma, for one, gladly returned to racing. He briefly served at Dayton's McCook Field during the war but quickly discovered he preferred motor sport's excitement to flying's monotony. Speed was more apparent—and exciting—on the ground. "Every minute has its problem and its thrill," he confessed; "I prefer to be down on the ground, smelling the gas, eating the dirt, in contact with my rivals and the crowd." Weeks before the race, De Palma showed off his daredevil temperament during a Denver auto show, driving a Packard powered by a Liberty engine on the streets of Colorado's capital at speeds up to one hundred twenty miles per hour, while thirty thousand spectators watched. In Indiana, he raced a Packard with an aviation engine and a body influenced by wartime fuselage designs.[52] Although *National Geographic* editor John La Gorce asserted in 1919 that "competitive tests on the Speedway [were] largely responsible for the successful

Pace lap, 1919, with referee Eddie Rickenbacker as passenger in the pace car. Note that spectators in foreground appear to be gazing up at aircraft. (IMS Photo Archive)

establishment of the automobile motor for aircraft use," stunts like De Palma's seemed to invert his assertion: aviation engines developed during the war, when no races were held at the speedway, may have fueled motor sport's sensational postwar competitions.[53]

Mixing military and theatrical metaphors, the *Los Angeles Times* said spectators in 1919 would see "one of the most remarkable speed battles ever staged."[54] *Battle* may have been an appropriate term, since the grim reaper made an impressive showing at the 1919 race. The brick oval had been fine for racers topping out around eighty miles per hour, but it was too dangerous for "speed demons" capable of one hundred twenty. Officials were "apprehensive" and drivers were already saying engines had to be smaller.[55] Their fears were well founded. Arthur Thurman was the first to perish on May 31. On the forty-fourth lap, his vehicle flipped; he was crushed and died instantly. His wife, watching from the stands, reportedly fainted. Thurman's mechanic, Nicholas Molinaro, suffered a fractured skull yet survived. On the ninety-sixth lap, Louis LeCocq's car flipped and its fuel tank ignited. He and his mechanic, Los Angeles native Robert Bandini, burned alive as the speedway band "played briskly to distract" the crowd from the dark plumes of smoke emanating from the crash site. Driver Elmer Shannon was also seriously injured. The race's winner was Indiana native Howdy Wilcox. His Peugeot finished in 5:44:24.75, averaging 87.12 miles per hour, before a record crowd estimated at 125,000.[56]

Reflecting on the race, Rickenbacker said he found himself "in the same frame of mind" as many nights on the Western Front. The "burst of flames and ugly black smoke" from LeCocq's crash resembled a "battle zone." Though not as violent, the race was a "kaleidoscope of thrills" moving even faster than armed conflict. "The period of combat of this memorable battle which I have just witnessed was limited to five dramatic hours into which have been rushed all the sensational thrills that come from a day of fatalities, tottering champions, cars in ashes and 100,000 electrified spectators cheering their favorites to go a little faster." Deaths were tragic, said Rickenbacker, yet he rationalized them as collateral damage incurred while satisfying the male nervous system's innate desire for conflict: "As long as men with fighting spines will post their lives to prove their valor and ability and thereby capture the honors of the victor some will have to pay the unnamed price." Rickenbacker claimed the Liberty Sweepstakes would "go down in the pages of racing lore as having featured more wonderful drivers and indescribable thrills than any event in all the annals of motor driven competition." Wilcox could be considered the "patron saint of Indianapolis and the recognized ace of American and European racers."[57]

Even if the speedway fueled modern masculinity's maniacal quest for technological progress, its return to racing illustrated significant issues that had to be fixed. Starter E. C. Patterson observed numerous problems with timing and record-keeping systems, recommended changes, and suggested erecting additional scoreboards to keep drivers and spectators informed of the race's progress. He lamented Thurman's and LeCocq's deaths but shunted blame onto them by accusing both of "reckless driving."[58] Critics again recommended outlawing the sport, but others resisted any hint of abolition. Rickenbacker said racing played an "indispensable role" in "development of automobile design, engineering and metallurgical discovery, as applied both to the automobile and the airplane." Each event "test[ed] every part of a motor car's mechanism more severely than two years of ordinary usage." Although the war was supposedly over after Versailles, the specter of conflict made it impossible "to ignore automobile racing" and its impact on national security. State-of-the-art aircraft would be necessary in future wars, and Indianapolis's speedway was a place for testing aviation technology.[59] Rickenbacker was not alone. The *New York Times* claimed Europe had "better airplane motors" in 1914 because racing had pushed its "motor industry" to "a higher degree of speed efficiency." Americans had to continue racing "to keep pace."[60] Advertisers picked up this theme. In 1920, Marmon promoted passenger cars with efficient engines born of "battles of the laboratory and factory," designed by engineers who, pressured by "necessities of war," were compelled "to win victories of mental and productive effort to adequately back up the great men on the fighting fronts."[61] In 1922, a Prest-O-Lite ad invited fans to tour the company's factory in Speedway City, where they could see "the Laboratory, chosen by the government during the war as the finest obtainable for battery testing." In this fine industrial facility, "some of the best engineers and scientists in the country" were diligently working to improve technologies necessary for everyday motoring.[62]

The war had a tremendous impact. In 1919, Fisher decided to host short exhibition races to entertain wounded veterans then being treated at Fort Benjamin Harrison, and he hoped to convince the army's Motor Transport Corps to provide hundreds of cars needed to bring the men, along with nurses, to the speedway. Fisher felt he could not do enough "for these poor devils who are all shot up," and so he planned to enlist Ralph De Palma, Barney Oldfield, and Howdy Wilcox to put on races. De Palma was unavailable, but an exhibition featuring Wilcox, Joe Dawson, and Tommy Milton was held shortly before the fort's hospital closed. Attendance was limited to wounded soldiers, their guests, nurses, and men in military uniform.[63]

Throughout the next decade, by contrast, racing was open to the multitude. And while it might help develop auto technology, the spectacle likely had a bigger impact on technologies developed explicitly for motor sport, which grew even more precise and rational. In response to 1919 malfunctions, Odis Porter created an improved timing device powered by a Prest-O-Lite battery. Cars passing over a one-eighth-inch-thick wire broke an electrical circuit, causing "metal hammers" to imprint "a ribbon much like that used on a computing machine." The device recorded precise times to one five-hundredth of a second; all the operator had to do was mark down which car had crossed the wire.[64] Crowds watched numbered cars whiz around the track while monitoring big scoreboards staffed by hundreds of men announcing "through amplifiers the correct information" coming from the judge's stand and the Speedway Press Bureau. These press facilities were now "the most complete of any big sporting event in the world."[65]

In light of the speedway's wartime role, it may seem surprising that aviation declined in importance there after World War I. In 1920, for instance, an international balloon contest was moved to Birmingham, Alabama, after Indianapolis's Citizens Gas Company refused to supply gas because of a shortage. Nevertheless, some aviation events were still held at the track, including a 1923 balloon competition to determine participants for an international contest in Brussels. Perhaps more representative of the postwar decade were the airborne newspaper photographers who captured aerial images of big races. And, although Indianapolis remained a commercial hub, other places became sites for international aviation. Fisher, for his part, saw Florida as a potential base for a Latin American aviation and shipping network. He imagined Miami as a hub with connections to Jacksonville, Havana, and Nassau, and even pondered an annual Pan American Aerial Derby with contestants traveling from Florida to Cuba, then Central and South America, before returning to Miami. He also saw Miami as an ideal connection point for steamships traveling between New York and the West Indies. Still obsessed with space-annihilating technologies, Fisher realized there were more profitable places to launch them than Indiana.[66]

Infrastructure pulled places together and put them within reach of tourists and developers. Before the war, Fisher created the roots of a transcontinental highway network, but, during the conflict, it became clear that the nation still needed better roads. In 1919, the US Army sent a convoy across the country, with nearly three hundred men driving six dozen vehicles westward, largely over the Lincoln Highway. Right before it set out, one associate assured Fisher that this "army truck train" would effectively "nail the Lincoln Highway on the map forever" and possibly give the route priority as a new, federally funded highway. Although Fisher worried the Lincoln Highway Association might get taken over by the government, it was clear to many people by 1919 that federal intervention was needed to build a national highway system. After all, big trucks driven by inexperienced soldiers frequently destroyed bridges—which military personnel then rebuilt, at government expense. The Lincoln Highway got the job done, but just barely; the convoy took two months to cover more than three thousand miles between New York City and San Francisco. Something had to change. One member of that 1919 expedition who may have begun to realize the need for federal highways was Lieutenant Colonel Dwight Eisenhower, later a World War II general and, in the 1950s, US president. Federal funding ultimately resulted in successive grids of numbered highways, first a 1920s network that included legendary Route 66 and US Highways 31 and 41—main stems of the old Dixie Highway—and then the 41,000-mile Interstate Highway System that was promoted by Eisenhower and authorized by Congress in 1956. The era when crossing the nation by car had been a challenging and strenuous ordeal was coming to an end, thanks in large part to government-funded roadbuilding.[67]

From US entry into World War I to the armistice, Indianapolis's speedway made significant contributions to the Allied war effort as an aviation center and also served as an important node in Fisher's nascent aviation network. Once the racing spectacle returned in 1919, it became clear that wartime advances had made motor sport deadlier than ever. As fatalities rose, proponents argued that driving at breakneck speeds was not about amusement; it was about technological progress, manly nerves, and national power. Yet, in the 1920s, as Fisher grew increasingly involved in real-estate development, racing grew into a bigger pop-culture spectacle than ever before.

6

SPORTS OF TITANS

A Golden Age of Racing and Development

The 1920s was a Golden Age of Sports, when new technologies turned sport into mass spectacle and transformed athletes into celebrities. Motor sport celebrities included Tommy Milton and Peter De Paolo, but not, for most Americans, Black driver Charlie Wiggins. Racing may have been more popular than ever, but this was the era when space annihilation yielded to legend creation, a shift that occurred partly by necessity, since Indianapolis speedway racing faced an existential threat. As traditionalists tried to shut down the oval and Carl Fisher focused on developing places for leisurely living, the speedway increasingly looked to its own golden era, becoming a place built on fond glances backward to a time and place of modern progress.

Around 1920, racing fans developed nostalgia for a speedway that seemed a quaint relic of earlier times. Indianapolis's decade-old bricks were no longer smooth, and racing enthusiasts saw the track as a prewar relic, a "historic Hoosier oval" that sponsored a now-classic race. Officials reacted to the deadly 1919 race by imposing limits on weight and tires and by reducing maximum piston displacement from 300 to 183 cubic inches (or three liters). New rules tried to make Indianapolis auto racing safer for prewar pavement. Some motor minds, though, were starting to think beyond brick. German industrialists considered building a five-mile steel-plate track over concrete trusses, surrounding an infield containing an industrial park.[1]

Early-1920s thinkers already anticipated midcentury spaces, which John Findlay calls *magic lands*, built on intertwined visions of industry, spectacle, and residential life, and they used welfare capitalism to navigate the competitive postwar labor market. By building "model homes, a new hotel and a community center," Speedway City echoed the suburban spaces near Henry Ford's plants.[2] For Fisher, though, housing was not enough; leisure activities were also needed to retain workers. He told a Union Carbide official that he and Allison would improve evening and weekend amusements in Speedway City to reduce excessive labor turnover, which cost Prest-O-Lite and Allison Engineering Company tens of thousands of dollars per year. Fisher thought the speedway might host a movie theater, "a small gymnasium, a basket ball [sic] court and a hand ball [sic] court, as well as a billiard room and café with up-to-date soda fountain attachments."[3] Jane Fisher later wrote that even though Carl would not allow a single "damned horse" on Speedway City's streets, he encouraged fun, which he saw "as important as food."[4]

As Speedway City matured and leisure became a central aspect of life, Fisher envisioned other purposes for the big tract of land on which the oval sat. In fact, he may never have intended the track to last more than a few years, and Pop Myers later said as much. As Fisher's Miami Beach developments took off and he considered developing a resort on Grosse Isle near Detroit, he introduced ideas that already attracted tourists and residents to South Florida. The speedway's infield was ideal for polo, he thought, big enough for twelve fields similar to those created alongside the exclusive golf course at Miami Beach. Fisher outlined plans for a Speedway Polo Club, and Allison observed that airplane hangars or garages could be converted into horse barns if enough dirt was put down over the concrete. The Army even removed its aviation repair depot from Speedway City because airplanes could no longer land on the polo fields' manicured grass.[5]

Fisher did not want workhorses on the streets of his auto-themed town, but he did not mind expensive polo ponies on the speedway infield. He hoped to convince a thousand Hoosiers to join his new polo club at fifty dollars each, an ambitious strategy that could gross $50,000. More generally, the speedway might become the centerpiece of an Indianapolis-area sporting complex. In 1921, at a time when Fisher thought racing was declining, he told Allison they could transform the grounds into "a big golf course, play grounds, swimming pools and polo fields." It took a while to generate interest in polo, he admitted, but golf would quickly make the racing plant into a "center of athletic diversions." Fisher's experience in Miami convinced him that golf links could generate about $20,000 per year, and pools would make money during the summer and yield "a barrel of publicity." Recreation facilities could turn a profit until the track was "cut up" in four or five years. Fisher may have planned to develop the speedway's real estate by the mid-1920s. He clearly had little, if any, sentimental attachment to it.[6]

For the foreseeable future, long-distance racing would continue at the speedway, even though some observers thought shorter events would eventually take over. Oval-track racing seemed like ideal sport because it pushed modern men to physical limits. Highly trained drivers could not stop for food or drink and they needed days to recover. Racing was "as strenuous as any other sport" and it approximated "the heat of battle."[7] Military metaphors were still common, with one account saying pace-car driver Barney Oldfield led "the fliers to the war." In 1920, Gaston Chevrolet won the big race in a Michigan-made Monroe, averaging 88.16 miles per hour (5:40:16.64). The crowd of 120,000 saw crashes involving Louis Chevrolet and Joe Boyer, yet neither was injured. Gaston was not so lucky in November when he crashed in a two-hundred-fifty-mile race at California's Beverly Hills Speedway. He was driving a green car when he died, perhaps inaugurating the custom of banning cars of that color from racing at Indianapolis.[8]

Sport became a central part of American life in the 1920s, when the New York Yankees won their first three World Series titles and football became a national obsession. Universities such as Ohio State and Stanford erected huge football stadiums, and some campuses—including Indiana and Illinois, each located a short drive from Indianapolis—styled new facilities as war memorials. The speedway even became a reference point for big sporting structures. In 1922, the New York Times said that new Yankee Stadium would be America's "biggest athletic arena"—except, of course, for the speedway.[9] Racing may not have had stars as famous as Yankees slugger Babe Ruth, but it did have legends who, like Ruth, endorsed consumer goods. Barney Oldfield worked with Firestone in 1919 to develop and market an eponymous line of tires. Chicago's biggest sporting goods store sold Oldfield Tires at its retail center in the Loop, alongside other motoring accessories, including tow ropes, tire gauges, seat covers, and dusters.[10]

Consumerism was a key part of 1920s life, but so was mobility, as postwar highways facilitated movement of people, goods, and capital. The Lincoln Highway Forum said it was as if American society had developed a romantic relationship with concrete. By the early 1920s, a so-called Ideal Section of the Lincoln Highway was built in Dyer, Indiana. This concrete roadway featured lighting, drainage, landscaping, and pedestrian walkways, almost like a section of racetrack. Soon, additional sections were paved with concrete, while sturdy bridges elevated the roadway above railroad tracks in places as remote as rural Wyoming, thus eliminating dangerous grade crossings—the same thing Indianapolis had done on city streets in the 1910s.[11] Progress in infrastructure was spreading beyond automotive metropolises. As Fisher told the Dixie Highway Commission, good roads helped people see new places and spend money. Henry Joy saw the Lincoln Highway as a "river" moving a "great flow of traffic" into the West, especially to national parks. As rails had once done, highways now integrated remote regions into a cultural and economic grid. By the 1930s, as the web of roads spread, some conservationists worked to keep pavement and cars out of remote places they hoped to maintain as wilderness.[12]

Spectacle and improvement were intertwined, with correspondents invoking races in the same conversations in which they discussed highway business. Fisher never seemed pleased with the progress on the Lincoln and Dixie Highways, especially when he thought auto executives did not contribute enough money. Their apathy, however, may have resulted from an increase in government funding. With better roads now becoming common, enthusiasts saw improvements every time they drove to a race. By the 1920s, Chicago motorists heading to Indianapolis could take an old macadam route, via Lafayette, Indiana, but a better option was to head southward along the Dixie Highway to Danville, Illinois, then east to Crawfordsville, Indiana. Nearly every major town within several hours' drive of Indianapolis featured campsites with lights, running water, bathrooms, and grills, precursors to inexpensive motor courts and, eventually, motels. By the early 1920s an estimated ten thousand cars traveled to Indianapolis each May.[13]

In 1921, hundreds of cars thronged the speedway gates, and a crowd of 135,000 saw Tommy Milton, driving an Indianapolis-made Frontenac (a company started by the Chevrolet brothers) win the race in 5:34:44.65, or 89.62 miles per hour.[14] Six months later, French general Ferdinand Foch visited Indianapolis during a trip to America for the conference that negotiated the Washington Naval Treaty. Foch presided at the cornerstone dedication for the million-dollar Indiana War Memorial that later became

Indiana World War Memorial, pictured here in 1930. (W. H. Bass Photo Co. Collection, Indiana Historical Society)

a focal point of the American Legion's headquarters. After speaking at the Claypool Hotel, Marshal Foch and twenty-five thousand others ventured to the speedway to watch a twenty-five-mile race. It would not be long, however, before critics tried to end Memorial Day racing, claiming it disrespected veterans.[15]

The 1922 500-mile race featured Jules Goux, De Palma, Howdy Wilcox, and Milton, as well as newer names, including Hollywood movie star Wallace Reid. Unlike Victoria Prescott in 1914, who was not welcome at the track, Reid was seen as a serious contender, even though he ended up bowing out because of a filming commitment.[16] Before the race, a thousand-piece brass band with flag-toting veterans led a parade around the track. Then the record crowd watched racer Frank Davidson become the first to race with no riding mechanic since Ray Harroun in 1911. Winner Jimmy Murphy, driving a car built by Los Angeles's Harry Miller, virtually never trailed. Aided by an efficient pit crew, Murphy won about $30,000 in prize money and set a world record time of 5:17:30.79, averaging 94.48 miles per hour and shattering De Palma's 1915 record. One writer said the race was a "five hour acid [litmus] test" that fueled technological progress. Some manufacturers did, in fact, return to racing in the 1920s, claiming a desire for progress, yet they perhaps also craved the publicity and competitive advantages that victory might bring.[17]

Racing thrived, but would the big event still be held on Memorial Day? Postwar social changes prompted reactions against modernity, represented most famously by the 1925 Scopes Trial in Tennessee, which tested the legality of a state law forbidding the teaching of evolution in public schools. In Indiana, meanwhile, a Methodist group fought to enforce the Sabbath, outlaw tobacco, and ban Memorial Day racing. This was a time when the Ku Klux Klan gained a dominant presence in Indiana and other midwestern states, pushing for immigration bans and a return to traditional (i.e., white Protestant) social mores. Indiana's General Assembly considered a bill, supported by some American Legion chapters, to outlaw Memorial Day sporting events. Fisher was incensed but did not think the measure would become law. He predicted Indianapolis would fight to protect its famous race. Either the bill would get shot down—because the holiday was traditionally recognized as a time for amusements—or the speedway would lobby for laws permitting the race a few days before or after Memorial Day. The issue was not easily brushed aside, though, and it soon became clear it would emerge in the upcoming legislative session.[18]

The showdown came in January 1923. State Senator Robert Moorhead, a veteran of the Spanish-American War and World War I, introduced Senate Bill 31, which outlawed all sporting events charging admission on Memorial Day, including races between animals, cars, boats, or aircraft. The Anti-Saloon League supported the bill, as did recently reelected Mayor Lewis Shank, who claimed quiet reflection on the holiday limited political radicalism. Members of veterans groups like the Grand Army of the Republic, Veterans of Foreign Wars, and American Legion tended to divide along generational lines: proponents of the law tended to be older Civil War veterans, while some opponents were younger World War I veterans. The Indiana House of Representatives narrowly passed the bill despite opposition from Marion County's delegation, and then the measure moved to the desk of Republican governor Warren McCray. Speedway manager Pop Myers claimed the big race would leave Indiana if the bill became law, but Allison echoed Fisher by saying it would simply move to another day. Still, when eight hundred acres sold at Glen Allen, Virginia, near Richmond—midway between Boston and Atlanta—some observers speculated that Indiana and New York investors had bought the land to build a two-mile track, seating seventy-five thousand, where the embattled Hoosiers might relocate.[19]

Fisher seemed genuinely concerned about the speedway's future, and so he tried to sell his shares to the other owners for $640,000, just slightly below the $648,000 at which Allison, Newby, and Fisher had apparently considered selling the entire facility the previous year. (Frank Wheeler, tragically, had taken his own life days before the 1921 race.) Allison, always playing the hard-nosed businessman, firmly asserted he would *not* pay such a high price. Instead, he carefully calculated the liquid value of the real estate. Allison reckoned the southern half of the grounds, a 160-acre quarter section, might be worth $1,200 per acre, a total of $192,000. The comparably sized northern half, though, was only worth about $400 per acre, or $64,000. A 40-acre (quarter-quarter section) tract south of Thirtieth Street was valued at around $500 per acre, totaling $20,000, while a 72-acre piece of land (nearly a half-quarter section) between the speedway and the railroad tracks was worth $700 per acre, or $50,400. Allison said the total, $326,400, seemed high, perhaps by 10 percent, meaning the land might be worth only $294,000. If "buildings and grandstands" were "sold to wreckers," he conceded, they might garner another $4,000 or $5,000, while salvaged bricks might defray demolition costs. To Allison, at least, the speedway was worth around $300,000, less than half of what it would sell for in just four years.[20]

Despite the fear implied in Fisher's contemplated sale, the controversial bill's passage was no sure bet. Indiana's American Legion supported the antiracing law, but two local chapters opposed it. A member of Indiana's legislature who worked to defeat the measure was Russell Harrison, son of former president Benjamin Harrison. A Spanish-American War veteran, he argued that if the state outlawed racing, it should also ban other pop-culture events, including theatrical performances or the brass bands that inhibited solemn Memorial Day observances at the Soldiers and Sailors Monument. Ultimately, Governor McCray, a Klan opponent, vetoed the bill on advice of Attorney General Ulysses S. Lesh, who deemed it unconstitutional. With the legislative session ending soon, there was no chance of the bill passing over McCray's veto. For the time being, racing was safe. The legislature again considered outlawing Memorial Day racing two years later, but that time the bill did not even pass the assembly. Still, animosity lingered. Days before the 1923 race, Mayor Shank, reacting in outrage when a ticket agent refused entry to Ohio's Republican senator Simeon Fess, said the city would not oil roads leading to the track and would provide no police or ambulances—only fire protection. After Allison apologized, Shank reluctantly agreed to provide usual city services, albeit only in the name of public safety.[21]

Fallout from the attempt to end Memorial Day racing was significant. Fisher was already spending more time in Miami, but now he seriously considered selling the track. The dustup may also have prompted racing fans to be even more prone to see the speedway as legendary. One year after he advocated outlawing Memorial Day races, Mayor Shank said the oval was Indianapolis's "best single advertisement," with its annual race promoting a heartland city the same way as Louisville's Kentucky Derby. Harry Stutz, likewise, said the speedway made Indianapolis known around the world as a place of "invention, industry, and sports." While some thought the Memorial Day spectacle was not patriotic, Stutz said it paid "utmost respect" to the nation's "fallen heroes."[22] Others stressed the track's role as a laboratory. It was, according to one colorful metaphor, "the Aladdin's lamp of the gasoline transportation genie!" The oval's impact on modern time and space seemed immeasurable: It had "helped bridge space in minutes instead of hours" and "stimulated suburban growth, relieved the congestion of crowded cities, given children wholesome home environments, lightened the monotony of the farmer and his family, [and] increased the value of his land." The speedway was a metonym for automobility itself, a signifier of the many ways cars and roads had transformed American society.[23]

Racing grew in international popularity. Japanese fans requested tickets, while German companies hoped to enter the race for the first time since the war. Foreign drivers vying to compete at Indianapolis came from Argentina, England, France, Italy, and Poland. Cars were expensive sporting goods, with owners spending up to $200,000 to develop each one, and drivers were valuable athletes. Milton and Wilcox each carried $10,000 insurance policies taken out by Harry Stutz, who insisted—perhaps not convincingly—that the policies were "merely a matter of business" and not based on any fear of deadly crashes.[24] All US-made cars were now single-seaters, a change that Peter De Paolo said "took a lot of the picturesqueness out of racing." Spectators no longer watched a "mechanic sitting on the right of the driver, perhaps jerking vigorously at a pump to maintain the air pressure on the gasoline tank, or pumping oil into the crank case of the car from the main reservoir, as was done in the old days." Modern technology augmented motor sport while simultaneously instilling nostalgia for old-time races.[25]

Despite cloudy skies, a huge crowd showed up in 1923. Eddie Ricken-backer was the starter, while Fred Duesenberg drove the pace car. Tommy Milton, starting in the pole position, finished in 5:28:06.27, or 91.44 miles per hour, becoming the 500-mile race's first two-time winner. At the time, the crowd was probably the biggest ever to witness an American sporting event. Fans stood on top of cars in the infield to watch the race as photographers snapped pictures from airplanes. Representing the era's sensational sports reporting, James Bennett proclaimed on the *Chicago Tribune*'s front page that racing was a "sport of Titans, with Vulcan as its promoter." This colorful phrasing, vividly invoking racing's sights and sounds, may have been influenced by the emergent technology of radio. Bennett said the "roar of the devil's perambulators" filled the air as racers appeared "like a troupe of harlequins gone speed crazy."[26]

The day after the race, Fisher called a meeting to discuss the track's future. Some thought the speedway might be shuttered or relocated, and Fisher added grist to the rumor mill when he said it needed $200,000 worth of improvements. Since he claimed he had already accomplished what he planned to do when he built the track, selling or substantially altering it was not out of the question. Fisher repeated the old chestnut about the speedway being conceived as a place for testing cars. But now, he said, 500-mile races had proven American machines were better than European ones, which meant races had become more or less extraneous.[27] Fisher's claim held a grain of truth, yet it may have been a selective origin story. The desire for popular spectacle appears to have been a primary feature of the track from day one, but, by 1923, Fisher's nationalistic tone and tight focus on motor developments echoed postwar discourses.

Fisher's role diminished in 1923, when Allison replaced him as speedway president. Soon it was rumored they would sell the track to a California investment group led by Russell "Cliff" Durant, head of the Beverly Hills Speedway and millionaire son of General Motors founder William Durant.[28] Yet even as its future seemed uncertain, the speedway continued hosting events. In July, veterans celebrated the fifth anniversary of the Second Battle of the Marne with a parade in downtown Indianapolis and exhibition races at the track. The next month, Argentinian prizefighter Luis Firpo dismantled Cincinnati's Joe Downey in ten rounds. During a pause in the fighting, with the crowd of ten thousand in an uproar, Mayor Shank, who moonlighted as an auctioneer and vaudeville performer, entered the ring to declare that he would order the boxers and promoters arrested unless they resumed the fight.[29]

Meanwhile, the speedway's mythical status only grew. One observer called the 500-mile race "the oldest motor race classic of the new world and the greatest speed event" on the globe. Yet it kept evolving, with new rules continuing to reduce engine size. One 1924 entrant had a piston displacement of just 91.5 cubic inches (1.5 liters), which became the new maximum in 1926. Cars with engines up to 122 cubic inches had to weigh a minimum of fourteen hundred pounds, while those with engines of 91.5 cubic inches or less had to be at least twelve hundred pounds. Riding mechanics were no longer allowed, but innovative balloon tires were introduced and the track itself saw updates. Speedway superintendent Harlan Sample and his crews remodeled the facility by building better grandstands, relocating pits, and improving the infield.[30]

Racing occupied a liminal space between technology and spectacle. The 1924 field included Antoine Mourre, a French aviator and cavalry officer who also competed in rugby, pole vault, and road races; it did *not* include Ralph De Palma, who was barred from AAA contests for racing in unsanctioned events. Henry Ford refereed that year's race, with his duties resembling the control he imposed at company towns stretching from Dearborn, Michigan, to Fordlandia, Brazil. Ford held "power to stop cars, disqualify or reinstate them, and make all decisions." The local chamber of commerce touted the mogul's presence as a sign of Indianapolis's importance in the motoring world. The day before the race, sixty-year-old Ford inspected the course on foot, walking the entire track in thirty-eight minutes. Newspapers later reported he had taken out a life insurance policy on each driver, although the men did not learn about it until after the fact.[31]

Racing's biggest 1920s innovation may have been radio. Although Indianapolis's WOH broadcast the 500-mile race earlier in the decade, far-off listeners did not hear it until 1924, when they tuned to a broadcast sponsored by Prest-O-Lite and transmitted on Chicago's WGN radio. Microphones and an AT&T cable transmitted the sounds of pit crews and spectators, as well as A. W. "Sen" Kaney's play-by-play, from Indianapolis to Chicago and then into homes around America. Racing was no exception to the radio boom that helped create celebrities like Red Grange, whose WGN-disseminated performance in the 1924 Illinois-Michigan game made him a legend.[32] Some racers even used a "wireless telephone" to talk to pit crews.[33] WGN again broadcast the race in 1925, just weeks after Louisville's famed Kentucky Derby was first transmitted via airwaves. On May 30, fans tuned to WGN at 10:15 a.m. to hear the cars, the crowd, and the 1,075-piece band. Among those who listened were nine hundred patients at the Edward Hines Jr. Veterans' Hospital, on the former site of Chicago's Speedway Park. A public-address system disseminated the broadcast, and each bed had headphones linked to a "central receiving set."[34]

In 1924, the first-ever cowinners, Indianapolis's Lora L. "Slim" Corum and Detroit's Joe Boyer, set a track record of 98.24 miles per hour in a Duesenberg, with Boyer driving the last ninety laps in relief.[35] Under AAA rules, Corum won first prize, although Boyer gained a significant amount in lap prizes. The crowd was estimated at 140,000, while many more virtually "saw" the race via WGN's "vivid word picture." Memorial Day sports were a hit, with nearly nine hundred thousand Americans attending events on May 30.[36] Sports venues were quasi-public spaces. At the speedway, a force of twelve hundred guards kept order under the leadership of Indiana National Guard officers. In one 1920s account, a guard threw rocks at an African American man who climbed a tree in an attempt to watch the race for free. Reportedly, after forcing him to come down, the guard then gave the man some cash to buy a ticket. Whether or not the guard really acted in this paternalistic manner, the message was clear: the speedway was a place for making money, and its private security force controlled access.[37]

Nativism and racism were common features of 1920s racing. The post–World War I era was a time of red scares, immigration restriction, and white supremacy. Newspapers sometimes used ethnic slurs when referring to drivers, and one account even claimed that Ralph De Palma and Dario Resta—who had migrated to the United States and England, respectively, as small children—represented Italy, not their actual countries of residence. Anti-Black sentiment, which was even worse, was part of the radio program on Memorial Day. A blackface-minstrel-style performance by Sam 'n' Henry, WGN's "comic colored boys," precursors to the racist duo Amos 'n' Andy, was a component of the 1927 broadcast.[38] For his part, Carl Fisher had complicated racial views. Although some accounts stress his kind treatment of individual African Americans—and he did give monetary donations to Black colleges, churches, hospitals, and charities—Fisher also created two virtually all-white towns and seems to have helped initiate the speedway's unofficial ban on nonwhite racers when Jack Johnson was barred in 1910. He may have been kind to many people of color, but he did virtually nothing to challenge segregation.[39]

Racing was still a segregated affair in an era when the Ku Klux Klan was strong in the Midwest and Indianapolis formally segregated its schools and hospitals, leaving the city's large Black population severely underserved by public institutions. Yet racism did not prevent African American speedsters from partaking in motor sports. In 1924, an Indianapolis-based Colored Speedway Association began hosting annual one-hundred-mile races on a dirt track at Indiana's state fairgrounds. Frank A. "Fay" Young of the *Chicago Defender* dubbed these races the "Gold and Glory Sweepstakes." Prizes were not as big as those at whites-only speedway races, yet drivers and spectators came from all over the Midwest, especially Chicago, Detroit, and St. Louis, even though segregation often made long-distance travel difficult. One of the best Black racers was Charlie Wiggins, an Evansville, Indiana, native and whiz mechanic who owned a shop in Indianapolis. Wiggins won the 1926, 1931, 1932, and 1933 races, becoming known as the "Negro Speed King." But tragedy struck in 1936, when his car skidded on the dirt track and slammed into a fence. Wiggins was thrown from his self-built car and crushed; he ended up losing a leg and an eye after eight hours of painstaking surgery in the segregated wing of a local hospital. The Gold and Glory Sweepstakes was never held again after 1936. Without Jim Crow, one can only imagine what Wiggins—or other legendary Black drivers, such as "Rajo Jack" DeSoto, Malcolm Hannon, "Wild Bill" Jeffries, Sumner "Red" Oliver, Bob Wallace, and Leon "Al" Warren—might have accomplished on the legendary Hoosier bricks.[40]

Although they were still excluded from competition, white women's visibility at the speedway increased in the 1920s. A local newspaper profiled Eloise Dallenbach, who worked as Pop Myers's secretary and had helped prepare for all races since the second annual event in 1912. The detail-oriented Dallenbach reportedly knew "every nook and cranny of the gigantic Speedway plant," possessed meticulous records of the races, and corresponded with ticket buyers all around the world. She had extensive knowledge of cars and racing. Yet, on the day of the big event, "Dolly" could not "pass to the paddock or into the judge's pagoda." A strict track rule said no women could enter this "sanctum" on Memorial Day.[41] It is unclear whether such rules were a holdover from early-twentieth-century concerns about women's bodies, or if it was just plain male chauvinism, or a combination thereof. Nevertheless, the speedway was happy to sell tickets to spectators of all sexes, even if officials thought female nerves were not quite strong enough to watch races. Myers claimed women got "more excited than men" during races and frequently had "to leave the stands because of the nervous strain of watching the cars speed by each other."[42]

The 1923 race saw Herbert Shoup, a sixteen-year-old spectator from La-fayette, Indiana, become the speedway's first post-1919 fatality; he was killed when Tom Alley struck a fence near the spot where Shoup and two friends stood. The following year, a spate of deadly races occurred at other tracks. In September, Joe Boyer died of injuries sustained at a new speedway in Altoona, Pennsylvania. The next day Dario Resta, who had won the 1916 three-hundred-mile race, died at Brooklands while driving a Sunbeam at 120 miles per hour. Resta was nearly decapitated when his car "dashed over a bank and crashed into an iron fence, nose-dived into the ground, . . . and burst into flames." Two weeks later, former champion Jimmy Murphy died in a one-hundred-fifty-mile event at the New York state fairgrounds near Syracuse, when his car smashed into a fence and his chest was pierced by wood fragments. At least five thousand witnessed Murphy's fatal wreck.[43] Only three died at Indianapolis in the 1920s, but the next decade was devas-tating: twenty-four drivers, mechanics, or spectators perished at the track between 1930 and 1940.

Speeds increased in the mid-1920s, even though the aging bricks made Indianapolis's oval America's "roughest and most dangerous." By 1926, the speedway set maximum piston displacement at 91.5 cubic inches and mini-mum vehicle weight at twelve hundred pounds, while raising qualifying speeds to eighty-five miles per hour.[44] Speed fever seemed to be spread-ing, on the water as well. Back in 1911, Carl Fisher had bought a mahogany speedboat and began staging races in Biscayne Bay. He loved the water so much that some of his friends called him "Skipper," and in 1925 he held a promotional regatta featuring $10,000 in prizes and ten racers, including two-time 500-mile-race winner Tommy Milton. Milton had no experience with motorboats, yet years of racing supposedly showed he had enough "nerve" to pilot a fast watercraft.[45]

The 1925 race was the last one Fisher attended for several years, engrossed as he was with his Florida developments, but that year's pace-car driver was future owner Eddie Rickenbacker, who kicked off the race in a car made by his own company, a firm that soon folded and left him indebted to the tune of a quarter-million dollars. Peter De Paolo, nephew of Ralph De Palma, won the race in a Duesenberg; he finished in 4:56:39.47, breaking records and averaging 101.13 miles per hour before an estimated 145,000 spectators. This race was the first in which De Paolo attached his son's baby shoes to his dashboard, which he believed prevented crashes, but De Paolo did not rely only on superstition alone. In a *Saturday Evening Post* article, the Italian American racer explained how he personally examined engine parts "with a high-power microscope" to determine whether they were capable of performing at high speeds.[46] Yet observers also reported that his "iron nerve" was aided by a supercharger.[47]

Automobiles advanced significantly in the 1920s, but so did roads. The *Chicago Tribune* now published maps with a mere paragraph outlining the

Peter De Paolo, July 1925. The Italian American speedster had just won a 250-mile race at the Baltimore-Washington speedway in Laurel, Maryland. Note the board track. (Library of Congress, National Photo Company Collection)

quickest routes to Indianapolis, rather than detailed, turn-by-turn directions. Big motor jaunts were possible in large part because of two decades'
worth of good pavement. Indiana's roads appeared to be falling behind
those of nearby states, especially Illinois, yet with the rise of federal funding, state-by-state differences mattered less than before. Race cars capable
of speeds topping a hundred miles per hour seemed to foreshadow future
passenger cars, and motor vehicles were already replacing streetcars. In
1925, the Indianapolis Street Railway Company began running a motor bus
out to Speedway City.[48]

Cars changed American life. In 1925, University of Chicago sociologists
Robert Park, Ernest Burgess, and Roderick McKenzie said automobiles
were a powerful factor in population shifts and the reorientation of places
formerly based on horses. New York scholars Robert and Helen Lynd also
showed, in a landmark study of Muncie, Indiana, how dramatically urban life
had changed since the 1890s. One resident of pseudonymous Middletown
exclaimed, "I can tell you what's happening in just four letters: A-U-T-O!"
Muncie saw its first motorcar in 1900, but by 1923 the town had more than
six thousand vehicles registered. Some people even mortgaged their houses
to buy cars. Automobiles decentralized urban space and changed social patterns. City dwellers needed cars to get to work, the grocery store, or the
golf course. Some even worried that a "motor insanity" or "automobilitis"
infected society. It is not surprising that automobility became a motif of
Speedway City, where the Catholic parish was named for Saint Christopher,
patron saint of motorists, and four public schools were ultimately named for
the track's founders. By the time the town incorporated in 1926, it sprawled
over hundreds of acres, with modest middle-class houses—and garages, of
course—set back from tree-lined streets.[49]

Speedway City represented a type of industrial-era space organized
around mobility, production, and consumption, one of two cases in which
Carl Fisher created a town with no preautomotive history. Yet it was never
as famous or as glamorous as its Florida counterpart. Miami Beach tourists stayed at Fisher's hotels, the Lincoln (1917), Flamingo (1920), Nautilus
(1924), and King Cole (1925). These structures catered to upscale transients
who wanted to spend winters "in comfort with modern conveniences."[50]
Miami Beach's opulence fostered a mentality of leisure and year-round
sport embodied in its "polo fields, tennis courts, bathing casinos," and golf
courses. Yachting, horseback riding, swimming, flying, and jai alai were

Carl Fisher's Nautilus Hotel in Miami Beach, with golfers. The hotel was designed by New York architects Schulze and Weaver and opened in January 1924. (Claude Carson Matlack Collection, 155–8, HistoryMiami Museum)

available, as were theaters showing the latest Hollywood films. Miami Beach spectators even watched Boston Braves spring-training games in the late 1910s. Promotional materials claimed that tourists arriving on well-paved roads were "dazzle[d]" by "lavish" recreation activities and the "panorama of ever-changing scintillating stage settings" at the hotels. It was almost as if modern infrastructure had turned south Florida into a theater. Fisher, who was especially concerned with appearances, insisted Miami clean up its waterfront so it could offer fine views for luxury yachts. He even devised an elaborate plan by which music could be piped directly from radio station WIOD (Wonderful Isle of Dreams) to speakers located strategically around the island, which included his several hotels and the grand causeways crossing the bay.[51]

Miami Beach lots sold for astronomical prices at the height of Florida's land boom, especially in frenetic 1925, but Fisher was not the only transplant who profited by reengineering south Florida space. Aviation pioneer Glenn Curtiss built an expensive racetrack at Hialeah and pitched attractions such as greyhound races, jai alai, "a hired Seminole village," and "cabarets" filled with Broadway stars. In Coral Gables, meanwhile, former

Pennsylvanian George Merrick transformed his family's citrus plantation into a City Beautiful town that became home to the University of Miami in 1925. Even earlier, Henry Flagler, who had made his fortune in nineteenth-century railroads, fostered Miami's development and transformed St. Augustine from an old Spanish outpost into a Yankee tourist paradise.[52] Seeing himself as a latter-day Flagler, Fisher raised lot prices by 10 percent each year, touting Florida as a place where salty sea air washed away respiratory maladies, including the persistent hay fever that had helped drive him away from Indiana. Ever the pitchman, Fisher said that Miami Beach, with its resplendent baths and polo fields, hosted more tourists "than any other place in the entire South."[53]

If Speedway City was a place where auto parts and motor spectacles were produced and consumed, Miami Beach was a place of *vacation*, where people enjoyed time away from work. Such places were largely accessible only because people used modern technologies to travel hundreds or thousands of miles from financial or industrial centers where they maintained comparatively mundane lives. One promoter said Miami was a "Mecca of motorists" since it was located at the terminus of several transcontinental routes, including the Dixie Highway and Old Spanish Trail.[54] William Anderson, editor of the *Macon Telegraph* and a good roads proponent, was amazed at the region's transformation. On a 1925 trip to Florida, Anderson saw how the "vast wilderness, sand beds and quagmires" that challenged 1910s motorists had been replaced by "an unending line of buildings and paved roads." Between 1921 and 1928, Miami Beach's population boomed, from 650 to more than 10,000, with assessed property valuation skyrocketing from $5,540,112 to $44,087,050. Infrastructure, too, grew by leaps and bounds: 551 telephones to 5,371; five hotels to sixty-one; fifteen miles of concrete sidewalks to eighty-six, and thirty miles of paved streets to ninety. The fancy island's growth was outstanding.[55]

South Florida could not have grown as it did without automotive infrastructure. By 1920, a county-financed causeway connected downtown Miami to South Miami Beach, giving drivers another way to get to Fisher's sensational sandbar. Even before its completion, advertisers assured investors the new causeway would inflate real-estate values in Miami Beach the same way Chicago's elevated trains had once fueled suburban growth. Fisher advertised Miami's mild winter climate on a massive, illuminated billboard at Fifth Avenue and Forty-Second Street in Midtown Manhattan. It might be winter in New York, but it was June in Miami. Like the optometrist's billboard in F. Scott Fitzgerald's 1925 novel *The Great Gatsby*, with faceless eyes gazing down on discontented Long Islanders trying to be anywhere or anyone else, a vivid sunset beckoned to motorists who sought escape from dreary northern winters. At some point, though, advertisement no longer seemed necessary. Instead, said Fisher, Miami should simply invest in "promotion of high-grade sports or entertainment."[56] Fisher was "selling real estate with sport." Initially, he tried to promote Miami Beach as a "paradise of rest" but then realized it was more profitable as "a place not to idle but a place to play." Turning an entire town into a playground was expensive, but big expenditures could mean big profits. Five polo fields took $100,000 of clay brought from twenty miles away, while motorboat races required a half-million dollars' worth of boats and $10,000 in prizes. Fisher claimed he spent $350,000 per year on golf, tennis, and aquatic sports.[57]

Although they were located more than a thousand miles apart and occupied different climates, Miami Beach and Speedway City were two sides of the same coin. Men such as Fisher, Curtiss, and Merrick created nearly

La Gorce Country Club building and golf course, Miami Beach, which opened in 1928 as a private golf club. It was named after John La Gorce, a leader of the National Geographic Society. (Claude Carson Matlack Collection, 92–27, HistoryMiami Museum)

magical spaces, accessible via cars or trains or airplanes, where they sold industrial-era Americans—who grew accustomed to the benefits of welfare capitalism—a vision of distant residential life saturated with cultural amenities. In the process, they so effectively annihilated space that they transformed it beyond recognition. By the late 1920s, tourists and real-estate investors traveled along the Tamiami Trail, a 275-mile section of the Dixie Highway between Tampa and Miami, graded with shards of rock blasted from the immense limestone shelf lying under the Everglades. Finished in 1928, the roadway effectively served as a dike, almost totally blocking the southward flow of water from Lake Okeechobee. Natural space yielded to artificial space, with potentially disastrous results. Car-focused suburbs became even more ubiquitous after World War II, when developers carved giant swamps into thousands of lots and sold them to retirees from the Northeast and Midwest. Sunshine State land-development schemes imposed a modern, car-focused, and environmentally destructive order on the land. Even though some developments remained nearly devoid of human inhabitation, they still exhibited residue of annihilated space: irreparable damage to animal habitats, lower water tables inviting forest fires, and crumbling roads serving as illicit runways for drug smugglers.[58]

Geography was altered, but so was temporality, with some places becoming resorts where people mainly relaxed and spent money. The progressive reinvention of 1910s Indianapolis seemed a quaint memory in light of Miami Beach's creation story. More generally, America's producer-based industrial economy yielded to a consumer-focused service economy. In the 1920s, writes historian Rebecca Cawood McIntyre, ambitious developers transformed parts of the Old South into "a place where leisure was permissible, a region where one could indulge in recreational pursuits with no fear of losing a commitment to hard work."[59] Florida's post–World War I growth was so phenomenal it created an economic bubble that popped after a Category 4 hurricane slammed into Miami in September 1926. The previous year, Fisher had predicted a fall, privately comparing Florida's land boom to the Yukon gold rush and Oklahoma's oil boom: quick growth with potential for "a great many disappointments."[60] In a letter to James Cox, publisher of the *Miami Daily News* and a former Ohio governor who ran as the Democratic nominee for president in 1920, Fisher complained about the influx of money coming into Florida from northern speculators who purchased marginal lands with little prospect of developing them any time soon. Yet even as he privately decried the swindlers—some of whom were surely lured by his own stunts—Fisher maintained a remarkably positive stance in public. In spring 1926, before the hurricane, he continued touting Florida's wonderful climate, which could continue attracting millions of new residents as long as they had access to "better roads, better transportation facilities and better housing." Florida's future was promising, thought Fisher, if people could just *get* there. Year-round warm weather in the tropics meant people never had to stop playing; they just had to migrate. Florida snowbirds could avoid cold and icy northern winters and instead enjoy the beach, go fishing, or play golf and tennis.[61]

Perhaps Fisher should have listened when he boasted about the intrinsic value of tropical climates. By the mid-1920s, he turned his attention to a development at Montauk Point, Long Island. Although it may have appeared that Fisher simply got bored with Miami Beach, or hoped to duplicate his Florida successes near New York City, he may in fact have been looking to diversify his investments before the bubble burst. He also had the potential to control sales in Montauk, unlike at Miami Beach, where other promoters owned portions of the sandbar. In the 1800s, Long Island had become a fashionable address for the rich and famous, and by the 1900s, transportation technologies drew it closer to the city. In 1925, Fisher and a group of thirty-four investors—including members of the Midwest's so-called "gasoline aristocracy" who also contributed to Miami Beach—bought almost ten thousand acres for $2.5 million. When friends warned Fisher that he was getting in over his head, he responded with a mixture of ambition and indignation. Biographer Mark Foster writes that the tycoon admitted "he felt a real need to 'see a place every two or three weeks where the steam shovels are throwing dirt and the buildings are going up.'" Indeed, Fisher jumped into Montauk just as he jumped into the Indianapolis Motor Speedway, the Lincoln and Dixie Highways, Speedway City, and Miami Beach. Seeing Long Island's eastern tip as a vacation spot and embarking point for travelers, with lower development costs than a Florida swamp, he built a giant Tudor-style manor for himself and again replaced local flora and fauna with more desirable species—including, of course, polo ponies. Montauk Beach, just a short drive from New York City, could be the world's "most complete sporting center," with something for everyone: golf, polo, tennis, swimming, and yachting. Long Island's climate seemed ideal for water sports, at least for part of the year. The timing, though, was not right. Even before the 1929 stock market crash, Montauk chipped away at Fisher's once-significant fortune; after the onset of the Great Depression, it virtually wiped him out.[62]

In 1925, though, Fisher seemed unstoppable. The famous Hoosier had almost single-handedly created the modern sport of speedway racing before then initiating construction of the nation's first transcontinental highways and reconfiguring machine-oriented space from Indiana to New York, California, Michigan, and Florida. With fast cars on hard pavement, it seemed possible not just to sell a motor spectacle signifying spatial annihilation but actually to eliminate space such that any number of distant points could be reached more quickly and, as a result, sold as consumer goods to people with increasing amounts of money and leisure time. Any place could be a commodity. Just after World War I, an impatient Fisher had said that Tennessee, like Florida, was "worth billions of dollars in real estate value." Its mild climate and hilly topography made for "a fine lot of scenery." If the Volunteer State would just cooperate in building its portions of the Dixie Highway, it, too, could become a haven for well-off northerners.[63]

In 1925, Fisher predicted Miami and Miami Beach, which topped out around 30,000 combined population in 1920, would have 100,000 (an increase of more than 330 percent) by 1930. In actuality, the metro area had more than 115,000 by then, even after the disastrous hurricane. He seemed to be working wonders. According to his close friend, Cherokee humorist Will Rogers, Fisher was second only to Henry Ford in terms of his impact on American mobility. Fisher was "the man that took Miami away from the Alligators and turned it over to the Indianians [sic]." He "fixed up the chug-holes so the Fords could get in"—both literally and figuratively paving the way to Miami Beach. Without Fisher, cracked Rogers, Florida would be the "Turpentine State." But now it was uncertain what the storied space annihilator might accomplish on Long Island. Considering Fisher's history with infrastructure, joked Rogers, the famous Hoosier might make Montauk into "the terminal for a Subway to Europe." Or maybe he would build more golf courses, which in turn might convince some Miami "pleasure seekers" to move back up to the Empire State. After two wild decades, Fisher's next move was anybody's guess.[64]

Rogers's description, if tongue-in-cheek, was based on astute observation of Fisher's guiding principle: spend money to develop modern technologies and infrastructures that allowed people to go more places, enjoy themselves, and, in the process, spend more money. Between the 1910s and 1920s, the Hoosier industrialist accomplished amazing things. Yet, like many Jazz Age Americans, Fisher spread himself too thin. By the time his seventy-eight-year-old mother died at his New York home in 1925, around the same time he and Jane separated, Fisher had shifted his attention away from Indiana to build elite, leisure-focused communities at Miami Beach and Montauk.[65] Eventually, nature and the economy intervened to cause Fisher's land-and-leisure empire to come crashing down. To mitigate the damage, he and Allison unloaded the aging track, with its decrepit, and uneven—yet legendary—bricks, right as the Roaring Twenties peaked.

7

SELLING THE SPEEDWAY

A Place at the Center of American Culture

As the Twenties roared to their destructive climax, Indianapolis's speedway was as famous as ever, but its owners sought to divest themselves of an aging track needing costly repairs. In 1927, they found a potential buyer: World War I ace and faltering auto tycoon Eddie Rickenbacker. Backed by an anonymous Detroit investment group, the war hero bought the speedway right at the decade's climax. By this time, the track was a site of cultural consumption in more ways than one, with the legendary races attracting more than a hundred thousand fans each year, and the first Hollywood film about it debuted in 1929. The brick oval was being sold, both literally and figuratively and was assuming a central place in American culture.

By the 1920s, Indianapolis was the speed capital of North America and, perhaps, the world. It was an identity Hoosier scribes relished. Writer William Herschell contributed heavy-handed poems to official programs, including one celebrating the cosmopolitan and "jovial" crew passing through the gates on race day.[1] In another, he wrote that although thoroughbred racing and aviation were appealing, there was nothing quite like "the feel of the wheel of a racing car!" Herschell's folksy verse proclaimed that what was really tested on the track was not the machine, but the inner man. Engine, steering wheel, and distance combined to put "man in a man, for it takes an ace/In the gripping grind of the Speed's hard pace." A *real* man could tune out the roar of the crowd and the brass bands and complete the dangerous task at hand. Lap after lap, a winning driver enjoyed the satisfaction of sitting behind "the wheel of a Victor's Car!"[2]

Indianapolis may have been synonymous with racing in the 1920s, but it was not the only place. From his humid perch in Miami, Fisher encouraged Havana to host races that could lure legions of visitors from Florida, at a time when Cuba, with its bars and brothels, was a major tourist destination. Around the same time, Texas promoters planned a 1.25-mile track near Houston and Galveston, built like a bowling alley with 4.5 million board-feet of pine and 150,000 pounds of nails. Stands and bleachers would seat twenty thousand, while the infield could accommodate eight thousand cars.[3] Fisher constructed a similar track in Fulford-by-the-Sea, a tony development north of Miami. The steeply banked track was built on deep pilings, with a "board-walk promenade, massive grand-stands, and a mound-like infield." Its first event was postponed when the sinking of *Prinz Valdemar* in January 1926 caused a bottleneck that delayed shipments of building materials and foreshadowed Florida's coming real-estate bust. Once racing finally got underway, Pop Myers brought one of the speedway's proprietary timing machines from Indianapolis, along with timekeeper Odis Porter, who recorded Peter De Paolo's three-hundred-mile world record of 129.29 miles per hour.[4] In theory, the new raceway was an asset to the community, but not all agreed. Real-estate ads for residential lots in working-class North Fulford boasted of the town's proximity to the speedway, but a federal official said the track was "an unsightly affair" that devalued lots in swanky Fulford-by-the-Sea. In any case, neither the track nor the nearby towns lasted long. In September 1926, a massive hurricane, with winds up to one hundred fifty miles per hour, destroyed much of Miami and other nearby communities. The wooden track, like Florida's 1920s boom, lay in ruins. Miami Beach was not a total loss, as first reported, but it sustained significant damage, as did Fisher's fortune. One estimate calculates his Miami holdings declined by roughly a third, from $30 million to $20 million, literally overnight.[5]

After the hurricane, Fisher shifted focus to rebuilding Miami Beach, a decision that negatively affected his Long Island development. For years, he had assured investors that Montauk would be even bigger than Miami Beach. Eastern Long Island's summertime climate seemed ideal for leisure activities and sports, and it held potential as a transportation hub. The reputed origin of "Montauk" was a Native American word meaning "place for seeing far off," and Fisher—always looking to move people and dollars rapidly from place to place—was enchanted with the idea of transatlantic liners or airplanes docking at Long Island's eastern tip, where passengers might be able to travel directly to Boston or other cities without first going through Manhattan.[6] Rear Admiral William Moffett even considered placing a "mooring mast" for dirigibles at Montauk.[7] With infrastructure for transportation, hospitality, and leisure, Montauk might be ideal for conventions. People did not want to be confined to stuffy, crowded downtowns in the summer, figured Fisher, so that left Atlantic City, which was controlled by African Americans and therefore, in his mind, undesirable for "the good class of people." Montauk, with its wealthy landowners and Anglophile architecture, could be the world's "great convention city."[8]

Besides Montauk and Miami Beach, Fisher still had the speedway, which, as a large piece of more-or-less open land fairly close to downtown Indianapolis, also held potential for transportation. In 1926, the Indianapolis Chamber of Commerce proposed turning the infield's northeast quadrant into Circle City's airport. The speedway seemed ideal for an airfield, since it was flat and "well drained," and accessible from the city center by automobile or streetcar. It was the perfect time to build an airport, said the chamber, since aviation routes were still being established. Cities with high-quality fields would be essential for commercial aviation and airmail. Boosters said Indianapolis was located "at the cross-roads of the nation and must have an adequate airport . . . to take her place as one of the great flying centers." Initially, Fisher and James Allison agreed to the arrangement, as long as the airfield did not operate on race day, but the plan was nixed. Pop Myers publicly pointed out how difficult it would be to conduct races at a facility with a municipal airport, and the promise of a one-day annual shutdown was impractical. Even more important, speedway officials required a clause allowing removal of the airport with only six months' notice, as well as an insurance policy indemnifying them against damages. Insurance companies were unwilling to underwrite such a policy, and so the city looked elsewhere. It leased 234 acres of farmland near Mars Hill, another industrial town established in the 1910s.[9]

Had Indianapolis built an airport at the speedway, it would have joined Atlanta and Minneapolis as cities that converted prewar racetracks into aviation fields. Instead, the oval remained a place for space-annihilating spectacle. Between 1925 and 1931, Henry Ford and his son, Edsel, sponsored annual aviation endurance contests, known as Ford Tours. In August 1926,

Ford Tour participants flew a winding circuit from Detroit to Chicago, St. Paul, Wichita, Kansas City, Indianapolis, Cleveland, and Fort Wayne, among other cities, before returning to the Motor City. In each town, pilots stopped overnight to exhibit their machines to people who might want to purchase similar models. The Ford Tours increased in scope as aviation infrastructure improved. In 1928, twenty-six participants—including a woman, Memphis's Phoebe Fairgrave Omlie—competed in a four-week-long tour encompassing 6,300 miles (about four thousand miles more than in 1926) and featuring more than $12,000 in prizes. Pilots stopped in thirty-two cities and flew above seventeen states, including Texas, California, Oregon, and North Dakota.[10] Rickenbacker predicted "boys and girls" would one day "be driving flying machines" as if they were cars.[11]

As Indianapolis considered where to build the airport, it also hoped to annex several suburbs, including newly incorporated Speedway. Council member Walter Dorsett said it was "ridiculous" that such towns, clearly part of the metro area, were not located within municipal boundaries or paying city taxes. With annexation, Indianapolis might see tax rates decrease and bond limits increase, while former suburbs gained services. But Speedway City residents, aided by Prest-O-Lite and Allison Engineering Company, resisted. Fisher and Allison likely opposed higher taxes and supported home rule, especially in wake of the 1923 attempt to outlaw Memorial Day racing. Speedway voted to incorporate four months after the airport proposal first surfaced, around the same time that the plan fizzled, and annexation never happened. Even after Indianapolis merged with Marion County in 1969 to create Unigov—a consolidated metropolitan government similar to those in Nashville-Davidson and Miami-Dade—Speedway remained an autonomous enclave.[12] By the late 1920s, ads for residential developments like Speedway Terrace said the town combined "city conveniences" with "suburban pleasures." It had schools, churches, and stores, as well as owner-occupied homes on big lots with two-stall garages, curbs, and sidewalks and easy access to downtown Indianapolis by bus or car. It was a "fine community in which to live." Such assertions emerged from a context in which homeownership was seen as thoroughly American and, as historian LeeAnn Lands argues, homebuyers were encouraged to think of finely landscaped neighborhoods as exclusive reserves for white residents.[13]

While Speedway matured into an independent municipality, motor sport continued at its namesake track. Before the 1926 race—the first in which engines displaced no more than 91.5 cubic inches—the 1913 pagoda was replaced with a new structure that stood until Tony Hulman built a steel-and-glass tower in the 1950s. In time trials, tens of thousands watched as Herbert Jones hit the wall at 105 miles per hour and fractured his skull; he later died at Methodist Hospital. Rain postponed the race after 175 miles and, although it resumed after a seventy-minute delay, the event was finally stopped at 400 miles. Los Angeles's Frank Lockhart won the truncated race in 4:13:37.78, averaging 94.63 miles per hour. The crowd was reportedly the second-largest for a global sporting event in 1926, after a Paris horse race.[14]

At this time, Fisher had not attended a race in two years and his personal life was unraveling. Carl and Jane grew estranged after their infant son died in 1921; five years later, Jane attained a divorce in Paris in 1926 and soon remarried—by chance, on the same day as the Miami hurricane. A few months later, in May 1927, Carl married his secretary. The 1920s were wearing thin, and racing underwent changes too. Tiny engines on paved tracks seemed boring, and so racing's future seemed to lie in riskier dirt tracks.[15] Still, Indianapolis remained a place for innovation. Fisher and Allison announced a 1927 competition, with a $15,000 purse, for diesel-engine cars.

Carl Fisher, circa 1920s. (Carl Fisher Papers, 1963–015–153, HistoryMiami Museum)

Publicist Steve Hannagan optimistically predicted many entrants, but the race generated little enthusiasm. At one point, Indiana's Cummins Engine Company was the only manufacturer expressing interest. The hyped event was postponed and apparently never conducted.[16]

Automobility became mundane. Between 1919 and 1929, all forty-eight states initiated gasoline taxes to fund roads. Newly numbered federal routes included US Highways 31 and 41, main branches of the Dixie Highway, while US 30 followed Fisher's old Lincoln Highway and US 40 superseded portions of the old National Road. Many roads were good enough by 1927 that a *Chicago Tribune* article outlining routes to Indianapolis had few details, and its map was just a humorous cartoon. But if roads had improved, even to the point of approximating racetracks, some motorists figured they would never reach speedway-level paces. One car company official mused, "Just imagine trying to drive an automobile at the rate of eighty miles an hour on the highway."[17] Racers had to watch the track, monitor tires, and keep an eye on the tachometer and oil gauge, all while paying attention to pit crews and race officials. Doing so much at once was unnerving, and one physician said even experienced racers could hardly keep up. For a novice racing at 110 miles per hour, "his eyes rattle in their sockets, his teeth chatter and he neither sees, hears nor thinks." Typical drivers, it seemed, could not survive such speeds.[18]

By the end of the decade, though, some people started to think that with the right roads, even ordinary passenger cars could reach speedway-level velocities. In 1928, one Californian claimed the nation needed "a network of specially constructed high-speed roadways" like those in Italy or Wayne County, Michigan. A good, fast road that was similar to a racetrack, by limiting access and banning pedestrians, might cut driving times in half.[19] Studebaker's Paul Hoffman, a major highway proponent who helped bankroll the Albert Russel Erskine Bureau for Street Traffic Research at Harvard University, agreed, saying "super-highways" would allow motorists to drive at constant speeds up to sixty miles per hour.[20] In this way, drivers might trim excessive gasoline usage, which university studies dubbed a "bad roads tax." Fast roads were appealing at a time when Americans invested so much in cars. Auto insurance premiums surpassed $400 million in 1928, a year that saw the nation's eighty-seven largest cities add more than eight hundred total miles of pavement, with the majority of increases concentrated west of the Appalachians. Los Angeles paved about one hundred sixty miles, while

Seattle added seventy-five and Chicago added sixty-five. Indianapolis, then America's twenty-first largest city (with 350,000 residents, about the same as Seattle), paved sixteen miles that year.[21]

Someday, it seemed, people might practically *live* on the road. In 1928, Fisher collaborated with Glenn Curtiss to form the Aerocar Company. Historian Mark Foster calls Aerocar "a glorified trailer, which could be hitched up behind an automobile," but Fisher was enthralled with the vehicle. He opened a factory near Miami in 1929, hoping to sell hundreds of thousands of units, but the Depression interrupted his plans. People were migrating by road, just not in grandiose style. Aerocar may have been one of Fisher's latter-day "marginal projects," but he saw it as revolutionary—or at least hoped to convince others it was.[22] In an enthusiastic letter to Charles Kettering, founder of Dayton-based Delco and a top General Motors (GM) researcher, Fisher said Aerocar would change the world. Speaking as a real-estate developer and salesperson, he thought it would "revolutionize automobile traffic." Highways were no longer mere pathways. They were actually becoming ribbons of mobile residential and leisure space.[23]

Fisher still had one more race as part-owner of the Indianapolis Motor Speedway, in 1927, and it may have been the pinnacle of 1920s racing. Racers included three past winners (Milton, Lockhart, and De Paolo), as well as Hollywood stunt driver Cliff Bergere, who entered a car designed by dominant 1920s builder Harry Miller. George Souders, a former Purdue University student whose only racing experience was on dirt tracks, entered an Indiana-made car. In time trials, most drivers attained speeds well over a hundred miles per hour, speeds that were fueled by new technologies. When Peter De Paolo discovered his supercharger was broken, replacement parts were sent by air from Los Angeles to Chicago, then driven by car to Indianapolis.[24] On race day, a crowd of about 145,000 saw Souders, the rookie dark-horse racer, drive two hundred laps without relief in 5:07:33 (97.54 miles per hour) and win about $30,000. Souders's mother, who understood racing's dangers, refused to watch her twenty-six-year-old son race. She later claimed, not quite convincingly, that although she "knew he could do it," she wanted to forgo the nervous tension: "I was afraid the first time on a brick track would be too much for George." Souders was welcomed as a hero back in Lafayette, especially at Purdue.[25]

Media-reported perceptions of motor sport differed by gender. In an informal poll taken in downtown Chicago in May 1927, men saw racing as

The second pagoda, built 1926. It is pictured here in 1948, a decade before Tony Hulman replaced it with the modern, steel-and-glass Master Race Control Tower in 1957. (IMS Photo Archive)

an adjunct to technological development, while women saw it as entertainment. When asked whether they would rather attend an Indianapolis auto race or the Kentucky Derby, male Chicagoans picked wheels over hooves. A speedway was a "testing ground" for engineers and auto racing was an "instructive" activity demonstrating modern, technological "progress." Some women, though, chose a third option: none of the above. One homemaker did not like either type of racing and thought it impractical to travel out of state for track events. An unmarried clerk said she had seen both animal and auto races and would rather "dance, swim, or go to a good show." It is impossible, of course, to take such a small sample at face value. As historian Virginia Scharff argues, many 1920s Americans simply presumed women and men held divergent ideas or desires about automobiles.[26] Yet opinions expressed on a busy street corner may have illustrated a genuine range of opinions: for some people, racing signified technological modernity, while for others it signified cultural spectacle.

Links between motor sport and masculinity permeated 1920s racing, even among those who claimed the spectacle improved technology. Adman Homer McKee proclaimed that racers, just like US Marines, were "brave

men," but instead of going to battle they stared down death "for six deliri-
ous hours" to improve passenger cars. Racing was "a kind of happy hell
that hairy men come back to year after year" because they were "GUINEA
PIGS." Speedway racing was like a vaccine, and drivers were the volunteers
who took "the deadly germ of ACCIDENT in their own blood and build up
for us the ANTI-TOXINS that keep you and me and our families—ALIVE."
Modernity, it seemed, could not exist without a dangerous spectacle in
which some men courageously took risks so fellow patriarchs might enjoy
enhanced mobility.[27]

At some point, repeated assertions that speedways were built and operated for technological progress sounded like post-hoc justifications, just-so
stories trotted out whenever folks had to defend Memorial Day crowds or
tragic fatalities. Spectators read in their twenty-five-cent programs that
racing was a big science experiment, not a "gigantic sporting event."[28] Such
articles protested too much. Speedway races might fuel technological advances, but was that why drivers risked their lives and spectators flocked
to races? Oft-repeated claims about the sport's role—reportedly, at least
three-quarters of all advances in auto technology came from racing—may
have been part smoke screen. By the late 1920s, the bumpy track surface
was better for testing vehicular durability than for setting speed records.
If that was truly the case, then why were the old bricks still hosting races,
rather than less risky endurance contests? Fans' desire for speed carnivals
meshed with track officials' desire to sell it to them, a pop-culture tango
dating back to the speedway's earliest days. And by this time, nostalgia for
the races—suspended during World War I and nearly canceled in 1923—was
growing. The 1927 program featured a retrospective feature by Steve Hannagan, who recounted dramatic stories from the event's previous decade and
a half. If anything, the quest for speed innovation appears to have migrated
around this time, with young men in other places, especially Southern California, using aftermarket parts to turn old Model T Fords into souped-up
hot rods.[29]

The Roaring Twenties may have peaked in 1927, and the crowd at that
year's race was even bigger than the one for the legendary Jack Dempsey–
Gene Tunney match at Chicago's Soldier Field. For Fisher, whose Montauk
development sucked most of his time and cash, it was time to sell. He first
offered the track to two-time winner Tommy Milton, who declined. Next,
he and Allison targeted Eddie Rickenbacker. According to his ghostwritten

1967 memoir, Rickenbacker initially approached Allison about buying Allison Engineering Company, but the older man said that even though he spent a lot of time in Florida, he wanted to keep his engine company. "But I have a better idea, one tailor-made for you," Allison said. "Why don't you take over the Speedway?" Rickenbacker claimed he had never thought about buying the track but considered it right away: "Owning and operating the Indianapolis Speedway, home of the world's greatest automotive event, would be a thrill." He was impressed by the potential value of the land, which was no longer quite so far from downtown: "When the Speedway had been built in 1909, it had been far out in the country, and its 320 acres had been acquired for $72,000. But now it was practically surrounded by the city, and its real-estate value alone had multiplied." Rickenbacker recalled that Allison "strongly hinted" the track might "be sold to real estate speculators."[30]

Newspapers first reported the speedway's impending sale in late July. Rickenbacker was a good target, because of his record as a racer, flyer, referee, and pace-car driver. By 1927, he was based in Detroit, head of the failing Rickenbacker Motor Company, one of that city's many manufacturers to overestimate the 1920s market for luxury vehicles. But he needed money to buy the track. Rickenbacker later said that he initially hoped to find the cash in Indianapolis, but he could not locate enough investors. The Circle City had once been a font of automotive ingenuity, but the Motor City now controlled the auto industry, and so he turned to Detroit's deeper pockets. Rickenbacker claimed he was motivated by nostalgia for the old track and its role as the "world's greatest testing laboratory." Also, he was deep in debt, and taking over the legendary speedway where he had once raced might be a path to solvency.[31]

The first investment group Rickenbacker assembled lost interest in June 1927, but he quickly assembled another. Although it is unclear which other Detroit investors backed the purchase, some were certainly involved in the auto industry. In any case, the speedway's owners were eager to sell. As negotiations grew protracted, Fisher told Rickenbacker to get his affairs in order; he and Allison did not want the track "shopped around" like a used car.[32] Rickenbacker arranged with the American Appraisal Company in Milwaukee to evaluate the property while accountants examined the speedway's finances. In Detroit, Union Guardian Trust Company agreed to "take up $100,000.00 of bonds immediately on closing the deal, and at least an additional $100,000.00 each thirty days with a payment in full" delivered by November 9. The deal was finalized by August 15. The first payment of $100,000 came through on September 1; the next, totaling over $540,000, was made on November 1. The final payment, of about $32,000, came on December 6. According to papers now located in a Miami archive, the total amount came to $672,690.92, including fees and interest. James Allison received $263,952, Fisher got $146,640, and Arthur Newby got $58,656. Pop Myers gained $25,000, while Lem Trotter earned $43,700 and two others made small sums. Myers remained vice president and general manager, while Eloise Dallenbach stayed on as secretary and Fisher and Allison remained on the board. Rickenbacker was taken aback when the ever-precise Myers said the new owners had to take over maintenance immediately. Fletcher National Bank of Indianapolis extended a loan, but in the meantime, Rickenbacker needed stable income. Early in 1928, Cadillac announced his appointment as sales manager for its La Salle division. The next year, after Allison died suddenly of pneumonia, Rickenbacker helped General Motors acquire an interest in Allison's engine firm, as well as a share of German airplane manufacturer Fokker. It appears that at least some backers of the 1927 speedway purchase were associated with GM.[33]

According to one Rickenbacker biographer, at the time of the purchase, publicist Steve Hannagan "suggested calling the speedway 'the world's greatest outdoor testing laboratory for the automotive industry.'"[34] Yet Fisher offered Rickenbacker advice belying any notion that the speedway was simply a place for testing. Always the showman, he suggested getting fellow "bird man" Charles Lindbergh to be referee or starter. Lucky Lindy's presence, said Fisher, could augment ticket sales by up to $75,000. He also recommended pushing the marching band up to fifteen hundred members, even if a tenth were incompetent musicians; simply advertising such a big band would bring people to the track. He also once again recommended swimming pools and golf links. Fisher admitted the speedway's program had grown stale, and so Rickenbacker might infuse "younger blood and more spirit," while also maintaining ties to "old timers." Fisher told Henry Joy he was pleased the new owner was enthusiastic about both aviation and racing, which echoed his own space-annihilating past. But Fisher needed cash more than he needed an aging brick track in Indiana. Each year, he told Joy, the speedway made about $150,000 profit. Fisher's five-sixteenths share ownership meant perhaps $47,000 per year, a mere one-third of the $146,000-plus he earned from the 1927 sale. That capital immediately went

Eddie Rickenbacker, pictured at the speedway in 1935. (IMS Photo Archive)

to help pay off a large note, held at the First National Bank of Miami, taken out to fund Montauk development.[35]

At the time of the sale, details were fuzzy. Newspapers overestimated the figures, guessing Rickenbacker spent $1–1.9 million for the facility. Rickenbacker, who now claimed he had long dreamed of being part of "the greatest race in the world," announced the big event would still be held on Memorial Day.[36] He also quashed rumors—which Pop Myers took as literally as possible—that the speedway would relocate to Detroit. The 500-mile race was now a global icon for racing and for Indiana. It would not be moved. "We paid a huge sum for the property," said Rickenbacker, "and a great portion of that sum represented the good will, prestige and popularity of the Speedway." Detroit might one day have its own track, but it would not get "the Indianapolis Motor Speedway."[37] Rickenbacker did not relocate the track, of course, but he did make changes, including implementing one of Fisher's ideas by installing a one-hundred-fifty-acre, semiprivate, eighteen-hole golf course, with nine holes located within the infield. Golf helped make the facility "a year-round recreational center."[38] The course, operated by Speedway Golf Corporation, advertised itself as one of the Midwest's "sportiest." Fairways and putting greens, like polo fields, may have gentrified the speedway's clientele insofar as it attracted men who played a game that, if growing more mainstream by the 1920s, was still coded as exclusive and white. Although there were a few Black golfers by the late 1800s, by the early 1900s, African Americans were still often limited to serving as caddies or groundskeepers.[39]

The speedway was a legendary entertainment center, but there were now better places for sheer velocity. In February 1928, Frank Lockhart attempted to break the former land speed record of 203.79 miles per hour at Florida's Daytona Beach. (By comparison, Indianapolis's record speed as of that May was 124.018 miles per hour.) Before shipping his Stutz Blackhawk Special to Florida, Lockhart tested the car at Indianapolis, but he did not accelerate it past 80 miles per hour on the bricks. At Daytona, even with less-than-ideal weather, Lockhart pushed the car much harder, and the Stutz somersaulted into the Atlantic at 225 miles per hour, before thousands of spectators. Rescuers rushed to pry him from the car and, miraculously, the twenty-five-year-old was not seriously injured. He was not so fortunate two months later. On April 25, again seeking a record at Daytona, Lockhart blew a tire. He was thrown from the car and rushed to the hospital, but doctors pronounced him dead on arrival. Pallbearers at the funeral included three 500-mile champions: Slim Corum, Peter De Paolo, and George Souders. Wilbur Shaw, who witnessed the tragic crash in Florida and later played a key role in saving the speedway, recalled that Lockhart's death "was a terrific blow"—but it did not stop Shaw from racing.[40]

Indianapolis's old bricks saw some longer events in 1928. In a twenty-four-hour run supervised by the Hoosier Motor Club, a six-cylinder Whippet, produced by Toledo's Willys-Overland, drove 1,357.5 miles, averaging more than 56 miles per hour. Around the same time, a $25,000 bet at a Paris auto show resulted in a twenty-four-hour showdown pitting a Stutz against a Hispano-Suiza. Hispano-Suiza's president tried to stop the event, but the car was shipped across the Atlantic and the contest began on the afternoon of April 18. After seventeen hours of persistent engine troubles, the Stutz finally dropped out and the Hispano-Suiza, averaging 70.14 miles per hour, claimed victory.[41] That same year, Marmon reentered racing for the first time since 1911, reportedly to test "advanced engineering ideas" on enclosed tracks.[42]

Marmon ads may have been right to call Indianapolis's speedway "the greatest and most severe proving ground in the world," yet the track's severity did not deter racers or spectators. Four days before the 1928 race, superfan Theron Kilander parked outside the speedway gates, hoping to secure a good spot in the infield; he would sleep in his car and eat sandwiches from a vendor's stand.[43] The night before the race, streets were "clogged with unending lines of motor cars" honking their horns, the "din and clamor" filling the evening air.[44] Folks were in a "carnival mood."[45] It was unclear whether motor sport was "funny business, sport, [or] game," but whatever it was, people loved it, and in 1928 they could hear the race's final hour on the National Broadcasting Company radio network.[46] The next year, Fisher recommended raising admission prices. After all, he had attended "at least fifteen or twenty-five different types of entertainment" more expensive than a 500-mile race, yet none beat "the Speedway show." He thought that skydivers jumping from airplanes might justify more expensive tickets.[47]

Speed was paradoxical, pushing people so quickly into the future they could not help but look back to the past. As writer W. F. Fox put it in 1928, people now lived longer and moved so rapidly they were "actually lapping Time"—going forward so quickly they could almost regain what had been lost. Racecars were like time machines, practically turning back the clock. It was a revolution, and drivers heralded a new era; they were the "Paul Reveres of the Automobile industry." If 1775 Boston was too archaic of a reference for some readers, Fox also used a more recent analogy: each car in the big race was just like the *Spirit of St. Louis*, the airplane Charles Lindbergh had flown across the Atlantic in 1927.[48] But according to "a Speedway Fan," Memorial Day races were not just about technological progress. Sure, the speedway was a "testing laboratory" where engineers improved cars, but more important was that it was a place for spectacle. The race was a "great speed pageant" that excited more than a hundred thousand spectators who assembled for all kinds of reasons, none of which could easily be pinned down.[49]

Winner of the 1928 race, witnessed by about 140,000, was Louis Meyer, a twenty-three-year-old Los Angeles mechanic who finished in 5:01:33.75, or 99.482 miles per hour, a track record for 91.5-cubic-inch engines. In an amazing show of efficiency, Meyer made only one pit stop and used no relief driver. This was Rickenbacker's first race as owner, and he did what he could to build the speedway's legend, proclaiming this the best race in track history. It might have been a great event, but at least one spectator decided enough was enough. Peter De Paolo, who had crashed in the time trials, reportedly fainted while watching the race and announced his retirement:

"I love my wife and [four-year-old son] too much to risk my life again. I am going to work from now on only as an automotive engineer. I believe I can make just as much that way as racing." Motor sport's siren song came calling, however, and by May 1929 De Paolo was back.[50]

The speedway's founders, meanwhile, continued passing into history. On August 3, 1928, fifty-five-year-old James Allison died after a brief bout with pneumonia. He had not updated his will after marrying his secretary at Fisher's Long Island house a few days earlier, and so his first wife, whom he had recently divorced, sued the new widow for $2 million, a major portion of Allison's estimated $3.5–6 million fortune. At the same time, Fisher was desperate for cash. He planned to sell shares of various investments—including Speedway Realty Company and Globe Realty—to fund developments in Miami Beach and Montauk. In one case, he hoped to unload a seventy-acre tract south of the speedway, but he discovered it had little value because it was located on a stream and so only a portion of it could be developed. Real estate outside the central business district was not selling especially well at this time, but a Fletcher National Bank official went out to inspect some of Fisher's other properties in Speedway to determine their value.[51]

Meanwhile, the AAA Contest Board, headed by Rickenbacker, announced a switch to two-man cars with riding mechanics—and bigger engines, up to 366-cubic-inch displacement—for 1930. This shift, reportedly meant to make races safer, develop young drivers, and improve stock passenger vehicles, may have actually been spurred by Rickenbacker's Detroit investment partners, who had gotten crowded out of racing by specialist builders like Harry Miller and wanted back in. It may also have had the effect of making the aging speedway seem less obsolete, or of introducing more nostalgia. Rickenbacker assured skeptical fans that bigger racers would surpass the smaller vehicles that had set speed records in the 1920s, yet critical observers debated whether these changes would really improve racing or whether they would just lead to the scrapping of hundreds of thousands of dollars' worth of fine machines. Although some racing fans refer to the 1930s as the era of the junkyard, in 1929, the 500-mile race was rebranded as the "Grand Prize of America," and the track announced a forthcoming "permanent challenge cup." By 1936, the sterling-silver Borg-Warner Trophy immortalized Indy's speedway champions.[52]

The 1929 race was the last contest run with 91.5-cubic-inch (1.5-liter) engines. Drivers had to average at least 90 miles per hour for four laps in trials, and they also had to be in good shape. Cliff Durant, multimillionaire GM heir and racetrack owner, wanted to race, but first the overweight thirty-eight-year-old had to lose some pounds. Durant trained in Florida and Indiana, driving more than fifty miles per day, but he could not quite cut it; Durant withdrew and conceded racing was a sport for younger men.[53] Pole position went to Chicago's Cliff Woodbury, who averaged 120.5 miles per hour in the trials, while drivers with the second- and third-fastest times in the trials were Leon Duray and Ralph Hepburn, both of Los Angeles. The City of Angels saw a rising number of native sons racing in the 1920s as it grew in size and prominence and, like Indianapolis, rebuilt its sprawling metropolitan infrastructure for cars. It helped that Southern California's mild climate fostered year-round racing. After 1924, Legion Ascot Speedway, which was also among the first tracks to schedule nighttime races, "developed many of the western drivers that later became successful at Indianapolis."[54]

Spectators at the 1929 race may have glimpsed Charles Lindbergh and his new bride, the former Anne Morrow, who were rumored to be in attendance. Despite Prohibition, liquor was easy to find, and at least a dozen drunk drivers were arrested on race day.[55] To facilitate the flow of more than a hundred thousand presumably less-intoxicated motorists, Indianapolis again turned two-way streets into one-way streets, and some out-of-state visitors may have gotten ideas about traffic regulation. One Chicagoan observed an "experiment" on Meridian Street, where signs directed slower drivers to right-hand lanes and faster drivers to center lanes. Many were at first perplexed but soon figured it out. Maybe Chicago could learn something about traffic flow. The Windy City, said the *Tribune*, might widen some streets, add lane markers, and sort traffic by speed. As usual, the lines between spectacle and progress blurred on Hoosier pavement.[56]

Radio again offered what one source confusingly called a "birdseye view" of the race, and since Harvey Firestone served as referee in 1929, it was only fitting that Firestone Tire and Rubber sponsored the broadcast. A more literal bird's-eye view was provided by a Goodyear-Zeppelin dirigible, which some observers even then called a blimp. The helium-filled *Puritan* flew from Akron by way of Dayton, picking up passengers in Indianapolis, including reporters and photographers, and hovered over services at the Soldiers and Sailors Monument before circling over the speedway and landing in the infield. Aware this race was the last for single-seat cars with

91.5-cubic-inch engines, media reports intoned an air of finality, as if motor sport teetered on the verge of change. Rickenbacker, who said the 1929 race featured the fastest-ever cars and drivers, personally invited Fisher to come from Montauk to see the race's last running with small engines.[57] It seemed 1929 might never be topped. The record crowd of about 160,000 saw Pennsylvania's Ray Keech, holder of a land speed record set at Daytona, win in 5:07:25:42, averaging 97.585 miles per hour, in a race where only twelve drivers finished. Cliff Woodbury crashed early but later returned as a relief driver. Frenchman Jules Moriceau flipped his car in the twenty-fifth lap, and Deacon Litz flew off the track in the fifty-sixth. The worst crash came in lap sixteen, when twenty-two-year-old Bill Spence of Los Angeles hit the wall, fracturing his skull; he died before reaching the hospital. The *Los Angeles Times* said Keech's "steady, consistent and nervy driving" recalled the greatest drivers in Indianapolis history.[58]

By the late 1920s, a time when cars and movies were linked in the American mind as "twin products of a modern world speeding out of control,"[59] the legendary track became a veritable film set. This was just a few years after Fisher—who understood film's potential for selling representations of places to mass audiences—discussed the possibility of filming movies at Miami Beach. He figured his pet elephant and speedboats, along with "good looking diving girls" and "stunts" by Black residents, would make for a "corking film."[60] A portion of the 1929 race was immortalized in the Metro-Goldwyn-Mayer silent film *Speedway*, directed by Harry Beaumont and featuring William Haines, Anita Page, Ernest Torrence, and John Miljan. Besides on-site filming, the movie featured scenes filmed at Burbank's Central Airport. Haines played young mechanic Bill Whipple, whose adopted father is hard-luck racer Jim "Mac" MacDonald (Torrence), who has run the 500-mile race sixteen times without winning. Rival driver Lee Renny (Miljan) suckers Whipple into leaving Mac by promising a chance at glory, but Renny eventually reveals he is just using Whipple for his mechanical expertise. Aviator Patricia (Page) "teaches Whipple a lesson by taking him up in an airplane and showing him Mother Earth at a variety of strange angles" and ultimately talks Mac, whose heart condition will not allow him to finish the race, into forgiving Bill and letting him drive in relief. Bill sacrifices glory by pulling into the pit at the last minute to let Mac take over and win. Bill gets the girl, of course, once she sees his selfless action. The plot, if contrived, drew on enduring racing tropes, including aviation and motor sport's health risks. It also anticipated later speedway-themed feature films.[61]

Real-life races, though, did not always have Hollywood endings. Red-headed speedster Ray Keech had only about two weeks to enjoy victory before his life ended in a two-hundred-mile Flag Day race on the one-and-a-quarter-mile board track at Altoona. As twenty-five thousand watched, a car smashed into the rail and slid into the infield, causing Keech's machine to swerve and flip. He suffered a fractured skull, crushed chest, and severed leg as his car was engulfed in flame. Officials stopped the race immediately and Keech posthumously won the $4,500 first prize. In wake of this tragedy, the AAA Contest Board recited a litany of motor-sport utility: "Racing has done far more than any other factor to provide the laboratory, the crucible, out of which has emerged the handsome, speedy, relatively simple and mechanically marvelous motor car of today." It was still safer than "ordinary street traffic" or other risky activities. By the 1930s, such assurances—which echoed football apologists who downplayed that sport's dangers in the early years of the twentieth century—frequently followed reports of racing deaths.[62]

Despite casualties, speedways remained places to demonstrate elision of space. Days before the 1929 event, twenty-four airplanes raced from airfields in Buffalo, Denver, Fargo, Jacksonville, and San Antonio to East St. Louis, Illinois. On Memorial Day, the top nine sped from East St. Louis to Indianapolis and back, with the winner receiving a $5,000 trophy.[63] In June, two stock Marmon Roosevelts drove around the clock in an attempt to break a record for internal-combustion engines, and the contest finally ended when high winds hit the speedway. The one Marmon still going had run continuously for over 440 hours, or more than eighteen days. Marmon ads asked readers to imagine a car driving "from New York to Los Angeles, immediately turning around and coming back to New York; then after arriving in New York immediately going to Miami; from Miami to Detroit; then from Detroit to Dallas, and doing all this without the motor once being shut off or the wheels stopped."[64] The speedway concentrated space annihilation in one place, with or without spectators. As one humorist put it, this was an "age o' speed," when a "feller kin git a letter to an aunt in Balboa, Panama, almost as quick as he kin receive a stove pipe or revolver from Sears & Roebuck." Cars, trains, and planes made it possible, with "professional men" whizzing to workplaces "over wide, smooth highways, often arrivin' an hour an' a half ahead o' business." Everything, it seemed, was moving faster.[65]

In the heady days before the stock market crash, motoring's possibilities seemed endless. Science allowed a thin stream of fossil fuel to power cars or airplanes on "scientifically built" roads or wings.[66] Yet lurking in coverage of 1929 motor events was a fear that progress could not endure. Financial markets, weakened by the demise of Florida's real-estate boom three years earlier, collapsed in late October, sparking the Great Depression. All was not well in Fisher's empire, to say the least, with bankers advising him to unload his remaining shares of Speedway Realty. Desperate for cash, he finally sold his stock for a low-ball figure of $112,500 in April 1930. Fisher had also left the speedway's board of directors by this time. After the former owner offered detailed suggestions for improvements, Rickenbacker called a board meeting and Fisher submitted his resignation shortly thereafter. He rarely visited the track anymore, he admitted, and surely "some of those Indianapolis people would feel very proud" to serve. It is unclear whether Fisher felt forced out by the new owners or whether he just no longer cared. Either way, the board accepted his resignation and expressed regret for his departure.[67]

As the 1920s wound to a close, Indianapolis entered a new era. Fifty-five-year-old Carl Fisher was done with racing, apparently for good, and his fortune dwindled as he tried to satisfy his Montauk debts. James Allison and Frank Wheeler were dead, elderly Arthur Newby was out of the picture, and a nearly anonymous group of Detroit investors fronted by Rickenbacker had taken over the speedway. Yet racing continued at a track located in a city some considered a geographical and cultural common denominator, a place the local Merchants Association called the Pivot City. Indianapolis was North America's population center, said boosters, as well as a "continental center of distribution." A full decade before the slogan became Indiana's official motto, a writer in 1927 called the intersection of Meridian and Washington Streets, one block south of Monument Circle, "the cross roads of America." People reputedly sought out this provincial capital located at "the very center of the world's most prosperous continent." Like a modern-day Rome, all roads seemed to lead to Indianapolis. On Memorial Day, residents and hotels continued a Circle City tradition by welcoming the world to their doorsteps.[68]

Hoosier modernity was based on industrial production, geographic centrality, and spectacular rituals symbolizing space annihilation. With fewer than half a million people, said Jonathan Brooks in *The New Republic*, Indianapolis was not a "superlative" city, yet it boasted "the world's largest railroad shops, the world's greatest motor race course, the biggest silk hosiery mills in the world, and the greatest per capita production of reading matter in this or any other world." The city had more than six hundred miles of paved streets, two hundred fifty miles of streetcar tracks, and the globe's most extensive interurban system. Indianapolis's factories could not quite compete with Detroit's, but each year they produced cars worth a hundred thousand dollars. The city was "a little better than average" with "fine wide streets and boulevards." It may not have exactly been a city of champions, yet a "good average fellow" (presumably, a white fellow of some means) could enjoy it as either a resident or a visitor. Indianapolis might not *quite* be "the crossroads of America," yet it was clearly a central "economic point."[69] Blithe assertions of Indianapolis's central-place status were common by this time. Nicholas Noyes, head of the chamber of commerce, said Indianapolis's "location" was important for its success, but so was its pro-business atmosphere and near-suburban amenities: neighborhoods, churches, schools, and recreation. "In all these respects," said Noyes, "Indianapolis is truly favored."[70]

Indianapolis may or may not have actually been America's central place, but the Roaring Twenties was as good a time as any to make such assertions. Modern places benefited from the production of durable goods as well as cultural signifiers, and this was the era when German scholars transformed Johann Heinrich von Thünen's ideas about urban hinterlands and production zones into central-place theory. In a 1933 book whose title translates to *Central Places in Southern Germany*, geographer Walter Christaller argued that economic activity took place within regions focused on centrally located towns. Size was important, but a town's true significance was based on the goods and services it produced. What mattered was the number of potential consumers located in proximity to a town, plus the quality of infrastructure over which they had to travel. How good, in other words, were the roads between a marketplace and its customers? Better transportation yielded a natural division of labor, which meant some towns developed specialized economic roles. Christaller argued that more prosperous regions contained greater wealth, which could be spent on various orders of goods, ranging from basic necessities to luxury items and cultural products—including tourism, a topic the geographer focused on later in his career.[71] Members

8

JUST CALL IT THE "500"

Forging Traditions in the Depression Era

Speedway racing had to compete with other amusements during the Great Depression. Regulations on engines and fuel fluctuated and, for the first time, some of the bricks were covered with asphalt, but maybe the most innovative thing about 1930s Indianapolis was the range of new sporting traditions created. The Borg-Warner trophy debuted in 1936, as did the ritual of the champion drinking milk. It was a dynamic time, when people looked backward to move forward, not unlike Ray Harroun's fabled rearview mirror back in 1911. Races had become iconic cultural rituals. As driver Rex Mays declared in 1939, "We just call it the '500'."[1]

In theory, new rules opened racing to more competitors, especially Detroit companies that had stopped racing when the sport became dominated by specialist builders like California's Harry Miller, a "top-notch manufacturer of high-performance carburetors and custom-built racing engines." With a new formula announced in 1929, which may have been influenced by Rickenbacker's Detroit ties, it was now easier for big manufacturers to enter the race. Starting in 1930, the AAA sanctioned a field of up to forty cars. Unlike 1920s-style single-man machines with tiny motors, cars now carried a riding mechanic, as in the old days, and engines displaced up to 366 cubic inches. The sport was seemingly democratized, with a larger, more international mix of speedsters.[2] Many were still banned, though, including women, supposedly for lack of physical stamina. Charlie Merz

asserted a 500-mile race was "a great test of men, motors and materials";
it was not for "molly-coddles." Some men thought women could drive fast
over short distances but could not endure longer races. Women could not
even serve as relief drivers, even though events at Brooklands had shown
they were capable of driving as fast as men.[3] Some sources implied women
should be procreating, not racing. When a nest of rabbits was found at
the track, the *Chicago Tribune* reminded readers that female racers were
banned, "but not Mrs. Rabbit" and her babies. (It was rumored a publicist
planted rabbits each year to generate such accounts.)[4] Still, women made
inroads into the sport. Indianapolis's Elfrieda Mais, a racer and stunt pilot,
hoped to enter the 1931 race but was rejected, and so she set her sights on
California's Legion Ascot Speedway. Tragically, Mais perished in a race at
Birmingham, Alabama, in 1934.[5]

Indianapolis boosters estimated fifty million people heard the city's name
"once a minute for five hours" on race day, especially via radio. At the track,
crowds as big as 32,000 watched trials in 1930, and the race-day crowd was
estimated at around 150,000. They saw twenty-three-year-old Billy Arnold

Start of the 1930 race. (IMS Photo Archive)

win in 4:58:39:72, driving his Miller-Hartz Special 100.448 miles per hour. They also saw Paul Marshall, riding mechanic for brother Cy, perish in a crash when their car flipped over the wall. Cy suffered a fractured skull and jaw yet survived to race again. The next year, thirty-eight cars topped 100 miles per hour in trials, while a diesel-powered racer built by Clessie Cummins reached 96.871. After rain delayed the 1931 race for two hours, the crowd of 120,000 saw Cummins's car finish without a single pit stop. The winner was Louis Schneider, a former motorcycle cop, who finished in 5:10:27:94 (96.629 miles per hour) and earned nearly $40,000. Billy Arnold escaped a crash with burns, bruises, and a broken hip, but one of his wheels struck eleven-year-old spectator Wilbur Brink, who died of a fractured skull.[6]

Automobility was becoming an essential, if uneasy, part of American life. In *Middletown in Transition*, a sequel to their earlier study, sociologists Robert and Helen Lynd noted that in Muncie, cars were more necessary than ever. Registrations in the county jumped from 9,721 in 1925 to 14,661 in 1935, and many people now used motor vehicles to earn extra cash. Some might "give up everything in the world but their car."[7] Yet critics questioned the car-oriented built environment. In *Technics and Civilization* (1934), Lewis Mumford lamented that the same "mistakes" made "in the railroad building period were made again with this new type of locomotive." In his next book, *The Culture of Cities* (1938), Mumford conceded that planners had effectively incorporated highways into the landscape, but now he saw communications as being even more important than transportation. Radio and television reduced the need for fully cohesive cities and might eventually eliminate urban congestion altogether. Transmission of sounds and images heralded an era when people could congregate via epistemic rather than physical means.[8] Mumford's observation was prescient. In coming years, space annihilation would be carried out over airwaves even more than on streets or highways.

As Mumford speculated about the impact of communications, racing remained fodder for Hollywood. In 1932, James Cagney and Joan Blondell filmed *The Crowd Roars* at Indianapolis and other tracks. Besides featuring cars "thundering down the stretch" and "bursting into flame while the great crowd of spectators roars," the movie also included a love story. Cagney plays a champion who falls apart when his friend dies in a race, but his love interest (Blondell) prompts his revival.[9] Speedway movies became a standard, even clichéd, genre in the 1930s. Jimmy Stewart's first starring role was *Speed* (1936), a weakly reviewed, B-grade MGM film about a racer. In 1939, Warner Brothers released *Indianapolis Speedway*. Critic Frank Nugent called it "another of those racing melodramas" that tended to "roll around as regularly as the Indianapolis classic itself." The film's nonracing portions, he said, were "stereotripe."[10]

By 1932, the Depression neared its lowest point, with an estimated 25 percent unemployment, and the economic crisis affected racing. Ralph De Palma declared bankruptcy in 1931, and races were not broadcast for several years because sponsors could not afford the price speedway officials demanded. General admission tickets dropped from $2.50 to $2.00 in 1933, while the purse shrank to $10,000. Yet, even during the depths of the Great Depression, other cities still tried to emulate Indianapolis. In 1932, a corporation announced plans to build a $250,000 speedway with a 1.25-mile oval seating up to sixteen thousand at a 232-acre site in Los Angeles. Later in the decade, plans were drawn up for four-hundred-acre-plus Metropolitan Park, seating more than thirty-two thousand for speedway races and aviation contests, in Southern California's quickly growing San Fernando Valley.[11] Meanwhile, as Detroit edged back into racing, motor scions oversaw the revised spectacle at Indianapolis. Edsel Ford was the pace-car driver in 1932, while Harvey Firestone Jr. was referee. Fred Frame won in 4:48:03.79, his 103.144-miles-per-hour speed besting De Paolo's 1925 record. There were several crashes in the race, watched by an estimated 150,000 spectators, and only ten cars finished.[12]

Why did people keep watching? The *New York Times* said they were attracted by "the thrill of the sound, the roar of horsepower at the massed start; the nerve-tingling, iterated noise like torn silk as each car of a spread field comes down the brick homestretch," plus "the sight of flashing racers zooming around the banked turns and eating up the straightaways, wheel to wheel, with only inches and an iron hand between triumph and disaster.[13] Others, however, found motor sport boring. "Five hours is too long for anyone to concentrate upon a sporting event. The cars roar and whine around the oval in a whirl that becomes monotonous. A spectator can't tell who is leading without looking at the score board where laps are recorded for each of the contestants."[14] But if racing were abolished, claimed AAA president Thomas Henry, young men would ultimately reinvent it, "driven by the eternal instinct that no speed is so swift that it cannot be beaten, no performance so brilliant that it cannot be surpassed."[15]

The quarter-century-old bricks were bumpy and virtually obsolete by 1930, but that did not stop racing men from using the track to fulfill the purported need for speed. Ernie Triplett drove a lap at 120.34 miles per hour in 1933, while Wild Bill Cummings drove the fastest ten laps ever run at the speedway. High speeds were dangerous. In trials, Al Aspen and mechanic Mitz Davis crashed into the wall at more than 109 miles per hour but sustained only minor injuries; three days later, Speed Gardner struck the wall at 108 miles per hour and broke a femur. The next day, Virgil Livengood smashed into a guard rail.[16] The 1933 race was among the deadliest ever. Two drivers and one riding mechanic died, while three others were seriously injured. In one crash, Mark Billman hit the wall and died at the infield hospital. In another, Malcolm Fox threw a wheel and was hit by Lester Spangler; both their riding mechanics perished. About one hundred thousand spectators saw Louis Meyer finish with a record speed of 104.162. The second driver to win twice, Meyer earned the $12,000 first prize plus $1,150 in lap prizes. Newsreels featuring "hideously realistic and blood-chilling" crashes were frequently shown at theaters.[17]

Racing officials tinkered with rules at a time when many sports worked to maintain fan interest. Major-league baseball inaugurated the All-Star Game at Chicago's Comiskey Park in 1933, and two years later it emulated the Negro and minor leagues by playing its first game under lights—a Reds-Phillies night game at Cincinnati's Crosley Field. Meanwhile, some universities fostered publicity by increasing athletic commercialization and broadcasting football games on radio.[18] At Indianapolis, qualifying speed increased to 100 miles per hour in 1932, up from ninety the year before, and around the same time new rules limited fuel usage. Tanks could hold no more than fifteen gallons, a restriction that supposedly made races safer while also adding excitement, since drivers now had to make more pit stops. In 1934, drivers were limited to forty-five gallons of fuel for the entire race, and then the limit was reduced to 42.5 gallons in 1935 and 37.5 in 1936. After racers protested, the AAA eventually relented, allowing as much standard, commercial-grade fuel as drivers wanted.[19]

Speedway racing competed with other motor sports during the Depression, especially midget car racing, which debuted in Southern California in 1933. Midget cars were almost like a mockery of modernity, a sardonic throwback to the little cars of the 1920s. The earliest of these diminutive racers were reportedly made of parts "from antiquated automobiles, motorcycles, and washing machines."[20] It was simple, relatively low-tech racing. There were "no elaborate track layouts, no banked curves, [and] no well-equipped pits to supply instant service." Midget racing merely required a track and "cars from back-yard workshops and garages, with their daredevil drivers." These fast little cars, with lightweight aluminum bodies and engines maxing out at a hundred cubic inches, cost a fraction of standard racers, but it was dangerous to race the two types of cars on the same track. In 1936, after a racer died in a nonmidget event, the National Midget Racing Car Association warned that anyone participating in unsanctioned events would be expelled. That same year, disputes over whether a midget car could compete in the Gold and Glory Sweepstakes led to an hours-long delay, which may have contributed to the terrible crash that ended Charlie Wiggins's racing career. Tragically, Los Angeles's Bob Swanson died in 1940, two weeks after the 500-mile race, when he was fatally injured in a Toledo midget race.[21]

Indianapolis's death toll increased throughout the 1930s. Although some considered the era's heavier cars safer, making them less likely to roll, the extra weight may have actually been dangerous. In May 1931, Joe Caccia and Clarence Grove took a turn at 104 miles per hour and flipped over the wall; the flaming wreck fell near the men, burning them alive. Some brushed aside the danger. Hal Foust said racing was a "proving ground" for "tires, shock absorbers, steering gears, valves, lubricants," and fuel. Dangerous accidents merely showed what should be improved.[22] Yet it was growing more difficult to excuse fatalities. Driver Benny Benefield suffered a concussion and mechanic Harry Cox died when their car, the same one in which Caccia and Grove died the previous year, crashed into a tree. Two days later, Milton Jones died in a crash and mechanic Harold Gray was badly injured. In 1933 trials, fifteen thousand watched as William Denver's car crashed over the wall at 110 miles per hour, struck a tree, and burst into flames; he and riding mechanic Bob Hurst died. The following year, Pete Kreis and riding mechanic Bob Hahn died in a similar crash. Critics said the oval had to be reengineered or the races had to end; Indianapolis was no longer safe. In response to mounting criticism, racing officials continued simply offering platitudes that lives were sacrificed for the "advancement of automotive engineering." Some observers pointed out in rebuttal that by now many manufacturers had established their own "laboratories and proving grounds."[23]

As one writer put it, every racecar carried an extra rider: the grim reaper. Doctors and nurses set up shop at the track in the 1930s, with pints of blood in four types. Yet drivers continued risking death and fans kept flocking to races. University of Southern California psychologist Milton Metfessel said that spectators craved racing's thrills; the sport was relaxing because it distracted fans from "pressing circumstances and daily obligations." Just by watching races, he claimed, spectators could safely experience the same dangers as drivers. It was "a matter of vicarious living." Some 1930s racers, though, saw the risk as just part of their jobs. Lou Meyer said high-speed driving was "a lot of hard work." After all, "When you're traveling more than 100 miles an hour your senses don't catch up with thrills." Racing was just "a steady, hard grind"; it was a "business."[24] Mid-1930s racing was briefly regulated by the New Deal's short-lived National Recovery Administration, which stabilized markets, and Indianapolis's purse rose back to $50,000 in 1934, close to pre-1930 levels. Rickenbacker saw the bigger prize as an attempt to contribute "to the nation-wide drive for a complete return to good times."[25]

The good-times business was happy to serve up consumer spectacle. Sportswriter Paul Gallico, who compared the speedway to Ancient Rome's Circus Maximus, said race day was a "fiesta," with fans flocking to concession stands to buy hot dogs and lemonade and "enjoy the doggonedest eating party you ever did see." It was the world's largest picnic.[26] Once ratification of the Twenty-First Amendment ended Prohibition in 1933, money could be made on liquor, too. Gambling was also a risky way to make money during the Depression. In 1931, police arrested leaders of an Indiana syndicate operating an illegal speedway lottery in Illinois, Kentucky, Michigan, and Ohio. Later in the decade, an official estimated that a raid on a similar operation saved Indiana residents $50,000—as well as, one supposes, a lucky winner.[27] By the late 1930s, Indiana considered legalizing pari-mutuel gambling, a move that racer Wilbur Shaw supported; he thought it would bring in additional spectators and thus be good for the sport's health.[28]

William Herschell's 1934 retrospective observed that, back in 1909, critics predicted the speedway would last only a few years before "return[ing] to its original employment as an Indiana cornfield." But now, the track anticipated its biggest crowds ever. Why was it built, and why did fans still show up? Herschell claimed Fisher, Allison, Newby, and Wheeler had planned the speedway as a "practical proving ground," yet he also echoed his own flowery poems by saying the races "tested" men's "intestinal stamina."[29] By calling the speedway a "brick-paved farm," Herschell juxtaposed Indiana's agricultural past with its industrial present, implying that modernity was about transforming pastoral land into machine space.[30] The oval, in other words, represented modern progress. In 1937, the year of the big race's twenty-fifth running, Herschell said long-time spectators were "drawn by the lure that crept into their hearts back in the days when cars 'went like sixty' and actually didn't do much more."[31]

Modernity brought all kinds of changes. Bill Cummings won the 1934 race in 4:46:05.21, or 104.865 miles per hour, before about 140,000 spectators. Legend says that, before the race, he was aided by Black racer and mechanic Charlie Wiggins, who was snuck into a garage to work on Cummings's engine. If skilled, nonwhite labor did help the 1934 winner, it was in violation of the speedway's Jim Crow gentleman's agreement—and the racer who ended up taking credit was white. Cummings owned an Indianapolis night club, and in the victory lane he asked for a cigarette and a beer. It goes without saying that this post-Prohibition request, unlike Lou Meyer's chaste request for milk two years later, did not start a tradition. Cummings was even featured in cigarette ads, claiming Camels eliminated fatigue and would "*never* jangle healthy nerves."[32]

A big surprise for the 1935 race was the referee, Amelia Earhart, then resident aviator at Purdue University, who served as the track's first-ever female official. Rickenbacker said the speedway broke precedent because Earhart had "broken all precedent in invading man's field of aviation and fighting her way to a well-established position among the best flyers in the world." Back in 1931, Earhart had circled the speedway in an autogiro, an early helicopter, and not long after that gained fame with a transatlantic solo flight. Earhart was not the only female flyer present at Indianapolis in 1935. A few days before the race, aviator Laura Ingalls (cousin of the famous writer) and photographer Margaret Bourke-White rode with Lou Meyer at speeds topping 100 miles per hour. The track saw a renaissance in aviation during the 1930s, possibly because that was the new owner's main business. In 1934, after passage of the federal Air Mail Act, General Motors sold several airlines but held onto Eastern Airlines and asked Eddie Rickenbacker to be general manager. When the airline was nearly sold out from under him in 1938, Rickenbacker again tapped into his credit networks; this time he found the money in New York to purchase Eastern Airlines for $3.5 million. He remained president until 1953.[33]

Women attended Indianapolis races in the 1930s but still could not compete. In one poem, Herschell portrayed a female spectator as the "driver in the stands," living vicariously through male drivers and competing with other women for attention from the "man behind the wheel."[34] Women may have sought affection from manly drivers, but many also became motorists themselves. Weeks before the 1936 race, Grace and Flora Ford of Peoria, Illinois, camped out near the speedway; three years later, a woman slept in her car as she waited to enter the gates. Women were taking the wheel. Champion racer Lou Meyer confessed that he did not drive routine trips around town; his wife did. The Associated Press essentially reversed traditional gender roles when it reported that the 1936 victor's wife drove him to their hotel in the new car he had just won, with the "hysterical [riding] mechanic and his girl friend" in back.[35] Considering the calm woman behind the wheel—while a male racer was hysterical—one questions the notion that men, and only men, could withstand grueling races with bodies and minds intact.

A tipping point may have been reached on May 21, 1935, when three racers perished in trials. Johnny Hannon, an inexperienced driver from Pennsylvania, skidded into the wall at 117 miles per hour and was thrown; he died immediately, and his mechanic, Oscar Reeves, was seriously injured. Later that day, California's William "Stubby" Stubblefield crashed over the retaining wall at 116; he and mechanic Leo Whittaker died on the way to the hospital. One local resident even sued to stop the race, echoing early-1910s critics by alleging the races exhibited "all the evils of a prize fight or a bull fight." The track rendered the lawsuit moot by securing an injunction postponing a hearing until after the race.[36] The track made small changes, such as installing electric signal lights to replace a hand-operated flag system. One observer quipped that now "even traffic cops" might not be able to tell the speedway from "a first-class boulevard."[37]

Cavino "Kelly" Petillo, who was born in Pennsylvania but moved to Southern California with his family at the age of sixteen, won the 1935 race with a record 106.240-miles-per-hour speed. The crowd of 155,000 saw the month's fourth fatality when Clay Weatherly crashed through a fence at 110 miles per hour and flew into the infield. He suffered a fractured skull, while riding mechanic Ed Bradburn fractured two vertebrae.[38] It even became common in the 1930s for newspapers to report the track's all-time death toll. Weatherly, for instance, was the thirty-first fatality. Some critics wondered whether there were safer ways to satisfy the supposedly innate desire to risk one's life, while others insisted that racers died for technological progress. Paul Gallico said racing was "laboratory work" that resulted in safer cars.[39] Of course, there was some truth to the idea that technological progress was made at the track, but tests were typically conducted outside competitions. Tire companies measured heat generated on the bricks; Standard Oil tested products like a paraffin-based motor oil; and Studebaker tested a stock car that drove more than 60 miles per hour for fifteen thousand miles. Crosley, a Cincinnati firm, even exhibited a new line of low-cost, lightweight, aerodynamic, and fuel-efficient cars at the speedway.[40]

Engineers studying 1935 crashes determined the problem was with the turns and retaining walls, especially near the stands, where drivers maintained unsafe speeds in an attempt to please the crowd. Small imperfections in the brick made it hard for racers to control machines at high speeds, and the turns themselves were poorly engineered. The outer ten feet of each turn rose sharply, with a retaining wall perpendicular to the ground but obtuse in relation to grade. To correct the problem, the grade was made consistent throughout the turn and walls were rebuilt at a ninety-degree angle to grade. Carl Fisher, no longer formally connected to the speedway, was not sure these changes mattered. "I used to sit and shudder at the possibility of some of the cars hurtling through the air and landing in the grandstand," he confessed, "and setting it afire and killing off God knows how many people, and every year I have been fearful of what might happen." Pop Myers assured Fisher that now there was virtually no chance of racecars flying into the grandstands.[41] By 1936, Myers said the rebuilt turns had "a profound psychological effect" on drivers, who could now "coax greater speed out of their mounts all through the long grind." By comparison, unskilled and "nervous drivers" had a hard time even controlling passenger cars when driving on highways at speeds topping 60 miles per hour.[42]

The track was safer, yet still dangerous. On May 15, 1936, Tony Gulotta and riding mechanic Carl Riscigno were injured in a crash involving Mauri Rose and mechanic Earl Frost. In 1937, two perished and five more were injured in practice. Spectator George Warford was killed and pit crew members Otto Rohde and Tony Caccia were critically injured when Overton Phillips's car caught on fire and crashed into a racer parked at one of the pits; Phillips and his unauthorized passenger, Walter King, were seriously injured, and Rohde died several days later. In another crash, mechanic Albert Opalko was thrown from a car driven by Frank McGurk, who was badly injured. In

1939, riding mechanic Lawson Harris died when Babe Stapp's car crashed during a test run. Detroit's George Bailey died in a 1940 practice run when he hit the guardrail and his fuel tanks ignited in flames. Succumbing to third-degree burns, Bailey was the track's last prewar fatality. Rickenbacker claimed in his memoir that as a racer he had never liked the brick surface, so as owner he ordered it "completely resurfaced with Kentucky rock asphalt." The statement was not true. By the late 1930s, 650 yards of exposed bricks remained on the straightaway. The track was not totally repaved until 1961, years after Rickenbacker sold it to Tony Hulman.[43]

Americans continued excusing racing fatalities as "martyrs to progress." One newspaper reader insisted Americans should be "grateful" for speedways because, without them, they might "still be dependent upon the buggy and spring wagon for transportation."[44] Another said that without racing, the "modern pleasure car" would not exist: "Springs, ignition, tires and the front-[wheel] drive car are the results of the speedway tests, and, as is to be expected, many lives are lost in racing as well as in any sport where high speed is required." Speed facilitated the "march of civilization." Racers paved the way for passenger cars able to drive on "superhighways."[45] Racers might seem like "reckless adventurers," said the president of the AAA, but in truth their "recklessness and ambition" were simply "the rarely minted coins which all heroes pay out with a superb gesture to the high gods of adventure in the hope of buying human advancement."[46]

Racing discourse got so tied up in technological progress that some began to question whether it was even sport at all. Sportswriter Arch Ward said a 500-mile race hardly qualified as "a sporting event," and he repeated the half-true chestnut that the oval was built as a "laboratory . . . where daredevils could compete for cash awards in the interest of scientific research."[47] Another writer agreed the speedway served as a laboratory, but he also said that it hardly compared with normal road conditions. If car companies wanted to make real progress, they should operate dedicated testing grounds.[48] The rub was that when the bricks were laid in 1909, the oval had featured both cutting-edge motors *and* state-of-the-art pavement. By the interwar era, cars had advanced dramatically while the track remained largely the same. The races were so deadly, in part, because 1930s engines should not have been racing on 1909 bricks.

Americans continued seeing racetracks as models for better highways. Some predicted races would prompt development of aerodynamic cars capable of attaining highway speeds of 100 miles per hour.[49] Some even imagined a transcontinental "speedway" crossing North America from New York to San Francisco—basically, the Lincoln Highway, except with a much better surface than that which stymied Emily Post back in 1915. The Pittsburgh Chamber of Commerce, inspired by Interior Secretary Harold Ickes, envisaged a wide road with "high-speed" bypasses and no grade crossings, an innovative type of roadway that Lincoln Highway promoters had discussed as early as the 1920s. Drivers could enter from "feeder" roads at ramps located every ten miles, so that getting on and off the highway was almost like entering or exiting the pits at a racetrack. This superhighway—an "immense concrete ribbon across America"—would cost $300–400 million, but it would theoretically create jobs and pay for itself, with an ambitious toll structure that foresaw motorists paying one-dollar tolls every hundred miles.[50] The first segment of the limited-access Pennsylvania Turnpike, which later influenced the design of postwar Interstate Highways, opened in 1940. On such roads, cars could move "unimpeded like water in a river."[51] Indiana's nineteenth-century dream—making people, goods, and capital flow over land as if they were moving, with scarce friction, on water—seemed to have become reality.

Despite the economic crisis, or perhaps because of it, automobiles became an essential part of American life during the Depression. At one point, Carl Fisher criticized the Pullman Company's high rates for railroad passage, observing that those who could afford to take a train to Miami Beach would simply drive their own cars and seek inexpensive accommodations along the way. Although Fisher declared bankruptcy in 1933—he was a sloppy bookkeeper, better at spending money than at managing investments—he still paid close attention to his developments. In 1935, he touted an expensive road to Montauk Beach, as well as the Long Island Parkway recently developed by New York parks commissioner Robert Moses. In South Florida, meanwhile, Fisher contributed to a push to build better airport and harbor facilities. If tourists could not get to Miami and Miami Beach, he feared, they would instead spend their money in Cuba, Bermuda, or the Bahamas, which then would hurt his hotel business even further.[52]

As infrastructure improved and the speedway aged, Indianapolis grew into a site for nostalgia. The 500-mile race seemed to be the only one that still had "the flavor of the old-time road races" with "old-time throttle pushers."[53] By this time, though, the speedway's founders were nearly gone—Newby having died in 1933—and it might have been time for new traditions. In 1935, Robert Stranahan of Toledo's Champion Spark Plug, with Rickenbacker and Myers, formed a 100-Mile-an-Hour Club for racers who had driven the entire race faster than the century mark. Before 1930, the club's only member would have been Peter De Paolo, but by 1937, there were about twenty members, including Kelly Petillo, Bill Cummings, Mauri Rose, Louis Meyer, Fred Frame, Howdy Wilcox, Floyd Roberts, Cliff Bergere, Wilbur Shaw, and Lou Moore. Yet racing was so dangerous that, as the club's membership grew, it also declined. By 1940, eight members had died, seven of whom perished with "hands on the wheel, throttle pressed hard against the floor board." The eighth, Bill Cummings, died in a 1939 crash on Indiana Route 29, along the alignment of the old Michigan Road. New members joined the club until it disbanded in 1969, when averaging a hundred miles an hour was no longer a rare feat.[54]

Endurance also became an important trope in the 1930s. Lou Meyer was racing's "iron man" because he had won the big race three times and had driven more miles in the event than anyone else, reaching 4,385 by 1938, thus passing De Palma's 4,061. Ralph Mulford and Tony Gulotta also topped 4,000 miles, while Cliff Bergere approached that figure. Pop Myers admitted that although he "loved the old days," he had to admire the "dominance" of newer drivers such as Meyer, whom he called "the greatest 500-mile racer of all time."[55] Shaw, one of twelve drivers who had been racing at Indianapolis for at least a decade, said, "Why, we last as long as the headliners in any sport." Some racers compared themselves to baseball players, only a few of whom—such as Lou Gehrig, eventual holder of baseball's ironman record after 1939—were still playing after ten years in the game. Lifetime winnings, of course, were an important indicator of racing success. By 1940, Shaw topped the list with $71,300 in total prizes.[56]

Scholar Eric Hobsbawm has argued that new rituals or symbols that signify "continuity with the past" emerge at times when society undergoes major changes. Depression-era Indiana was a place for such "invented traditions" and their related mementos.[57] One such item was the Borg-Warner Trophy, a fifty-two-inch-tall sterling-silver, art-deco cup featuring bas-relief images of the sweepstakes race champions. It was first revealed in New York in February 1936, and by late May it was presented at a prerace dinner, attended by Rickenbacker and Indiana's Democratic governor, Paul McNutt. The trophy was, according to one account, "designed in the modern tempo."

Each race's winner received a miniature copy, with his visage added, plus $100 per week for as long as he defended the championship. Lou Meyer was the trophy's first winner, as well as the epic race's first three-time champion. He finished in 4:35:3.39, earning a total of $29,850 plus a new car. An estimated crowd of 166,000 saw Meyer set a new speed record of 109.069 miles per hour. Immediately after finishing the 1936 race, he started a tradition by requesting and drinking a bottle of buttermilk. Supposedly, his mother had told him the beverage would quench his thirst better than any other. Meyer was a thirty-two-year-old husband and father with a mild persona; newspapers reported he would hold a quiet celebration that evening. Such images clearly contrasted Bill Cummings's 1934 request for a beer and cigarette.[58]

Lou Meyer (center) receiving the new Borg-Warner Trophy, 1936. (IMS Photo Archive)

Although Meyer's buttermilk seemed to portray him as a prohibition-ist—his 1936 win came just a couple of years after repeal of the Eighteenth Amendment—one newspaper reported him enjoying a beer on his front porch the day after that famous request. Whatever the reality, images of Meyer's record-setting win and milk bottle were quickly disseminated around the nation. Within sixteen minutes of the race's conclusion, the Associated Press (AP) distributed a photo of Meyer via Wirephoto, its new, proprietary telephotography technology. "Never before had any picture been transmitted by wire in such a short time after a camera recorded a news event." The AP photo was published in evening papers on the Pacific Coast and in morning papers in the East—just a few weeks after Dorothea Lange's iconic *Migrant Mother*, immortalizing Dust Bowl migrants, first appeared in a San Francisco newspaper.[59] More than the mere act of drinking milk, it was the memorable photo of Meyer and its rapid, widespread transmission that created Indianapolis's most idiosyncratic tradition. Partly at the urging of the dairy industry, the champion has drunk milk after subsequent races, with the exception of the early Hulman years (1947–55), when Wilbur Shaw delivered a jug of ice water to each winner. In 1993, Emerson Fittipaldi infamously insisted on drinking orange juice to promote his citrus plantations in Brazil, yet even he finally agreed to take a sip of milk at the urging of distraught racing officials.[60]

Trophies and traditions grew more important as media mythologized the speedway and Hoosier auto manufacturing declined. In the early 1900s, car companies thrived in more than fifty Indiana cities and towns, but eventually production was consolidated by Detroit's Big Three: Chrysler, Ford, and General Motors. The stock-market crash and Great Depression killed off most Hoosier carmakers: Marmon closed in 1933, while Stutz went bankrupt in 1937, the same year Auburn and Duesenberg ceased production. Others, including Cole, Haynes, and National, had already shut down in the 1920s. Soon, Indiana's only remaining automaker was Studebaker in South Bend, which was weakened by the Depression but held on until the 1960s, a decade after its merger with Detroit-based Packard. In general, only parts companies persisted in Indiana after the Depression. As production was ceded to Michigan—before, eventually, migrating largely to Japan, Germany, Korea, and the US South—Indiana's visible association with motors was based largely on consumer spectacle and nostalgia. And it was right around this time, in early 1937, when the State of Indiana officially declared itself the

"Crossroads of America." The term—once used to designate the downtown intersection of Meridian and Washington Streets, a place that by the 1930s saw "automobiles racing by and airplanes [flying] overhead"—had become a synecdoche for the entire state.[61]

The 500-mile race was now an Indianapolis institution, hardly something that hidebound traditionalists could even consider outlawing. In fact, one veteran racing fan and *Indianapolis Star* staff writer, Mary Bostwick, said someone should write a guidebook for novice racegoers so they could under-stand the ritual's distinctive customs, lingo, and traditions. She portrayed the speedway as an exotic land requiring an anthropologist's keen ethnography skills. But even then, the place was *not* like a foreign country, where a "tour-ist can stand around inside museums and cathedrals . . . and gape about." Visitors did not have access to the track or the pits, so they could not "chat with the native Speedwayites as they pursue their native arts and crafts." It was even harder if a tourist was a woman, for the oval was like "one of those monasteries in Europe where they won't allow . . . any female" to enter. A woman could not talk her way into the pagoda, even if she had a press pass and was accompanied by a man. Bostwick's frustration was tangible, but she and other women would have to continue to wait for access.[62]

Grandstand B, 1938, photographed by Arthur Rothstein. (Library of Congress, Farm Security Administration Collection)

As much as it might have seemed like a foreign country, Indianapolis's legendary oval had only a few years of racing before war closed it again. In 1937, Wilbur Shaw narrowly bested Ralph Hepburn before 170,000 fans. His record time of 4:24:07.81 (113.580 miles per hour) earned him roughly $36,000. After the race, Shaw and his mechanic, Jigger Johnson, celebrated in victory lane, mugging for the camera and speaking over the radio.[63] Meanwhile, officials kept tinkering with rules. Fuel restrictions were lifted in 1938, as was the regulation requiring a riding mechanic. Now, though, cars had to have side mirrors, and supercharged engines had to displace less than 183 cubic inches, while others were limited to 274. Indianapolis "adopted the international racing formula" by following the rules of Paris-based Association Internationale des Automobile Clubs Reconnus. Racing, like other sports, was globalizing, with spectators coming from as far away as Shanghai and Western Australia. As historian Barbara Keys has shown, sports created international regulatory bodies and competitions in the 1930s, including the World Cup of Fédération Internationale de Football Association (FIFA), while media coverage transformed Olympiads in Los Angeles (1932) and Berlin (1936) into global spectacles.[64]

As the Depression began to lift, diverse spectators flocked to races from all over, including H. B. Brady, an officer of Chicago's Colored Chamber of Commerce. The big crowd saw the purse rise to $100,000 in 1938, when thirty-eight-year-old Floyd Roberts, a Southern California aviation engineer and dirt-track racer, gave racing its own Cinderella story. Roberts, who made a spectacular showing in time trials, finished the 500-mile race in 4:15:58, a record speed of 117.200 miles per hour, before 140,000 spectators. The victory netted him $31,950. Roberts's first major win was a godsend. His wife said she had always supported her husband in his dangerous line of work, and now the prize money meant a new home for their family. "We have planned a long time for this moment and now, like a dream, it has come true."[65]

The Roberts family's happy story, though, came to a tragic end just one year later. Rickenbacker predicted the "fastest race in the history of the classic" in 1939, when boxer Gene Tunney was honorary starter. Members of an Indianapolis Citizens' Speedway Committee distributed tens of thousands of posters and maps to help out-of-town visitors navigate the area.[66] Finishing in 4:20:47.41, or 115.035 miles per hour, Shaw won his second 500-mile race while driving a Maserati, the first non-US-made winning car

Crowds at the 1938 race, photographed by Arthur Rothstein. (Library of Congress, Farm Security Administration Collection)

since 1919. The crowd, estimated at 145,000, saw Shaw's victory, but they also witnessed a tragedy. More than halfway into the race, Floyd Roberts was passing Bob Swanson when they collided. Roberts was mauled by a board fence and suffered serious head injuries; he later died at Methodist Hospital. Swanson and Chet Miller were also injured in the three-car crash, as were two spectators: Martha Ponelite of Collinsville, Illinois, and Mrs. Bruce Milliken of Thorntown, Indiana. To make the tragedy even more poignant, Roberts had declared the 1939 race would be his last.[67] The popular California racer was the speedway's thirty-seventh fatality. Although the *New York Times* still insisted racing improved motor technology, the *Los Angeles Times* questioned the value of high-speed races: "Except to demonstrate where ultimately lie the limits of endurance of flesh and steel—if that is of value—it is hard to see the practical benefit of these sacrifices to the idea of speed."[68]

Speeds were higher than ever by the late 1930s, but Indianapolis was nowhere near the world's fastest place. In 1939, Englishman John Cobb set a new land-speed record of 368.85 miles per hour on Utah's Bonneville Salt Flats, a prehistoric lakebed even better for overland speed than the fine sands of Daytona Beach.[69] Without the nostalgia and invented traditions of the interwar years, Indiana's urban track, once the world's most innovative, might have faded into oblivion. Instead, it became a global institution. As if to underscore the speedway's passage into legend, just six weeks after the 1939 race, on July 15, sixty-five-year-old Carl Fisher died in Miami Beach. In his later years, Fisher carried out regular correspondence with Tommy Milton, and although the two men intermittently encouraged each other to cut down on their drinking, it may have been too late for Fisher, who battled diabetes and cirrhosis of the liver, taking insulin and having fluid drained from his abdomen with increasing frequency. He had not drunk much before Prohibition, but he hated the idea of the government telling him what to do, and so he became a hard drinker and bootlegger who imported huge quantities of alcohol from the Caribbean. It did not help that his second wife, Margaret Collier Fisher, also liked to drink. Obituaries focused on Carl's real-estate and roadbuilding efforts, tending to mention the speedway as an afterthought or as a sideshow to his other enterprises, especially Miami Beach. Some Indianapolis papers, though, did portray him as a sportsman proud of having founded the speedway. Journalists stressed how far Fisher had fallen after Florida's real-estate bubble burst in 1926. Formerly worth somewhere between $20 million and $100 million in the heady 1920s, Fisher's estate was valued at an estimated $55,000–141,000 at the time of his death. Nevertheless, he had had a sensational career. Some people at the time thought Miami Beach might soon erect a monument to the man who "would have made a great circus owner" and "had an agile mind for devising unusual ideas to amuse and interest the public."[70]

Commemorations of Fisher's life could have better portrayed the heartland speedway as the center of the fallen tycoon's vertically integrated motor empire: a sprawling network of roads, racetracks, and real-estate developments built on the idea of deploying speed and leisure in the service of capitalism. Fisher eliminated spatial fetters so that he could rebuild space in his own modern, playful image. The speedway was a place that visibly undermined the constricting realities of distance, a site for spectacles that proved the importance of technologies for getting from here to there—and in the process made distance between geographical points seem less relevant, even as it made some of those points more profitable, more *legendary*, than others.

The speedway only saw two more races before World War II, and in one of them a woman speed enthusiast finally entered the race as an owner. In

9

TRADITION NEVER STOPS

The Cultural Logic of Sports Capitalism

During World War II, the Indianapolis Motor Speedway fell into disrepair and was on the verge of permanently closing, but traditions created before the war may have saved it. After 1945, Tony Hulman modernized the speedway, turning it into a viable, postwar sporting facility, while also building its mystique, embodied most clearly in the museum that first opened in the 1950s. Such developments displayed the cultural logic of sports capitalism—the idea that modern sports profit from selling nostalgia as much as from selling athletic achievement.

Surprisingly little commemorative space is devoted to Carl Graham Fisher, who was nearly as good at abandoning projects as he was at starting them. In 1941, two years after his death, a crowd gathered in Miami Beach to dedicate a memorial to the Hoosier Barnum, a man who "carved a great city out of a jungle." This cenotaph is virtually the only monument to Fisher anywhere. Although memory of his achievements lives on in Florida, Fisher was actually buried in Indianapolis's Crown Hill Cemetery. Perhaps it is fitting that a man who spent much of his life showing Americans how to use modern means of travel between points as if the space between did not matter is now best remembered as a developer some twelve hundred miles from his burial place. In 1924, fifteen years before he died, Fisher built a concrete mausoleum on a man-made island near Miami Beach, but even then it was unclear where he would rest. "It doesn't make any difference to me whether the last of me is left in New York, Miami or Indianapolis," he scoffed. After all, he owned a mausoleum in Indiana, too, and might build another one in Miami Beach. Appropriately, just a few years after building the mausoleum in Florida, Fisher traded the island—now known as Fisher Island—to William K. Vanderbilt II for a two-hundred-fifty-foot yacht.[1]

In Speedway, Indiana, which had a population of more than fourteen hundred residents, war loomed on the horizon. Allison Engine Company—a division of General Motors after 1929—built a 41,000-square-foot plant in 1935 and expanded it to 300,000 square feet four years later. Allison cranked out engines for fighter planes and bombers at a $6 million factory made of brick, steel, concrete, and glass. The state-of-the-art plant was illuminated at night, guarded around the clock, and secured by an electric fence. Two former racers who worked there were Harry Hartz and Mauri Rose.[2] Perceived links between motor sport, aviation, and militarism endured. Although the Treaty of Versailles prohibited Germany from building an air force, that nation had embraced a potent combination of gliders and auto racing. To catch up with Germany, Eddie Rickenbacker suggested making American commercial pilots fly airmail routes with bombers or fighters. Sounding like Carl Fisher in 1917, Rickenbacker said that if industrialists could just be freed of "political red tape," they could build more military aircraft. In March 1941, however, he was seriously injured in an airliner crash and was stuck in an Atlanta hospital, unable to travel to Indiana to inspire drivers who might one day become fighter pilots.[3]

In 1941, no non-US drivers were in the big race. Two French drivers who hoped to compete, René Le Bègue and Jean Tréveaux, received approval from the Vichy regime and arrived at Indianapolis in May, but neither qualified. Rickenbacker said that driver Susan Paley aspired to be the first woman to enter the race, but in fact it would be another thirty-six years before a female driver, Janet Guthrie, qualified in 1977. That year, the starting command was changed to "In company with the first lady ever to qualify at Indianapolis, gentlemen, start your engines!" When Lyn St. James became the second woman to qualify in 1992 she requested a gender-neutral starting command, yet the language of ladies-and-gentlemen persisted until 2017.[4] As of 2022, nine women drivers have qualified for the Indy 500.

Getting to the 1941 race was affected by the budding war effort when Chicago motorists were advised to avoid Rantoul, Illinois, the traffic-congested site of the Army Air Corps's Chanute Field. Meanwhile in Indianapolis, the race was delayed by a fire that burned twenty-four garages, destroyed a racecar, injured seven people, and damaged the electrical timer. Once the fire was put out and the timer repaired, a big crowd estimated at 162,000 saw relief driver Mauri Rose win in 4:20:36:34, splitting almost $30,000 with cowinner Floyd Davis. Their speed of 115.117 miles per hour was the second-fastest ever, despite almost one hundred miles under a yellow flag. Three-time champion Wilbur Shaw was badly injured, the result of a defective wheel that had been mistakenly installed on his car. He never raced again. Earlier in the event, Emil Andres and Joel Thorne collided, and rookie Everett Saylor was badly injured when his car crashed into the wall and hit two vehicles parked in the infield; Saylor survived but perished on a dirt track in Missouri the next year. Just days after this last prewar race, sixty-two-year-old Louis Chevrolet died in Detroit and was interred at Indianapolis, near his brother Gaston's gravesite.[5]

One writer gave fans a nuanced idea of why drivers competed in the risky spectacle. Some men sought money, hoped to become celebrities, or were attracted by love for the sport. Cliff Bergere, the Hollywood stuntman, said the race was a relaxing break from his dangerous day job. Other racers acknowledged more complex reasons, some tied to various ideals of manliness. Billy Devore, son of 1927 second-place finisher Earl Devore, said he raced to honor his late father's memory. Reportedly, when Earl lost to George Souders, he came to the pit and told his sixteen-year-old son, "Billy, I wanted to win more than anything else in the world today. If I never have this chance again, I want you to drive here and keep trying till you do win it." (Billy Devore started seven times at Indianapolis, but never finished higher than seventh.) Wilbur Shaw figured he became a racer because he grew up near the speedway and "worshipped" the famous racers. "Meeting some of these 'big shots' was an unforgettable thrill for me." Shaw, who became the speedway's head of racing operations after the war, wanted to emulate those drivers. None of the racers quoted said they entered motor sport to develop or test cars, although certainly many of them were enchanted with the technology of motors and speed.[6]

But now, in 1941, the sport faced an uncertain future. As Mauri Rose invested his prize money in war bonds, some whispered the 1942 race would be canceled. Pop Myers tried to quash the rumors, but his optimism was undermined by Rickenbacker's assertion that there would be no rules changes in 1942 because of wartime supply-chain issues. By December 7, 1941, Japan's

attacks on Pearl Harbor and the Philippines made it harder to act as if racing would not be affected. At the end of the month, Rickenbacker finally
proclaimed, "Tradition and priorities demand that we again voluntarily
abandon the annual 500-mile race." The war effort seemed equivalent to
a race of ten thousand miles, said one writer, and so the Allies needed all
racers to contribute. Although Rickenbacker offered the speedway to the
federal government as an aviation center, its facilities were no longer suited
to the era's large, sophisticated aircraft.[7]

Americans debated the wartime role of sports, which provided recreation
and morale but also used essential resources. Some sports, such as baseball, did continue, albeit with a shrunken talent pool: the St. Louis Browns
signed a one-armed outfielder, for instance, while the All-American Girls
Professional Baseball League fielded teams composed of female players.
Racing machines, though, were too closely tied to military needs. Journal-
ist Bob Considine wrote that Rickenbacker "did the right thing in calling
it a day for the old gas derby." But who knew when racing would resume?
On January 5, 1942, sixty-eight-year-old Pop Myers announced his retirement, as did Eloise "Dolly" Dallenbach. They no longer had any duties at
the track. News coverage recounted the speedway's glory days in the past
tense, while Rickenbacker, speaking from West Palm Beach, denied rumors
that the grounds would be subdivided and developed.[8] The Indianapolis
Automobile Racing Association hoped a big dirt-track race might be held at
the state fairgrounds, but in July 1942 the Office of Defense Transportation
banned all "contests between persons or against time, distance, or previously established records," except "tests conducted for and at the request
of the armed forces."[9] Were events open to paying spectators truly essential
for developing auto technology, or were they only necessary in a mindset,
like Fisher's, which always prioritized private enterprise and competition?

Memorial Day 1942 was the first time since 1918 the speedway had not
hosted a 500-mile race. Instead, former racers and mechanics contributed
to the war effort. Deacon Litz built airplane engines in Africa, while Art
Herrington worked with tanks in India. Ray Harroun served on a "bomb-
loading wagon." Wilbur Shaw was "an aviation fuel tank expert," while Harlan Fengler worked for Packard, instructing US Army Air Forces personnel
how to maintain Rolls-Royce Merlin engines produced in Detroit. Peter De
Paolo taught mechanics at a California air base, and he later received the
Legion of Merit for his work with aircraft forced to land in Switzerland.[10]

At the same time, Al Putnam and George Souders, two former racers working in a Curtiss-Wright plant, looked back fondly on old racing days, now that the oval was "deserted, silent, and almost forgotten." The main activity there during the war was golf. As a potential air-raid target, Speedway implemented blackouts and dimouts. In contrast with World War I, when the track had become an aviation facility, it now lay fallow. The United States had established air bases in warm-weather locations, including Texas, and the Civilian Pilot Training Program, created in 1939, taught aviators at college campuses and airports.[11]

Because of wartime rationing, Americans did not drive as much as before. In May 1942, motor traffic in Indiana was down 22 percent, in part because there were no races to drive to. In September, a group of elite drivers, including 500-mile champions Billy Arnold, Howdy Wilcox, and Wilbur Shaw, pledged to hold the accelerator under 35 miles per hour, the wartime speed limit, to conserve gas and rubber encouraging civilians to do the same. War prompted the development of charcoal- or alcohol-based fuels, as well as synthetic rubber. In 1943, the *Chicago Tribune* and Goodyear sponsored a trial of synthetic tires at Indianapolis's "famous old track." These "Tribbuna" tires, made with butadiene manufactured from waste wood pulp, demonstrated wear comparable to that of latex rubber and could withstand speeds up to 100 miles per hour. At wartime speed limits, they might last more than 27,000 miles.[12]

It was a good thing so many miles could be squeezed out of tires, because soon Americans would be driving more than ever. Planning for federally funded highways began in 1936, before the war, when US officials visited Germany to inspect that nation's Autobahn. Three years later, they issued a report, *Toll Roads and Free Roads*, exhorting America's need for a system of toll-free, high-speed roadways funded by gas taxes. Meanwhile, Americans visiting the 1939 world's fair in New York got a glimpse of auto utopia courtesy of Futurama, a GM-sponsored exhibit touting the coming auto-focused society. The impending war, though, altered priorities, with the desire for "superhighways" evaporating by 1940.[13] In 1944, officials of the AAA and Public Roads Administration set out from Indianapolis on a nearly 24,000-mile tour of a potential road network stretching 33,920 miles, about 20 percent fewer miles than the system the US Congress ultimately authorized in 1956. This expedition investigated routes for highways resembling the limited-access Pennsylvania Turnpike—with no turns, grade crossings, or traffic-control devices. Such roads, with pleasant landscaping to "relieve the strain of traveling," could augment safety, reduce vehicle wear, move farm goods efficiently, and link military bases. Officials thought a system built with federal matching funds might take twenty years to complete and cost $15 billion. Aircraft landing strips might even be built alongside the roads.[14]

Even Rickenbacker, who figured cars would benefit from wartime developments, might not have been able to predict the tremendous changes in postwar motoring. Parking and transit woes pushed retail to suburban fringes by 1946, devaluing downtown real estate. As streetcars yielded to buses, private motor vehicles became nearly the only way to get anywhere. Automobility was the nation's new spatial reality. The Serviceman's Readjustment Act of 1944 (GI Bill) and the Federal Housing Administration (FHA) fueled suburban growth, with many neighborhoods catering exclusively to white homebuyers, especially veterans and parents of Baby Boomers. As early as January 1945, Speedway's developers implored people to buy

Truck driving on recently completed Pennsylvania Turnpike with grade separation (overpass), 1942, photographed by Arthur Rothstein. (Library of Congress, Farm Security Administration Collection)

"an excellent family home": a "POSTWAR HOME!" They advertised the growing town as a convenient place with shopping centers, churches, schools,
movie theaters, and golf courses. As with other postwar developments,
from Levittown, New York, to Orange County, California, Indianapolis's
outskirts were sprawling.[15]

Some tests were conducted at the speedway during the war, but without
spectators. The track's *raison d'être* had disappeared. The bricks sprouted
weeds while "ancient wooden grandstands looked as if they were about to
fall apart." Looking over the track in 1944, Al Rickenbacker (Eddie's brother)
assured fans the big race would return after the war, yet even he admitted
the facility needed serious work. But who would carry it out? In August
1945, newspapers reported that a component of the Indianapolis-based
American Legion might (ironically) buy the track and continue racing there,
but the Rickenbackers claimed no knowledge of such a deal. By that time,
the federal government was allowing horse racing but not motor racing.

Deteriorating stands at the Indianapolis Motor Speedway, circa 1945, around the
time Wilbur Shaw and Tony Hulman teamed up to save the track. (IMS Photo
Archive)

It would be another year before fans again witnessed the big race. In the meantime, just as during World War I, motor enthusiasts had to settle for nostalgic looks backward, recalling Kelly Petillo's win in 1935 or Peter De Paolo's dramatic 1925 victory.[16]

Eddie Rickenbacker anticipated a spectacular postwar future. He thought the 1946 race might involve "cars testing jet propulsion and gasoline turbine engines for ground transport on synthetic tires." Nuclear-powered cars might even compete one day.[17] Drivers whizzing by at up to 600 miles per hour could use shortwave radios to talk with pit crews. Rickenbacker anticipated no shortage of racers or mechanics. "The thousands of World War II pilots, with perfect coordination and reflexes," he said, would provide "a tremendous supply of drivers." The sport, said Rickenbacker, would soon be taken over by "those kids who have been driving half-tracks, jeeps and artillery at night, under fire."[18] Mauri Rose made a similar prediction. Pilots who "got their start running the tails off 'Zekes and Bettys'" (nicknames for Japanese planes) might prove to be "too tough" for racing's old-timers, but their skills would appeal to fans.[19]

The Office of Defense Transportation finally lifted its racing ban in August, a week after the atomic bombing of Nagasaki and two weeks before Japan surrendered aboard the USS *Missouri*. But the speedway's future was uncertain, and Rickenbacker may not have believed his own fantastic predictions. In November 1945, newspapers reported the businessman had sold the track to Terre Haute's Anton "Tony" Hulman Jr., scion of a grocery wholesaling family and a talented marketer who built Clabber Girl Baking Powder into a national brand before investing in commercial real estate, utilities, and media stations throughout the Ohio basin. This time, the capital that bought the track originated within Indiana. The speedway's reported price was $750,000, slightly more than what Rickenbacker had paid in 1927. Septuagenarian Pop Myers returned as vice president and Wilbur Shaw became president. Rickenbacker proclaimed, "It is fitting that Hoosier management and Hoosier capital should continue the most famous venture in mechanical competition." In the 1920s, he recalled, Carl Fisher had been distracted by Miami Beach, and so Detroit investors swooped in to rescue the speedway. For eighteen years, he had maintained the facility's finances and paid for $250,000 of improvements and added the golf course. But now Rickenbacker was focused on Eastern Airlines, and so it was time to return the "great State institution" to Hoosiers. He believed Hulman and Shaw would provide the "'home-town' and 'home-State' ownership" the track needed. Hulman, for his part, said his priority was to enhance "spectator comfort and convenience" while "provid[ing] a track and competition that should be an invitation and a challenge to the best race drivers in the world."[20]

Shaw—who was at that time one of only three living champions to know the feeling of drinking milk or hoisting the Borg-Warner Trophy in victory lane—was instrumental in arranging the purchase. Toward the end of the war, he appeared in a promotional film, *The Crucible of Speed*, about tire tests at the speedway. In his autobiography, Shaw recalled the facility's sorry state: cracked asphalt, weeds growing between the bricks, and decaying grandstands. He recalled, "The depressing scene actually haunted me in my dreams for several nights." Other tracks were being converted into housing developments, Shaw knew, but he saw Indianapolis's speedway as "the world's last great speed shrine, which must be preserved at any cost." He started thinking about buying the track, but first he had to find capital, just as Rickenbacker did in 1927. At first, Shaw pitched the idea to auto-industry

Tony Hulman (left), Hoosier capitalist and consummate sportsman, with Wilbur Shaw. (IMS Photo Archive)

leaders, who wanted to promote their own brands at the oval, but that was not what Shaw envisioned for the legendary track. Pursuing a tip from a local investor, Shaw contacted Hulman. The two met in Terre Haute, where Shaw outlined what he knew about the track's finances. Hulman reportedly said he was not interested in profits—he simply wanted the speedway and its epic annual race to remain a statewide tradition, like the Kentucky Derby. Hulman bought the speedway, named Shaw president, and got to work.[21]

The deteriorating track, which had seemed destined for a residential subdivision, needed about a quarter-million dollars' worth of updates, which were funded by selling ten years' worth of concession rights for $1 million. Workers replaced termite-riddled grandstands with steel-reinforced concrete, bringing permanent seating up to 87,000, and added new concession stands, scoreboards, and a public-address system. Meanwhile, technological marvels—like a rocket booster based on wartime German technology, as well as communications equipment developed by Massachusetts defense contractor Raytheon—seemed poised to change racing forever.[22] The 1946 race even featured a "Fly to the Speedway" event coordinated by the speedway's chaplain, along with Shaw, Hulman, local newspapers, and the chamber of commerce. On race day, hundreds of planes flew to Indianapolis from all around America.[23]

The classic race, revived on May 30, 1946, was won by Los Angeles's George Robson in 4:21:16.7, or 114.82 miles per hour. The estimated crowd of 175,000 saw few crashes, although Mauri Rose fractured a hip in one; he would return to win back-to-back races the next two years. Robson won nearly $49,000, as well as an international, all-expenses-paid vacation from Trans-World Airlines (TWA). Tragically, just three months later, he died in a race in Atlanta. Motor sport was still deadly, but its harsh edges were buffered by nostalgia. Racing's return seemed to indicate "good old days" were "peeking around the corner." Spectators got a whimsical glance backward before the 1946 race, when an antique-car parade featured early-1900s vehicles, as well as names resonating with automotive history: Harvey Firestone Jr., Henry Ford II, Ralph De Palma, and Tommy Milton. The crowd reportedly chuckled at ancient cars and turn-of-the-century fashions. One writer pointed out that the average 1946 sedan could demolish records set at speedway races held forty years earlier.[24] Another enduring tradition was inaugurated that year when tenor James Melton of New York's Metropolitan Opera sang "(Back Home Again in) Indiana" accompanied by Purdue

University's marching band. The nostalgic tune was written and recorded right before US entry to World War I, and a brass ensemble had played it during the closing laps of the 1919 race. Melton's 1946 performance stunned the big crowd, many of whom may have just returned from several years of overseas service. In later years, folksy comedic actor Jim Nabors sang the standard at many races between 1972 and 2014.[25]

Two weeks after racing resumed, the sport's one-time, would-be integration pioneer Jack Johnson perished in a car crash on US Highway 1 in North Carolina. Obituaries in major dailies recounted and implicitly criticized Johnson's lavish spending habits, marriages to white women, 1913 Mann Act conviction, and exile to Europe, but they did not mention his attempt to race at Indianapolis in 1910. In the *Chicago Tribune*'s portrayal, Johnson just seemed to be an aging motorist who perhaps should not have been operating an automobile. The sixty-eight-year-old boxing legend was driving from Texas to New York, returning from a speaking tour, when he swerved and struck a telephone pole.[26] At the time of Johnson's death, sports color lines were largely still in place, but Black athletes were breaking through. Between 1946 and 1950, pro football, baseball, and basketball began desegregating, with Jackie Robinson's April 1947 debut with the Brooklyn Dodgers being the most famous instance. Baseball may have had the oldest color line in big-league sports—dating back to Reconstruction-era debates about the exclusion of Black teams from interstate leagues, as well as a racist "gentlemen's agreement" forged by Cap Anson and other white National League players—but racing was nearly as bad. By 1952, stock-car driver Joie Ray became the first AAA-licensed Black racer, paving the way for Wendell Scott, who competed in a National Association for Stock Car Auto Racing (NASCAR) event in 1953 and was inducted into NASCAR's Hall of Fame in 2015. Scott was the first Black driver to win a Grand National Series event, but because of a scoring error—and, most likely, racism too—he was not credited with the win; his family finally received the trophy two decades after he died.[27]

It was never easy for Black racers, but Indianapolis's de facto color line persisted even longer than NASCAR's. It was finally broken in 1991 by Willy T. Ribbs, who qualified for the Indy 500 with backing from boxing promoter Don King and comedian Bill Cosby. As was the case with every racial pioneer, Ribbs faced pushback, although his often came in the form of microaggressions. Using a well-worn trope about Black bodies, one newspaper portrayed Ribbs as a natural athlete. With "good hands, quick reflexes, [and] a strong back," California-born Ribbs could have starred in the NFL, NBA, or MLB. So what was he doing in a sport like auto racing? Ribbs, understandably, seemed miffed by the question, which appeared to echo the scientific racism often deployed in discussions about Black athletes. So he patiently explained that his father had been a racer, and ever since his childhood he had worked on cars and dreamed of driving at Indianapolis—a story similar to that of many white drivers. As of 2022, the last Black driver in the Indy 500 was George Mack, who competed in 2002. Ribbs has been quoted as saying that, while IndyCar may not oppose Black drivers, it does little to cultivate them.[28]

As racing returned after World War II, spectators may have asked who, exactly, was the speedway's new owner? *Sports Illustrated* published a profile of Tony Hulman in 1958. Robert Shaplen introduced the Terre Haute businessman, then worth about $100 million, as "a 57-year-old, boyishly handsome Hoosier," one of America's "most versatile and accomplished sportsmen." Hulman had been a member of Yale's undefeated 1923 football team, coached by Tad Jones, and had won an honorable mention for Walter Camp's final All-American team. He had earned a bachelor's degree from Yale's Sheffield Scientific School, was a former track and field star, and now was a big-game hunter, deep-sea fisherman, and swimmer; he also could play "a crackerjack game of bridge or billiards." In the decade after 1946, this consummate sportsman invested $3 million in the Indianapolis Motor Speedway, building bleachers, grandstands, fences, cafeteria, paddock, walls, and drainage ditches. He preserved a three-foot stretch of the 1909 bricks while repaving the rest of the oval with Kentucky Rock asphalt, or Kyrock, manufactured by a company Carl Fisher had once controlled. Hulman reportedly spent a quarter of his time on track affairs and enjoyed his role as an "automotive Pied Piper." The shy businessman embodied qualities of boxing promoter Tex Rickard and circus impresario P. T. Barnum. In other words, he was a midcentury version of Carl Fisher, although he was a much more careful investor.[29]

While some claimed Hulman had never witnessed a 500-mile race before buying the track, he asserted that he had, in fact, watched his first race in 1914 and saw at least a dozen more by the time it closed in 1941. Hulman was no stranger to speedway traditions. The Hoosier capitalist reflected on growing up within Indianapolis's hinterland and transportation networks. "Race day was always a big day for us kids in Terre Haute," Hulman recalled.

"Even if we weren't goin', we'd stand at the bridge on the side of town—it was the Old National Road then, dirt, before it got to be U.S. 40—and we'd watch the cars go by to Indianapolis, 70 miles away. Foreign makes and all. It was pretty darn impressive." In other words, he had witnessed firsthand the annihilation of space by early 1900s automobiles heading to the track, which he believed "should remain a home-grown Indiana enterprise."[30] Ignoring the many improvements he had made since taking over in 1946, Hulman proclaimed in the late 1950s, "This is the way it was built originally, and this is how we ought to keep it."[31] In reality, however, the spectacle was changing in important ways. Around this time, in fact, the term "Indy 500" first gained common usage. Using keyword searches, it is practically impossible to find the phrase prior to 1959.[32]

Shaplen's *Sports Illustrated* piece said a 1950s race had virtually all the "attributes of a circus, a clambake and a county fair." Tickets ranged from $3 to $30, with the purse topping $300,000. On race day, Hulman—Pied Piper or mild-mannered Barnum, choose your analogy—personally greeted patrons traveling from afar, and he handed out passes granting admission for a lucky few to visit his multimillion-dollar, glass-and-concrete Master Race Control Tower, which replaced the three-decades-old pagoda in 1957. For many folks, getting to Indianapolis was half the experience. What could be more American than seeing "thousands of cars with their multifarious license plates lined up and waiting for the signal to enter the huge enclosure"? Or driving five hundred miles to watch a race of that many miles—and then turning around to drive back home again? Nostalgia, too, was part of the attraction. Patrons now visited the museum to see champion cars driven by Ray Harroun or Mauri Rose, along with photos of past races. The museum reportedly received tourists from as far away as Outer Mongolia.[33]

Perhaps sport's past was its future, its future its past. Rickenbacker had chaired the sports committee of the 1939 New York World's Fair, where Harroun's Marmon was part of a display of old trophies and artifacts in the fair's Academy of Sports. One observer thought it ironic that while the fair focused on the "World of Tomorrow," its sport exhibit was focused on yesterday.[34] The 1930s was a good time for looking backward, as Henry Ford discovered when he opened his museum and Greenfield Village in Dearborn, Michigan. Historian Kenneth Bindas observes that such 1930s attractions embodied modernity, which itself was based, paradoxically, on nostalgia: "The past was necessary in order to understand the present and project the

Wilbur Shaw with the 1909 Prest-O-Lite Trophy and a poster diagramming modern telephone installations at the speedway. (Indiana Historical Society, P0569)

future, and a usable past was essential to maintaining the conformity of belief in modernity." The Depression was a time of rapid change, generating an overwhelming longing for the past. Only by looking backward could Americans move forward, especially as another global conflict brewed. And once the war was over, looking back to simpler times must have seemed incredibly appealing.[35]

Nostalgia was good for business. Hulman first broached the idea of a museum in 1947, at a time when an estimated quarter-million visitors dropped by throughout the year. After Shaw died in an airplane crash in 1954, Hulman decided to build it. By 1955, the planned facility had acquired two cars—Shaw's Maserati, the 1939 and 1940 victor, and 1932 champion Fred Frame's Miller-Hartz—and sought more items. In July 1955, ground was broken for the $125,000 museum and office structure, with Boots Shaw (Wilbur's widow) turning one of the first shovels of earth. The air-conditioned museum opened the next year, a few days before the 1956 race, and within a month the guest book showed visitors from all forty-eight states

Indianapolis Motor Speedway office building and museum, pictured in 1960. (IMS Photo Archive)

and at least two dozen nations. The exhibits included six racecars, a display of historic tires courtesy of Firestone, the Wheeler-Schebler trophy, and photos of old champions. Over time, some predicted, such artifacts would "illustrate the evolution of racing cars and engines from the first days to the present" and show "highlights of a half century of motor sport."[36] Museum artifacts starkly contrasted with the 7,200-square-foot, brick-stone-and-glass structure, which also housed Indianapolis Motor Speedway (IMS) offices in fluorescent-lit rooms with acoustic-tile ceilings. The "hub of auto racing" no longer looked as it had in the 1940s, when chipped paint and collapsing grandstands gave it the appearance of a war zone. The speedway was once again modern, and now it was surrounded by postwar shopping centers, motels, and suburban homes built on former agricultural fields.[37]

If capital, as scholar Jonathan Levy argues, is an asset invested with an expectation of future profits,[38] then the speedway's long-term transformation made sense. In the twentieth century, the land on which the oval sat had been converted into liquid assets three times: first, when Fisher, Allison,

Newby, and Wheeler bought it in 1909; second, when they sold it to a group of Detroit investors led by Eddie Rickenbacker in 1927; and, finally, when Tony Hulman bought it in 1946. Back in 1909, this farmland could have been transformed into residential or industrial use, but instead it became a site for a popular spectacle illustrating modern annihilation of space. Two decades later, it had the potential to continue as a pop-culture site or be turned into something else, most likely a residential development or an airport. During the interwar years, however, modern media technologies and invented traditions so transformed the old brick track that even though postwar development was not out of the question, it made more sense to maintain the land as a site for legendary spectacle. With the increase in longevity of the races—as more years were invested in maintaining the land as a place for famous and classic sporting events—the speedway grounds became increasingly profitable as a site of sporting memory. Something similar can be seen in legendary professional baseball stadiums, especially Boston's Fenway Park (1912) and Chicago's Wrigley Field (1914), as well as the many retro ballparks that now mimic them.

By the 1950s, motor sport technology advanced so quickly that it destroyed its own utility almost immediately. A racecar only one or two years old was already an artifact, and things only sped up in the 1960s, when winning cars were relegated to relic status almost immediately. It was hard for the museum to keep up. By 1962, curator Karl Kizer, an Indianapolis tire-company owner and former racer, oversaw a collection of seventeen cars, including seven 500-mile-race winners. He kept adding to the menagerie, sometimes tracking down old cars in rural Indiana and Texas. Among the museum's prized possessions was Fisher's 1903 Premier (the one in which workers had drilled holes yet nevertheless was rejected for the Vanderbilt Cup). Each year in the late 1950s, about 250,000 people visited the museum, and Hulman initiated bus tours of the track in 1960. The museum was open with free admission every day but Christmas, yet it may not have seemed welcoming to all visitors. Journalists sometimes gendered the museum as a male place, one that women might join in visiting reluctantly. It was a "Museum for Dad and the Boys," as the *Chicago Tribune* put it. "Men can spend hours inside the museum and women find it interesting, too."[39] By the time of the 1976 Bicentennial, a moment when many Americans came to value public history, a sleek, $5.5-million museum, built of prestressed concrete, quartz, steel, and glass, opened in the infield, opposite the large viaduct off Sixteenth Street. The modern facility, which charged a one-dollar admission fee, was sizable and had ample parking. And gender expectations may have been changing in the era right before Janet Guthrie became the first woman to qualify. Although one newspaper photograph of the museum showed boys ogling an antique racecar, another pictured a more heterogeneous crowd of young men and women streaming out of the museum.[40]

In the 1950s, the first speedway museum opened the same week in which postwar America made an enduring investment in speedwaylike superhighways. On May 29, 1956, one day before the fortieth running of the famous sweepstakes race, the Federal Aid Highway Act passed the US Senate. The federal government provided 90 percent funding for more than forty thousand miles of limited access, high-speed, divided highways, while states paid the rest. This federal Interstate Highway System was the culmination of an idea Fisher concocted forty years earlier, with one big exception: the new interstates were government-funded. These highways reshaped American society. As urban planners advocated decentralized cities less susceptible to nuclear attack, many white Americans, including some who feared school integration, moved to suburbs, from which they drove to work, church, shopping, leisure, and just about everything else. This was the "golden age" of family vacations, when cheap gas facilitated road trips to national parks, historic sites, and theme parks like Disneyland or Six Flags over Texas. Midwesterners trekked to attractions such as Indiana Beach or Abraham Lincoln's southern Indiana boyhood home, which became a National Park Service site in 1962. Many Black Americans, though, remained trapped in inner cities, a result of poverty and real-estate and banking practices that perpetuated segregation. Those who had the means to buy cars and travel did not have the same access to restaurants, hotels, or roadside attractions. Black motorists used *Green Books* and similar publications to find lodging or food; as Martin Luther King Jr. recounted in 1963, during a "cross country drive" they had "to sleep night after night in the uncomfortable corners of [an] automobile." Automobility changed America, but color lines, both official and unofficial, meant unequal spatial access.[41]

Not everyone was happy with the new roadways. In 1958, cultural critic Lewis Mumford argued that highways should be one part of a coherent transportation infrastructure, along with footpaths, rails, and aviation. Americans were too reliant on cars, he said, and soon autos would choke freeways as they once choked central business districts. He predicted calamity. By the 1970s, Americans would figure out how much damage superhighways had done to urban and rural areas, as well as to "the efficient organization of industry and transportation." Highways made the same impact "upon vegetation and human structures as the passage of a tornado or the blast of an atom bomb."[42] Roadbuilding did not result just in annihilation of *distance*, but rather the actual obliteration of *space*, a geographical sacrifice to the modern desire to move quickly.

Historian Jeremiah Axelrod argues that early-1900s automotive parkways were based on scenery, not shared public space. Drivers watched attractive landscapes pass by windshields as if watching a movie screen; roadside environments tailored to motorists were consumable. By the 1940s, however, parkways gave way to freeways, efficient yet unaesthetic ribbons of commerce like those Mumford criticized.[43] By the time of President Lyndon Johnson's Great Society, the Highway Beautification Act of 1965 ("Lady Bird's Bill") made it so motorists could now watch a pleasant panorama as they cruised at 65 miles per hour. Perhaps Americans were already primed for autopia. For decades, they had paid to watch cars race around tracks where speed was made legible or viewed films of the races or read newspaper accounts of the thrilling yet deadly races held at Indianapolis and elsewhere. There were many ways to consume spatial mobility.

Better roads fostered tourism. Even before the museum opened, people could visit the speedway six days a week, invariably asking (in vain) to drive a lap or two on the bricks. But after the war, the Circle City contemplated turning the track into a year-round attraction. In 1946, the head of the Indianapolis Convention and Visitors' Bureau suggested making the famous race the centerpiece of a weeklong celebration to "keep visitors in the city a little longer"—and presumably, spend more money. The festival could feature boxing matches and baseball games, along with parades, aerial contests, and exhibits of Hoosier agriculture and industry. It would be like a world's fair, or maybe Indianapolis's own version of Mardi Gras.[44] This vision, which sounded like a promotion Carl Fisher would have dreamed up twenty years earlier, foreshadowed the way late-1900s cities thought about sports and tourism. Indianapolis wanted to "keep visitors pleasantly bemused all summer, and all year if possible."[45] It was like Miami Beach, which itself provided a template for other perpetual leisure spaces, including postwar Las Vegas. By the 1960s, visitors drove cars fueled by cheap gasoline to Speedway, where they stayed at a motel with "air conditioned rooms, swimming pool, lounge, dining room, and private party rooms all decorated in a motif of the lore of the track."[46] This was the same decade when pro football's Hall of Fame opened in Canton, Ohio (1963), giving fans a "pilgrimage site" similar to the Baseball Hall of Fame that opened in Cooperstown in 1939. Similarly, the Hockey Hall of Fame (established in 1943) moved to Toronto in 1961, while the Naismith Memorial Basketball Hall of Fame (1959) later opened its facility in Springfield, Massachusetts, in 1968.[47] Such places, historians note, often "cater to the nostalgia market" for a particular sport's "golden age."[48]

The speedway museum, like these other facilities, embodied the cultural logic of sports capitalism. Modern sports make money not just by selling tickets or media rights promising access to unscripted athletic drama. Rather, they are profitable largely because modern transportation and communications technologies allow fans to make pilgrimages to legendary venues and consume a pleasing variety of history in which generations pay fealty to aging grandstands or relics associated with sports icons. Yet it is best to remember that historical narratives can be oversimplified and mythologized at these sites of memory—*lieux de mémoire*, in Pierre Nora's terminology—and the narrative is sometimes coded as white and male, with scarcely nuanced analysis.[49] Women and nonwhite men desired to race at Indianapolis as early as the 1910s, but it took decades for them to gain entry. This story has slipped into obscurity. A visitor to the Indianapolis Motor Speedway Museum in 2021 could view a large wall panel about Willy Ribbs, titled "Breaking Barriers," which made no mention of Jack Johnson or the complex history of the speedway's unofficial color line. The attractive exhibit simply recounted Ribbs's achievements as a Black racer and his admirable "perseverance" in the face of post-Jim Crow racism: "Due to the color of his skin, Willy had to overcome prejudice and work harder to achieve his dream" as a budding racer in the 1980s. Neither would that same visitor have seen exhibits dedicated to pioneer female drivers, such as Janet Guthrie or Lyn St. James.[50]

The story so often told about the speedway focuses on its role as "an important part of Hoosier heritage," a place "built to provide a testing ground for Indiana's burgeoning automobile industry." In fact, this was the story written into the *Congressional Record* by Republican Senator Dick Lugar in April 1996. The 500-mile race, said the proclamation, became "a rite of spring for millions of Americans" after 1911, while Indianapolis itself became home to a different kind of production: the "IndyCar racing industry."[51] In 2009, concurrent Senate and House resolutions (the latter introduced by André Carson, an African American Democrat from Indianapolis) recognized the oval's centennial, noting its 1987 designation as a National Historic Landmark "as the oldest continuously operated automobile race course" in the world. The speedway was a "great source of pride to all Hoosiers" for having "played an enormous part in shaping and defining the City of Indianapolis, the State of Indiana, United States motorsports, and the United States auto industry." The resolution highlighted the achievements of Janet Guthrie, Willy Ribbs, and Danica Patrick—who in 2005 became the first woman to lead the race—without discussing the origins of the gender and color barriers such racers had to confront.[52]

Speedway nostalgia fit postmodern Indianapolis. Around 1970, the Hoosier capital—now surrounded by a fifty-three-mile bypass loop, Interstate 465—began transforming itself into an urban center focused on sport and tourism. Indiana marketed itself as a place where "the good life is better," an economically progressive state no longer focused only on farming and industry, and team sports were part of this identity. Indianapolis became home to the American Basketball Association (later NBA) Pacers in 1967,

In 1977, Janet Guthrie became the first woman to qualify for the Indy 500. Here she receives 188 silver dollars, in recognition of her 188-mile-per-hour qualifying time. (IMS Photo Archive)

the Indianapolis Capitals of the Continental Football League from 1968 to 1978, and the World Hockey Association's short-lived Indiana Racers in 1974. Hulman, a former Yale football player, even considered building a football stadium on a portion of the speedway's infield. Instead, big-league football came to Indianapolis in 1984 in the form of the NFL Colts. Indianapolis had built a $78 million dome in the early 1980s, certain the NFL would grant it a team, but when an expansion franchise was not forthcoming, Mayor William Hudnut spoke with Baltimore Colts' owner Robert Irsay and offered an attractive, low-rent deal that convinced the Colts to move to Indiana. Irsay's storied team packed up its equipment and left literally in the middle of the night in March 1984, angering Baltimore football fans and shocking the sports world. The Colts played in the Hoosier Dome (later the RCA Dome) for twenty-four seasons, until Lucas Oil Stadium opened in 2008.[53]

Indianapolis has not had an MLB team since the 1880s, yet it does have the Class AAA Indians, a team that plays in a downtown stadium, Victory Field (1996), which followed the trend of retro ballparks that make nostalgia marketable by deploying a sense of what scholar Daniel Rosensweig calls "instant history" within an artificial yet pleasantly commodified setting that historian Benjamin Lisle calls "urbanoid" space. Sports teams and stadiums are valuable, especially if they have been in one place for a very long time—or at least appear to have been. Pro teams are an important part of Indianapolis's identity, but the city also hosted the amateur Pan Am Games in 1987 and became home to the National Collegiate Athletic Association (NCAA) a decade later, after that organization moved from metro Kansas City to White River State Park in 1999. Indianapolis has hosted the NCAA Final Four multiple times, most recently in 2021, when the entire tournament was held at six venues in central Indiana.[54]

The speedway was as much about consuming myths associated with the Sport of Titans as it was about watching drivers push cars two hundred laps around a 2.5-mile track. Scholar Annie Gilbert Coleman argues that "memories" of legendary racers "have made the Indianapolis 500 the most tradition-bound race in the world." It is practically a "religious ritual."[55] Historian Philip O'Kane portrays the Indy 500 as one of three open-wheel races with "iconic status" in global motor sports. People make "annual pilgrimage[s]" to Indianapolis to see the race, visit the museum, and kiss the bricks.[56] As racing technology constantly outstripped its own novelty, meaningful glances backward were all but inevitable. Postmodern cultural critic Fredric Jameson posited the "Cultural Logic of Late Capitalism," arguing that culture itself has become commodified in late capitalism, with society trading on rituals and nostalgia.[57] Annihilated temporal space can render profit for the annihilators. Even Carl Fisher once predicted that time would "be the most precious commodity of the future."[58]

By the post-1945 era, another layer of meaning accrued to America's speed capital. The speedway was a proto-postmodern site for celebrating rituals characterizing a modern society starting to pass into memory. In the 1970s—as Indianapolis remade its economy and image for a postindustrial world—the US auto industry declined. By the following decade, Rust Belt cities such as Gary, Indiana, and Youngstown, Ohio, shed residents at precipitous rates, scrambling to replace industrial jobs with low-paying positions in service or tourism. Indeed, the ill-fated AutoWorld theme park of Flint, Michigan, may have been the most notorious case of the shift to a symbolic economy. Around the same time, health care displaced manufacturing as the biggest economic sector in former industrial cities.[59] As Eddie Rickenbacker realized in 1927, a legendary brick track could not be relocated or outsourced—at least not the same way an auto factory could be.

Perhaps because Indianapolis's auto industry declined in the 1930s and subsequently retooled for sports and tourism, Indiana's capital city did not suffer the same fate as bigger, and formerly richer, industrial neighbors, such as Detroit or Cleveland. In recent years, some wits have even called Indianapolis the "Diamond in the Rust." Even if it was located in the so-called Rust Belt, Indianapolis more closely resembled the emergent cities of the Sunbelt, sprawling metro areas in the Southeast and Southwest that built reputations on pro-corporate labor laws, carefully managed urban sprawl, warm climates tempered by air conditioning, and year-round recreation.[60] In fact, Indianapolis's city-county government, Unigov, resembled combined metro areas in the South more than it did crazy-quilt jurisdictions in the Northeast. Indianapolis mixed old and new economic realities, continuing to be a place for technological innovation even as it became a signifier for cultural rather than industrial production. When early-twenty-first-century Americans visited the sleek speedway museum or consumed televised races contested by global carmakers, they could feel as if they were reliving an era when heartland innovators transformed the United States into a global leader in automobility and consumer spectacle.

"Where Tradition Never Stops," 2021. (Author photo)

In the wake of a global pandemic that once again disrupted a long history of Memorial Day races, the Indianapolis Motor Speedway affixed to the stands along Sixteenth Street a huge billboard proclaiming it as the place "WHERE TRADITION NEVER STOPS."[61] The legendary track's gaze back at the past would seemingly continue perpetually into the future. Fans could drive into the infield, pay admission to enter the museum, and buy a keychain or a hat or a sliver of historic brick. The twenty-first-century speedway was a sight to behold: century-old bricks covered with asphalt and surrounded by vast expanses of grandstands. But it behooves us to remember not just the legendary drivers or race day's overwhelming sights and sounds. We should understand Indianapolis's origins amid US expansion and the rise of modern transportation infrastructure, as well as the Progressive Era context that produced motor sport. What people consume at such places is not just sporting achievement but rather a complex web of sporting spectacle mixed with consumerism and nostalgia for events, heroes, and structures dating from the industrial era. Racing fans should be aware of how some individuals were prevented from participating in the races—restrictions that still resonate. And, truth be told, we need to consider the environmental impact of technologies that brought motor-fueled spectacle to a landlocked city in the center of Indiana—a speed capital, a central place for America's putative central place. The Indianapolis Motor Speedway grew out of the idea that transportation technology and infrastructure could bring people and places closer together while facilitating a type of entertainment that generated profits by selling representations of spatial annihilation. We have to understand, in short, how society not only consumed Carl Fisher's vision for modern mobility and space as signified at a world-famous track, but actually tried as hard as possible to *become* it.

NOTES

Abbreviations

CT	*Chicago Tribune*
Fisher Papers	Carl Fisher Papers, HistoryMiami Research Center, Miami, Florida
IMS	Indianapolis Motor Speedway, Speedway, Indiana
IndNews	*Indianapolis News*
IndSJ	*Indiana State Journal*
IndyStar	*Indianapolis Star*
IndSun	*Indianapolis Sun*
LAT	*Los Angeles Times*
NYT	*New York Times*
WP	*Washington Post*
WSJ	*Wall Street Journal*

In citations of the Carl Fisher Papers ("Fisher Papers"), numbers refer to box/microfilm reel and frame number. For instance, "1: 676" denotes box/reel 1 and frame 676.

Introduction

1. "Speedway Opens at Indianapolis," *CT*, Aug. 19, 1909, 7.

2. On the demonym "Hoosier," see Jonathan Clark Smith, "Not Southern Scorn but Local Pride: The Origin of the Word *Hoosier* and Indiana's River Culture," *Indiana Magazine of History* 103, no. 2 (2007): 183–94; Katie Mettler, "'Hoosier' Is

Now the Official Name for Indiana Folk. But What Does It Even Mean?" *WP*, Jan. 13, 2017, https://www.washingtonpost.com/news/morning-mix/wp/2017/01/13/hoosier-is-now-the-official-name-for-indiana-folk-but-what-does-it-even-mean/?utm_term=.616b71580985.

3. Accounts dismissing the balloons' significance include Mark S. Foster, *Castles in the Sand: The Life and Times of Carl Graham Fisher* (Gainesville: University Press of Florida, 2000), 75–76, 92; Charles Leerhsen, *Blood and Smoke: A True Tale of Mystery, Mayhem, and the Birth of the Indy 500* (New York: Simon and Schuster, 2011), 22–24.

4. Clifford Geertz, *The Interpretation of Cultures* (New York: Basic Books, 1973), 9–10, 417, 453.

5. Ronald J. Horvath, "Machine Space," *Geographical Review* 64, no. 2 (April 1974): 167–88; John A. Jakle and Keith A. Sculle, *Lots of Parking: Land Use in a Car Culture* (Charlottesville: University of Virginia Press, 2004), 9–12.

6. On the urban leisure economy, see John M. Findlay, *Magic Lands: Western Cityscapes and American Culture after 1940* (Berkeley: University of California Press, 1992); Andrew M. Busch, *City in a Garden: Environmental Transformations and Racial Justice in Twentieth-Century Austin, Texas* (Chapel Hill: University of North Carolina Press, 2017); Alex Sayf Cummings, *Brain Magnet: Research Triangle Park and the Idea of the Idea Economy* (New York: Columbia University Press, 2020).

7. William Cronon, foreword to Christopher W. Wells, *Car Country: An Environmental History* (Seattle: University of Washington Press, 2012), x.

8. Antonio Gramsci, *Selections from the Prison Notebooks*, ed. Quintin Hoare and Geoffrey Nowell Smith (New York: International, 1971), 9; Karl Marx, *Grundrisse*, trans. Martin Nicolaus (New York: Penguin, 1973), 524. This idea is developed further in Brian M. Ingrassia, "Annihilating Space: Motor Sport and the Commodification of Movement," *Journal of Sport History* 50, no. 1 (Spring 2023).

9. Henri Lefebvre, *The Production of Space*, trans. Donald Nicholson-Smith (Oxford, UK: Blackwell, 1984); Eric Hobsbawm and Terence Ranger, eds., *The Invention of Tradition* (Cambridge: Cambridge University Press, 1983).

10. Steve Marston, "Spectacles of Speed: Modernity, Masculinity, and Auto Racing in Kansas, 1909–1918," *Kansas History* 38 (Autumn 2015): 193.

11. "Eddie Pullen to Try Again," *LAT*, May 1, 1921, VI13.

12. Robert Markus, "Janet Wins Right to Laugh," *CT*, May 23, 1977, E1.

13. For sport history overviews, see Allen Guttmann, *Sports: The First Five Millennia* (Amherst: University of Massachusetts Press, 2004), and Elliott Gorn and Warren Goldstein, *A Brief History of American Sports* (Urbana: University of Illinois Press, 2004). On racing, see Allen Guttmann, *From Ritual to Record: The Nature of Modern Sports*, rev. ed. (New York: Columbia University Press, 2004), 7; Guttmann, *Sports*, 3; Daniel S. Pierce, *Real NASCAR: White Lightning, Red Clay, and Big Bill France* (Chapel Hill: University of North Carolina Press, 2012); Randal Hall, "Before NASCAR: The Corporate and Civic Promotion of Automobile Racing in the American South, 1903–1927," *Journal of Southern History* 68, no. 3 (2002): 629–68; Pete Daniel, *Lost Revolutions: The South in the 1950s* (Chapel Hill:

University of North Carolina Press, 2000), 91–120; David N. Lucsko, "American Motor Sport: The Checkered Literature on the Checkered Flag," in *A Companion to American Sport History*, ed. Steven A. Riess (Hoboken, NJ: Wiley Blackwell, 2014), 313–33; Daniel J. Simone, "Racing, Region, and the Environment: A History of American Motorsports" (PhD diss., University of Florida, 2009). For examples of racing being called a "sport" or "game," see "Eddie Pullen to Try Again," *LAT*, May 1, 1921, VI13; "Ralph De Palma, Darling of Fans, Enters Classic," *LAT*, April 30, 1922, G3. On 1800s men's pastimes, see Melvin L. Adelman, *A Sporting Time: New York City and the Rise of Modern Athletics, 1820–70* (Urbana: University of Illinois Press, 1990); Howard P. Chudacoff, *The Age of the Bachelor: Creating an American Subculture* (Princeton, NJ: Princeton University Press, 1999). On technoscientific sport, see Rayvon Fouché, *Game Changer: The Technoscientific Revolution in Sports* (Baltimore: Johns Hopkins University Press, 2017).

14. H. F. Moorhouse, *Driving Ambitions: A Social Analysis of the American Hot Rod Enthusiasm* (Manchester, UK: Manchester University Press, 1991); Robert C. Post, *High Performance: The Culture and Technology of Drag Racing, 1950–2000*, rev. ed. (Baltimore: Johns Hopkins University Press, 2001); David N. Lucsko, *The Business of Speed: The Hot Rod Industry in America, 1915–1990* (Baltimore: Johns Hopkins University Press, 2008); Gary S. Cross, *Machines of Youth: America's Car Obsession* (Chicago: University of Chicago Press, 2018).

15. A Progressive Era overview is Maureen Flanagan, *America Reformed: Progressives and Progressivisms, 1890s-1920s* (New York: Oxford University Press, 2006). On international influences, see Daniel T. Rodgers, *Atlantic Crossings: Social Politics in a Progressive Age* (Cambridge, MA: Harvard University Press, 1998). On athletic reform, see Brian M. Ingrassia, *The Rise of Gridiron University: Higher Education's Uneasy Alliance with Big-Time Football* (Lawrence: University Press of Kansas, 2012).

16. On the Midwest, see Kristin L. Hoganson, *The Heartland: An American History* (New York: Penguin, 2019); Jon K. Lauck, *From Warm Center to Ragged Edge: The Erosion of Midwestern Literary and Historical Regionalism, 1920–1965* (Iowa City: University of Iowa Press, 2017); William Cronon, *Nature's Metropolis: Chicago and the Great West* (New York: Norton, 1991).

17. On spatial unification, see Robert Wiebe, *The Search for Order, 1877–1920* (New York: Hill and Wang, 1967), xiii. On the Progressive Era public, see Shelton Stromquist, *Reinventing "The People": The Progressive Movement, the Class Problem, and the Origins of Modern Liberalism* (Urbana: University of Illinois Press, 2006).

18. On automobility, see Wells, *Car Country*; David Blanke, *Hell on Wheels: The Promise and Peril of America's Car Culture, 1900–1940* (Lawrence: University Press of Kansas, 2006); Cotten Seiler, *Republic of Drivers: A Cultural History of Automobility in America* (Chicago: University of Chicago Press, 2008); Brian Ladd, *Autophobia: Love and Hate in the Automotive Age* (Chicago: University of Chicago Press, 2008); Peter D. Norton, *Fighting Traffic: The Dawn of the Motor Age in the American City* (Cambridge, MA: MIT Press, 2008); Virginia Scharff, *Taking the Wheel: Women and the Coming of the Motor Age* (Albuquerque: University of New Mexico Press, 1992); Beth L. Bailey, *From Front Porch to Back Seat: Courtship in*

Twentieth-Century America (Baltimore: Johns Hopkins University Press, 1988); John B. Rae, *The American Automobile: A Brief History* (Chicago: University of Chicago Press, 1965); James J. Flink, *America Adopts the Automobile, 1895–1910* (Cambridge, MA: MIT Press, 1970). John A. Jakle and Keith A. Sculle's numerous books on automobiles include *Motoring: The Highway Experience in America* (Athens: University of Georgia Press, 2008). On the Good Roads Movement, see Bruce E. Seely, *Building the American Highway System: Engineers as Policy Makers* (Philadelphia: Temple University Press, 1987); Michael R. Fein, *Paving the Way: New York Road Building and the American State, 1880–1956* (Lawrence: University Press of Kansas, 2008); Howard Lawrence Preston, *Dirt Roads to Dixie: Accessibility and Modernization in the South, 1885–1935* (Knoxville: University of Tennessee Press, 1991); Tammy Ingram, *Dixie Highway: Road Building and the Making of the Modern South, 1900–1930* (Chapel Hill: University of North Carolina Press, 2014). On races that promoted roadbuilding campaigns, see Brian M. Ingrassia, "Rousing Sentiment for Good Roads: The Spectacles of Atlanta's 1909 Automobile Week," *Georgia Historical Quarterly* 102, no. 1 (Spring 2018): 25–58; and Hall, "Before NASCAR." For city-level studies, see Scott L. Bottles, *Los Angeles and the Automobile: The Making of the Modern City* (Berkeley: University of California Press, 1987); Jeremiah B. C. Axelrod, *Inventing Autopia: Dreams and Visions of the Modern Metropolis in Jazz Age Los Angeles* (Berkeley: University of California Press, 2009); Paul Barrett, *The Automobile and Urban Transit: The Formation of Public Policy in Chicago, 1900–1930* (Philadelphia: Temple University Press, 1983); Howard L. Preston, *Automobile Age Atlanta: The Making of a Southern Metropolis, 1900–1935* (Athens: University of Georgia Press, 1979); William R. Worley, *J. C. Nichols and the Shaping of Kansas City* (Columbia: University of Missouri Press, 1990).

19. Gabrielle Esperdy, *American Autopia: An Intellectual History of the American Roadside at Midcentury* (Charlottesville: University of Virginia Press, 2019), 1–4; Axelrod, *Inventing Autopia*. See also Reyner Banham, *Los Angeles: The Architecture of Four Ecologies* (Baltimore: Penguin, 1971), 213–22.

20. Foster, *Castles in the Sand*; Ingram, *Dixie Highway*; Annie Gilbert Coleman, "Making Time and Place at the Indy 500," *Environmental History* 16 (April 2011): 323–35; Jerry M. Fisher, *The Pacesetter: The Untold Story of Carl G. Fisher* (Fort Bragg, CA: Lost Coast Press, 1998).

21. Sean Dinces, *Bulls Markets: Chicago's Basketball Business and the New Inequality* (Chicago: University of Chicago Press, 2018); Jerald Podair, *City of Dreams: Dodger Stadium and the Birth of Modern Los Angeles* (Princeton, NJ: Princeton University Press, 2017), 63. On using sport to analyze the past, see Michael Oriard, *Reading Football: How the Popular Press Created an American Spectacle* (Chapel Hill: University of North Carolina Press, 1993).

22. Brian M. Ingrassia, "Speed Attractions: Urban Mobility and Automotive Spectacle in Pre–World War I Amarillo," *Southwestern Historical Quarterly* 123, no. 1 (July 2019): 60–86. On the "unbuilt environment," see Kathryn J. Oberdeck, "Archives of the Unbuilt Environment: Documents and Discourses of Imagined

Space in Twentieth-Century Kohler, Wisconsin," in *Archive Stories: Facts, Fictions, and the Writing of History*, ed. Antoinette Burton, 251–73 (Durham, NC: Duke University Press, 2005).

23. David Monod, *Vaudeville and the Making of Modern Entertainment, 1890–1925* (Chapel Hill: University of North Carolina Press, 2020), 9, 22 (quotation).

24. On Ford and Barnum, see Steven Watts, *The People's Tycoon: Henry Ford and the American Century* (New York: Vintage, 2005); Neil Harris, *Humbug: The Art of P. T. Barnum* (Chicago: University of Chicago Press, 1973); Bluford Adams, *E Pluribus Barnum: The Great Showman and the Making of U.S. Popular Culture* (Minneapolis: University of Minnesota Press, 1997); Ray E. Boomhower, "Carl Fisher: The Hoosier Barnum," *Ray E. Boomhower's Books*, Nov. 16, 2020, http://rayboomhower.blogspot.com/2020/11/carl-fisher-hoosier-barnum.html (accessed Sept. 26, 2021).

Chapter 1. Crossroads of America

1. Indiana Historical Bureau, "Emblems and Symbols," accessed Sept. 26, 2021, https://www.in.gov/history/about-indiana-history-and-trivia/emblems-and-symbols/.

2. Peter Onuf, *Statehood and Union: A History of the Northwest Ordinance* (Bloomington: Indiana University Press, 1987), 14; Andrew R. L. Cayton, *Frontier Indiana* (Bloomington: Indiana University Press, 1996), 103–5.

3. Gregory Evans Dowd, *A Spirited Resistance: The North American Indian Struggle for Unity, 1745–1815* (Baltimore, MD: Johns Hopkins University Press, 1992), 181–85; Cayton, *Frontier Indiana*, 220–25; Robert M. Owens, *Mr. Jefferson's Hammer: William Henry Harrison and the Origins of American Indian Policy* (Norman: University of Oklahoma Press, 2007); Walter Johnson, *The Broken Heart of America: St. Louis and the Violent History of the United States* (New York: Basic Books, 2020), 41–71; Richard C. Wade, *The Urban Frontier: The Rise of Western Cities, 1790–1830* (Cambridge, MA: Harvard University Press, 1959).

4. Jerry M. Fisher, *The Pacesetter: The Untold Story of Carl G. Fisher* (Fort Bragg, CA: Lost Coast Press, 1998), 3; James H. Madison, *Hoosiers: A New History of Indiana* (Bloomington: Indiana University Press, 2014), 46; Nicole Etcheson, *The Emerging Midwest: Upland Southerners and the Political Culture of the Old Northwest, 1787–1861* (Bloomington: Indiana University Press, 1996).

5. Donald F. Carmony, *Indiana, 1816–1850: The Pioneer Era* (Indianapolis: Indiana Historical Bureau/Indiana Historical Society, 1998), 108–9 (quotations); Jon C. Teaford, *Cities of the Heartland: The Rise and Fall of the Industrial Midwest* (Bloomington: Indiana University Press, 1993), 27–28.

6. On Ralston, see Emmett A. Rice, "A Forgotten Man of Indianapolis," *Indiana Magazine of History* 34, no. 3 (Sept. 1938): 286–91; Carmony, *Indiana*, 109–14. On early settlers, see Robert G. Barrows and Leigh Darbee, "The Urban Frontier in Pioneer Indiana," *Indiana Magazine of History* 105, no. 3 (Sept. 2009): 271–73. On L'Enfant, see James Sterling Young, *The Washington Community, 1800–1828* (New

York: Harcourt, Brace, World, 1966), 3–7. On the 1825 relocation, see Mildred C. Stoler, "Documents: The Removal of the State Capital to Indianapolis," *Indiana Magazine of History* 27, no. 3 (Sept. 1931): 240–43.

7. William Cronon, *Nature's Metropolis: Chicago and the Great West* (New York: Norton, 1991), 48–50.

8. Ralph D. Gray, "Transportation," in *Encyclopedia of Indianapolis*, ed. David J. Bodenhamer and Robert G. Barrows (Bloomington: Indiana University Press, 1994), 189; George E. Amick, "Post Roads in Southern Indiana," *Indiana Magazine of History* 30, no. 4 (Dec. 1934): 333; Barrows and Darbee, "Urban Frontier in Pioneer Indiana," 279; George Rogers Taylor, *The Transportation Revolution, 1815–1860* (New York: Rinehart, 1951), 18–19; Daniel Walker Howe, *What Hath God Wrought: The Transformation of America, 1815–1848* (New York: Oxford University Press, 2007), 212; Theodore Sky, *The National Road and the Difficult Path to Sustainable National Investment* (Newark: University of Delaware Press, 2011), 86–88; Cayton, *Frontier Indiana*, 286–87; Roger Pickenpaugh, *America's First Interstate: The National Road, 1806–1853* (Kent, OH: Kent State University Press, 2020), 53–61; "Indiana," *NYT*, Nov. 30, 1852, 2. On Whigs and their ideas about growth, see Daniel Walker Howe, *The Political Culture of the American Whigs* (Chicago: University of Chicago Press, 1979), 20–21.

9. Giles R. Hoyt, "Germans," in *Encyclopedia of Indianapolis*, 618–19; Michelle D. Hale, "Indiana Avenue," in *Encyclopedia of Indianapolis*, 730; Tyrone McKinley Freeman, *Madam C. J. Walker's Gospel of Giving: Black Women's Philanthropy during Jim Crow* (Urbana: University of Illinois Press, 2020).

10. Rebecca S. Shoemaker, "Michigan City, Indiana: The Failure of a Dream," *Indiana Magazine of History* 84, no. 4 (Dec. 1988): 319, 327, 328, 336–42; Teaford, *Cities of the Heartland*, 21–22; James H. Madison, *The Indiana Way: A State History* (Bloomington: Indiana University Press, 1986), 81.

11. Taylor, *Transportation Revolution*, 33–35, 45–46; Carol Sheriff, *The Artificial River: The Erie Canal and the Paradox of Progress, 1817–1862* (New York: Hill and Wang, 1996), 32–35, 52–54; Howe, *What Hath God Wrought*, 117–19, 219; Richard H. Gasson, *The Birth of American Tourism: New York, the Hudson Valley, and American Culture, 1790–1830* (Amherst: University of Massachusetts Press, 2008), 97–100; Cayton, *Frontier Indiana*, 284.

12. Paul Fatout, *Indiana Canals* (West Lafayette, IN: Purdue University Studies, 1972), 72–73; Madison, *Indiana Way*, 82–85; Cayton, *Frontier Indiana*, 284–85; Taylor, *Transportation Revolution*, 47–48.

13. Sheriff, *Artificial River*, 173 (quotation); Craig Miner, *A Most Magnificent Machine: America Adopts the Railroad, 1825–1862* (Lawrence: University Press of Kansas, 2010), 4–5, 19, 28; Taylor, *Transportation Revolution*, 80; Cronon, *Nature's Metropolis*, 86–87.

14. David E. Nye, *American Technological Sublime* (Cambridge, MA: MIT Press, 1994), 53.

15. Quoted in Etcheson, *Emerging Midwest*, 53–54; see also Carmony, *Indiana*, xi.

16. Etcheson, *Emerging Midwest*, 52–53.

17. Scott Reynolds Nelson, *Oceans of Grain: How American Wheat Remade the World* (New York: Basic Books, 2022); Taylor, *Transportation Revolution*, 79. In 1850, 6,578 miles of America's railroads (74%) were located east of the Mississippi and in the northern states. Indiana's 1850 mileage was only 2.5 percent of the national total, but in 1860 its 2,163 miles comprised 7 percent of the nation's 30,636 miles.

18. Barrows and Darbee, "Urban Frontier in Pioneer Indiana," 276, 280 (*Journal* quotation); Teaford, *Cities of the Heartland*, viii, 38–39; Mansel G. Blackford, *Columbus, Ohio: Two Centuries of Business and Environmental Change* (Columbus: Trillium/Ohio State University Press, 2016), 17; Cronon, *Nature's Metropolis*; Madison, *Indiana Way*, 96.

19. Carl Abbott, "Indianapolis in the 1850s: Popular Economic Thought and Urban Growth," *Indiana Magazine of History* 74, no. 4 (Dec. 1978): 294–314; Emma Lou Thornbrough, *Indiana in the Civil War Era, 1850–1880* (Indianapolis: Indiana Historical Bureau/Indiana Historical Society, 1965), 318 (quotation), 323–32; "Rail-Road News," *Scientific American*, Apr. 26, 1851, 249.

20. Wolfgang Schivelbusch, *The Railway Journey: The Industrialization of Time and Space in the 19th Century* (Berkeley: University of California Press, 1977), 35 (quotation); Cronon, *Nature's Metropolis*, 92.

21. Thornbrough, *Indiana in the Civil War Era*, 318, 321; Taylor, *Transportation Revolution*, 29–31.

22. Cayton, *Frontier Indiana*, 268, 275–76, 287; Thornbrough, *Indiana in the Civil War Era*, 1; Frederick D. Kershner Jr., "From Country Town to Industrial City: The Urban Pattern in Indianapolis," *Indiana Magazine of History* 45, no. 4 (Dec. 1949): 337; "The West," *NYT*, Sept. 22, 1852, 2 (quotations). See also William Oliver, *Eight Months in Illinois, with Information to Immigrants* (Carbondale: Southern Illinois University Press, 2002), 205–6.

23. "Indiana," *NYT*, Nov. 30, 1852, 2 (quotations); "Financial: Indiana Central Railway Company," *NYT*, Mar. 5, 1857, 7.

24. "Indiana," *NYT*, Jan. 31, 1853, 2 (quotation); Victor M. Bogle, "Railroad Building in Indiana, 1850–1855," *Indiana Magazine of History* 58, no. 3 (Sept. 1962): 215–16; Madison, *Indiana Way*, 154.

25. Quoted in Abbott, "Indianapolis in the 1850s," 315.

26. Abbott, "Indianapolis in the 1850s," 294–95, 300 (quotation), 302–3, 308–10, 314; Mary Ellen Gadski, "Union Station," in *Encyclopedia of Indianapolis*, 1363. On aspiring central cities, see Adam Arenson, *The Great Heart of the Republic: St. Louis and the Cultural Civil War* (Cambridge, MA: Harvard University Press, 2011); Amahia Mallea, *A River in the City of Fountains: An Environmental History of Kansas City and the Missouri River* (Lawrence: University Press of Kansas, 2018), 3.

27. William G. Thomas, *The Iron Way: Railroads, the Civil War, and the Making of Modern America* (New Haven, CT: Yale University Press, 2011), 105–8; Wendy Hamand Venet, *A Changing Wind: Commerce and Conflict in Civil War Atlanta* (New Haven, CT: Yale University Press, 2014); Leonard P. Curry, *Blueprint for Modern America: Nonmilitary Legislation of the First Civil War Congress* (Nashville: Vanderbilt University Press, 1968), 124, 131–32; Richard White, *Railroaded: The Transcontinentals and the Making of Modern America* (New York: Norton, 2011), 17; Thornbrough, *Indiana in the Civil War Era*, 318; "A New Railroad Enterprise," *NYT*, Oct. 4, 1870, 8.

28. Adam Criblez, *Parading Patriotism: Independence Day Celebrations in the Urban Midwest, 1826–1876* (DeKalb: Northern Illinois University Press, 2013), 117; Peter C. Bjarkman, "Baseball," in *Encyclopedia of Indianapolis*, 300–301; Matthew Dennis, *Red, White, and Blue Letter Days: An American Calendar* (Ithaca, NY: Cornell University Press, 2002), 98–100. On the YMCA, see Clifford Putney, *Muscular Christianity: Manhood and Sports in Protestant America, 1880–1920* (Cambridge, MA: Harvard University Press, 2001), 64–72.

29. "Indianapolis as a Railroad Centre," *NYT*, June 10, 1873, 2 (quotations); Rebecca Edwards, *New Spirits: Americans in the "Gilded Age," 1865–1905*, 3rd ed. (New York: Oxford University Press, 2015), 27.

30. Eric Foner, *Reconstruction: America's Unfinished Revolution, 1863–1877* (New York: Harper and Row, 1988), 583–84; Richard White, *The Republic for Which It Stands: The United States during Reconstruction and the Gilded Age, 1865–1896* (New York: Oxford University Press, 2017), 346–53; "Lines Entering Indianapolis," *NYT*, July 25, 1877, 5; "Indiana," *CT*, July 24, 1877, 2.

31. "Passing Events in Indiana," *NYT*, Jan. 22, 1882, 2; Gadski, "Union Station"; James A. Glass, "The Gas Boom in East Central Indiana," *Indiana Magazine of History* 96, no. 4 (Dec. 2000): 314–15, 326–27, 329; Clifton J. Phillips, *Indiana in Transition: The Emergence of an Industrial Commonwealth, 1880–1920* (Indianapolis: Indiana Historical Society, 1968), 192–97; Frank Felsenstein and James J. Connolly, *What Middletown Read: Print Culture in an American Small City* (Amherst: University of Massachusetts Press, 2015), 19–30.

32. Kenneth T. Jackson, *Crabgrass Frontier: The Suburbanization of the United States* (New York: Oxford University Press, 1985), 39–42, 105–15; Phillips, *Indiana in Transition*, 251–52; Teaford, *Cities of the Heartland*, 73–74; Charles Johnson Taggart, "Streetcars," in *Encyclopedia of Indianapolis*, 1305.

33. Timothy J. Sehr, "Three Gilded Age Suburbs of Indianapolis: Irvington, Brightwood, and Woodruff Place," *Indiana Magazine of History* 77, no. 4 (Dec. 1981): 305–32; Jackson, *Crabgrass Frontier*, 112–13; Sam B. Warner Jr., *Streetcar Suburbs: The Process of Growth in Boston, 1870–1900* (Cambridge, MA: Harvard University Press, 1962); Dolores Hayden, *Building Suburbia: Green Fields and Urban Growth, 1820–2000* (New York: Vintage, 2003), 71–79; Blake McKelvey, *The Urbanization of America, 1860–1915* (New Brunswick, NJ: Rutgers University Press, 1963), 51–52.

34. Connie J. Zeigler, "Street Railway Strikes (1892 and 1913)," in *Encyclopedia of Indianapolis*, 1303–4; Brian J. Cudahy, *Cash, Tokens, and Transfers: A History of Urban Mass Transit in North America* (New York: Fordham University Press, 1990), 144. On New York's strike, see Edward O'Donnell, *Henry George and the Crisis of Inequality: Progress and Poverty in the Gilded Age* (New York: Columbia University Press, 2015), 173–82, 233–34.

35. Teaford, *Cities of the Heartland*, 77–78; "An Event for the Veteran," *IndSJ*, Aug. 17, 1889, 8; "His Joyful Homecoming," *CT*, Aug. 22, 1889, 1; "At Harrison's Home," *WP*, Aug. 23, 1889, 1; "Indiana's War Monument," *NYT*, Aug. 23, 1889, 1; "Two Games in Indianapolis," *NYT*, Aug. 23, 1889, 3; "The Meaning of the Monument," *IndSJ*, Aug. 26, 1889, 4; "Row in the Indianapolis G.A.R.," *NYT*, Mar. 22, 1893, 1; "Shaft to Heroic Dead," *WP*, May 16, 1902, 3; William L. Selm, "Soldiers and Sailors Monument," in *Encyclopedia of Indianapolis*, 1278–79. On the GAR, see David W. Blight, *Race and Reunion: The Civil War in American Memory* (Cambridge, MA: Belknap, 2001); Stuart McConnell, *Glorious Contentment: The Grand Army of the Republic, 1865–1900* (Chapel Hill: University of North Carolina Press, 1992).

36. Charles Mulford Robinson, "City Beautiful and Its Meanings," *IndNews*, Aug. 22, 1903, 12; "Women Speak Their Views on Making the City Beautiful," *IndSJ*, Dec. 27, 1903, 20; "The City Beautiful," *IndNews*, Apr. 13, 1907, 6; Michelle D. Hale, "Parks," in *Encyclopedia of Indianapolis*, 1077; "George Edward Kessler and the Park System," *National Park Service*, https://www.nps.gov/nr/travel/indianapolis/kessleressay.htm (accessed Sept. 11, 2021). See also William H. Wilson, *The City Beautiful Movement* (Baltimore: Johns Hopkins University Press, 1989). On the Emrichsville Bridge, see William Gulde, "Bridges," in *Encyclopedia of Indianapolis*, 351; Nathan Bilger, "Preservation Denied: Emrichsville Bridge," *HistoricIndianapolis.com*, https://historicindianapolis.com/preservation-denied-emrichsville-bridge/.

37. Phillips, *Indiana in Transition*, 252–56; H. Roger Grant, *Interurbans and the American People* (Bloomington: Indiana University Press, 2016), 11–15; "Electric Through Lines," *NYT*, June 24, 1903, 2; "Indiana Traction Merger," *WP*, Nov. 27, 1906, 11; "New York to Chicago by Trolley Lines," *NYT*, Apr. 6, 1909, 6.

38. Christopher W. Wells, "The Changing Nature of Country Roads: Farmers, Reformers, and the Shifting Uses of Rural Space, 1880–1905," *Agricultural History* 80, no. 2 (Spring 2006): 152.

39. Connie J. Zeigler, "Street Paving Exposition," in *Encyclopedia of Indianapolis*, 1302; Sheryl D. Vanderstel, "Tomlinson Hall," in *Encyclopedia of Indianapolis*, 1336–37.

40. Evan Friss, *The Cycling City: Bicycles and Urban America in the 1890s* (Chicago: University of Chicago Press, 2015), 125 (quotation), 128–33, 144–45, 158.

41. Steven A. Riess, *City Games: The Evolution of American Urban Society and the Rise of Sports* (Urbana: University of Illinois Press, 1989), 62–65; Stephen Hardy, *How Boston Played: Sport, Recreation, and Community, 1865–1915* (Knoxville: University of Tennessee Press, 2003), 147–67; Roger Gilles, *Women on the Move: The*

Forgotten Era of Women's Bicycle Racing (Lincoln: University of Nebraska Press, 2018); Phillips, *Indiana in Transition*, 310–11; Michael Taylor, "The Bicycle Boom and the Bicycle Bloc: Cycling and Politics in the 1890s," *Indiana Magazine of History* 104, no. 3 (Sept. 2008): 237–38; "First of the Meet," *IndNews*, Aug. 9, 1898, 1–2; "National Meet of the L.A.W.," *NYT*, Aug. 10, 1898, 5 (quotations); Tiffany Benedict Browne, "Newby Oval: The Track before the Track," *Indianapolis Monthly*, May 19, 2016, https://www.indianapolismonthly.com/arts-and-culture/circle-city/newby-oval.

42. Joseph J. Corn, *The Winged Gospel: America's Romance with Aviation, 1900–1950* (New York: Oxford University Press, 1983), 5–8; Robert Wohl, *A Passion for Wings: Aviation and the Western Imagination, 1908–1918* (New Haven, CT: Yale University Press, 1994), 10 (quotation).

43. Phillips, *Indiana in Transition*, 311–16; Ralph D. Gray, *Alloys and Automobiles: The Life of Elwood Haynes* (Indianapolis: Indiana Historical Society, 1979); John Jakle and Keith Sculle, *Motoring: The Highway Experience in America* (Athens: University of Georgia Press, 2008), 12. On Wheeler, see "Frank Wheeler Takes Own Life," *IndyStar*, May 28, 1921, 1.

44. Mark S. Foster, *Castles in the Sand: The Life and Times of Carl Graham Fisher* (Gainesville: University Press of Florida, 2000), 10–15 (quotation); Carl G. Fisher LAW membership card, ca. 1897, 4: 567, Carl Graham Fisher Papers, HistoryMiami Research Center, Miami, Florida [hereafter, Fisher Papers]; George M. Dickson, "Members of the Zig[-]Zag Cycling Club," Nov. 15, 1929, 2: 405–7, Fisher Papers; Lisa Lorentz, "Friday Favorite: Zig-Zag Cycling Club," *Historic Indianapolis*, June 13, 2014: https://historicindianapolis.com/friday-favorites-zig-zag-cycling-club/. On Ford, Fordism, and Detroit's auto industry, see Steven Watts, *The People's Tycoon: Henry Ford and the American Century* (New York: Vintage, 2005); Thomas P. Hughes, *American Genesis: A Century of Invention and Technological Enthusiasm, 1870–1970* (Chicago: University of Chicago Press, 2004); Donald Finlay Davis, *Conspicuous Production: Automobiles and Elites in Detroit, 1899–1933* (Philadelphia: Temple University Press, 1988). For a comparison of cars' and railroads' ability to annihilate space, see Christopher W. Wells, *Car Country: An Environmental History* (Seattle: University of Washington Press, 2012), 142–55.

45. Foster, *Castles in the Sand*, 18–44; Jane Fisher, *Fabulous Hoosier: A Story of American Achievement* (New York: Robert McBride, 1947), 43. Jane Watts actually was born on March 29, 1887.

46. Watts, *People's Tycoon*, 64–82 (quotation on 64).

47. Jerry Fisher, *Pacesetter*, 23–24; "Life of Uncle John Goodwin Is Hanging in the Balance," *Times Recorder* (Zanesville, OH), Sept. 10, 1903, 1, 5; "Death Victor," *Times Recorder* (Zanesville, OH), Sept. 15, 1903, 7; Jane Fisher, *Fabulous Hoosier*, 48–49; "Carl Fisher's Vanderbilt Cup Premier," *The First Super Speedway*, accessed Sept. 26, 2021, https://www.firstsuperspeedway.com/photo-gallery/carl-fishers-vanderbilt-cup-premier. Some sources claim fourteen casualties in the 1903 Zanesville race, apparently an exaggeration.

48. "James A. Allison, Capitalist, Dies," *IndNews*, Aug. 4, 1928, 1–2; Foster, *Castles in the Sand*, 46–55.

Chapter 2. America's Brooklands

1. C. G. Fisher, "Advantages of a Big Circular Track," *Motor Age*, Nov. 15, 1906, 31 (quotation); Jerry M. Fisher, *The Pacesetter: The Untold Story of Carl G. Fisher* (Fort Bragg, CA: Lost Coast Press, 1998), 45–46. Detailed accounts of some events analyzed in this chapter are in D. Bruce Scott, *Indy: Racing before the 500* (Batesville, IN: Indiana Reflections, 2005).

2. Al Bloemker, *500 Miles to Go: The History of the Indianapolis Speedway* (New York: Coward-McCann, 1961), 11–12; Reed L. Parker, "Stage Set for Speedway[']s Greatest Racing Event," *CT*, May 23, 1915, E8 (quotation); Mark S. Foster, *Castles in the Sand: The Life and Times of Carl Graham Fisher* (Gainesville: University Press of Florida, 2000), 72–74; Nicholas H. Lancaster, *Brooklands: Cradle of British Motor Racing and Aviation* (Oxford, UK: Shire, 2009), 7–11. On overseas influences, see Daniel T. Rodgers, *Atlantic Crossings: Social Politics in a Progressive Age* (Cambridge, MA: Harvard University Press, 1998). On the twenty-four-hour race, see Sigur E. Whitaker, *James Allison: A Biography of the Engine Manufacturer and Indianapolis 500 Cofounder* (Jefferson, NC: McFarland, 2011), 28.

3. Daniel J. Simone, "Racing, Region, and the Environment: A History of American Motorsports" (PhD diss., University of Florida, 2009), 35; Fisher to Albert L. Judson, Oct. 17, 1919, 8: 659–60, Carl Graham Fisher Papers, HistoryMiami Research Center, Miami, Florida; Annie Gilbert Coleman, "Making Time and Place at the Indy 500," *Environmental History* 16 (Apr. 2011): 328 (quotation); "Motor Racing Sport Holds Its Popularity," *NYT*, Jan. 12, 1913, XX13; "Plan to Revive Auto Classics," *NYT*, Oct. 26, 1913, S3.

4. Clay McShane, *Down the Asphalt Path: The Automobile and the American City* (New York: Columbia University Press, 1994), 34–40 (quotations); David Schuyler, *The New Urban Landscape: The Redefinition of City Form in Nineteenth-Century America* (Baltimore: Johns Hopkins University Press, 1986), 126–46; Charles Mulford Robinson, *The Improvement of Towns and Cities; or, The Practical Basis of Civic Aesthetics* (New York: G. P. Putnam's Sons, 1906), 157–58, and *Modern Civic Art; or, The City Made Beautiful*, 3rd ed. (New York: Arno, 1970), 312; Brian M. Ingrassia, "Modeling 'Civic Effectiveness' in the Midwest: Charles Mulford Robinson's Progressive Era Urban Planning, 1907–1915," in *The Sower and the Seer: Perspectives on the Intellectual History of the American Midwest* (Madison: Wisconsin Historical Society Press, 2021), 125–39. In 1911, New Yorkers considered converting the Harlem speedway for automobiles; "Autoists Want Speedway," *NYT*, July 2, 1911, C8.

5. "Statement of Purchase of 240A. from D. A. Chenoweth, et al.," "Statement of Purchase of 80A. from Kevi Munter," and Indiana Department of State Proclamation, Mar. 20, 1909, Folder "Speedway Papers," unprocessed collection, IMS; Foster, *Castles in the Sand*, 73–75; "Greatest Auto Course Planned for This City," *IndNews*, Jan. 6, 1909, 3; "Greatest Automobile Racing Track in the World

Planned," *IndNews*, Jan. 19, 1909, 13; "Early Start on Auto Show," *CT*, Jan. 24, 1909, B4; "Proposed Auto Speedway at Indianapolis, First 2-Mile Track," *CT*, Jan. 24, 1909, B4; "Indianapolis to Have the Most Remarkable Course in the World," *WP*, Jan. 31, 1909, M3; "Motor Speedway to Be Best in World," *IndyStar*, Feb. 7, 1909, 34; "Indiana's Auto Speedway," *NYT*, Feb. 8, 1909, 7; "Sure of a Motor Speedway," *CT*, Feb. 8, 1909, 14; "Big Speedway Nearly Ready," *LAT*, May 18, 1909, I6; "Indianapolis Speedway," *LAT*, May 24, 1909, I12. On lighting, see John A. Jakle, *City Lights: Illuminating the American Night* (Baltimore: Johns Hopkins University Press, 2001), 38–48. On French Lick's limited railroad connections, see maps in Clifton J. Phillips, *Indiana in Transition: The Emergence of an Industrial Commonwealth, 1880–1920* (Indianapolis: Indiana Historical Society, 1968), 227–55.

6. C. C. King, Bros. and Son General Contractors bid, Mar. 11, 1909, folder "Speedway Papers," unprocessed collection, IMS; "Motor Cup Offered Is Finest in World," *IndyStar*, Mar. 18, 1909, 7; "Speedway Work Begun," *NYT*, Apr. 4, 1909, S4 (quotation); Whitaker, *James Allison*, 49.

7. "Strang Expects Record," *IndyStar*, Mar. 21, 1909 8; "Auto Dealers Ask for Reorganization," *IndyStar*, Mar. 30, 1909, 9; "Revise Plans for Motor Speedway," *IndyStar*, Mar. 31, 1909, 9; Motor Men Meet Here," *IndyStar*, Apr. 24, 1909, 7; "Indianapolis Speedway," *LAT*, May 24, 1909, I12 (quotation); "Hold Your Hats, It's Doin' 6 Per!" *IndNews*, May 29, 1946, 26. On stadiums, see G. Edward White, *Creating the National Pastime: Baseball Transforms Itself, 1903–1953* (Princeton, NJ: Princeton University Press, 1996), 21–29.

8. "Aeronauts to Try for Balloon Title," *NYT*, May 16, 1909, S3; "Fisher Tests Speedway," *IndyStar*, May 22, 1909, 9 (quotation).

9. "New Auto Speedway Nearing Completion," *NYT*, May 2, 1909, S4.

10. Charles Leerhsen, *Blood and Smoke: A True Tale of Mystery, Mayhem, and the Birth of the Indy 500* (New York: Simon and Schuster, 2011), 22–24 (quotation); Foster, *Castles in the Sand*, 75–76; "National Balloon Race," *NYT*, Apr. 18, 1909, S1; "Championship Balloon Cup," *NYT*, May 30, 1909, S3; "Six Starters in Balloon Race from Speedway Grounds," *IndSun*, June 3, 1909, 6; "Nine Balloons Start Flight," *Atlanta Constitution*, June 6, 1909, B4. On ACA, see Tom D. Crouch, *The Eagle Aloft: Two Centuries of the Balloon in America* (Washington, DC: Smithsonian Institution Press, 1983), 532.

11. "Aeronauts to Try for Balloon Title," *NYT*, May 16, 1909, S3; "Participants in the Balloon Race," *IndSun*, June 3, 1909, 6; "Race Balloons Fly by Night," *CT*, June 6, 1909, 1; "Balloons Preparing for National Race at Indianapolis and Local Contestant," *Atlanta Constitution*, June 7, 1909, 7; Joseph J. Corn, *The Winged Gospel: America's Romance with Aviation, 1900–1950* (New York: Oxford University Press, 1983), 114 (quotation). On Glidden, see Tammy Ingram, *Dixie Highway: Road Building and the Making of the Modern South, 1900–1930* (Chapel Hill: University of North Carolina Press, 2014), 38–39.

12. "Asks Permission to Lay Pipe," *IndNews*, Feb. 25, 1909, 8; "Speedway Work Begun," *NYT*, Apr. 4, 1909, S4; "Will Test Gas Pipes," *IndyStar*, May 21, 1909, 9;

"Special Service," *IndSun*, June 3, 1909, 4; "Interesting Is Start of Balloon Race," *IndSun*, June 4, 1909, 6 (quotation); "Six Huge Gas Bags Fly the Skies for Prize Cup," *IndyStar*, June 6, 1909, 9; Indianapolis Gas Company, "Talks on Gas, No. 37," advertisement, *IndyStar*, June 7, 1909, 4.

13. "National Balloon Race Has Many Entries," *Atlanta Constitution*, Mar. 7, 1909, D6; "Championship Balloon Cup," *NYT*, May 30, 1909, S3; "Six Starters in Balloon Race from Speedway Grounds," *IndSun*, June 3, 1909, 6; "Interesting Is Start"; "Nine Balloons Race from Indianapolis," *NYT*, June 6, 1909, 1; "Nine Balloons Start Flight"; James Craig Reinhardt, *The Indianapolis 500: Inside the Greatest Spectacle in Racing* (Bloomington: Red Lightning Books/Indiana University Press, 2019), 10.

14. "Balloons Tug at Leashes Ready for a Great Race," *IndSun*, June 5, 1909, 1; Foster, *Castles in the Sand*, 76; "Race Balloons Fly by Night," *CT*, June 6, 1909, 1; "Sky High Racers," *LAT*, June 6, 1909, I1; "Nine Balloons Race from Indianapolis"; "Four Balloons Sailing South," *Atlanta Constitution*, June 7, 1909, 7; "All Balloons Come to Earth," *Atlanta Constitution*, June 8, 1909, 11; "The Indianapolis Balloon Races," *Scientific American*, June 19, 1909, 459. On sporting records, see Allen Guttmann, *From Ritual to Record: The Nature of Modern Sports*, rev. ed. (New York: Columbia University Press, 2004), 40–44.

15. "All Balloons" (quotation); "University City Balloon Wins," *Atlanta Constitution*, June 9, 1909, 5; "Indianapolis Balloon Races"; Foster, *Castles in the Sand*, 41. On rural communities' reactions, see Kristin L. Hoganson, *The Heartland: An American History* (New York: Penguin, 2019), 246–47. On Civil War balloons, see Crouch, *Eagle Aloft*, 335–69.

16. On the contests as publicity stunts, see Leerhsen, *Blood and Smoke*, 22; Foster, *Castles in the Sand*, 75–76, 92. On the Wrights, see Jenifer Van Vleck, *Empire of the Air: Aviation and the American Ascendancy* (Cambridge, MA: Harvard University Press, 2013), 18.

17. "Balloons to Play Part in New Arctic Dash," *Miami Herald*, Sept. 8, 1909, 1; "Balloons Will Aid Speed of the Railroads," *Miami Herald*, Sept. 10, 1909, 1; "Kurzon [*sic*] Explains Aeroplane Flight," *IndyStar*, Oct. 17, 1909, 32 (quotation); Foster, *Castles in the Sand*, 88, 93–94; Crouch, *Eagle Aloft*, 536; Cotten Seiler, *Republic of Drivers: A Cultural History of Automobility in America* (Chicago: University of Chicago Press, 2008), 43.

18. "F.A.M. Annual Run," *LAT*, Aug. 1, 1909, VI8; "Motor Cyclists at Odds," *NYT*, Aug. 9, 1909, 5; "Hard Motorcycle Test Ends," *CT*, Aug. 12, 1909, 7; "In the Automobile World," *WP*, Aug. 13, 1909, 8; "Rain Prevents Cycle Races," *CT*, Aug. 14, 1909, 11; "Fred Huyck First in 3 Races," *CT*, Aug. 15, 1909, C2; "Ripping Clip Almost Fatal," *LAT*, Aug. 15, 1909, VI1; Scott, *Indy*, 29–36.

19. "$5,000 Cup for Indianapolis Race over 8 Feet in H[e]ight," *IndNews*, Mar. 19, 1909, 14; "Speedway Plans for Accurate Time," *IndyStar*, July 18, 1909, 21; "Great Speed Carnival on New Race Course Will Start on Thursday," *NYT*, Aug. 15, 1909, S4; "Warner's 'Newfangled' Speedometer," *Wisconsin Historical Society*, accessed Sept. 26, 2021, https://www.wisconsinhistory.org/Records/Article/CS2689.

20. "Plan Auto Road to Connect Indianapolis with Chicago," *CT*, May 29, 1909, 4; "Relic of Navy for City," *IndyStar*, July 24, 1909, 10; "Many Clubs Plan Runs," *IndyStar*, Aug. 13, 1909, 12 (quotation); "Indianapolis Speedway," *NYT*, Aug. 13, 1909, I12; "Interest in Hoosier Races," *CT*, Aug. 15, 1909, C3; "Many Cars in Run to Indianapolis," *CT*, Aug. 17, 1909, 6; "Local Autoists Leave Today," *CT*, Aug. 18, 1909, 9; "Motor Speedway Opening," *NYT*, Aug. 19, 1909, 5. Urban parking lots emerged in the 1910s (John A. Jakle and Keith A. Sculle, *Lots of Parking: Land Use in a Car Culture* [Charlottesville: University of Virginia Press, 2005], 35, 48–49, 67).

21. Cathleen Donnelly, "Claypool Hotel," in *Encyclopedia of Indianapolis*, ed. David J. Bodenhamer and Robert G. Barrows (Bloomington: Indiana University Press, 1994), 448; A. K. Sandoval-Strausz, *Hotel: An American History* (New Haven, CT: Yale University Press, 2007), 229 (quotation), 314; John A. Jakle, Keith A. Sculle, and Jefferson S. Rogers, *The Motel in America* (Baltimore: Johns Hopkins University Press, 2002).

22. "First Accident to Speedway Race Rider," *IndNews*, Aug. 18, 1909, 3; "Fall under Auto May Prove Fatal," *CT*, Aug. 18, 1909, 9; Betty Blythe, "'Wild Bob' Burman Takes First Woman around the Motor Speedway in a Racer," *IndyStar*, Aug. 18, 1909, 5 (quotation).

23. "Juvenile Auto Races at Ascot," *LAT*, May 29, 1914, III1; "Indianapolis Race Bulletins Today," *LAT*, May 30, 1913, III1; "New Speedway Proves Fast," *CT*, Aug. 16, 1909, 11; "Speedway Opens at Indianapolis," *CT*, Aug. 19, 1909, 7 (quotation).

24. "Motor Speedway Opened at Indianapolis," *CT*, Aug. 20, 1909, 7; "Two Auto Racers Hurled to Death," *CT*, Aug. 20, 1909, 1 (quotation); "Motor Speedway Opened at Indianapolis," *CT*, Aug. 20, 1909, 7; "Two in Racing Auto Killed before 10,000," *NYT*, Aug. 20, 1909, 1. See also Brian M. Ingrassia, "Shattered Nerves and Broken Bodies: Violence in Intercollegiate Football and Automotive Racing during America's Progressive Era," in *Sports and Violence: History, Theory, and Practice*, ed. Craig Hovey, Myles Werntz, and John B. White (Newcastle, UK: Cambridge Scholars, 2017), 22–34.

25. "Lower Records at Indianapolis Races," *NYT*, Aug. 21, 1909, 5; "Three More Slain by Racing Autos," *CT*, Aug. 22, 1909, 1 (quotation); "Racing Car Kills 3," *WP*, Aug. 22, 1909, 1; Remy Brassard donor contract, folder "Speedway Papers," and Prest-O-Lite Trophy gift deed, unprocessed collection, IMS.

26. "In the Automobile World," *WP*, Aug. 24, 1909, 4.

27. "Three More Killed in Auto Carnival," *NYT*, Aug. 22, 1909, 1; "Revise Rules to Prevent Killing," *CT*, Aug. 24, 1909, 9; "Explosion of Auto Tire Caused Speedway Deaths," *IndyStar*, Aug. 25, 1909, 1; "Auto Race Deaths Due to Bad Track?," *CT*, Aug. 26, 1909, 7; "Speedway Held for Deaths," *CT*, Aug. 28, 1909, 1; "Speedway Company Held," *LAT*, Aug. 28, 1909, I112; "Blame for Auto Deaths," *NYT*, Aug. 28, 1909, 1; "Coroner Blames Motor Speedway," *IndyStar*, Aug. 28, 1909, 14. The speedway appears to have paid a settlement to Jolliffe's family; see Omer D. Jolliffe suit, Johnson County, Indiana, Mar. 2, 1910, unprocessed collection, IMS.

28. "Fatal Accidents End Two Firms' Racing," *LAT*, Aug. 25, 1909, I1; "Protests against Auto Track Racing," *NYT*, Aug. 29, 1909, S4 (quotations).

29. "Motor Racing," *LAT*, Aug. 26, 1909, II4.

30. G. Henri Bogart, "An Incident of Progress" (letter to editor), *IndyStar*, Sept. 21, 1909, 6.

31. "Slaughter as a Spectacle," *NYT*, Aug. 30, 1909, 6.

32. "Fatal Accidents," I7; "Precautions in Auto Races," *CT*, Aug. 29, 1909, C3; C. H. Underwood to Indianapolis Motor Speedway, Sept. 25, 1909, folder "Speedway Papers," unprocessed collection, IMS. On Chicago's boulevards, see Paul Barrett, *The Automobile and Urban Transit: The Formation of Public Policy in Chicago, 1900–1930* (Philadelphia: Temple University Press, 1983), 70–72.

33. Untitled document, 1909, folder "Speedway Papers," unprocessed collection, IMS Museum.

34. Wabash Clay Company contract, Sept. 14, 1909, folder "Speedway Papers," unprocessed collection, IMS; Scott, *Indy*, 74–75.

35. "Speedway Will Be Paved with Brick," *IndyStar*, Sept. 16, 1909, 9; "Wanted—Male Help," *IndyStar*, Sept. 20, 1909, 9 (quotation); "Push Work on Speedway," *IndyStar*, Oct. 3, 1909, 7; "Speedway Nearly Ready," *NYT*, Dec. 6, 1909, 7.

36. "The Indianapolis Track," *Good Roads Magazine*, Sept. 1909, 320 (quotations); "Brick for the Indianapolis Speedway," *Good Roads Magazine*, Oct. 1909, 344.

37. "Speedway Paving Example for City," *IndyStar*, July 19, 1910, 3; Whitaker, *James Allison*, 66; "Speedway Will Be Paved with Brick," 9 (quotation); Logan W. Page, "The Construction of Automobile Roads," *SAE Transactions* 6 (1911): 141. On Page, see Bruce E. Seely, *Building the American Highway System: Engineers as Policy Makers* (Philadelphia: Temple University Press, 1987), 24–45.

38. Jane Fisher, *Fabulous Hoosier: A Story of American Achievement* (New York: Robert M. McBride, 1947), 64.

39. Jackson Automobile Company, advertisement, *CT*, Oct. 31, 1909, A3.

40. Buick, advertisements, *CT*, May 28, 1910, 7, and July 3, 1910, 4.

41. Firestone Tire, advertisement, *New York Times*, Aug. 22, 1909, C5; Nordyke and Marmon, advertisement, *CT*, Feb. 6, 1910, 11 (quotations); Michelin, advertisement, *CT*, June 5, 1910, 12, and *NYT*, May 28, 1910, 2; Remy Electric, advertisement, *CT*, May 31, 1911, 6; Monogram Oil, advertisement, *NYT*, June 4, 1911, C6; Studebaker, "Common Sense on the Automobile Question," advertisement, *CT*, Jan. 28, 1912, K16; Jackson Lears, *Fables of Abundance: A Cultural History of Advertising in America* (New York: Basic Books, 1994), 212–15.

42. "Plan Big Motordrome on Jersey Meadows," *NYT*, Aug. 29, 1909, S4 (quotation); "Motor Speedway for Detroit?," *Detroit Free Press*, Oct. 23, 1909, 8; "$500,000 Motor Speedway for Detroit Almost Sure," *Detroit Free Press*, Oct. 24, 1909, 17; "Local Speedway for Autos," *CT*, Nov. 17, 1909, 14; "Two Tickets in Motor Club," *CT*, Nov. 21, 1909, C4; Brian M. Ingrassia, "Rousing Sentiment for Good Roads: The Spectacles of Atlanta's 1909 Automobile Week," *Georgia Historical Quarterly* 102, no. 1 (Spring 2018): 25–58.

43. "Precautions"; "Speedway Will Be Paved with Brick," 9; "Carl Fisher Here," *LAT*, Nov. 7, 1909, VII1; "Finish Speedway This Week," *CT*, Dec. 6, 1909, 14.

44. "Aviators at Indianapolis," *NYT*, Sept. 4, 1909, 4; "Current Notes Picked Up from Sporting Arena," *WP*, Sept. 19, 1909, S4; "Curtiss Will Fly Here Next Month," *IndyStar*, Oct. 13, 1909, 10; "Wins Honor of Naming Bumbaugh's Dirigible Balloon," *IndyStar*, Nov. 15, 1909, 5.

45. "Kurzon [*sic*] Explains" (quotations); "Aviation Meet Opens To-Day," *NYT*, June 13, 1910, 2. On neurasthenia, see David G. Schuster, *Neurasthenic Nation: America's Search for Health, Happiness, and Comfort, 1869–1920* (New Brunswick, NJ: Rutgers University Press, 2011), 1; Gail Bederman, *Manliness and Civilization: A Cultural History of Gender and Race in the United States, 1880–1917* (Chicago: University of Chicago Press, 1995), 84–92; Brian M. Ingrassia, *The Rise of Gridiron University: Higher Education's Uneasy Alliance with Football* (Lawrence: University Press of Kansas, 2012), 72–74.

46. "Aeroplane Flight Next Week," *IndNews*, Dec. 9, 1909, 12; "Aeroplane Fails to Fly Because of Balky Motor," *IndyStar*, Dec. 17, 1909, 6; "Designs Aerial Attire," *IndyStar*, Dec. 19, 1909, 23 (quotations).

47. "State Executive to Lay Gold Brick," *IndyStar*, Dec. 16, 1909, 8; "Motor Speedway Races," *NYT*, Dec. 17, 1909, 13; "Speed Trials Start Today," *CT*, Dec. 17, 1909, 17; "Aitken Shatters Many Auto Marks," *CT*, Dec. 18, 1909, 10; "New Speed Records for National Cars," *NYT*, Dec. 18, 1909, 11; "Strang Cuts Auto Record at Indianapolis Speedway," *CT*, Dec. 19, 1909, C1; "Strang Breaks World's Record," *NYT*, Dec. 19, 1909, S4; "Smashes Auto Mark," *WP*, Dec. 19, 1909, S2; "Speedway Faster Than Ever, Say Visiting Chicago Men," *CT*, Dec. 20, 1909, 14; "Hold Your Hats, It's Doin' 6 Per!" *IndNews*, May 29, 1946, 26; Hek, "Some Offside Plays," *CT*, Dec. 19, 1909, C1 (quotation).

48. Willis S. Thompson, editorial, *IndSun*, Jan. 10, 1910, 8 (quotations); Will H. Brown, "Motor Car Industry Is Boon to Entire Country," *IndSun*, July 9, 1910, 7. On discourses about automobility and health, see Brian Ladd, *Autophobia: Love and Hate in the Automotive Age* (Chicago: University of Chicago Press, 2008), 18–20; Reynold M. Wik, *Henry Ford and Grass-Roots America* (Ann Arbor: University of Michigan Press, 1972), 23–27.

49. "Prominent Citizens Praise Big Motor Speedway Recently Dedicated," *IndyStar*, Aug. 29, 1909, 13.

50. "Development of the Hoosier Capital from a Stage Coach Station to One of the Country's Greatest Motoring and Aviation Centers," *IndNews*, June 11, 1910, 15.

51. "Looks for More Speed," *IndyStar*, Dec. 19, 1909, 30 (quotation); Scott, *Indy*, 83.

52. "Speedway Promoters Would Like to Stage Olympian Games," *IndSun*, Oct. 11, 1909, 6; Willis S. Thompson, editorial, *IndSun*, Jan. 10, 1910, 8 (quotations); "Speedway Brings Fame," *IndSun*, Jan. 31, 1910, 14. On turn-of-the-century bigness, see Michael Tavel Clarke, *These Days of Large Things: The Culture of Size in*

America, 1865–1930 (Ann Arbor: University of Michigan Press, 2007). On the Olympics, see Mark Dyerson, *Making the American Team: Sport, Culture, and the Olympic Experience* (Urbana: University of Illinois Press, 1998).

53. "Attracts National Events," *Washington* (IN) *Gazette*, Oct. 16, 1909, 2 (quotation). On world's fairs, see Robert W. Rydell, *All the World's a Fair: Visions of Empire at American International Expositions, 1876–1916* (Chicago: University of Chicago Press, 1984).

54. "Speedway Brings Fame," *IndSun*, Jan. 31, 1910, 14 (quotation); "Increases Value of Speed Trophy," *IndyStar*, Apr. 21, 1910, 9.

55. "Los Angeles Track," *NYT*, Jan. 16, 1910, C6; "Wooden Saucer Track for Motors at Los Angeles, Latest Incentive to Speed," *NYT*, Mar. 27, 1910, S4 (quotation); "Motor Cars to Whiz on Los Angeles Track," *Atlanta Constitution*, Apr. 8, 1910, 11; "Automobile Gossip," *Atlanta Constitution*, Apr. 24, 1910, 8B. On board tracks, see Allen E. Brown, ed., *The History of America's Speedways: Past and Present,* 3rd ed. (Comstock Park, MI: America's Speedways, 2003), 39–46.

56. "Chicago Motorists Will Be Out in Force Today," *CT*, Apr. 3, 1910, I7; "Motorists Will Have Work Cut Out in Economy Run to be Held Thursday," *CT*, Apr. 24, 1910, C4; "Thursday Will Be Finest Day of All the Year for Motorists," *CT*, July 10, 1910, B5; "Indianapolis Track Fast," *NYT*, Apr. 24, 1910, S4. On Hawthorne, see Steven A. Riess, *City Games: The Evolution of American Urban Society and the Rise of Sports* (Urbana: University of Illinois Press, 1989), 184.

57. "Dates for Hoosier Speedway," *CT*, Jan. 16, 1901, C4; "Auto Driver Beall Fractures Rib," *NYT*, May 27, 1910, 11; "Indianapolis Speedway Gets 'Round Governor's Order," *LAT*, May 29, 1910, I8 (quotation); Matthew Dennis, *Red, White, and Blue Letter Days: An American Calendar* (Ithaca, NY: Cornell University Press, 2002), 226, 234; Adam Criblez, *Parading Patriotism: Independence Day Celebrations in the Urban Midwest, 1826–1876* (DeKalb: Northern Illinois University Press, 2014), 119, 122.

58. "More than 300 Flower Bedecked Motor Cars Will Parade Gayly over Chicago's Boulevard System Next Saturday Afternoon," *CT*, May 1, 1910, I5; "Vibrant Groans of the Chugging Racers Will Lure Motor Fans from Chicago to Indianapolis' Reconstructed Speedway This Week," *CT*, May 22, 1910, I5; "Auto Motors Hum in Wait for Flag," *IndyStar*, May 22, 1910, 11. To compare early-twentieth-century drives with later ones, see Hal Foust, "1911 Auto Trip Is a Breeze Today," *CT*, Aug. 7, 1961, 22.

59. "Cars Hum around Hoosier Track," *CT*, May 27, 1910, 15; "Row Mars Racing on Big Speedway," *CT*, May 28, 1910; "Two Winning Pilots in Motor Races at Indianapolis Speedway," *CT*, May 28, 1910, 9; "Many New Records at Indianapolis," *NYT*, May 28, 1910, 11; "New Automobile Records," *WP*, May 28, 1910, 2.

60. "Big Motor Race to Harroun," *CT*, May 29, 1910, C1; "Harroun in Marmon Wins Big Contest," *NYT*, May 29, 1910, S4; "Motor Records Go by Board," *CT*, May 31, 1910, 15; "Chilly Spring Breezes Have Not Stopped Motor Tourists," *CT*, June 5, 1910, 15.

61. "Plans Trip Abroad for Aerial Meet," *IndyStar,* Feb. 15, 1910, 8; "Big Aviation Meet for Indianapolis," *NYT,* Apr. 3, 1910, S2; "Indianapolis Will Make Air History," *IndyStar,* May 8, 1910, 31; "Development of the Hoosier Capital," *IndNews,* June 11, 1910, 15; "Wright Craft to Maneuver," *LAT,* June 12, 1910, VII1; "Try Indianapolis Course," *NYT,* June 12, 1910, 2; "World Record Won by Wright Pupil," *NYT,* June 14, 1910, 9; "Highest Flight," *LAT,* June 14, 1910, I1; "Sky Pilot Fails in Record," *CT,* June 15, 1910, 13; "Brookins Braves a Storm," *NYT,* June 16, 1910, 4; "Brookins in Airship Soars 4,503 Feet," *NYT,* June 18, 1910, 1; "Aero Glides 2 Miles," *WP,* June 18, 1910, 1; "The Aviation Meet at Indianapolis," *Scientific American,* June 25, 1910, 519; "A Novel Wind Wagon," *Scientific American,* July 23, 1910, 64; Scott, *Indy,* 113–31; Jane Fisher, *Fabulous Hoosier,* 24 (quotation).

62. "Flying Now the King of Sports," *WP,* Aug. 7, 1910, M3.

63. "Nine Balloonists to Start," *NYT,* Sept. 16, 1910, 5; "Balloons Start in Distance Sail," *CT,* Sept. 18, 1910, 2; "Balloons in Race Pass over Pittsburg[h]," *NYT,* Sept. 19, 1910, 1; untitled article, *NYT,* Sept. 20, 1910, 1; "Harmon and Other Balloonists Safe," *NYT,* Sept. 21, 1910, 5. On the vertical city, see Jeremiah B. C. Axelrod, *Inventing Autopia: Dreams and Visions of the Modern Metropolis in Jazz Age Los Angeles* (Berkeley: University of California Press, 2008), 142–48; Tom Standage, *A Brief History of Motion: From the Wheel, to the Car, to What Comes Next* (New York: Bloomsbury, 2021), 110–11.

64. "Cobe Cup Contest at Indianapolis," *NYT,* June 5, 1910, X10; "Automobilists Plan Huge Club Run and Week-End Tour to See Cobe Cub Race on Indianapolis Speedway," *CT,* June 19, 1910, 15; "New Auto Records at Indianapolis," *NYT,* July 2, 1910, 8; "Marks Fall in Motor Meet," *CT,* July 2, 1910, 9; "Three Events Eagerly Anticipated by Motorists: Elgin Race, Cobe Contest, and Reliability Run," *CT,* July 3, 1910, B7; "Dawson Drives Winning Cobe Car," *CT,* July 5, 1910, 15; "Hearne Is Speedway Star," *CT,* Sept. 4, 1910, C1; "Hearne Winner of Free-for-All," *NYT,* Sept. 4, 1910, C8.

65. Mia Bay, *Traveling Black: A Story of Race and Resistance* (Cambridge, MA: Belknap, 2021), 107. On Black respectability, see Louis Moore, *I Fight for a Living: Boxing and the Battle for Black Manhood, 1880–1915* (Urbana: University of Illinois Press, 2017), 110–11.

66. "Johnson in Shape for Early Battle," *IndyStar,* Nov. 16, 1909, 8; "Johnson Eager to Join Auto Racers," *IndyStar,* Nov. 19, 1909, 12; Walter H. Eckersall, "Johnson to Be Motor Pilot," *CT,* July 10, 1910, C2 (Johnson quotation); "Jack Johnson to Drive," *WP,* July 24, 1910, 8 (Chevrolet quotation and Burman quotation); H. G. Copeland, "Gossip of the Automobilists and Notes of the Trade," *NYT,* July 24, 1910, C8; "Refuse Johnson's Request," *WP,* July 27, 1910, 8; "Johnson Barred off Speedway," *NYT,* July 28, 1910, 10. On Johnson's career and Reno, see Randy Roberts, *Papa Jack: Jack Johnson and the Era of White Hopes* (New York: Free Press, 1983), 89–114; Theresa Runstedtler, *Jack Johnson, Rebel Sojourner: Boxing in the Shadow of the Global Color Line* (Berkeley: University of California Press, 2012). On baseball's color line, see Adrian Burgos Jr., *Playing America's Game: Baseball, Latinos, and the*

Color Line (Berkeley: University of California Press, 2007), 53–67; Ryan A. Swanson, *When Baseball Went White: Reconstruction, Reconciliation, and Dreams of a National Pastime* (Lincoln: University of Nebraska Press, 2014). On horseracing, see James C. Nicholson, *The Kentucky Derby: How the Run for the Roses Became America's Premier Sporting Event* (Lexington: University Press of Kentucky, 2012), 33–41; Katherine C. Mooney, *Race Horse Men: How Slavery and Freedom Were Made at the Racetrack* (Cambridge, MA: Harvard University Press, 2014).

67. "Jeffries and Party Visit Indiana's Big Auto Race Track," *IndyStar,* Nov. 28, 1909, 22; "James J. Jeffries and Party at the Indianapolis Motor Speedway," *LAT,* Jan. 2, 1910, VI9; Scott, *Indy,* 77.

68. "Oldfield Introduces His Auto at Cheyenne," *IndNews,* May 12, 1910, 12; "Brick Tracks Dot U.S. in All Parts," *IndyStar,* June 5, 1910, 27; "Speedway for Denver," *NYT,* July 10, 1910, S4; "Plans Motor Speedway," *NYT,* Oct. 9, 1910, XX7 (quotation); "Louisville Plans Motor Speedway," *IndyStar,* Dec. 28, 1910, 9; Brian M. Ingrassia, "Speed Attractions: Urban Mobility and Automotive Spectacle in pre–World War I Amarillo," *Southwestern Historical Quarterly* 123, no. 1 (July 2019): 60–86.

69. "25,000 in Auto Racers," *NYT,* Sept. 8, 1910, 10; "Twenty Cars Ready for Vanderbilt Cup Race," *CT,* Sept. 25, 1910, H4; "Plans Great Speed Race," *WP,* Nov. 13, 1910, A2; "To Make Race History," *NYT,* Dec. 18, 1910, C6 (quotation); "Steam Cars May Compete in Races," *NYT,* Dec. 25, 1910, C8.

70. "Guard Lives of Spectators," *NYT,* Dec. 11, 1910, C8; "Speedway Praised by Road Builders," *IndyStar,* Jan. 2, 1911, 10.

Chapter 3. Speed Carnivals

1. "Three More Killed in the Auto Races," *Des Moines Register,* Aug. 22, 1909, 1; "Sings Praises of Daring Mechanics," *IndyStar,* Jan. 1, 1911, 16; "Speedy Card for Piepan," *LAT,* Jan. 8, 1911, VII7; "Dawson to Drive in $25,000 Race," *NYT,* Mar. 19, 1911, S6.

2. Al Bloemker, *500 Miles to Go: The History of the Indianapolis Speedway* (New York: Coward-McCann, 1961), 11–12 (quotation); concessions contract, July 1909, folder "Indianapolis Motor Speedway," unprocessed collection, IMS.

3. "Five Thousand Chicagoans Will Witness Indianapolis Race," *CT,* May 28, 1911, 15 (quotation); "Facts about Indianapolis Speedway," *CT,* May 30, 1911, 6B; "Crowd Biggest in Station's History," *IndNews,* May 31, 1911, 12; "Will Hold Annual Event," *IndyStar,* June 3, 1911, 9; Nicholas W. Sacco, "The Grand Army of the Republic, the Indianapolis 500, and the Struggle for Memorial Day in Indiana, 1868–1923," *Indiana Magazine of History* 111, no. 4 (Dec. 2015): 365–66.

4. William Cronon, *Nature's Metropolis: Chicago and the Great West* (New York: Norton, 1991); Aaron Shapiro, *The Lure of the North Woods: Cultivating Tourism in the Upper Midwest* (Minneapolis: University of Minnesota Press, 2013); Colin Fisher, *Urban Green: Nature, Recreation, and the Working Class in Industrial Chicago* (Chapel Hill: University of North Carolina Press, 2015); Brian Hoffman,

Naked: A Cultural History of American Nudism (New York: New York University Press, 2015), 10, 53–54. On midways, see Robert W. Rydell, *All the World's a Fair: Visions of Empire at American International Expositions, 1876–1916* (Chicago: University of Chicago Press, 1984); James Gilbert, *Perfect Cities: Chicago's Utopias of 1893* (Chicago: University of Chicago Press, 1991); Gail Bederman, *Manliness and Civilization: A Cultural History of Gender and Race in the United States, 1880–1917* (Chicago: University of Chicago Press, 1995); Robin F. Bachin, *Building the South Side: Urban Space and Civic Culture in Chicago, 1890–1919* (Chicago: University of Chicago Press, 2004).

5. "Auto Club Lists Four Early Runs," *CT*, Mar. 16, 1911, 20; "Chicago Motorists Welcome," *CT*, Mar. 19, 1911, 7; John G. DeLong, "Start Work on Elgin Course," *CT*, Apr. 18, 1911, 23; DeLong, "Auto Club to LaPorte Today," *CT*, May 13, 1911, 10; DeLong, "National Circuit in Modified Form This Year," *CT*, May 14, 1911, 15; "Motors to Run to Milwaukee in Gasoline Economy Test," *CT*, May 21, 1911, 15; "Speedway Marks Highways," *IndyStar*, May 24, 1911, 9; DeLong, "Racers Qualify for Long Grind," *CT*, May 27, 1911, 13; "Five Thousand Chicagoans Will Witness Indianapolis Race," *CT*, May 28, 1911, 15; "Chicago Hosts Are Off to Race," *CT*, May 30, 1911, 6A.

6. "Plan Loop System to Avert Accidents," *IndyStar*, May 28, 1911, 28; "Chicago Hosts," (quotation). On clay roads and Eno, see Christopher Wells, *Car Country: An Environmental History* (Seattle: University of Washington Press, 2013), 69–71, 92.

7. John G. DeLong, "Hoosier Meet to Set New Record," *CT*, May 4, 1911, 22; "Entry Blanks Are Out for the Annual Algonquin Hill Climb," *CT*, May 7, 1911, 17; "Prepare for Rush at Indianapolis," *NYT*, May 15, 1911, 9; "Special Train for Indianapolis," *NYT*, May 16, 1911, 11; "Speedway Race Is Magnet for Fans," *IndyStar*, May 28, 1911, 28; "Vanguard of Motor Army Throngs City," *IndyStar*, May 29, 1911, 1; "Autos Ready for Race of Decade," *NYT*, May 29, 1911, 7; John G. DeLong, "Save Racing Car from Oil Blaze," *CT*, May 29, 1911, 12; "Train and Trolley Bear in Thousands," *IndNews*, May 30, 1911, 1; "Burman Lowers Speedway Records," *NYT*, May 30, 1911, 12; "Speed Thrills at Great Race," *LAT*, May 31, 1911, III3; "Indianapolis Meeting of the American Chemical Society," *Science* 33, no. 861 (June 30, 1911): 989.

8. Fred J. Wagner, "More Interest in Road Racing," *NYT*, Jan. 7, 1912, XX2; "Racing Drivers' Features," *NYT*, Mar. 17, 1912, C12; "Autos for Sweepstakes," *NYT*, May 16, 1911, 11 (quotation).

9. "Auto Race Circuit Is Now Assured," *NYT*, Mar. 5, 1911, C8; "National Circuit Automobile Dates," *NYT*, May 11, 1911, 8.

10. "Writes City's Name in Motor Archives," *IndyStar*, Feb. 26, 1911, 17; "Cobb Tries for Barney's Mark," *LAT*, Apr. 16, 1911, VII3; Reed L. Parker, "Plans for Indianapolis Memorial Day Motor Races Foreshadow Most Thrilling Event in History of Automobiling," *CT*, May 19, 1912, A7 (Parker quotation); John G. DeLong, "Forty Starters Awaiting Signal in Auto Contest," *CT*, May 30, 1911, 6A (DeLong quotation). On vaudeville, see Robert W. Snyder, *The Voice of the City: Vaudeville and Popular Culture in New York* (New York: Oxford University Press, 1989), 35–37;

Kathryn J. Oberdeck, *The Evangelist and the Impresario: Religion, Entertainment, and Cultural Politics in America, 1884–1914* (Baltimore: Johns Hopkins University Press, 1999), 194–98; David Monod, *Vaudeville and the Making of Modern Entertainment, 1890–1925* (Chapel Hill: University of North Carolina Press, 2020).

11. "Two Interclub Matches and Hill Climb Scheduled for June," *CT*, June 2, 1912, B7 (quotation); Reed L. Parker, "Plans for Great Auto Classic to Be Set in Motion on New Year's Day," *CT*, Dec. 29, 1912, B7.

12. "Dramatis Personae of the Speed Spectacle: No. 8—Ralph De Palma, Mercedes," *CT*, June 4, 1916, E6; 1913 Official Program, Eddie V. Rickenbacker Collection (unprocessed), IMS.

13. Walter H. Eckersall, "It's Hard to Change the Natural Gait," *CT*, May 16, 1911, 16; "Motorists to See Star Boxing Card," *IndyStar*, May 24, 1911, 9; "Ready for the 500 Mile Sweepstakes, *Miami Herald*, May 29, 1911, 1; "McFarland at Indianapolis," *NYT*, May 19, 1912, C6; "Mayor to Allow Boxing Show," *WP*, Apr. 12, 1914, 52; "Can't Hold Bouts at Indianapolis," *CT*, May 22, 1915, 11; "Boxing Ban in Indianapolis," *NYT*, May 23, 1915, S2 (quotation). On boxing's color line, see Meg Frisbee, *Counterpunch: The Cultural Battles over Heavyweight Prizefighting in the American West* (Seattle: University of Washington Press, 2016), 127–54; Louis Moore, *I Fight for a Living: Boxing and the Battle for Black Manhood, 1880–1915* (Urbana: University of Illinois Press, 2017), 140.

14. "Oldfield Quits Racing Game," *CT*, Mar. 2, 1911, 11; "Moross Buys Oldfield's Autos," *NYT*, Mar. 2, 1911, 10; "Race for Crown as Speedway King Comes Off Today," *CT*, May 30, 1911, 6A; "Oldfield Barred at Indianapolis," *NYT*, Jan. 5, 1912, 10; "In the Automobile World," *WP*, Jan. 6, 1912, 3; "Oldfield to Drive at Indianapolis," *NYT*, Apr. 3, 1914, 9. On Oldfield-Johnson, see Randy Roberts, *Papa Jack: Jack Johnson and the Era of White Hopes* (New York: Free Press, 1983), 119–20; Thomas H. Pauly, *Game Faces: Five Early American Champions and the Sports They Changed* (Lincoln: University of Nebraska Press, 2012), 174–76.

15. "Plan Loop System to Avert Accidents," *IndyStar*, May 28, 1911, 28; "Vanguard of Motor Army Throngs City," *IndyStar*, May 29, 1911, 1; "Pickpockets in Crowd Make Few Big Hauls," *IndNews*, May 31, 1911, 13 (quotation); "Visitors Victims of Bold 'Crooks'," *IndyStar*, May 31, 1911, 13; "Pickpockets Have No Chance at 'Leathers'," *IndNews*, May 30, 1912, 9.

16. Barney Oldfield, "Dread of Terrible Accidents Supercharges Speedway Air," *LAT*, May 28, 1911; "Gossip of the Automobilists and Notes of the Trade," *NYT*, May 28, 1911, C8; "Locate Death Curve," *WP*, May 28, 1911, 10; "Motor Racers Defy Fear; Jest at Death Prospect," *CT*, May 30, 1911, 6B (quotation).

17. "Chasing Death and a World's Record around the Rim of a Saucer!" *CT*, May 28, 1911, G4.

18. Walter H. Eckersall, "Skill of Pilot Big Factor," *CT*, May 30, 1911, 6B.

19. Reed L. Parker, "Plans Being Pushed for Big Elgin Road Races," *CT*, Apr. 6, 1913, B10 (Jenkins), and "Impossible to Pick the Winner of the 500 Mile Memorial Day Race," *CT*, May 25, 1913, B7 (De Palma).

20. Ralph De Palma, "Perils of Drivers in Auto Racing," *NYT*, Jan. 15, 1911, C8 (quotations); "Ralph De Palma, the Speed Idol, Will Race in the Big Indianapolis Event," *CT*, Apr. 20, 1913, B11; John G. DeLong, "Famous Drivers and Fast Cars Will Line Up in Speedway Race," *CT*, May 4, 1913, B10; Reed L. Parker, "Bragg's Machine Hits Top Speed," *CT*, May 26, 1914, 16; Brian M. Ingrassia, *The Rise of Gridiron University: Higher Education's Uneasy Alliance with Big-Time Football* (Lawrence: University Press of Kansas, 2012), 75.

21. "Two Men Injured Speeding Motor," *CT*, May 25, 1911, 13; DeLong, "Save Racing Car"; "Race for Crown"; "Speeders an Odd Lot," *WP*, Feb. 11, 1912, 16 (quotation); Reed L. Parker, "A Smile When Hurt Often Turns the Tide of Battle in Your Favor," *CT*, May 30, 1912, 10. On gambling, see Jackson Lears, *Something for Nothing: Luck in America* (New York: Viking, 2003), 187–227.

22. "Insurance against Rain," *NYT*, Apr. 23, 1911, C8; "Brokers Refuse Rain Risk for Elgin Stock Car Races," *CT*, Apr. 24, 1911, 17; "Gambler's Chance to Win," *WP*, Feb. 2, 1913, M8. On insurance in sports, see Ingrassia, *Rise of Gridiron University*, 166. On weather prediction, see Jamie L. Pietruska, *Looking Forward: Prediction and Uncertainty in Modern America* (Chicago: University of Chicago Press, 2017).

23. "Two Days' Racing," *Cincinnati Enquirer*, Apr. 20, 1911, 9.

24. "Disbrow Discusses Indianapolis Race," *NYT*, Mar. 5, 1911, C8 (quotation); "Pope Entered in Sweepstakes," *LAT*, Apr. 2, 1911, VII5; "Marmon Driver Punches Bag," *LAT*, Apr. 23, 1911, VII4; John G. DeLong, "Oil on Speedway to Be Burned Off," *CT*, May 28, 1911, C1; "Speed Kings Seek Country," *CT*, May 30, 1911, 6A. On football's rural retreats, see Ingrassia, *Rise of Gridiron University*, 88.

25. "To Fight Speedway Bar," *IndyStar*, Aug. 8, 1909, 29; "De Palma on Driving," *NYT*, Jan. 15, 1911, XX4; on temperance and progressivism, see James H. Timberlake, *Prohibition and the Progressive Movement, 1900–1920* (Cambridge, MA: Harvard University Press, 1963); David E. Kyvig, *Repealing National Prohibition*, 2nd ed. (Kent, OH: Kent State University Press, 2000), 7–10.

26. "Auto Race Pilots Are Not Developed," *NYT*, Feb. 5, 1911, C8; "Nine Entries for Big Auto Event," *NYT*, Feb. 26, 1911, C8; "Race Drivers to Organize," *NYT*, Mar. 19, 1911, S6; "Drivers on Edge for Motor Test," *CT*, May 26, 1911, 13; John G. DeLong, "Racers Qualify." *CT*, May 27, 1911, 13.

27. "Race for Crown," and "$225,000 Worth of Autos Entered for Indiana Races," *CT*, May 30, 1911, 6A; "Prize List Offered in 500-Mile Race," *CT*, May 30, 1911, 6B.

28. "Bar Girl Pilot at Speedway," *CT*, Apr. 10, 1913, 14 (quotation); "Woman Barred in Speedway Race," *NYT*, Apr. 10, 1913, 9; "Bar Girl from Auto Race," *WP*, Apr. 10, 1913, 5.

29. "Woman in Auto Race," *NYT*, Jan. 27, 1914, 10 (quotations); Alice Kessler-Harris, *Out to Work: A History of Wage-Earning Women in the United States* (New York: Oxford University Press, 1982), 186–87.

30. "Drivers Set for Speedway Trial," *CT*, May 23, 1911, 12; "Two Men Injured in Speeding Motor," *CT*, May 25, 1911, 13; "Forty-Four Cars Will Start in India-

napolis," *NYT*, May 28, 1911, C8; "Marmon Car Wins; Death Marked Race," *NYT*, May 31, 1911, 13 (quotations); "Cotton to Deaden Noise," *WP*, June 11, 1911, E10.

31. "'My Last Race; Too Dangerous'—Harroun," *CT*, May 31, 1911, 22.

32. "Ralph De Palma, the Speed Idol, Will Race in the Big Indianapolis Event," *CT*, Apr. 20, 1913, B11.

33. "Ready for the 500 Mile Sweepstakes," *Miami Herald*, May 29, 1911, 1; "2,000 to Record Auto Race," *CT*, May 30, 1911, 6C (quotations); "Forty-Four Cars Will Start in Indianapolis," *NYT*, May 28, 1911, C8; "Protest Speedway Race," *NYT*, June 1, 1911, 8; "Why Stock Car Racing Will Die," *NYT*, Aug. 6, 1911, C8; "How Accurate Timing of Auto Race Is Secured," *NYT*, June 6, 1915, X10.

34. Barney Oldfield, "Big Game Dead, Says Oldfield," *LAT*, June 6, 1911, III1.

35. "One Dead, 7 Hurt in Big Auto Race; Harroun Victor," *CT*, May 31, 1911, 1; "Clergy Protests against Indianapolis Motor Races," *CT*, Nov. 7, 1911, 11 (quotations).

36. Alex J. Sloan, "Speed-Mad Men Thrilled by Cars," *LAT*, June 7, 1911, III3.

37. Joe S. Jackson, "Sporting Facts and Fancies," *WP*, May 19, 1911, 8.

38. "Pilots for Motor Racing Reforms," *NYT*, June 12, 1911, 20; "First Entrants in the Elgin Automobile Races Are Announced," *CT*, June 25, 1911, B7; "Abandons Dirt Tracks," *NYT*, July 2, 1911, C8; "Why Stock Car Racing Will Die," *NYT*, Aug. 6, 1911, C8; Fred J. Wagner, "Must Keep Racing above Suspicion," *NYT*, Aug. 13, 1911, C8 (quotation); Fred J. Wagner, "Abolish Racing on Mile Dirt Tracks," *NYT*, Sept. 24, 1911, C8.

39. "Track and Road Races in Favor," *NYT*, June 4, 1911, C8; "Stock Touring Car Race," *NYT*, Apr. 12, 1915, 7 (quotation). On football, see Ingrassia, *Rise of Gridiron University*, 55–63.

40. Carl Fisher, "High Speed Real Test of Motors," *IndyStar*, May 26, 1912, 51.

41. Henderson Motor Car ad, *CT*, May 26, 1912, A4; National Motor Vehicle ad, *CT*, June 4, 1912, 9; Michelin ad, *CT*, Oct. 27, 1912, 8.

42. "Motor Speedway Gives Vitrified Bricks a Test," *CT*, Mar. 10, 1912, K1; "First Clay Show Marks New Era in Building Industry," *CT*, Mar. 10, 1912, K1 (quotation); Reed L. Parker, "Longer Race for Speedway Prize," *CT*, May 10, 1912, 8.

43. Wagner, "Must Keep Racing above Suspicion"; "$50,000 Auto Race," *NYT*, Nov. 5, 1911, C8; "Safety for Drivers and Spectators the Watchword at Speedway," *IndNews*, May 11, 1912, 11.

44. "Motor Enthusiasts Turn to Good Roads Conference," *CT*, Mar. 10, 1912, B7; "Speedway Is Motor Mecca," *LAT*, Mar. 17, 1912, VII3; Michael E. Fein, *Paving the Way: New York Road Building and the American State, 1880–1956* (Lawrence: University Press of Kansas, 2008).

45. Fred J. Wagner, "Racing Aids Good Roads Propaganda," *NYT*, Oct. 29, 1911, C8; "Lincoln Memorial Public Highway," *NYT*, Feb. 11, 1912, C11; Reed L. Parker, "Racing on Wane?," *CT*, Apr. 7, 1912, B7; "Indiana Classed as Poor Roads State," *IndNews*, Sept. 24, 1912, 13; L. M. Steffens, "Route Map and Log to and from In-

dianapolis Races," *CT*, May 23, 1915, E6; Mark S. Foster, *Castles in the Sand: The Life and Times of Carl Graham Fisher* (Gainesville: University Press of Florida, 2000), 101–2; "Progressive Party Platform of 1912," *American Presidency Project*, Nov. 5, 1912, https://www.presidency.ucsb.edu/documents/progressive-party-platform -1912.

46. "$10,000 Auto Race on Labor Day," *NYT*, Nov. 2, 1911, 12; "$50,000 Auto Race," *NYT*, Nov. 5, 1911, C8; "Few Entries for Auto Sweepstakes," *NYT*, Mar. 31, 1912, C10; "Many Changes in Auto Racing Rules," *NYT*, Apr. 28, 1912, X12; Reed L. Parker, "Longer Race for Speedway Prize," *CT*, May 10, 1912, 8; Fisher, "High Speed Real Test"; Brian M. Ingrassia, "Rousing Sentiment for Good Roads: The Spectacles of Atlanta's 1909 Automobile Week," *Georgia Historical Quarterly* 102, no. 1 (Spring 2018): 48.

47. "Big Demand for Speedway Boxes," *IndyStar*, Jan. 16, 1912, 9; "Famous Drivers for Sweepstakes," *NYT*, May 12, 1912, X15; "Noted Athlete Blossoms Out as Auto Salesman," *LAT*, May 25, 1912, I13; "Indianapolis Is Enthused over the 500-Mile Auto Race," *Miami Herald*, May 30, 1912, 5 (quotation); Parker, "Smile When Hurt"; "Plans Pathfinder Campaign," *LAT*, July 5, 1912, III5.

48. "Gauging Your Own Speed Is Essential to Success in Any Race," *CT*, May 31, 1912, 9 (quotations); Reed L. Parker, "Joe Dawson Wins Great Auto Race; New Record Set," *CT*, May 31, 1912, 1; "Dawson Makes New Speedway Records," *NYT*, May 31, 1912, 9; "Officials Recheck Speedway Racers," *IndNews*, May 31, 1912, 21.

49. Fred J. Wagner, "Wagner Describes Race," *NYT*, May 31, 1912, 9 (quotation); "Edythe Chapman to Reappear," *LAT*, Aug. 22, 1912, II5.

50. Reed L. Parker, "Important Lessons Learned by Manufacturers at Indianapolis," *CT*, June 9, 1912, A7; Parker, "De Palma Loses His Honors," *CT*, June 30, 1912, 11; Edward V. Rickenbacker, *Rickenbacker* (Englewood Cliffs, NJ: Prentice-Hall, 1967), 152–53 (quotation).

51. A. R. Pardington, "New York Needs Speedway Course," *NYT*, Jan. 1, 1911, C9; "Chicagoans Plan Auto Speedway," *CT*, May 30, 1911, 6D; Fred J. Wagner, "College Men Take Up Truck Building," *NYT*, Jan. 21, 1912, C8; Parker, "Important Lessons Learned"; Parker, "Elgin Road Race Decision Brings Slump in Motor Racing Circles," *CT*, July 7, 1912, A6 (quotations); "Auto Speedway for New York," *NYT*, Dec. 27, 1912, 6; "Motor Speedway Plan Is Dropped," *NYT*, Apr. 3, 1913, 7; "Auto Road Races Can Be Revived," *NYT*, Oct. 12, 1913, S5; "Plan to Revive Auto Classics," *NYT*, Oct. 26, 1913, S3.

52. William Herschell, "Speedway City, Which Carl G. Fisher Dreamed of Twenty Years Ago," *IndNews*, Apr. 13, 1929, 21.

53. W. M. Herschell, "Speedway the Horseless City, a New Idea in Industrial Centers," *IndNews*, June 15, 1912, 14 (quotations); "Factory City Is Rising Rapidly Near Speedway," *IndyStar*, Sept. 15, 1912, 29–30; Foster, *Castles in the Sand*, 55. On 1920s Los Angeles, see Jeremiah B. C. Axelrod, *Inventing Autopia: Dreams and Visions of the Modern Metropolis in Jazz Age Los Angeles* (Berkeley: University of California Press, 2009), 47–61. On Ebenezer Howard's Garden Cities, see Robert

H. Kargon and Arthur P. Molella, *Invented Edens: Techno-Cities of the Twentieth Century* (Cambridge, MA: MIT Press, 2008), 7–18. On parks and playgrounds, see Brian M. Ingrassia, "Modeling 'Civic Effectiveness' in the Midwest: Charles Mulford Robinson's Progressive Era Urban Planning, 1907–1915," in *The Sower and the Seer: Perspectives on the Intellectual History of the American Midwest*, ed. Joseph Hogan, Paul Murphy, and Gleaves Whitney (Madison: Wisconsin Historical Society Press, 2021), 125–39.

54. S. Paul O'Hara, *Gary, The Most American of All American Cities* (Bloomington: Indiana University Press, 2011), 50–51 (quotation); Heather B. Barrow, *Henry Ford's Plan for the American Suburb: Dearborn and Detroit* (DeKalb: Northern Illinois University Press, 2015), 92–102; Andrea Tone, *The Business of Benevolence: Industrial Paternalism in Progressive America* (Ithaca, NY: Cornell University Press, 1997), 91–94; Kathy Peiss, *Cheap Amusements: Working Women and Leisure in Turn-of-the-Century New York* (Philadelphia: Temple University Press, 1986).

55. James W. Loewen, "General: Indiana," *History and Social Justice*, accessed Sept. 26, 2021, https://sundown.tougaloo.edu/sundowntownsshow.php?id=910; Loewen, *Sundown Towns: A Hidden Dimension of American Racism* (New York: New Press, 2005). On race, class, and residential patterns, see David R. Roediger, *The Wages of Whiteness: Race and the Making of the American Working Class* (London: Verso, 1991), and *Working toward Whiteness: How America's Immigrants Became White: The Strange Journey from Ellis Island to the Suburbs* (New York: Basic Books, 2005).

56. A. S. Blakely, "Road across U.S. Proposed," *IndyStar*, Sept. 11, 1912, 1; "New American Road across Continent," *NYT*, Sept. 15, 1912, X11; Blakely, "Motor Club Boosts Road across U.S.," *IndyStar*, Sept. 18, 1912, 10; "Coast-to-Coast Road Is Given Big Boost," *IndNews*, Sept. 23, 1912, 17; Reed L. Parker, "Announce New Ocean to Ocean Highway," *CT*, Oct. 13, 1912, B11 (quotations); "Ocean-to-Ocean Highway," *NYT*, Nov. 24, 1912, X16.

57. Page quoted in "Welcomes Road Plan for Publicity Value," *IndyStar*, Sept. 15, 1912, 35.

58. Drake Hokanson, *The Lincoln Highway: Main Street across America* (Iowa City: University of Iowa Press, 1999), 6–7.

59. Reed L. Parker, "Announce New Ocean to Ocean Highway," *CT*, Oct. 13, 1912, B11 (quotation); "The Lincoln Highway: Reaching a Ten Million Dollar Ideal" (Detroit, MI: Lincoln Highway Association, 1914), 9: 395–400, Carl Graham Fisher Papers, HistoryMiami Research Center, Miami, Florida [hereafter, Fisher Papers].

60. "Congressmen Favor Federal Aid to Improve Country's Highways," *CT*, Feb. 16, 1913, B6; "Gilhousen to Meet Cross-Country Marmon," *LAT*, June 29, 1913, VII2; "Reed L. Parker, "Long Drive by Motorists," *CT*, July 1, 1913, 14; "Map Winter Auto Route to Pacific," *NYT*, July 23, 1913, 13; Jane Fisher, *Fabulous Hoosier: A Story of American Achievement* (New York: Robert M. McBride, 1947), 85 (quotations).

61. "Organize to Build Nation-wide Road," *IndNews*, Sept. 11, 1912, 12 (Allison quotation); Hokanson, *Lincoln Highway*, 8–13 (Hokanson quotation, 12).

62. "Boosted by the Hoosiers," *Chattanooga Daily Times*, Nov. 24, 1914, 6 (quotation); Foster, *Castles in the Sand*, 104.

63. "Way Down in Sunny Dixie They Are Boosting Good Roads Movement, More Particularly the Lincoln Tributary from Indiana to Florida," *IndNews*, Nov. 21, 1914, 13; "Indiana to Get Dixie Highway?," *CT*, Oct. 11, 1915, 8; Reed L. Parker, "Gossip of the Auto Trade," *CT*, Nov. 7, 1915, E6; "Dixie Highway Now Assured," *LAT*, Nov. 7, 1915, VI5; Fisher letters to Haines Egbert, Alex Wright, and D. C. Jenkins, Aug. 23, 1917, 4: 93–95, Fisher Papers; Foster, *Castles in the Sand*, 119–20, 126. Tammy Ingram, *Dixie Highway: Road Building and the Making of the Modern South, 1900–1930* (Chapel Hill: University of North Carolina Press, 2014), 43–52 (quotation, 48).

Chapter 4. Automotive Metropolis

1. "Many Tracks Washed Out," *IndNews*, Mar. 25, 1913, 11; "As Flames Sweep the Buildings People Jump into the Water and Drown," *Miami Herald*, Mar. 27, 1913, 1; "Vandals Plunder in Indianapolis," *Miami Herald*, Mar. 28, 1913, 1; Geoff Williams, *Washed Away: How the Great Flood of 1913, America's Most Widespread Natural Disaster, Terrorized a Nation and Changed It Forever* (New York: Pegasus, 2013), vii–ix, 157, 167–68, 172, 202; Cynthia J. Clendenon, "Flooding and Flood Control," in *Encyclopedia of Indianapolis*, ed. David J. Bodenhamer and Robert G. Barrows (Bloomington: Indiana University Press, 1994), 581–83.

2. "Roads to Auto Exhibit Are in Good Condition," *IndNews*, Mar. 25, 1913, 16; "Motor Boats Go to the Rescue," *Miami Herald*, Mar. 27, 1913, 8; "Caught in Swirling Mass of the Flood," *IndNews*, Mar. 27, 1913, 9; "Test Cars Used to Drag the Roads," *NYT*, May 11, 1913, X14; "Weidely Is Gaining Fame," *IndyStar*, May 18, 1913, 31; US Department of Agriculture, Office of Public Roads, *The Road Drag and How It Is Used*, Farmers' Bulletin 597 (Washington, DC: Government Printing Office, 1914); Kevin Rozario, *The Culture of Calamity: Disaster and the Making of Modern America* (Chicago: University of Chicago Press, 2007); Warren James Belasco, *Americans on the Road: From Autocamp to Motel, 1910–1945* (Baltimore: Johns Hopkins University Press, 1997), 8–9, 20–25.

3. "The Next Summer Meeting," *SAE Transactions* 7, pt. 2 (1912): 213; Reed L. Parker, "Plans Being Pushed for Big Elgin Road Races," *CT*, Apr. 6, 1913, B10; "How to Motor to Indianapolis Race," *NYT*, May 25, 1913, X11; "Arrest New York Autoists," *NYT*, May 28, 1913, 1; "Cross Desert to See Race," *LAT*, June 8, 1913, VII3; "How to Reach the Indianapolis Motor Speedway," 1913 Official Program, Eddie V. Rickenbacker collection, IMS [hereafter, Rickenbacker collection].

4. "Guyot to Drive a Sunbeam Car in Big Race at Indianapolis," *CT*, Feb. 16, 1913, B7; "Peugeots and Isottas for Indianapolis Race," *LAT*, Feb. 16, 1913, VII4; "Gossip in Motor Contest Field Centers around Indianapolis," *CT*, Mar. 9, 1913, B9; Reed L. Parker, "Charles P. Root Is Made the Starter for 500 Mile Sweepstakes Race," *CT*, Mar. 16, 1913, B11; "Foreign Car for Big Motor Race," *CT*, Apr. 18, 1913, 18; John G.

De Long, "Pillette Sails on Saturday," *CT*, Apr. 21, 1913, 10; De Long, "Thirty-One Cars for Motor Grind," *CT*, May 6, 1913, 10; De Long, "Trucco Entered for Motor Grind," *CT*, May 8, 1913, 10; "Great Throng for Classic," *LAT*, May 25, 1913, VII9; "Indianapolis Speed Tests," *NYT*, May 26, 1913, 8; "Indianapolis Speed Tests," *NYT*, May 26, 1913, 8. On the pagoda, see James Craig Reinhardt, *The Indianapolis 500: Inside the Greatest Spectacle in Racing* (Bloomington, IN: Red Lightning/Indiana University Press, 2019), 25.

5. "The Next Summer Meeting," *SAE Transactions* 7, pt. 2 (1912): 213; Reed L. Parker, "New Ruling Will Make Speedway Races Closer," *CT*, Apr. 27, 1913, B9.

6. "Smaller Cars for Indianapolis Race," *LAT*, Jan. 26, 1913, VII2; Reed L. Parker, "French Peugeot, Piloted by Goux, Auto Race Winner," *CT*, May 31, 1913, 13; "French Flyer First with American Cars Close Up," *LAT*, May 31, 1913, B1; "Goux, in French Car, Winner of the Five Hundred Mile Race," *Miami Herald*, May 31, 1913, 1; "Dunning Fails to Improve," *CT*, June 2, 1913, 13; Parker, "Waukesha to Be Objective Point of Interclub Race," *CT*, June 8, 1913, B6; "60,000 Can View Auto Event," *WP*, Oct. 10, 1913, 9.

7. "Congressmen Favor Federal Aid to Improve Country's Highways," *CT*, Feb. 16, 1913, B6; "Gossip in Motor Contest Field Centers around Indianapolis," *CT*, Mar. 9, 1913, B9; Reed L. Parker, "Charles P. Root Is Made the Starter for 500 Mile Sweepstakes Race," *CT*, Mar. 16, 1913, B11; John G. DeLong, "C.A.C. after Foreign Cars to Compete in the Big Elgin Race in August," *CT*, Mar. 30, 1913, B11 (quotation); "Ralph De Palma, the Speed Idol, Will Race in the Big Indianapolis Event," *CT*, Apr. 20, 1913, B11; "Laurens Enos Makes Plea for National Highway," *CT*, June 22, 1913, B8. On the 1913 convention, see Richard F. Weingroff, "The National Old Trails Road, Part 1: The Quest for a National Road," *Highway History*, updated 08/21/2018, https://www.fhwa.dot.gov/infrastructure/trails.cfm (Washington, DC: US Highway Administration, US Department of Transportation). On Dunne, see Richard Allen Morton, *Justice and Humanity: Edward F. Dunne, Illinois Progressive* (Carbondale: Southern Illinois University Press, 1997), 77. On roadbuilding, see Michael R. Fein, *Paving the Way: New York Road Building and the American State, 1880–1956* (Lawrence: University Press of Kansas, 2008). On convict labor, see Alex Lichtenstein, *Twice the Work of Free Labor: The Political Economy of Convict Labor in the New South* (London: Verso, 1996); Jeffrey Alan John, *Progressives and Prison Labor: Rebuilding Ohio's National Road during World War I* (Akron, OH: University of Akron Press, 2022).

8. "Curtailed Service Result of Strike," *IndNews*, Nov. 1, 1913, 1–2; "Fierce Car Riots in Indianapolis," *NYT*, Nov. 2, 1913, 1; "Police Idle as the Rioting Continued," *IndNews*, Nov. 3, 1913, 4; "Deputy Sheriffs Will Aid Police in Strike Duty," *Indy-Star*, Nov. 3, 1913, 1; "Indianapolis Riots Laid to Politicians," *NYT*, Nov. 4, 1913, 5; "Indianapolis Asks for State Troops," *NYT*, Nov. 6, 1913, 7; "3,000 State Troops Hold Indianapolis," *NYT*, Nov. 7, 1913, 1; Connie J. Zeigler, "Street Railway Strikes (1892 and 1913)," in *Encyclopedia of Indianapolis*, 1303–5; William Doherty, "Police Mutiny (Nov. 1913)," in *Encyclopedia of Indianapolis*, 1122–23. On the ILGWU, see

Nan Enstad, *Ladies of Labor, Girls of Adventure: Working Women, Popular Culture, and Labor Politics at the Turn of the Century* (New York: Columbia University Press, 1999), 84–118.

9. "Car Strike Ends in Indianapolis," *NYT*, Nov. 8, 1913, 10; "Indianapolis Cars Running," *NYT*, Nov. 9, 1913, 3; "Indianapolis Police Check Strike Riots," *NYT*, Dec. 2, 1913, 8; "20,000 May Strike at Indianapolis," *NYT*, Dec. 3, 1913, 5; *Report, Findings and Award of the Public Service Commission of Indiana in the Arbitration Proceedings between the Indianapolis Traction Company and Its Employees* (Indianapolis: Public Service Commission of Indiana, 1914), 2; Richard W. Worth, "Teamsters Union," in *Encyclopedia of Indianapolis*, 1325 (quotations); William Doherty, "Wallace, Harry R.," in *Encyclopedia of Indianapolis*, 1407; James R. Barrett, *Work and Community in the Jungle: Chicago's Packinghouse Workers, 1894–1922* (Urbana: University of Illinois Press, 1987), 177.

10. "Mail Service Hampered by the Car Situation," *IndNews*, Nov. 1, 1913, 2; "Special Notice," *IndNews*, Nov. 1, 1913, 25; Habich Bicycle ad, *IndyStar*, Nov. 2, 1913, 12 (quotation); "Street Car Strike Ties Up U.S. Mails," *IndyStar*, Nov. 2, 1913, 11; "Messengers Who Will Aid the News in Placing Election Returns Speedily before the Public," *IndNews*, Nov. 3, 1913, 9; "Notice to Agents," *IndNews*, Nov. 3, 1913, 12. On the 1905 Teamsters' strike, see Georg Leidenberger, *Chicago's Progressive Alliance: Labor and the Bid for Public Streetcars* (DeKalb: Northern Illinois University Press, 2006), 143–44.

11. "Auto Club Wants Streets to Be Safe," *NYT*, Dec. 25, 1913, 10 (quotation); Peter D. Norton, *Fighting Traffic: The Dawn of the Motor Age in the American City* (Cambridge, MA: MIT Press, 2008), 71–79.

12. E. R. L. "My Nearest Approach to Death Was When—," *CT*, Dec. 14, 1913, E8; L. L. R., "My Nearest Approach to Death," *CT*, Feb. 1, 1914, E8 (quotation); "Beware of Grafters Is Caution to Public," *IndNews*, May 29, 1915, 3. On industrial accidents, see Michael K. Rosenow, *Death and Dying in the Working Class, 1865–1920* (Urbana: University of Illinois Press, 2015). On dramatic death stories, see Sarah E. Igo, *The Known Citizen: A History of Privacy in Modern America* (Cambridge, MA: Harvard University Press, 2018), 32–33. See also Brian M. Ingrassia, "Shattered Nerves and Broken Bodies: Violence in Intercollegiate Football and Automotive Racing during America's Progressive Era," in *Sports and Violence: History, Theory, and Practice*, ed. Craig Hovey, Myles Werntz, and John B. White (Newcastle, UK: Cambridge Scholars, 2017), 32.

13. "Utility Cars Next to Show What the Motor Can Do," *CT*, Sept. 3, 1911, B7. On Chicago's boulevards, see Paul Barrett, *The Automobile and Urban Transit: The Formation of Public Policy in Chicago* (Philadelphia: Temple University Press, 1983), 70–72. On urban planning, see LeeAnn Lands, *The Culture of Property: Race, Class, and Housing Landscapes in Atlanta, 1880–1950* (Athens: University of Georgia Press, 2009), 58–59; Carl Smith, *The Plan of Chicago: Daniel Burnham and the Remaking of the American City* (Chicago: University of Chicago Press, 2006); John F. Bauman and Edward K. Muller, *Before Renaissance: Planning in Pittsburgh, 1889–1943* (Pittsburgh: University of Pittsburgh Press, 2006), 51–101.

14. William Doherty, "Bell, Joseph E.," in *Encyclopedia of Indianapolis*, 316–17; "To the President and Members of the Common Council," Jan. 19, 1914, folder 1, Mo711, Joseph E. Bell Papers, Indiana Historical Society, Indianapolis, Indiana [hereafter, Bell Papers]; "Department of Public Works—Cont. [Budget, 1914/1915]," Apr. 1, 1915, folder 2, Mo711, Bell Papers (quotation); Charles Mulford Robinson, *The Width and Arrangement of Streets: A Study in Town Planning* (New York: Engineering News Publishing, 1911); Kurt Culbertson, "George Edward Kessler: Landscape Architect of the American Renaissance," in *Midwestern Landscape Architecture*, ed. William H. Tischler, 99–116 (Urbana: University of Illinois Press, 2000); Robert B. Fairbanks, *For the City as a Whole: Planning, Politics, and the Public Interest in Dallas, Texas 1900–1965* (Columbus: Ohio State University Press, 1998), 25–27, 45–50; Amahia Mallea, *A River in the City of Fountains: An Environmental History of Kansas City and the Missouri River* (Lawrence: University Press of Kansas, 2018), 82–83; Clay McShane, *Down the Asphalt Path: The Automobile and the American City* (New York: Columbia University Press, 1994), 200. On antivice activism, see Brian Donovan, *White Slave Crusades: Race, Gender, and Anti-vice Activism, 1887–1917* (Urbana: University of Illinois Press, 2006). On street cleaning, see Daniel Eli Burnstein, *Next to Godliness: Confronting Dirt and Despair in Progressive Era New York City* (Urbana: University of Illinois Press, 2006).

15. "For Motorist and Motorcyclist," *CT*, Feb. 15, 1914, E8; "Auto Head Optimistic on Good Roads Prospect," *CT*, Mar. 8, 1914, E8; Reed L. Parker, "Yankees to Copy Peugeot Motor," *CT*, June 21, 1914, E8; John A. Jakle and Keith A. Sculle, *Motoring: The Highway Experience in America* (Athens: University of Georgia Press, 2008), 53; Clifton J. Phillips, *Indiana in Transition: The Emergence of an Industrial Commonwealth, 1880–1920* (Indianapolis: Indiana Historical Society, 1968), 266–70. On Fisher, see "Lawmakers Study Excise Tax Plan," *IndNews*, Feb. 20, 1917, 4; Drake Hokanson, *The Lincoln Highway: Main Street across America* (Iowa City: University of Iowa Press, 1999), 22–30.

16. "Auto Head Optimistic on Good Roads Prospect," *CT*, Mar. 8, 1914, E8; "Oldfield to Pilot Maxwell in 500 Mile Auto Classic," *CT*, Mar. 10, 1914, 16; "Foreign Drivers Coming," *NYT*, May 3, 1914, S2; Reed L. Parker, "Cars Qualify for Speedway Grind," *CT*, May 28, 1914, 15; Reed L. Parker, "Georges Boillot Hits Ninety Clip," *CT*, May 22, 1914, 15 (quotation); Parker, "All Set for the 500 Mile Race at the Indianapolis Speedway," *CT*, May 24, 1914, E9; Joe Dawson, "Driver Dawson Sees Chance for American to Win Grind," *CT*, May 30, 1914, 15.

17. "Goux Favorite at Gay Speedway," *CT*, May 30, 1914, 15.

18. Reed L. Parker, "Georges Boillot Hits Ninety Clip," *CT*, May 22, 1914, 15; "Record Time on Speedway," *NYT*, May 27, 1914, 13; Parker, "Cars Qualify for Speedway Grind," *CT*, May 28, 1914, 15; "Sets Mark in Auto," *WP*, May 28, 1914, 9; Parker, "Star Auto Pilots Throw in Clutch for Race Today," *CT*, May 30, 1914, 15 (quotation).

19. "Motor Race Special for Speedway Event," *LAT*, Mar. 15, 1914, VII2; "For Motorist and Motorcyclist," *CT*, May 24, 1914, E8; Marshall Field ad, *CT*, May 28, 1914, 16 (quotations); "Nab Motorists at South Bend," *CT*, May 30, 1914, 15;

"Tribunes Rushed to Indianapolis," *CT*, May 31, 1914, 5. On ads targeting women, see Virginia Scharff, *Taking the Wheel: Women and the Coming of the Motor Age* (Albuquerque: University of New Mexico Press, 1991), 120.

20. Reed L. Parker, "Thomas Passes All Speed Marks; Wins Wild Race," *CT*, May 31, 1914, 5; "Delage Car Wins; New Race Record," *NYT*, May 31, 1914, S3; "Sets Auto Mark," *WP*, May 31, 1914, 56; "Rene Thomas Won Five Hundred Mile Race," *Miami Herald*, May 31, 1914, 1; E. C. Watkins, "Dawson, Injured, Fights for Life," *IndyStar*, May 31, 1914, 1; "Expect Dawson to Recover," *CT*, June 2, 1914, 14.

21. "Auto Track at Hawthorne," *CT*, June 4, 1911, C2; "Germany after Race-course," *Austin Statesman*, Oct. 26, 1913, 31; Reed L. Parker, "It's Easy Enough to Make Mistakes without Assistance," *CT*, Mar. 5, 1914, 14, and "Chicago Assured Motor Speedway," *CT*, May 8, 1914, 16; "Auto Course at Hawthorne," *CT*, July 2, 1914, 14; Keene Gardiner, "Picks Chicago Men to Handle 500 Mile Race," *CT*, May 20, 1915, 11; Reed L. Parker, "Thompson Helps at Dedication of Auto Course," *CT*, June 15, 1915, 14 (quotation), and "Motor Derby Delayed Week; Strike Cause," *CT*, June 16, 1915, 13; Floyd P. Gibbons, "Resta Wins; Sets World Record," *CT*, June 27, 1915, 1; Jack Proctor, "Buenos Aires Men Plan Auto Course; Rickard in Scheme," *CT*, July 20, 1915, 12. On Chicago's speedway, see Stan Kalwasinski, "Speedway Park—A History," *Chicagoland Auto Racing.com*, accessed Sept. 26, 2021, http://www.kalracing.com/autoracing/Speedway_Park_History.htm.

22. Stutz ad, 1914 Official Program, Rickenbacker collection; "Improvements on Sioux City Track," *Des Moines Register*, May 3, 1914, 56; "Sioux City's Speedway a Surprise to Motorists," *CT*, July 12, 1914, G6; "Aviator to Defy Death at Speedway," *Des Moines Tribune*, July 20, 1915, 2; "Enthusiastic over New Motor Track," *Des Moines Register*, July 22, 1915, 9; Reed L. Parker, "Five New Speedways Planned for Next Year," *CT*, July 26, 1914, D8; "Winner of 300 Mile Motor Race at Des Moines," *CT*, Aug. 9, 1915, 11; "150 ICONS: Sioux City Auto Race Attracted Thousands to Mini Indy," *Sioux City Journal*, Jan. 5, 2015, https://siouxcityjournal.com/blogs/siouxland_history/150icons/icons-sioux-city-auto-race-attracted-thousands-to-mini-indy/article_c4cf9926-d80d-5d4b-9ca9-56e0e039ae63.html. On the racing team, see Edward V. Rickenbacker, *Rickenbacker* (Englewood Cliffs, NJ: Prentice-Hall, 1967), 66–67.

23. "Frisco and Toledo Are After Speedway," *IndyStar*, Nov. 30, 1911, 10; "Notes of the Automobile Trade," *NYT*, Nov. 8, 1914, XX6 (quotation); "Auto Racing Circuit," *NYT*, Nov. 28, 1914, 14; "Philadelphia Plans Most Modern Track for Motor Contests," *CT*, July 7, 1915, 10; "Plans $700,000 Speedway," *CT*, July 18, 1915, B4; "Narragansett Speedway Is Nearing Completion," *LAT*, Aug. 4, 1915, III4; J. G. Davis, Clarence E. Eldridge, "Speedway in Louisville," *WP*, Aug. 15, 1915, 17; "Burman's Fast Mile," *NYT*, Sept. 19, 1915, S2; "Concrete Track at St. Joseph," *LAT*, Oct. 26, 1915, III4; "Auto Racing News and Notes about Flyers in General," *IndNews*, May 6, 1916, 10.

24. "Races to Become Class Experiments in Future," *LAT*, June 14, 1914, VII4; "Sheepshead Speedway," *NYT*, Nov. 19, 1914, 9; "To Open Sheepshead Speedway

in June," *NYT*, Nov. 24, 1914, 11; Reed L. Parker, "Hoosiers Happy; Display No Fear of Local Track," *CT*, Dec. 17, 1914, 16; "More Seats at Speedway," *NYT*, Dec. 20, 1914, S2; "Sheepshead Bay to Be Auto Course," *NYT*, Mar. 9, 1915, 10; "The Fastest Auto Track," *NYT*, Mar. 11, 1915, 12; "140 Miles an Hour Motordrome Track," *NYT*, Apr. 15, 1915, 11; "27 Miles of Seats for New Speedway," *NYT*, Apr. 25, 1915, S4; "Fisher Inspects Speedway," *NYT*, May 2, 1915, 18; "World's Largest Sport Arena," *NYT*, May 2, 1915, SM18 (quotations); "Want Union Labor for the Speedway," *NYT*, May 16, 1915, 18; "Autoists Inspect Bay Motordrome," *NYT*, June 16, 1915, 13; "American Cup Race New Motor Derby," *NYT*, July 18, 1915, S3; "World's Record on New Speedway," *NYT*, Oct. 10, 1915, S2; "The 350-Mile Astor Cup Auto Race," *Scientific American* 113, no. 17 (Oct. 23, 1915): 357.

25. "Remarkable Speedway to Be Built in St. Paul," *LAT*, Sept. 14, 1914, III4; "Fisher Out of Speedway," *NYT*, Aug. 20, 1915, 8; Alvin W. Waters, "The Twin City Motor Speedway," *Minnesota History* 60, no. 8 (Winter 2007–8): 305–7; Daniel J. Simone, "Racing, Region, and the Environment: A History of American Motorsports" (PhD diss., University of Florida, 2009), 42–43; Sigur E. Whitaker, *James Allison: A Biography of the Engine Manufacturer and Indianapolis 500 Cofounder* (Jefferson, NC: McFarland, 2011), 119–20.

26. Untitled document, folder "Annual Statements," unprocessed collection, IMS; History Committee of the Speedway Civic Committee, *The Story of Speedway* (Indianapolis: Speedway, 1976), 95, 96, 99 (quotation).

27. Jane Fisher, *Fabulous Hoosier: A Story of American Achievement* (New York: Robert M. McBride, 1947), 132 (quotation); Polly Redford, *Billion-Dollar Sandbar: A Biography of Miami Beach* (New York: E. P. Dutton, 1970), 65–78; Mark S. Foster, *Castles in the Sand: The Life and Times of Carl Graham Fisher* (Gainesville: University Press of Florida, 2001), 145–57. Some accounts say attorney Frank Shutts introduced Collins and Fisher.

28. Fisher to C. W. Kotcher, Nov. 16, 1922, 10: 311, Carl Graham Fisher Papers, HistoryMiami Research Center, Miami, Florida [hereafter, Fisher Papers]; W. A. Kohlhepp to Fisher, Apr. 11, 1923, 10: 334–36, Fisher Papers; Fisher to Edward W. Bok, Feb. 13, 1925, 10: 200, Fisher Papers; H. E. Talbott to Fisher, Jan. 3 [unknown year], 10: 204, Fisher Papers; Fisher to Fred Hoerger, Apr. 3, 1930, 10: 205, Fisher Papers; "Fisher Tells How Flamingo May Come Back" (*Miami Daily News* clipping, Apr. 7, 1930), 10: 206, Fisher Papers; Whitaker, *James Allison*, 135–49; Christopher Knowlton, *Bubble in the Sun: The Florida Boom of the 1920s and How It Brought on the Great Depression* (New York: Simon and Schuster, 2020), 49–53 (first quotation); Fisher, *Fabulous Hoosier*, 169; Foster, *Castles in the Sand*, 161 (second quotation); Redford, *Billion-Dollar Sandbar*, 88–89.

29. W. E. Griffis to Fisher, Feb. 20, 1924, 10: 374–76, Fisher Papers; "Second Payment Blues," ca. 1927, 10: 838 (first quotation), Fisher Papers; "Miami Beach Bay Shore Company: Summary—Special Covenants and Stipulations," 11: 107–27 (second quotation), Fisher Papers; Foster, *Castles in the Sand*, 158–60, 208–9; Melanie Shell-Weiss, *Coming to Miami: A Social History* (Gainesville: University

Press of Florida, 2009), 67, 106. On Miami labor, see Thomas A. Castillo, *Working in the Magic City: Moral Economy in Early Twentieth-Century Miami* (Urbana: University of Illinois Press, 2022).

30. Fisher, *Fabulous Hoosier*, 144, 147 (quotations); Rebecca Cawood McIntyre, *Souvenirs of the Old South: Northern Tourism and Southern Mythology* (Gainesville: University Press of Florida, 2011), 140; Knowlton, *Bubble in the Sun*, 55–56.

31. "City Report to PMC Council," May 25, 1915, folder 3, Mo711, Bell Papers.

32. "Department of Public Works—Cont. [Budget, 1914/1915]," Apr. 1, 1915, folder 2, Mo711, Bell Papers (quotation); Connie J. Ziegler, "Pogue's Run," in *Encyclopedia of Indianapolis*, 1121.

33. "Man to Look after the Indianapolis Parks," *IndNews*, Jan. 4, 1908, 4 (quotation); "Doubters Given Parkway Proof," *IndyStar*, July 27, 1915, 7; "The Park Architect," *IndNews*, Jan. 3, 1916, 6; "City Report to PMC Council," May 25, 1915, folder 3, Mo711, Bell Papers; David G. Vanderstel and Connie Ziegler, "Riverside Amusement Park," in *Encyclopedia of Indianapolis*, 1197–98.

34. "Department of Public Works—Cont. [Budget, 1914/1915]," Apr. 1, 1915, folder 2, Mo711, Bell Papers; "City Report to PMC Council," May 25, 1915 (quotation), folder 3, Mo711, Bell Papers; Charles Zueblin, *American Municipal Progress*, rev. ed. (New York: Arno, 1974), 143; "To Protect Auto Race Starter," *NYT*, May 14, 1914, 12; "Important Improvements Made at the Indianapolis Motor Speedway Affecting Both Public and Drivers in the Great Gasoline Derby," *IndNews*, May 22, 1915, 17; Norton, *Fighting Traffic*, 49; Clendenon, "Flooding and Flood Control," 582; Miriam K. Geib, "Railroad Track Elevation," in *Encyclopedia of Indianapolis*, 1160.

35. Miller McClintock, *Street Traffic Control* (New York: McGraw-Hill, 1925), 36.

36. "City Report to PMC Council," May 25, 1915, folder 3, Mo711, Bell Papers; Arthur J. Slade, et al., "Meeting of the Standards Committee," *SAE Transactions* 11, pt. 1 (1916): 39; Charles Mulford Robinson, *Report of Charles Mulford Robinson for Fort Wayne Civic Improvement Association* (Fort Wayne, IN: Fort Wayne Printing, 1910), 16; John A. Jakle, *City Lights: Illuminating the American Night* (Baltimore: Johns Hopkins University Press, 2001), 228 (first quotation), 3 (second quotation).

37. Report to PMCC (City Report for 1917), Jan. 1, 1918 (quotation), folder 5, Mo711, Bell Papers; "City Report to PMC Council," May 25, 1915, folder 3, Mo711, Bell Papers; Vanderstel and Ziegler, "Riverside Amusement Park"; Charles Mulford Robinson, *City Planning: With Special Reference to the Planning of Streets and Lots* (New York: G. P. Putnam's Sons, 1916).

38. Reed L. Parker, "Six Changes in Speedway Code," *CT*, Nov. 20, 1914, 14; "Conditions Changed for Speedway Contest," *CT*, Nov. 22, 1914, E8; "500-Mile Race Postponed," *NYT*, May 29, 1915, 8; "Shattered Previous Records at the Indianapolis Speedway in Tremendous Speed Bursts," *Miami Herald*, June 1, 1915, 1; Reed L. Parker, "De Palma Wins 500 Mile Auto Race in Record Time," *CT*, June 1, 1915, 17.

39. "Indianapolis Speedway Still under A.A.A. Rule," *IndNews*, Oct. 29, 1914, 14; "Mud Is the Deciding Speedway Factor," *IndNews*, May 29, 1915, 1, 3 (quotation); "Merging of Bodies That Control Auto Racing Would Help Speedway Promoters' Game," *IndNews*, Sept. 11, 1915, 12; "Speedway Associations May Become Power in Racing Game and Dictate to Three A.'s," *IndNews*, Sept. 25, 1915, 10. On the NCAA, see Brian M. Ingrassia, *Rise of Gridiron University: Higher Education's Uneasy Alliance with Big-Time Football* (Lawrence: University Press of Kansas, 2012), 58–61.

40. Report to PMCC (City Report for 1917), Jan. 1, 1918, folder 5, Mo711, Bell Papers (quotation); David G. Vanderstel and Connie Zeigler, "Broad Ripple Park (White City Amusement Park)," in *Encyclopedia of Indianapolis*, 343–54. On White City parks, see James Gilbert, *Perfect Cities: Chicago's Utopias of 1893* (Chicago: University of Chicago Press, 1991), 218; Adam Mack, *Sensing Chicago: Noisemakers, Strikebreakers, and Muckrakers* (Urbana: University of Illinois Press, 2015), 95–112.

41. Theodore Dreiser, *A Hoosier Holiday* (Bloomington: Indiana University Press, 1997), 93, 169, 176, 385. Local critics, meanwhile, were not impressed with Dreiser's book and his assessment of their city; see "Theodore Dreiser Revisits Indiana," *IndyStar*, Dec. 11, 1916, 7.

42. Reed L. Parker, "Hoosiers Talk 1,000 Mile Race," *CT*, Mar. 11, 1915, 11; "Indianapolis Race Reduced," *LAT*, Oct. 5, 1915, III4 (quotation); "Shorter Speedway Race," *NYT*, Dec. 31, 1915, 10; "Auto Racing News and Notes about Fliers in General," *IndNews*, Apr. 1, 1916, 10.

43. "Indianapolis Racers Get Less Coin Than Last Year," *LAT*, Jan. 16, 1916, VI11; "Burman's Cars Are Unmanned," *LAT*, Apr. 30, 1916, VI8; "De Palma Barred at Indianapolis," *CT*, May 9, 1916, 18; J. C. Burton, "Exhaust Echoes," *CT*, May 10, 1916, 14; "Oldfield Smashes Motor Record," *NYT*, May 29, 1916, 12.

44. "Indianapolis Classic Goes," *LAT*, Nov. 30, 1915, III1; "Auto Speed Kings Arrayed for Race," *NYT*, May 30, 1916, 10; "Notes of Motor Derby," *CT*, May 31, 1916, 16; "Resta Wins 300 Mile Auto Derby at Indianapolis," *CT*, May 31, 1916, 15 (quotation); "Resta's Peugeot Wins Sweepstakes," *NYT*, May 31, 1916, 15; "Aitken in Clean-up on Auto Race Track," *WP*, Sept. 10, 1916, 14; "Rain Prevents Auto Race," *CT*, Oct. 20, 1916, 14.

45. "Test New Automobile Fuel," *NYT*, July 5, 1914, C6; "He Makes Gasoline," *WP*, July 26, 1914, 14; "1,000-Mile Test with New Auto Fuel," *NYT*, Nov. 20, 1914, 12; "New Auto Fuel Test Ends," *NYT*, Nov. 21, 1914, 17; "For Motorist and Motorcyclist," *CT*, Feb. 7, 1915, E6; "Automobile," *Scientific American* 111, no. 6 (Aug. 8, 1914): 95; "Zoline Will Not Take the Place of Gasoline," *Bessemer Monthly* 109 (Jan. 1915): 4; "Footwear for Auto Big Rubber Item," *NYT*, Apr. 23, 1916, XX2; "Exports $97,464,381," *NYT*, Aug. 6, 1916, XX2.

46. J. C. Burton, "Exhaust Echoes," *CT*, Oct. 22, 1916, F9; Templar Motors Company ad, 1922 Official Program, Rickenbacker collection; Floyd P. Gibbons, "Resta Wins; Sets World Record," *CT*, June 27, 1915, 1.

47. Report to PMCC (City Report for 1917), Jan. 1, 1918, folder 5, M0711, Bell Papers.

48. Booth Tarkington, *The Magnificent Ambersons* (Garden City, NY: Doubleday, Page, 1918), 394, 414–22 (quotations on 272). On fictional Midland's relation to Indianapolis, see "Booth Tarkington's 'The Magnificent Ambersons'," *IndNews*, Oct. 26, 1918, 9.

49. Tarkington, *Magnificent Ambersons*, 392.

Chapter 5. Finest Flying Field in America

Parts of this chapter appear in Brian M. Ingrassia, "A 'Splendid Flying Field' in Indianapolis: Aviation and Speedway Spectacles in the Great War Era," *Middle West Review* 8, no. 1 (Fall 2021): 109–32.

1. "Entry Blanks for Race Out," *LAT*, Nov. 15, 1914, VII3; "Auto Drivers at Front," *NYT*, Nov. 15, 1914, S4 (quotation); Reed L. Parker, "Motor Drivers Shatter Marks," *CT*, Dec. 27, 1914, B1.

2. Reed L. Parker, "Chicago Track May Get Stars," *CT*, Feb. 7, 1915, B1; "Roads Are Cut Up during War," *LAT*, Apr. 4, 1915, VII8; "Thomas Quits War for 300-Mile Race," *IndNews*, Feb. 22, 1916, 12; "Rene Thomas Coming Over," *LAT*, Feb. 23, 1916, III2; "Porporato Dodging German Shrapnel," *CT*, Mar. 12, 1916, F1.

3. "Packard to Use Speedway Oval in Record Test," *CT*, July 9, 1915, 10; F. E. Moskovics, "Trend of Automobile Design," *LAT*, Oct. 24, 1915, VI14; "Asserts Auto Racing Has Been Aided by Aviation Experiments," *IndyStar*, Jan. 17, 1916, 8; "Auto Racing News and Notes about Flyers in General," *IndNews*, Apr. 29, 1916, 11; Harold Whiting Slauson, "Making a Sport of Speed," *Leslie's Weekly*, May 18, 1916, 8: 642, Carl Graham Fisher Papers, HistoryMiami Research Center, Miami, Florida [hereafter, Fisher Papers]; J. G. Vincent, "Detroit Section Papers: Twelve-Cylinder Engines," *SAE Transactions* 11, pt. 1 (1916): 201; Arthur J. Slade, et al., "Meeting of the Standards Committee," *SAE Transactions* 11, pt. 1 (1916): 21; J. B. Entz, "Electric Transmission on Owen Cars," *SAE Transactions* 11, pt. 2 (1916): 512.

4. "Cincinnati Gets Auto Speedway; Ready Next Fall," *CT*, Apr. 10, 1915, 8; "Fisher Offers Speedway for Use as Aviation Camp," *IndNews*, June 15, 1916, 17; "Indianapolis Auto Races May Be Moved to Cincy," *CT*, Dec. 17, 1916, A4; "Balk at High Hotel Rates," *WP*, Dec. 18, 1916, 7.

5. David M. Kennedy, *Over Here: The First World War and American Society* (New York: Oxford University Press, 2004), 13–14.

6. "Indianapolis Race in Air," *LAT*, Mar. 7, 1917, III1.

7. "Hoosiers Drop Big Motor Race as War Measure," *CT*, Mar. 24, 1917, 11; "Calling Off Big Classic Praised," *IndyStar*, Mar. 24, 1917, 12; "War May Mean Curtailment of Racing Season," *CT*, Mar. 25, 1917, D7; "Speedway Offered as Aviation Camp," *IndNews*, Mar. 29, 1917, 1; "Aviation Grounds Offered," *WP*, Apr. 5, 1917, 4; "Fisher against Racing While Great War Rages," *IndNews*, Nov. 21, 1917, 14; Fisher to J. G. Vincent, Mar. 31, 1917, 1: 683, Fisher Papers (quotation); Nichols

H. Lancaster, *Brooklands: Cradle of British Motor Racing and Aviation* (Oxford, UK: Shire, 2009), 20–21.

8. Kennedy, *Over Here*, 59–63; David O. Levine, *The American College and the Culture of Aspiration, 1915–1940* (Ithaca, NY: Cornell University Press, 1986), 26–32; Carol S. Gruber, *Mars and Minerva: World War I and the Uses of the Higher Learning in America* (Baton Rouge: Louisiana State University Press, 1975), 213–52; *The Students Army Training Corps: Descriptive Circular*, corrected to October 14, 1918, 2nd ed., accessed June 5, 2023, 12–13, https://cudl.colorado.edu/MediaManager/srvr?mediafile=MISC/UCBOULDERCB1–58-NA/1511/i7375352x.pdf.

9. "Indiana Automobile Plants Are Running at Top Speed These Days," *LAT*, Aug. 26, 1917, VI1; Sheppard Butler, "Exhaust Echoes," *CT*, May 23, 1917, 12; Donald Finlay Davis, *Conspicuous Production: Automobiles and Elites in Detroit, 1899–1933* (Philadelphia: Temple University Press, 1988), 142.

10. "Carl Fisher Offers Fast Speed Boat as Submarine Chaser," *IndNews*, Mar. 3, 1917, 2; "Home Products on Sale Today," *IndyStar*, Oct. 8, 1917, 8; Fisher to A. H. Godard, Nov. 16, 1917, 15: 259, Fisher Papers; Mark E. Schneider, "World War I," in *Encyclopedia of Indianapolis*, ed. David J. Bodenhamer and Robert G. Barrows (Bloomington: Indiana University Press, 1994), 1460–61; John Bodnar, *Remaking America: Public Memory, Commemoration, and Patriotism in the Twentieth Century* (Princeton, NJ: Princeton University Press, 1992), 83.

11. Report to PMC Council, Apr. 23, 1917, folder 4, M0711, Joseph E. Bell Papers, Indiana Historical Society, Indianapolis, Indiana [hereafter, Bell Papers] (quotation); Report to PMCC (City Report for 1917), Jan. 1, 1918, folder 5, M0711, Bell Papers; Stephen E. Bower, "Fort Benjamin Harrison," in *Encyclopedia of Indianapolis*, 593.

12. "War Will Bring Cancellation of Almost All Fixtures in American Sports," *NYT*, Mar. 28, 1917, 10; Butler, "Exhaust Echoes," *CT*, May 23, 1917, 12; B.F. Goodrich ad, *CT*, May 29, 1917, 8 (quotations; original emphasis).

13. "War Plans Hold Up Auto Racing," *NYT*, Apr. 1, 1917, XX5; "Cincinnati Tour Is Unsurpassed in Middle West," *CT*, May 27, 1917, D6 (quotations); Butler, "Exhaust Echoes," *CT*, May 29, 1917, 16.

14. "Speedway Asks Memorial Day Date for Derby," *CT*, Mar. 25, 1917, A3; "Original Date of June 9 for Chicago's Motor Derby," *CT*, Mar. 31, 1917, 11; "No Auto Race for Chicago," *WP*, Apr. 1, 1917, S1 (quotation); Butler, "Exhaust Echoes," *CT*, Apr. 19, 1917, 9; "Speed Stars Will Meet on Saturday," *NYT*, Sept. 16, 1917, S5; Alvin W. Waters, "The Twin City Motor Speedway," *Minnesota History* 60, no. 8 (Winter 2007–8): 310–11; Stan Kalwasinski, "Speedway Park—A History," *Chicagoland Auto Racing.com*, accessed Sept. 26, 2021, http://www.kalracing.com/autoracing/Speedway_Park_History.htm.

15. Aircraft Board (Washington, DC), to Fisher, Jan. 4, 1917, 2: 07, Fisher Papers; Fisher to Henry Souther, Mar. 20, 1917, 1: 677, Fisher Papers; Fisher to Society of Automobile Engineers, with summary of response, Mar. 21 and 28, 1917, 1:

670–71, Fisher Papers; Fisher to Society of Automotive Engineers, Mar. 28, 1917, 1: 676, Fisher Papers; Fisher to John Oliver La Gorce, Mar. 28, 1917, 1: 674–75, Fisher Papers; Fisher to Henry Souther, Mar. 28, 1917, 2: 235, Fisher Papers; Fisher to John Oliver La Gorce, Mar. 28, 1917, 1: 674–75, Fisher Papers; Fisher to J. G. Vincent, Mar. 31, 1917, 1: 683, Fisher Papers; Fisher to A. G. Batchelder, Apr. 26, 1917, 1: 685–86, Fisher Papers (quotation); Jane Fisher, *Fabulous Hoosier: A Story of American Achievement* (New York: Robert M. McBride, 1947), 112–13; Mark S. Foster, *Castles in the Sand: The Life and Times of Carl Graham Fisher* (Gainesville: University Press of Florida, 2000), 87.

16. Fisher to J. G. Vincent, Mar. 31, 1917, 1: 683, Fisher Papers.

17. Fisher to Henry Souther, Mar. 28, 1917, 2: 235, Fisher Papers.

18. Ibid.; Fisher to J. G. Vincent, Mar. 31, 1917, 1: 683 (quotations), Fisher Papers; Fisher to George O. Squiers [*sic*], Aug. 6, 1917, 2: 27–28, Fisher Papers; [Fisher], "Suggestions on Air Routes, Signals, and Map-Making" (ca. 1917), 2: 18–21, Fisher Papers.

19. Fisher to A. G. Batchelder, Apr. 26, 1917, 1: 685–86, Fisher Papers; "Asks to Inspect Speedway Field," *IndyStar*, Apr. 14, 1917, 11; "Report against Speedway Site," *IndyStar*, Apr. 29, 1917, 13; "They're Tuning 'em Up Again at the Indianapolis Motor Speedway," *IndNews*, May 24, 1919, 17.

20. Pomilio Brothers Corporation ad, *IndNews*, July 12, 1919, 7; "DeHavilands Now Made in Quantity, Ryan Declares," *NYT*, Aug. 29, 1918, 1; N. H. Gilman to Fisher, Sept. 18, 1918, 8: 645–46, Fisher Papers. On labor, see classified ads: *IndyStar*, Sept. 1, 1918, 23; *IndNews*, Sept. 2, 1918, 14; *IndNews*, Oct. 2, 1918, 14 (quotation); *IndyStar*, Jan. 22, 1919, 13; *IndNews*, Mar. 6, 1919, 24. On contract negotiations, see "Case No. 81: *In re* Claim of Ottorino Pomilio, Alessandro Pomilio, Amedeo Pomilio, and Ernesto Pomilio," in US Department of War, *Decisions of the War Department Board of Contract Adjustment*, vol. 1, January 22 to June 12, 1919 (Washington, DC: US Government Printing Office, 1919), 602–20.

21. Fisher to Henry E. Talbot, Aug. 14, 1918, 1: 733, Fisher Papers; "Italian Aerial Experts Leave," *IndyStar*, July 13, 1919, 24 (quotation); Waldemar Kaempffert, "Aviation Spreads Its Wings over the Earth," *NYT*, Dec. 16, 1928, A3.

22. Aircraft Board, Washington, DC, to Fisher, Jan. 4, 1917, 2: 07, Fisher Papers; George O. Squiers [*sic*] to Fisher, July 12, 1917, 2 :10, Fisher Papers (quotation); "Confers with Officers," *IndNews*, Aug. 24, 1917, 9.

23. [Fisher], "Suggestions on Air Routes," Fisher Papers; [Fisher], "Flying Fields—Location, Size & Equipment," ca. 1917, 2: 17, Fisher Papers (quotations). On drainage tile, see Kristin L. Hoganson, *The Heartland: An American History* (New York: Penguin, 2016), 200–205.

24. Fisher to Jesse G. Vincent, Mar. 31, 1917, 1: 683, Fisher Papers; Fisher to Howard E. Coffin, July 16, 1917, 2: 11, Fisher Papers (quotations). See also Foster, *Castles in the Sand*, 87–90.

25. Fisher to David Beecroft, Nov. 22, 1917, 2: 68–69, Fisher Papers.

26. Fisher to C. F. Kettering, July 16, 1917, 2: 13, Fisher Papers (quotations); "First Flight across Indiana of Uncle Sam's Military Airplanes," *IndNews*, Oct. 13, 1917, 15.

27. Fisher to C. F. Kettering, July 16, 1917, 2: 13, Fisher Papers; Fisher to S. D. Waldon, July 23, 1917, 2: 22, Fisher Papers; Fisher to S. D. Waldon, July 30, 1917, 2: 24, Fisher Papers; "Numbers on Roofs to Show Landing Places," *IndNews*, July 25, 1917, 1; "First Aviation Training Field," *IndNews*, July 25, 1917, 18.

28. Jason Weems, *Barnstorming the Prairies: How Aerial Vision Shaped the Midwest* (Minneapolis: University of Minnesota Press, 2015), 135–36.

29. Fisher to C. F. Kettering, July 16, 1917, 2: 13, Fisher Papers (quotations); "Progress Has Its Penalties," *IndyStar*, July 29, 1917, 16.

30. Fisher to C. F. Kettering, July 16, 1917, 2: 13, Fisher Papers; Fisher to S. D. Waldon, July 23, 1917, 2: 22, Fisher Papers; Waldon to Fisher, July 27, 1917, 2: 23, Fisher Papers; Fisher to W. F. Durand, Aug. 20, 1917, 2: 30, Fisher Papers (quotations); "Senator New in Aeroplane," *WP*, June 9, 1918, 2.

31. Fisher to Coffin, Aug. 21, 1917, 2: 31, Fisher Papers; Fisher to Reginald Sullivan, Aug. 24, 1917, 2: 42, Fisher Papers (quotation); Fisher to Coffin, Aug. 29, 1917, 2: 47, Fisher Papers; "Lighthouses Will Mark Aero Routes," *IndNews*, Aug. 20, 1917, 1.

32. Fisher to Eaton City Council, Aug. 23, 1917, 2: 36–37, Fisher Papers (quotation). Fisher wrote similar letters to Dunreith, Indiana, and Cambridge City, Indiana.

33. Fisher to W. F. Durand, Oct. 30, 1917, 10: 513, Fisher Papers.

34. Fisher to Coffin, Aug. 19, 1917, 2: 29, Fisher Papers; Fisher to W. F. Durand, Aug. 20, 1917, 2: 30, Fisher Papers (quotation); Fisher to Coffin, Sept. 22, 1917, 2: 45–46, Fisher Papers; Fisher to Lt. H. W. Schroeder, Oct. 13, 1917, 2: 48–49, Fisher Papers; Fisher to Coffin, Oct. 26, 1917, 2: 52–53, Fisher Papers; Fisher to David Beecroft, Nov. 22, 1917, 2: 68–69, Fisher Papers; Fisher to Coffin, Dec. 26, 1917, 2: 75–76, Fisher Papers.

35. Fisher to Lt. M. A. Sharp, Feb. 4, 1919, 1: 754, Fisher Papers.

36. Fisher to Col. E. Lester James, Sept. 19, 1918, 1: 738–39; Gilman to Fisher, Sept. 18, 1918, 8: 645–46, Fisher Papers; "Middle West News in Brief," *LAT*, June 20, 1919, I3.

37. N. H. Gilman to Fisher, Sept. 18, 1918, 8: 645–46, Fisher Papers; Fisher to Gen. Charles Lee, Sept. 23, 1918, 1: 742, Fisher Papers; "Flyer Falls 500 Feet to Death at Ball Game," *CT*, June 3, 1918, 3; "Plunges to Death in 'Flying Circus'," *NYT*, Aug. 25, 1918, 12; "Two Killed in Nose Dive," *NYT*, Sept. 23, 1918, 4; "British Royal Birdman Falls near Speedway," *IndyStar*, Sept. 23, 1918, 1.

38. "How They Work behind Scenes in Big Races," *CT*, Jan. 27, 1918, B4; "Name Auto Race Dates," *NYT*, Mar. 10, 1918, S3; Butler, "Exhaust Echoes," *CT*, Apr. 4, 1918, 13; "Auto Racers Plan an Active Season," *NYT*, May 12, 1918, 30. On SAA, see Robert Dick, *Auto Racing in the Shadow of the Great War: Streamlined Specials*

and a New Generation of Drivers on American Speedways, 1915–1922 (Jefferson, NC: McFarland, 2019), 64.

39. "Motor Racing History Told in National's Scrap Book," *CT*, Jan. 27, 1918, B11. On nostalgia, see Peter Fritzsche, *Stranded in the Present: Modern Time and the Melancholy of History* (Cambridge, MA: Harvard University Press, 2004). On scrapbooks, see Ellen Gruber Garvey, *Writing with Scissors: American Scrapbooks from the Civil War to the Harlem Renaissance* (New York: Oxford University Press, 2012).

40. "Speedway Boxers and Fort Mixers Ready for Bouts," *IndyStar*, July 18, 1918, 9; "Soldiers Have Wild Time in Ring at the Speedway," *IndyStar*, Aug. 3, 1918, 10; "Ten Battles On at Boxing Show," *IndyStar*, Aug. 23, 1918, 4; John W. Head, "Rosengarten Is Given Decision," *IndyStar*, Aug. 24, 1918, 4. On military boxing, see Wanda Ellen Wakefield, *Playing to Win: Sports and the American Military, 1898–1945* (Albany: State University of New York Press, 1997), 7, 23, 26.

41. "Builders Getting Back into Stride," *CT*, Mar. 23, 1919, D11; "Gossip of the Auto Trade," *CT*, May 11, 1919, E10; "Order Enlarged by Health Board," *IndNews*, Oct. 11, 1918, 27; Butler, "Exhaust Echoes," *CT*, Oct. 16, 1918, 11; Fisher to M. M. Allison, Nov. 17, 1921, 4: 175, Fisher Papers; Kennedy, *Over Here*, 189n119; John M. Barry, *The Great Influenza: The Epic Story of the Deadliest Plague in History* (New York: Penguin, 2004).

42. "1919 Auto Racing Season to Surpass 'Good Old Days'," *CT*, Dec. 4, 1918, 15; "Big Race for Indianapolis," *LAT*, Dec. 15, 1918, VI5.

43. Robert Wohl, *A Passion for Wings: Aviation and the Western Imagination, 1908–1918* (New Haven, CT: Yale University Press, 1994), 203; Peter Fritzsche, *A Nation of Flyers: German Aviation and the Popular Imagination* (Cambridge, MA: Harvard University Press, 1994), 59–101; Edward V. Rickenbacker, *Rickenbacker* (Englewood Cliffs, NJ: Prentice-Hall, 1967), 58–76, 96–135; John F. Ross, *Enduring Courage: Ace Pilot Eddie Rickenbacker and the Dawn of the Age of Speed* (New York: St. Martin's Griffin, 2014), 51–58, 76–78, 83–84; "Americans Drive Down Enemy Plane," *WP*, May 2, 1918, 4.

44. "1919 Auto Racing Season to Surpass 'Good Old Days'," *CT*, Dec. 4, 1918, 15.

45. "Great Interest in Sweepstakes," *LAT*, Mar. 16, 1919, VI10 (quotation); Butler, "Exhaust Echoes," *CT*, May 8, 1919, 19; "3 Die in Auto Race at Indianapolis," *NYT*, June 1, 1919, 18; T. E. Myers to Fisher, Mar. 20, 1919, 15: 497, Fisher Papers.

46. "Urges Erection of Aerodrome," *IndyStar*, May 31, 1919, 16.

47. T. E. Myers to Fisher, Jan. 16, 1919, 8: 647, Fisher Papers; T. E. Myers to Fisher, Feb. 11, 1919, 8: 649, Fisher Papers; T. E. Myers to Fisher, Mar. 10, 1919, 8: 652, Fisher Papers; Carl [Peltier] to Fisher, Nov. 17, 1919, 15: 265, Fisher Papers (quotation); "Seven Cars Now Entered," *NYT*, Mar. 16, 1919, 24.

48. "They're Tuning 'em Up Again."

49. T. E. Myers to Fisher, Feb. 11, 1919, 8: 648, Fisher Papers; Myers to Fisher, Feb. 22, 1919, 8: 651, Fisher Papers; IMS Corporation to Fisher (telegram), Apr. 2, 1919, 8: 653, Fisher Papers. See also "Drivers Sail for America," *LAT*, Apr. 23, 1919, III10; "Eight European Racing Drivers Ready to Try for Speedway Honors,"

LAT, May 25, 1919, VI1; "3 Die in Auto Race at Indianapolis," *NYT*, June 1, 1919, 18 (quotation).

50. "The World's Great Speed Event," *IndyStar*, May 31, 1919, 6 (quotation); "French Entries Race Favorites at Indianapolis" and "Road Bulletins," *CT*, May 25, 1919, E9; "Indianapolis Auto Race Plans," *WP*, May 26, 1919, 6; Sheppard Butler, "American Cars near French in Speed Surprise," *CT*, May 29, 1919, 13; "Auto Race Kings Ready for Big Sweepstake Race at Indianapolis," *WP*, May 31, 1919, 10.

51. "Allies in Speedway Race," *NYT*, Dec. 22, 1918, 25 (quotation); "American Car May Win," *LAT*, Jan. 12, 1919, VI14; "Fiat to Enter Hoosier Race," *CT*, Jan. 19, 1919, D6; "Foreign Cars for Big Race," *LAT*, Feb. 2, 1919, VI8; "Foreign Drivers Favored," *NYT*, May 18, 1919, 30; Sheppard Butler, "Exhaust Echoes," *CT*, May 22, 1919, I5; "Dario Resta Out of Race," *LAT*, May 27, 1919, III1.

52. "Prefers Auto to Plane," *NYT*, Mar. 2, 1919, 26 (quotation); "Remarkable Motor Drive," *LAT*, Apr. 3, 1919, III1; "De Palma at Indianapolis," *LAT*, May 19, 1919, I5; "French Entries Race Favorites at Indianapolis," *CT*, May 25, 1919, E9.

53. John Oliver La Gorce to Albertine Rossiter, July 15, 1919, 12: 417, Fisher Papers.

54. "Entry List over the Top," *LAT*, May 11, 1919, VI16.

55. Butler, "Exhaust Echoes," *CT*, Mar. 24, 1919, 19, and "Greater Hazards of Speed in Indianapolis Race Today," *CT*, May 31, 1919, 18 (quotations); "Greatest Event in History of Auto Racing Promised at Indianapolis Speedway Today," *LAT*, May 31, 1919, II9.

56. Sheppard Butler, "Three Killed in Auto Race; Wilcox Wins," *CT*, June 1, 1919, 1 (quotations); "3 Die in Auto Race at Indianapolis," *NYT*, June 1, 1919, 1; "Three Killed at Indianapolis in Wildest Race in Track's History," *LAT*, June 1, 1919, VI1; Butler, "Fourth Driver at Death's Door from Hoosier Motor Race," *CT*, June 2, 1919, 21.

57. Capt. Eddie Rickenbacker, "Most Wonderful of All the Contests," *WP*, June 1, 1919, 1.

58. E. C. Patterson to Fisher, June 3, 1919, 8: 654–55, Fisher Papers.

59. "Good in Auto Races," *WP*, July 27, 1919, R9.

60. "Great Auto Drivers in Duel of Speed," *NYT*, June 29, 1919, 20.

61. Nordyke and Marmon ad, *CT*, Jan. 26, 1920, 13 (quotation). After the war, Marmon tested cars on the oval ("Tested on Famous Track," *LAT*, May 16, 1920, VI6).

62. Prest-O-Lite ad, 1922 Official Program, Edward V. Rickenbacker collection (unprocessed), IMS [hereafter, Rickenbacker collection].

63. Fisher to Ralph De Palma, July 22, 1919, 8: 656, Fisher Papers (quotations); De Palma to Fisher, Aug. 7, 1919, 8: 657, Fisher Papers; "Hospital to Close Sept. 1," *IndyStar*, Aug. 12, 1909, 18; "Public Will Not Be Admitted to Big Speed Fest," *IndyStar*, Aug. 16, 1919, 16; "Speed Clashes at Brick Oval," *IndyStar*, Aug. 19, 1919, 11.

64. "Timing Device to Be Used at Races," *LAT*, Feb. 15, 1920, VI13; William F. Sturm, "A View of Automobile Racing through a Champion's Eyes: An Interview

with Peter De Paolo, 1925 A.A.A. Title Holder," *Saturday Evening Post*, Aug. 28, 1926, 146 (quotations).

65. "Who Is in the Lead?" 1922 Official Program, Rickenbacker collection.

66. "Refuses to Supply Gas for Balloon Racers," *NYT*, Aug. 7, 1920, 16; "Ballooners Change Dates," *IndNews*, Sept. 2, 1920, 25; "Tribune Airplane Picture of Big Auto Classic," *CT*, May 31, 1921, 22; "Indianapolis Gets Air Race," *NYT*, Mar. 28, 1923, 21; "13 Balloons Get Away in National Air Derby," *NYT*, July 5, 1923, 18; Fisher to S. Bobo Dean, Mar. 29, 1920, 2: 236–37, Fisher Papers; Benjamin F. Castle to Fisher, Oct. 8, 1920, 2: 278, Fisher Papers; Fisher to Averil Harriman, Nov. 8, 1923, 14: 374, Fisher Papers. On intercontinental flight, see Alex Bryne, "The Potential of Flight: U.S. Aviation and Pan-Americanism during the Early Twentieth Century," *Journal of the Gilded Age and Progressive Era* 19, no. 1 (Jan. 2020): 48–76.

67. Fisher to Roy D. Chapin, Dec. 26, 1917, 3: 318, Fisher Papers; Austin F. Bement to Fisher, Apr. 14, 1919, 9: 528, Fisher Papers (quotations); "Minutes of Annual Meeting of the Board of Directors of the Lincoln Highway Association," Dec. 30, 1919, 9: 563, Fisher Papers; Earl Swift, *The Big Roads: The Untold Story of the Engineers, Visionaries, and Trailblazers Who Created the American Superhighways* (Boston: Houghton Mifflin Harcourt, 2011), 65–69.

Chapter 6. Sports of Titans

1. "Racing Helps Motors," *WP*, June 22, 1919, A11; "Racing Rules Much Changed," *LAT*, July 27, 1919, VI16; "Germans Plan Steel Speedway for Racing Cars," *CT*, Jan. 30, 1921, D6; "Motordom," *CT*, May 15, 1921, F13 (quotation).

2. "Manufacturers, Short of Employe[e]s Because of House Shortage, Begin on Building Programs That Will Solve an Industrial Problem," *IndNews*, Apr. 3, 1920, 17 (quotations); classified ads, *IndNews*, Apr. 3, 1920, 21; John M. Findlay, *Magic Lands: Western Cityscapes and American Culture after 1940* (Berkeley: University of California Press, 1992).

3. Fisher to M. J. Carney, June 21, 1920, 8: 667–68 (quotations), Fisher Papers. On postwar labor, see David M. Kennedy, *Over Here: The First World War and American Society* (New York: Oxford University Press, 2004), 258–70.

4. Jane Fisher, *Fabulous Hoosier: A Story of American Achievement* (New York: Robert M. McBride, 1947), 76.

5. "Polo 1920–21 Outlined Plan," 8: 669–73, Carl Graham Fisher Papers, HistoryMiami Research Center, Miami, Florida [hereafter, Fisher Papers]; Allison to Fisher, Mar. 24, 1920, 1: 402, Fisher Papers; T. E. Myers to Fisher, May 6, 1937, 12: 768, Fisher Papers; "Polo Ponies for Team Already at Speedway," *IndNews*, June 9, 1920, 24; "Local Polo Squad Wins," *IndyStar*, June 18, 1920, 12; "Repair Depot Removal Approved; Starts Soon," *IndNews*, July 9, 1920, 1; Mark S. Foster, *Castles in the Sand: The Life and Times of Carl Graham Fisher* (Gainesville: University Press of Florida, 2000), 244.

6. Fisher to Allison, Mar. 27, 1920, 1: 404–5, Fisher Papers; Fisher to Allison, June 29, 1921, 8: 674 (quotations), Fisher Papers.

7. Roy H. Compton, "Great Year for Speed," *LAT*, Jan. 25, 1920, VI1; Harry Elliott, "Twenty-Four Drivers Will Start in 500-Mile Thriller at Indianapolis," *LAT*, May 31, 1920, I5; "What Would You Give for a Drink?" 1922 racing program, Edward V. Rickenbacker collection (unprocessed), IMS [hereafter, Rickenbacker collection] (quotations).

8. "Motordom," *CT*, May 23, 1920, G3 (quotation); "Chevrolet Wins 500 Mile Race," *CT*, June 1, 1920, 21; "Gaston Chevrolet Is Winner," *LAT*, June 1, 1920, III1; "Chevrolet Winner of 500-Mile Grind," *NYT*, June 1, 1920, 13; "De Palma, near Victory, Halted by Flaming Car," *WP*, June 1, 1920, 14; "$93,550 for Winners in 500-Mile Classic," *IndNews*, June 2, 1920, 17; "Gaston Chevrolet Killed in Race," *NYT*, Nov. 26, 1920, 1; "Deaths Fail to Affect Speedway Race Plans," *LAT*, Nov. 27, 1920, II5; Kelly Crandall, "The Superstition of the Green Race Car," *Bleacher Report*, Nov. 1, 2008, https://bleacherreport.com/articles/76249-the-superstition-of-the-green-race-car. Fisher reportedly was driving a green car at the time of his 1903 Zanesville crash.

9. "Work Begins Today on Yankee Stadium," *NYT*, May 6, 1922, 17. On Yankee Stadium, see Neil J. Sullivan, *The Diamond in the Bronx: Yankee Stadium and the Politics of New York* (New York: Oxford University Press, 2001). On college stadiums, see Brian M. Ingrassia, *The Rise of Gridiron University: Higher Education's Uneasy Alliance with Big-Time Football* (Lawrence: University Press of Kansas, 2012), 139–70.

10. Hess and Sackett ad, *LAT*, June 6, 1920, VI6; Oldfield Tire ad, *CT*, May 31, 1921, 10; Henry C. Litton and Sons ad, *CT*, Oct. 15, 1920, 13, and *CT*, June 19, 1923, 15.

11. *The Lincoln Highway Forum*, Dec. 1924, 9: 458–59, Fisher Papers; Drake Hokanson, *The Lincoln Highway: Main Street across America* (Iowa City: University of Iowa Press, 1999), 93–94.

12. Fisher to M. M. Allison, Apr. 25, 1919, 4: 107, Fisher Papers; "Minutes of Annual Meeting of the Board of Directors of the Lincoln Highway Association," Dec. 30, 1918, 9: 523 (quotation), Fisher Papers; Paul S. Sutter, *Driven Wild: How the Fight against Automobiles Launched the Modern Wilderness Movement* (Seattle: University of Washington Press, 2002).

13. Fisher to M. M. Allison, May 9, 1919, 4: 125, Fisher Papers; W. T. Anderson to Fisher, May 24, 1919, 4: 128, Fisher Papers; Fisher to F. A. Seiberling, Sept. 3, 1920, 9: 413, Fisher Papers; "Speedway Trails," *CT*, May 28, 1922, G2; "Tribune Tours," *CT*, May 27, 1923, A7; "Big Crowd to See Race," *NYT*, May 29, 1922, 16; "26 Motor Pilots Ready to Start 500 Mile Grind," *CT*, May 30, 1922, 16; "Jimmy Murphy Shatters World's Record in Indianapolis Auto Race," *LAT*, May 31, 1922, II11. On motor courts, see Warren James Belasco, *Americans on the Road: From Autocamp to Motel, 1910–1945* (Baltimore: Johns Hopkins University Press, 1997).

14. "Twenty-Three Cars Race," *LAT*, May 30, 1921, I5; "Tommy Milton Victor in Auto Classic," *CT*, May 31, 1921, 21; "Race Won by Milton," *LAT*, May 31, 1921, I1; "American Car Wins Indianapolis Race," *WP*, May 31, 1921, 11; "Milton Captures 500-Mile Classic," *NYT*, May 31, 1921, 25. On Frontenac, see David N. Lucsko, *The Business of Speed: The Hot Rod Industry in America, 1915–1990* (Baltimore: Johns Hopkins University Press, 2008), 35–36.

15. "Foch and Pershing Arrive Tomorrow," *NYT*, Oct. 27, 1921, 21; "Simple Splendor in Welcome to War Hero," *IndNews*, Nov. 4, 1921, 14; "Foch Says World Must Have Peace," *NYT*, Nov. 5, 1921, 12; John Bodnar, *Remaking America: Public Memory, Commemoration, and Patriotism in the Twentieth Century* (Princeton, NJ: Princeton University Press, 1992), 86; Thomas A. Rumer, "American Legion," and Richard G. Groome, "Marshal Foch Day," in *Encyclopedia of Indianapolis*, ed. David J. Bodenhamer and Robert G. Barrows (Bloomington: Indiana University Press, 1994), 254, 976.

16. "Picture Acting Is Too Prosaic," *LAT*, Apr. 2, 1922, VI9; "Thirty-Two Cars in Big Auto Race," *NYT*, May 6, 1922, 16; untitled photo of Wallace Reid, *WP*, May 13, 1922, 19.

17. "1,000-Piece Brass Band Will Open International Auto Race," *NYT*, May 13, 1922, 30; "One-Man Car in Speed Classic," *LAT*, May 21, 1922, VI3; "New Record Set for Race Attendance," *IndyStar*, May 31, 1922, 1; "Murphy Wins Great Auto Race Classic," *NYT*, May 31, 1922, 26; "Jimmy Murphy Shatters World's Record in Indianapolis Auto Race," *LAT*, May 31, 1922, II11; "Murphy's Spoils Close to $30,000," *NYT*, June 1, 1922, 25; "Motordom," *CT*, June 4, 1922, G2 (quotation); "Gives Credit to Engineer," *LAT*, June 11, 1922, VI2. "Packard Back in Race Game," *LAT*, Oct. 8, 1922, VI6.

18. "Favor Race Date Change," *IndyStar*, June 18, 1921, 7; Fisher to Allison, July 8, 1922, 8: 676, Fisher Papers; Allison to Fisher, Jan. 14, 1923, 1: 419–21, Fisher Papers. On Scopes, see Edward J. Larson, *Summer for the Gods: The Scopes Trial and America's Continuing Debate over Science and Religion* (New York: Basic Books, 1997). On the KKK, see James H. Madison, *The Ku Klux Klan in the Heartland* (Bloomington: Indiana University Press, 2020); Felix Harcourt, *Ku Klux Kulture: America and the Klan in the 1920s* (Chicago: University of Chicago Press, 2017).

19. "May Eliminate Auto Races Memorial Day," *WP*, Jan. 27, 1923, 17; "For New Motor Speedway," *NYT*, Jan. 31, 1923, 9; "Buy Motor Speedway Site," *WP*, Jan. 31, 1923, 5; "Big Hoosier Auto Race Target of Lawmaker's Bill," *CT*, Feb. 6, 1923, 19; "Would Change Holiday to Block Pro Sports," *WP*, Feb. 7, 1923, 14; "Passes Bill to Ban Auto Race May 30," *NYT*, Feb. 27, 1923, 17; "Governor Vetoes Memorial Day Bill," *NYT*, Mar. 6, 1923, 18; Albert B. Reed to Fisher, Jan. 4 and 19, 1923, 15: 332–33, Fisher Papers; Nicholas W. Sacco, "The Grand Army of the Republic, the Indianapolis 500, and the Struggle for Memorial Day in Indiana, 1868–1923," *Indiana Magazine of History* 111, no. 4 (Dec. 2015): 349–80.

20. Allison to Fisher, Jan. 14, 1923, 1: 419–21, Fisher Papers; "Motor Magnate a Suicide," *WP*, May 28, 1921, 1.

21. "Rift in Legion Grows over Speedway Issue," *WP*, Jan. 30, 1923, 10; "Ousts Legion Official," *NYT*, Jan. 30, 1923, 16; "Governor Vetoes Memorial Day Bill," *NYT*, Mar. 6, 1923, 18; "Mayor and Race Promoters Row in Indianapolis," *CT*, May 26, 1923, 15; "Mayor Declares War on Indianapolis Meet," *WP*, May 26, 1923, 10; "Police Protection for Race Crowds as Usual," *IndNews*, May 28, 1923, 1, 26; "Indiana House Bill Would Bar Auto Race on May 30," *CT*, Jan. 22, 1925, 14; Russell Harrison to Fisher, Apr. 9, 1923, 8: 677, Fisher Papers; Sacco, "Grand Army of the Republic," 373.

22. "City's Best Asset, Says Mayor Shank," *IndyStar*, May 30, 1924, 8 (Shank quotation); Harry C. Stutz, "H. C. Stutz Shows Speedway's Value," *IndyStar*, May 30, 1924, 9 (Stutz quotation). On Fisher's 1923 attitude, see Ralph Kramer, *Indianapolis Motor Speedway: 100 Years of Racing* (Iola, WI: Krause, 2009), 89–91.

23. George H. Mosser, "Regards Speedway as Industrial Aid to All Hoosierdom," *IndyStar*, May 30, 1924, 10 (quotations); The Pilgrim, "Motordom's Chiefs Acclaim Debt to Speedway Founders," *IndyStar*, May 30, 1924, 2.

24. "Ticket Sale Begins Today," *NYT*, Jan. 29, 1923, 13; "Motordom," *CT*, Apr. 22, 1923, A8; "Imports Own Fuel for Auto Classic," *WP*, May 7, 1923, 12; "Record Entry List Is Announced for Great Motor Classic at Indianapolis Speedway," *LAT*, May 13, 1923, VI2; "French Prince to Drive in Classic," *WP*, May 13, 1923, 60; Al G. Waddell, "Foreign Cars Too Slow for Yanks," *LAT*, May 22, 1923, III4; "Two Auto Drivers Insured for Race at Indianapolis," *NYT*, May 25, 1923, 27 (quotation); James O'Donnell Bennett, "Wasplike Cars Try for Speed and Fame Today," *CT*, May 30, 1923, 4.

25. William J. Sturm, "A View of Automobile Racing through a Champion's Eyes: An Interview with Peter De Paolo, 1925 A.A.A. Title Holder," *Saturday Evening Post*, Aug. 28, 1926, 142 (quotation); "One-Man U.S. Cars to Race Foreigners," *WP*, May 6, 1923, 73.

26. "Rickenbacker Starter," *LAT*, May 18, 1923, III2; "Duesenberg Chosen to Pace First Lap in 500-Mile Race," *NYT*, May 20, 1923, S3; "Milton Drives 108 Mi[les per] Hour in Speedway Trial," *CT*, May 27, 1923, A1; "23 Cars to Start in 500-Mile Race," *NYT*, May 30, 1923, 11; "Tommy Milton's Blistered Hands Guide Midget Racer to Victory," *LAT*, May 31, 1923, I13; James O'Donnell Bennett, "150,000 People See Tom Milton Win Auto Race," *CT*, May 31, 1923, 1 (quotations); untitled photo of crowd at the speedway, *CT*, May 31, 1923, 3.

27. Fisher quoted in "Famous Speedway May Be Dismantled," *NYT*, June 1, 1923, 16.

28. "Fisher Says New Rules May Govern Next Auto Classic," *IndyStar*, June 1, 1923, 1; "Indianapolis Again to Hold Auto Race," *NYT*, June 13, 1923, 15; "Durant Bids for Hoosier Speedway," *LAT*, Aug. 16, 1923, III1; "Confab Stirs Talk of Hoosier Oval's Sale," *CT*, Aug. 16, 1923, 12.

29. "Rainbow Veterans Keep Anniversary of Great Assault," *WP*, July 15, 1923, 2; "Indiana Governor Stops Firpo Bout," *NYT*, Aug. 9, 1923, 10; "Downey Is Cinch for Luis Firpo," *LAT*, Aug. 18, 1923, I5; "Refused to Enter the Ring Until Paid," *NYT*, Aug. 18, 1923, 6.

30. "Entry Blanks Issued for Speedway Classic," *WP*, Jan. 3, 1924, S3 (quotation); "Call Goes Out to Speed Kings for Hoosier Classic," *CT*, Jan. 20, 1924, A6; Sturm, "Automobile Racing through a Champion's Eyes," 150; "Entry Blanks Are Sent Out," *LAT*, Feb. 3, 1924, G6; "Indianapolis Track Being Kept in Repair," *LAT*, Feb. 13, 1924, B3; J. L. Jenkins, "In Motordom," *CT*, May 1, 1924, 20; J. L. Jenkins, "Motordom," *CT*, May 4, 1924, A8.

31. "De Palma Is Barred from Hoosier Classic for Outlaw Racing," *CT*, Apr. 6, 1924, A5; "Motordom," *CT*, Apr. 20, 1924, A8; "Henry Ford Will Referee Big Race," *LAT*, May 15, 1924, B1; "Henry Returns to Early Haunts as Speedway Referee," *CT*, May 18, 1924, A8 (quotation); "Ford Tries Out Speedway Oval as Pedestrian," *LAT*, May 30, 1924, 2; "Ford Speeds around Race Track," *NYT*, May 30, 1924, 10; Henry L. Dithmer, "C. of C. President Recites Benefits of Motor Classic," *IndyStar*, May 30, 1924, 6; "Henry Ford Insures Drivers in Race for $10,000 Each," *NYT*, May 31, 1924, 10. On Ford's enterprises, see Greg Grandin, *Fordlandia: The Rise and Fall of Henry Ford's Forgotten Jungle City* (New York: Metropolitan Books, 2009); Heather B. Barrow, *Henry Ford's Plan for the American Suburb: Dearborn and Detroit* (DeKalb: Northern Illinois University Press, 2015).

32. "W-G-N Will Give Auto Classic in All Its Thrills," *CT*, May 18, 1924, F13; "Layout of Race W-G-N Will Broadcast," *CT*, May 25, 1924, F10; Christy McKay, "WOH," in *Encyclopedia of Indianapolis*, 1401. On radio and sport, see Ronald A. Smith, *Play-by-Play: Radio, Television, and Big-Time College Sport* (Baltimore: Johns Hopkins University Press, 2001); Oriard, *King Football*; John Carroll, *Red Grange and the Rise of Modern Football* (Urbana: University of Illinois Press, 1999), 4, 70.

33. "To Use Wireless on Automobile in Race," *WP*, Apr. 9, 1922, 23 (quotation); "Motordom," *CT*, Apr. 23, 1922, G3.

34. "W-G-N Notes," *CT*, May 3, 1925, E12; "W-G-N to Bring Speedway Races to Your Homes," *CT*, May 24, 1925, H9 (quotation); R. W. C. Franch, "Sick Veterans Enjoyed Races," and Mrs. Mae McCullough, "Quin Ryan Half the Show," letters to editor, *CT*, June 4, 1925, 8; James C. Nicholson, *The Kentucky Derby: How the Run for the Roses Became America's Premier Sporting Event* (Lexington: University Press of Kentucky, 2012), 78.

35. Al G. Waddell, "Speed Kings Risk Death in Annual Indianapolis Classic Today," *LAT*, May 30, 1924, 9; Waddell, "Boyer Wins Indianapolis Auto Race," *LAT*, May 31, 1924, 9; J. L. Jenkins, "Joe Boyer Is Victor in 500 Mile Auto Race," *CT*, May 31, 1924, 11.

36. "140,000 Auto Fans See Corum Win Race," *NYT*, May 31, 1924, 10; "Thousands of Fans 'See' Boyer Win Auto Race via Trib[une] Radio," *CT*, May 31, 1924, 11 (quotation); "Million Persons See Holiday Sports throughout Country," *NYT*, May 31, 1924, 11.

37. "Speedway Guards, Semi-military Organization with One-Day Job," *Ind-News*, May 23, 1925, 21.

38. "De Palma Has Filed Name for May 30 Auto Race," *CT*, Feb. 27, 1921, G3; "Motordom," *CT*, May 15, 1921, F13; "Everything Set for Broadcast of Auto Classic," *CT*, May 29, 1927, G4 (quotation).

39. Foster, *Castles in the Sand*, 159–60; Jerry M. Fisher, *The Pacesetter: The Untold Story of Carl G. Fisher* (Fort Bragg, CA: Lost Coast, 1998), 21–22; Fisher correspondence on charities is in 3: 389–422, Fisher Papers.

40. Todd Gould, *For Gold and Glory: Charlie Wiggins and the African-American Racing Car Circuit* (Bloomington: Indiana University Press, 2002).

41. "All around the Town," *IndNews*, Nov. 3, 1922, 26; "She Helps to Run Speedway," *IndyStar*, May 30, 1924, 8 (quotations).

42. "Pa and Ma Public Take Son Bub to Speedway for Driver's Day," *IndNews*, May 22, 1922, 17.

43. "150,000 See Milton Win 500-Mile Race," *NYT*, May 31, 1923, 18; "Joe Boyer Dies of Race Crash Injuries," *LAT*, Sept. 2, 1924, 1; "Dario Resta Killed in Auto Speed Test," *NYT*, Sept. 4, 1924, 21 (quotation); "Jimmy Murphy Dies in Auto Race Crash," *NYT*, Sept. 16, 1924, 1; "Angelenos Mourn Pilot," *LAT*, Sept. 16, 1924, B1.

44. "Motordom," *CT*, June 22, 1924, A8; "Indianapolis Calls for Smaller Engines," *WP*, July 13, 1924, AA4; "Entry List Open for Auto Grind at Indianapolis," *CT*, Dec. 28, 1924, A3; "Balloon Tires Will Get Test at Indianapolis," *CT*, May 25, 1925, 22 (quotation).

45. "More Boats Arrive for Garden Show," *NYT*, Feb. 24, 1911, 11; "Miami Will Stage Speed Boat Regatta," *WP*, Dec. 9, 1924, S3; J. L. Jenkins, "Motordom Today," *CT*, Dec. 29, 1924, 17; "Milton to Lead Speed Kings in Novel Boat Race," *CT*, Feb. 22, 1925, A11 (quotation); "Milton Trying Car Changes," *LAT*, Apr. 12, 1925, H4; Foster, *Castles in the Sand*, 184–86.

46. "'Rick' Paces Speed Demons," *LAT*, May 31, 1925, H4; J. L. Jenkins, "500 Miles in 297 Minutes!" *CT*, May 31, 1925, 1; "De Paolo Smashes 500-Mile Auto Mark," *NYT*, May 31, 1925, S1; Sturm, "Automobile Racing through a Champion's Eyes," 11 (quotation). On Rickenbacker Motors, see Edward V. Rickenbacker, *Rickenbacker* (Englewood Cliffs, NJ: Prentice-Hall, 1967), 136–49.

47. "'Tornado' Helped," *LAT*, Dec. 13, 1925, B26 (quotation); Sturm, "Automobile Racing through a Champion's Eyes," 145.

48. "Tribune Tours," *CT*, May 23, 1926, A10; "Tribune Tours," *CT*, May 24, 1925, A10; "500-Mile Race Once Called Propaganda," *IndNews*, May 30, 1925, 12; "Two File Petitions Asking Bus Routes," *IndyStar*, Sept. 6, 1925, 16. On buses, see Brian J. Cudahy, *Cash, Tokens, and Transfers: A History of Urban Mass Transit in North America* (New York: Fordham University Press, 1990), 98–113.

49. Robert E. Park, Ernest W. Burgess, Roderick D. McKenzie, *The City* (Chicago: University of Chicago Press, 1967), 70, 107; Robert S. Lynd and Helen Merrell Lynd, *Middletown: A Study in Contemporary American Culture* (New York: Harcourt, Brace, 1929), 251 (first quotation), 258–59 (latter quotations), 64, 95, 137, 253, 254,

362. On Speedway City, see History Committee of the Speedway Civic Committee, *The Story of Speedway* (Indianapolis: History Committee of the Speedway Civic Committee, 1976), 101, 136, 155, 163; National Park Service, "Speedway Historic District," accessed Sept. 26, 2021, https://www.nps.gove/nr/travel/indianapolis/speedwaydistrict.htm.

50. Alton Beach Realty Company, "Birds-Eye Picture of Miami Beach," 10: 56, Fisher Papers (quotation); "From the Archives: Carl Fisher's Hotels," Miami Design Preservation League, archives, 2020, accessed Sept. 26, 2021, https://mdpl.org/archives/2020/10/carl-fishers-hotels-2/.

51. Carl G. Fisher Hotels pamphlet, 8: 525–32, Fisher Papers (quotations); Fisher to Charles B. Sommers, Oct. 5, 1920, and F. R. Humpage to Fisher, Oct. 11, 1920, 7: 267–69, Fisher Papers; Fisher to Frank B. Shutts, Mar. 26, 1919, 10: 555–56, Fisher Papers; WIOD memorandum, ca. 1929, 16: 784–92, Fisher Papers; Glenn Miller, "Playing Ball through the 1918 Pandemic," *Fort Myers Florida Weekly*, Feb. 10, 2021, https://fortmyers.floridaweekly.com/articles/playing-ball-through-the-1918-pandemic/.

52. Anne O'Hare McCormick, "Making a Speedway of De Soto's Trail," *NYT*, May 17, 1925, SM5, SM23 (quotations); Arva Moore Parks, *George Merrick, Son of the South Wind: Visionary Creator of Coral Gables* (Gainesville: University Press of Florida, 2015); Thomas Graham, *Mr. Flagler's St. Augustine* (Gainesville: University Press of Florida, 2014); Polly Redford, *Billion-Dollar Sandbar: A Biography of Miami Beach* (New York: E. P. Dutton, 1970), 117.

53. Fisher to C. Kucher, Dec. 20, 1919, 10: 126, Fisher Papers (quotation); Fisher to Harvey Firestone, Sept. 30, 1921, 10: 291, Fisher Papers.

54. "Miami-by-the-Sea," ca. 1918, 10: 98, Fisher Papers. On the concept of *vacation*, see Cindy S. Aron, *Working at Play: A History of Vacations in the United States* (New York: Oxford University Press, 1999), 3–10; Foster, *Castles in the Sand*, 305.

55. William T. Anderson to Fisher, Nov. 6, 1925, 10: 425–27, Fisher Papers (quotations); "The Growth of Miami Beach," 1928 flyer, 11: 72, Fisher Papers.

56. "Front Page Reader," ca. 1918, 10: 106–7, Fisher Papers; Alton Beach Realty Company ad, 1918–19, 10: 642, Fisher Papers; Fisher to Thomas J. Pancoast, Nov. 7, 1921, 10: 141, Fisher Papers; Fisher to Miss Whitney, Apr. 3, 1924, 10: 155, Fisher Papers (quotation).

57. Caroll Y. Belknap, "Selling Real Estate with Sport," unidentified magazine clipping ca. 1923, 16: 67–70, Fisher Papers; Redford, *Billion-Dollar Sandbar*, 115.

58. Christopher Knowlton, *Bubble in the Sun: The Florida Boom of the 1920s and How It Brought on the Great Depression* (New York: Simon and Schuster, 2020), 103–5; Jason Vuic, *The Swamp Peddlers: How Lot Sellers, Land Scammers, and Retirees Built Modern Florida and Transformed the American Dream* (Chapel Hill: University of North Carolina Press, 2021).

59. Rebecca Cawood McIntyre, *Souvenirs of the Old South: Northern Tourism and Southern Mythology* (Gainesville: University Press of Florida, 2011), 142.

60. Fisher to Mrs. E. Eldridge, July 21, 1925, 2: 845, Fisher Papers.

61. Fisher to James Cox, July 29, 1925, 2: 859, Fisher Papers; Fisher to Central Farmers' Trust Co., West Palm Beach, May 5, 1926, 2: 888 (quotation); Fisher to James J. Davis, May 11, 1926, 2: 890, Fisher Papers; Fisher, "Why I Still Have Faith in Florida," ca. Nov. 1929, 2: 920, Fisher Papers.

62. Foster, *Castles in the Sand*, 247–74 (first quotation, 250); Montauk Beach ad, 1928 Official Program, Rickenbacker collection; Fisher to Irving A. Collins, May 19, 1925, 12: 666, Fisher Papers; Fisher to Harvey S. Firestone, Nov. 5, 1926, 12: 684, Fisher Papers; Fisher to Roy D. Chapin, Dec. 30, 1927, 11: 148, Fisher Papers; "Montauk Beach: The New Summer City on Long Island's Slender Tip," 11: 516 (second quotation), Fisher Papers; Norman Taylor, *The Climate of Long Island: Its Relation to Forests, Crops, and Man*, Bulletin 458, Cornell University Agricultural Experiment Station, July 1926, 11: 686, Fisher Papers.

63. Fisher to V. D. L. Robinson, Apr. 29, 1919, 4: 110, Fisher Papers.

64. Fisher to James M. Cox, Apr. 19, 1925, 4: 18, Fisher Papers; Will Rogers, "Carl Took Florida from Alligators and Gave It Over to the Indianians [*sic*]," *WP*, Oct. 11, 1925, SM2 (quotations). On Rogers, see Amy M. Ware, *The Cherokee Kid: Will Rogers, Tribal Identity, and the Making of an American Icon* (Lawrence: University Press of Kansas, 2015), 130–74.

65. J. Fisher, *Pacesetter*, 289.

Chapter 7. Selling the Speedway

1. William Herschell, "The Click of the Turnstiles," 1927 Official Program, Edward V. Rickenbacker collection (unprocessed), IMS [hereafter, Rickenbacker collection].

2. William Herschell, "The Feel of the Wheel," 1922 Official Program, Rickenbacker collection.

3. Fisher to Antonio Giraudier, Mar. 25, 1920, 8: 664, Carl Graham Fisher Papers, HistoryMiami Research Center, Miami, Florida [hereafter, Fisher Papers]; "World's Largest Speedway Will Be Built in Texas," *Austin American*, Jan. 17, 1926, A9. On Cuba, see Christine Skwiot, *The Purposes of Paradise: U.S. Tourism and Empire in Cuba and Hawai'i* (Philadelphia: University of Pennsylvania Press, 2010), 4, 85.

4. "Build Florida Track," *LAT*, Dec. 25, 1925, B2 (quotation); "New Florida Speed Bowl Ready for Jan. 30 Classic," *CT*, Jan. 3, 1926, A5; "Date Switched for Florida 300-Mile Speedway Classic," *LAT*, Jan. 26, 1926, B2; "Speedway Experts Move South for New Track Premiere," *CT*, Feb. 28 [*sic*], 1926, A10 (this article may have been printed earlier, possibly on Feb. 21, since it refers to the upcoming race on Feb. 22); "De Paolo Triumphs, Sets World's Mark," *NYT*, Feb. 23, 1926, 31. On Florida's 1926 bust, see Mark S. Foster, *Castles in the Sand: The Life and Times of Carl Graham Fisher* (Gainesville: University Press of Florida, 2000), 224–30.

5. Donnelly Realty Co. ads, *NYT*, Oct. 26, 1925, 40, and *CT*, Oct. 27, 1925, 21; "Florida Lot Scheme Hit by Fraud Order," *NYT*, Aug. 4, 1926, 21 (quotation); Foster,

Castles in the Sand, 230–36; Daniel J. Simone, "Racing, Region, and the Environment: A History of American Motorsports" (PhD diss., University of Florida, 2009), 54; Christopher Knowlton, *Bubble in the Sun: The Florida Boom of the 1920s and How It Brought on the Great Depression* (New York: Simon and Schuster, 2020), 225–31, 274–75.

6. C. W. Chase Jr. to Fisher, June 27, 1927, 11: 753, Fisher Papers (quotation); Fisher to Edward N. Hurley, Sept. 26, 1927, 12: 68–69, Fisher Papers; Fisher to Joseph B. Thomas, Feb. 19, 1929, 12: 293, Fisher Papers.

7. Fred A. Britten to Fisher, Dec. 16, 1930, 12: 624, Fisher Papers.

8. Fisher to W. W. Atterbury, May 3, 1927, 11: 712, Fisher Papers (quotations); Montauk Beach Development Corporation ad, Nov. 1, 1928, 12: 229–31, Fisher Papers.

9. "Bryson Is Permanent Airport Group Head," *IndNews*, Mar. 30, 1926, 1; "Speedway Field Use for Airport Is Asked," *IndNews*, Apr. 2, 1926, 33; "Airport at Speedway May Soon Be Reality," *IndNews*, Apr. 7, 1926, 21, 36 (quotations); "Airport Supporters to Carry Out Plans," *IndNews*, Apr. 10, 1926, 7; "Motor Speedway Use for Airport Assured," *IndNews*, Apr. 13, 1926, 1, 18; "Incorporation Papers for Airport Are Filed," *IndNews*, Apr. 20, 1926, 14. "City Airport Will Be Established at Once," *IndNews*, Oct. 2, 1926, 33; "Pick Mars Hill for Airport," *IndyStar*, Oct. 2, 1926, 1.

10. "City Is Included in Airplane Tour," *IndyStar*, June 27, 1926, 1; "Plan Route for Planes to Visit City," *IndyStar*, July 25, 1926, 13; "Air Tour Planes Will Reach City at Noon Today," *IndyStar*, June 30, 1928, 1, 7; "25 Planes Start National Air Tour," *NYT*, July 1, 1928, 19.

11. Arthur Brisbane, "Today," *IndyStar*, May 31, 1926, 1.

12. "Speedway City Will Incorporate," *IndyStar*, Aug. 1, 1926, 26; "Candidates Speak at Speedway City," *IndyStar*, Aug. 11, 1926, 10; "Council to Act Soon to Annex Three Suburbs," *IndyStar*, Aug. 14, 1926, 1 (quotations); "Suburbs Opposed to Annexation, Report," *IndNews*, Aug. 14, 1926, 1; "Councilmen's Capers," *IndNews*, Aug. 16, 1926, 6; "Speedway Annexation Goes to Committee," *IndNews*, Aug. 17, 1926, 3; "Hold First Election at Speedway City," *IndyStar*, Aug. 19, 1926, 1; "Annexation of Our Suburbs," *IndyStar*, Aug. 19, 1926, 6; "City Planners Curbed in Bill before Council, *IndyStar*, Oct. 26, 1926, 22. On Unigov, see William Blomquist and Roger B. Parks, "Fiscal, Service, and Political Impacts of Indianapolis-Marion County's Unigov," *Publius* 25, no. 4 (Autumn 1995): 40–41.

13. Holloway Building Co. ad, *IndyStar*, July 15, 1928, 19; Schloss Bros. Investment Co. ad, *IndNews*, July 28, 1928, 35 (quotations); Speedway Realty Co. ad, *IndyStar*, Jan. 13, 1929, 31; Russell J. Clark, "Beautiful Speedway City Homes Open Today," *IndyStar*, June 30, 1929, 32; LeeAnn Lands, *The Culture of Property: Race, Class, and Housing Landscapes in Atlanta, 1880–1950* (Athens: University of Georgia Press, 2009), 111–20.

14. "New Small Auto, Speedy and Low, to Be Made Soon," *WP*, May 16, 1926, A3; J. L. Jenkins, "Pilot's Skull Fractured as Tiny Cars Whirl to Records," *CT*, May 28, 1926, 25; "Routes to Speedway," *IndyStar*, May 30, 1926, 1; "Hoosier City Agog

over Races," *WP*, May 31, 1926, 9; "Lockhart's Car Wins Race before 150,000," *NYT*, June 1, 1926, 32; "Record Crowds Again Featured the Year," *NYT*, Dec. 26, 1926, S5. On the pagoda, see James Craig Reinhardt, *The Indianapolis 500: Inside the Greatest Spectacle in Racing* (Bloomington, IN: Red Lightning Books/Indiana University Press, 2019), 25.

15. Fisher to George LeBoutillier, Apr. 26, 1927, 8: 688, Fisher Papers; Fisher to Rickenbacker, June 13, 1927, 8: 693–94, Fisher Papers; "Wife Divorces Carl G. Fisher, Rich Sportsman," *CT*, Aug. 14, 1926, 2; T. Von Ziekursch, "More Danger Is Needed to Save Motor Racing," *WP*, Jan. 23, 1927, A2; Jerry M. Fisher, *The Pacesetter: The Untold Story of Carl G. Fisher* (Fort Bragg, CA: Lost Coast, 1998), 279–95.

16. "Would Have Motor Show at Same Time as Big Race," *LAT*, June 27, 1926, G18; Steve Hannagan press release, undated, 8: 728, Fisher Papers. Variations were published in newspapers: "Oil Burners Will Race at Indianapolis," *LAT*, Jan. 3, 1927, 9; "Oil Burners to Vie Here," *IndyStar*, Jan. 3, 1927, 1. On lack of enthusiasm, see T. E. Myers to Fisher, Feb. 4, 1927, 8: 680, Fisher Papers; Fisher to Myers, Feb. 16, 1927, 8: 681, Fisher Papers.

17. Christopher W. Wells, *Car Country: An Environmental History* (Seattle: University of Washington Press, 2012), 185–88; Susan Croce Kelly, *Father of Route 66: The Story of Cy Avery* (Norman: University of Oklahoma Press, 2014), 86–87, 127–75; "High Speed Is Meaningless to Car Owner," *LAT*, Mar. 13, 1927, G11 (quotation); "Tribune Tours," *CT*, May 1, 1927, A12.

18. Myron R. Huff, "Where the Eyes Always Have It," *WP*, May 20, 1928, SM5.

19. "Stutz Stock Car Enters Speed Test for Stevens Prize," *WP*, Apr. 17, 1927, A4; "High-Speed Roads Urged," *LAT*, Apr. 22, 1928, G7 (quotation).

20. "News and Views of the Auto Trade," *CT*, Apr. 15, 1928, A11 (quotation). On Hoffman and the Erskine Bureau, see Peter D. Norton, *Fighting Traffic: The Dawn of the Motor Age in the American City* (Cambridge, MA: MIT Press, 2008), 163–69, 234–35.

21. Frederic J. Haskin, "Bad Roads Tax on Motorists Heavy," *LAT*, May 27, 1928, G8 (quotation); "Heaviest Year of Travel Assured," *LAT*, May 27, 1928, G5; "Car Insurance Totals Climb," *LAT*, July 29, 1928, G4; "U.S. Cities Busy Building Roads for Automobiles," *CT*, Apr. 28, 1929, A10.

22. Foster, *Castles in the Sand*, 286–87.

23. Fisher to C. F. Kettering, Apr. 8, 1929, 9: 35, Fisher Papers.

24. "Movie Daredevil Enters 500 Mile Speedway Test," *CT*, May 15, 1927, A2; "Former Purdue Youth Drives in Auto Classic," *WP*, May 15, 1927, 25; "Motordom," *CT*, May 22, 1927, A14; J. L. Jenkins, "Lockhart Spins at 120.10 Clip in Race Trials," *CT*, May 27, 1927, 23; "Milton Qualifies Car for Big Race Tomorrow," *LAT*, May 29, 1927, A3.

25. Charles W. Dunkley, "Souders, Ex-Purdue Student, Wins Auto Race," *LAT*, May 31, 1927, B1, B3; "145,000 See Youth Win Auto Classic," *NYT*, May 31, 1927, 29; "Mother 'Couldn't Stand' to See Son Win 500 Mile Race," *CT*, May 31, 1927, 1 (quotation); "Lafayette, Ind., Gives Souders Real Reception," *CT*, June 2, 1927, 17.

26. "The Inquiring Reporter," *CT*, May 13, 1927, 29 (quotations), and *CT*, May 22, 1927, A15; Virginia Scharff, *Taking the Wheel: Women and the Coming of the Motor Age* (Albuquerque: University of New Mexico Press, 1991), 119.

27. Homer McKee, "Saviors," 1922 Official Program, Rickenbacker collection.

28. "The World's Greatest Race Course," 1927 Official Program, Rickenbacker collection.

29. "Variations Countless," *LAT*, Mar. 11, 1928, G6; Steve Hannagan, "Do You Remember When?," 1927 Official Program, Rickenbacker collection; David N. Lucsko, *The Business of Speed: The Hot Rod Industry in America, 1915–1990* (Baltimore: Johns Hopkins University Press, 2008).

30. "145,000, Sport's Biggest Crowd of the Year, Saw 500-Mile Auto Classic at Indianapolis," *NYT*, Jan. 1, 1928, S5; Al Bloemker, *500 Miles to Go: The History of the Indianapolis Speedway* (New York: Coward-McCann, 1961), 169–70; Elmer W. Stout to Robert H. Tyndall, June 16, 1927, 8: 703, Fisher Papers; Edward V. Rickenbacker, *Rickenbacker* (Englewood Cliffs, NJ: Prentice-Hall, 1967), 151 (quotations). On the 1920s peak, see Charles J. Shindo, *1927 and the Rise of Modern America* (Lawrence: University Press of Kansas, 2010).

31. "Syndicate Seeks Speedway Stock of Carl Fisher," *IndyStar*, July 28, 1927, 1; "News of the Middle West," *LAT*, Aug. 5, 1927, 13; Rickenbacker, *Rickenbacker*, 153 (quotations). On Rickenbacker's company, see Donald Finlay Davis, *Conspicuous Production: Automobiles and Elites in Detroit, 1899–1933* (Philadelphia: Temple University Press, 1988), 33, 99.

32. Rickenbacker to Allison, July 7, 1927, 8: 697, Fisher Papers; Fisher to Rickenbacker, July 12, 1927, 8: 700, Fisher Papers (quotation); Rickenbacker to Fisher, July 18, 1927, 8: 704, Fisher Papers.

33. L. M. Langston to Allison, July 27, 1927, 8: 709, Fisher Papers (quotation); Rickenbacker to Allison, Sept. 1, 1927, 8: 714–15, Fisher Papers; "Motor Speedway Is Reorganized," *IndyStar*, Sept. 2, 1927, 20; Myers to Allison, Nov. 4, 1927, 8: 718, Fisher Papers; Allison to Fisher, Newby, and F. E. Sweet, Nov. 8, 1927, 8: 719, Fisher Papers; Myers to Allison, Dec. 7, 1927, 8: 722–23, Fisher Papers; Myers to Fisher, Dec. 8, 1927, 8: 726, Fisher Papers; "E. V. Rickenbacker Joins Sales Force of Cadillac Team," *WP*, Jan. 15, 1928, A9; "Indiana Race Draws Leaders," *LAT*, June 2, 1929, F1; Rickenbacker, *Rickenbacker*, 153.

34. Finis Farr, *Rickenbacker's Luck: An American Life* (Boston: Houghton Mifflin, 1979), 155.

35. Fisher to Rickenbacker, June 13, 1927, 8: 693–94, Fisher Papers (quotations); Fisher to Allison, July 12, 1927, 8: 696, Fisher Papers; Fisher to Rickenbacker, July 12, 1927, 8: 700, Fisher Papers; Fisher to Joy, Aug. 17, 1927, 8: 820–21, Fisher Papers; Robert H. Tyndall to Walter Kohlhepp, Sept. 12, 1927, 12: 57, Fisher Papers.

36. "War Ace Is Named Head of Speedway," *NYT*, Sept. 2, 1927, 10 (quotations); "Indianapolis Speedway Sold to Detroit Men," *CT*, Sept. 2, 1927, 23; "Rickenbacker Puts Money in Speedway," *LAT*, Sept. 2, 1927, 13.

37. "Speedway to Remain Here," *IndyStar*, Nov. 20, 1927, 67.

38. Rickenbacker, *Rickenbacker*, 154; "Golf Course Planned for Speedway Plant," *IndNews*, Mar. 19, 1928, 17 (quotation); William Herschell, "Speedway City, Which Carl G. Fisher Dreamed of Twenty Years Ago," *IndNews*, Apr. 13, 1929, 21; "Speedway Will Open Public Golf Grounds," *IndNews*, Apr. 17, 1929, 21.

39. "Incorporations," *IndyStar*, Mar. 24, 1928, 17; "The Speedway Golf Course," 1930 Official Program, Rickenbacker collection (quotation). On golf, see Richard J. Moss, *Golf and the American Country Club* (Urbana: University of Illinois Press, 2001); George B. Kirsch, *Golf in America* (Urbana: University of Illinois Press, 2009); Lane Demas, *Game of Privilege: An African American History of Golf* (Chapel Hill: University of North Carolina Press, 2017).

40. "Ship Lockhart's Car to Florida for Speed Test," *CT*, Feb. 13, 1928, 25; "Lockhart Car Crashes at Speed of 225 Miles," *WP*, Feb. 23, 1928, 1; "Lockhart Meets Death in Attempt at Record," *LAT*, Apr. 26, 1928, 1; "Lockhart Hurtles to Death Speeding 200 Miles an Hour," *NYT*, Apr. 26, 1928, 1; "Auto Race Drivers to Bear Lockhart's Body to Grave," *CT*, Apr. 29, 1928, A1; Putney Haight, "Racers Whiz to New Records in 500 Mile Trials," *CT*, May 27, 1928, A4; Wilbur Shaw, *Gentlemen, Start Your Engines* (New York: Coward-McCann, 1955), 83 (quotation). The *Los Angeles Times* reported that Lockhart's wife was "hysterical," but *New York Times* said she "bore [the news] with fortitude."

41. "Stutz and Hispano Plan 24-Hour Race," *NYT*, Mar. 27, 1928, 30; "French Auto Racer Here," *NYT*, Apr. 4, 1928, 9; "Pease Says He Barred Hispano-Suiza Racer," *NYT*, Apr. 5, 1928, 29; "Willys to Produce 6-Cylinder Whippet," *NYT*, Apr. 7, 1928, 22; "Car Pilots in Match Race Being Chosen," *LAT*, Apr. 8, 1928, G6; "Racing Car's Owner Appeals for Entry," *NYT*, Apr. 10, 1928, 11; Sterrett and Fleming ad, *WP*, Apr. 15, 1928, A8; "Auto Race Is Delayed," *NYT*, Apr. 15, 1928, 19; "Record Broken by French Car," *LAT*, Apr. 19, 1928, B4; "French Stock Car Is Victor," *LAT*, Apr. 20, 1928, B2.

42. "Factory to Again Enter Auto Races," *LAT*, Apr. 29, 1928, G8 (quotation); "Race Veteran Leads Team of Factory Drivers," *LAT*, May 6, 1928, G6.

43. "Auto Racer Hurt in Crash," *NYT*, May 25, 1928, 18; "De Paolo Hurt in Trial Spin," *LAT*, May 27, 1928, A1; "Relief Pilot Hurt in Speedway Crash," *NYT*, May 30, 1928, 14; "Fan Parks at Speedway Gates Four Days before Auto Race," *NYT*, May 27, 1928, 141; Chicago Motor Car Co. ad, *CT*, Mar. 31, 1929, 17 (quotation).

44. Putney Haight, "28 Cars to Face Starter's Flag at Indianapolis," *CT*, May 30, 1928, 17.

45. "Indianapolis 500-Mile Race Awaited by 31 Star Drivers," *WP*, May 30, 1928, 13.

46. "Great Automobile Race on Air Decoration Day," *WP*, May 23, 1928, 19; William S. Odlin, "Indianapolis Classic Victors Were Once Laurel 'Outlaws'," *WP*, June 9, 1929, A6 (quotation).

47. Fisher to Rickenbacker, Mar. 1 (quotation), Mar. 4, 1929, 15: 493–94, Fisher Papers.

48. W. F. Fox Jr., "And They Tell Us the Tempus, She Fugits," 1928 Official Program, Rickenbacker collection.

49. A Speedway Fan, "They Always Come Back," 1928 Official Program, Ricken-backer collection.

50. "Indianapolis 500-Mile Race Awaited by 31 Star Drivers," *WP*, May 30, 1928, 13; "Louis Meyer Wins 500-Mile Auto Race," *NYT*, May 31, 1928, 32; "Record Crowd Watches Race" and "New Speedway Chief Pleased," *IndyStar*, May 31, 1928, 8; "De Paolo Quits Racing for Sake of Family," *WP*, June 1, 1928, 13 (quotation); "De Paolo in Hoosier Race," *LAT*, May 6, 1929, 11.

51. "James A. Allison, Capitalist, Dies," *IndNews*, Aug. 4, 1928, 1–2; "Dies on His Honeymoon," *NYT*, Aug. 4, 1928, 6; "Founder of Speedway Dies of Bronchial Pneumonia," *CT*, Aug. 5, 1928, 12; "Widowed Bride Sued as Husband Is Being Buried," *CT*, Aug. 7, 1928, 3; Fisher to Elmer W. Stout, Sept. 4, 1928, 8: 727, Fisher Papers; M. E. Foley to Fisher, Jan. 9, 1929, 1: 471–72, Fisher Papers.

52. "Indianapolis Auto Race Officials Revise Rules," *WP*, Jan. 10, 1929, 17 (quotation); "Indianapolis to Eliminate Baby Racers in 1930," *CT*, Jan. 10, 1929, 19; "Racing Cars," *WP*, Jan. 12, 1929, 6; William Ulman, "Row in Automobile Racing Is Providing Stirring Debate," *WP*, June 16, 1929, A6.

53. "Cliff Durant to Seek Speed Classic Again," *CT*, Apr. 7, 1929, A14; "Forty-Six in Auto Classic," *LAT*, May 19, 1929, A4; "Indianapolis Autos Undergo Final Repair," *WP*, May 24, 1929, 13; "500-Mile Auto Race Will Be Held Today," *NYT*, May 30, 1929, 23.

54. "Cliff Woodbury Makes Fastest Time in Trials," *CT*, May 26, 1929, A10; Simone, "Racing, Region, and the Environment," 56 (quotation). On 1920s Los Angeles, see Jeremiah B. C. Axelrod, *Inventing Autopia: Dreams and Visions of the Modern Metropolis in Jazz Age Los Angeles* (Berkeley: University of California Press, 2009).

55. "Indianapolis Race Curtain for Pygmy Cars," *CT*, May 27, 1929, 28; "500-Mile Auto Race Will Be Held Today," *NYT*, May 30, 1929, 23; Putney Haight, "33 to Start in $80,000 Auto Race Today," *CT*, May 30, 1929, 21; "Hunt Lindy and Bride at Race; Fail to Find Pair," *CT*, May 31, 1929, 6; "Lindberghs Still Hidden," *NYT*, May 31, 1929, 21.

56. Putney Haight, "Indianapolis Shows Us Up in Auto Regulation," *CT*, June 2, 1929, A9. On one-way streets, see "Route Traffic to Speedway," *IndyStar*, May 29, 1921, 13; "Two One-Way Speedway Routes," *IndNews*, May 29, 1925, 1; "One-Way Routes to the Speedway," *IndyStar*, May 30, 1925, 1.

57. "Auto Race Broadcast on Memorial Day," *NYT*, May 26, 1929, XX18 (quotation); Ralph L. Power, "Hoover Speech on Ether Today," *LAT*, May 30, 1929, A6; "Goodyear-Zeppelin, Puritan, to Land at Speedway Today," *IndyStar*, May 30, 1929, 11; "Historic Auto Classic Today," *LAT*, May 30, 1929, B1, B4; Mary E. Bostwick, "Dirigible Riding Seems Just About like a Dream to Mary," *IndyStar*, May 31, 1929, 11; Rickenbacker to Fisher, May 9, 1929, 15: 499, Fisher Papers.

58. "Death Rides in Classic," *LAT*, May 31, 1929, 1 (quotations); "Keech Gets $31,900 as Auto Race Winner," *NYT*, June 2, 1929, S4.

59. Axelrod, *Inventing Autopia*, 78.

60. Fisher to John H. Levi, Aug. 13, 1919, 10: 114, Fisher Papers; Fisher to George Ade, Oct. 21, 1921, 10: 140, Fisher Papers.

61. "Hollywood Film Notes," *NYT*, June 23, 1929, X3; "Planes, Motors in 'Speedway'," *LAT*, July 14, 1929, 25; "Haines Wins a First and a Girl Here," *WP*, Sept. 1, 1929, A2; Mordaunt Hall, "The Screen," *NYT*, Sept. 21, 1929, 25 (quotations); "New Cinema Offerings," *NYT*, Sept. 22, 1929, X8.

62. "Ray Keech Killed as 4 Racers Crash," *NYT*, June 16, 1929, 1, 13; "Speed Test Scheduled at Daytona," *LAT*, July 21, 1929, E2 (quotations). On football apologists, see Brian M. Ingrassia, *The Rise of Gridiron University: Higher Education's Uneasy Alliance with Big-Time Football* (Lawrence: University Press of Kansas, 2012), 48–50.

63. "24 Planes Entered for Gardner Trophy," *NYT*, May 27, 1929, 2; "Nine Pilots Qualify for Thursday's Race," *WP*, May 29, 1929, 10; "Holman Winner in First Gardner Air Trophy Race," *CT*, May 31, 1929, 21.

64. "Marmon Cars Set Record," *WSJ*, June 21, 1929, 18; "Optimism Rules," *WSJ*, June 22, 1929, 1; Chicago Motor Car Co. ad, *CT*, July 1, 1929, 21 (quotation); "Storm Stops Roosevelt Run; 440-Hour Endurance Mark Set," *IndyStar*, July 1, 1929, 1; "Nonstop Roosevelt on Exhibition Here," *WP*, July 21, 1929, A6. See also Marmon ad, *NYT*, July 7, 1929, 50; A .C. Moses Motor Co. ad, *WP*, July 14, 1929, A9.

65. Abe Martin, "Speed," 1930 Official Program, Rickenbacker collection.

66. "Thin Stream Propels Cars," *LAT*, Aug. 18, 1929, E2.

67. Fisher to Rickenbacker, June 3 and 10, 1929, 15: 503–6, Fisher Papers; Myers to Fisher, June 10, 1929, 8: 730, Fisher Papers; Fisher to Myers, June 12, 1929, 8: 731, Fisher Papers (quotation); Myers to Fisher, Mar. 8, 1930, 8: 733, Fisher Papers; Stout to Fisher, Mar. 10, 1930, 8: 734–35, Fisher Papers; Fisher to Elmer Stout, Apr. 16, 1930, 1: 477, Fisher Papers.

68. Merchants Association, Indianapolis, "Visitors Welcome to Indianapolis," 1922 Official Program, Rickenbacker collection; Paul Q. Richey, "The Center of the Continent," 1927 Official Program, Rickenbacker collection (quotations). See also Indianapolis Hotels Association ad, 1941 Official Program, Rickenbacker collection.

69. Jonathan Brooks, "Indianapolis: A City of the Middle of the Road," *New Republic* 56, Nov. 14, 1928, 347–50.

70. Nicholas H. Noyes, "Progress of Indianapolis Healthful," *IndyStar*, Sept. 5, 1926, 57.

71. Walter Christaller, *Central Places in Southern Germany*, trans. Carlisle W. Baskin (Englewood Cliffs, NJ: Prentice-Hall, 1966).

Chapter 8. Just Call It the "500"

1. Rex Mays, "Speed Is My Business," *LAT*, May 28, 1939, I12.

2. "Tickets on Sale for Indianapolis Classic, May 30," *CT*, Jan. 26, 1930, G12; "Auto Racing Blossoms," *LAT*, Apr. 18, 1930, A11; "Record Entry Signed Up for Hoosier Race," *LAT*, May 3, 1931, F4; Hal Foust, "Indianapolis Race Has Entry List of 72 Cars," *CT*, May 22, 1932, A6; William Ullman, "New Machines and Drivers to Figure in Race Friday," *WP*, May 25, 1930, A8-A9; "$40,000, Fame Await Victor at

Indianapolis," *CT*, May 30, 1930, 19; David N. Lucsko, *The Business of Speed: The Hot Rod Industry in America, 1915–1990* (Baltimore: Johns Hopkins University Press, 2008), 44 (quotation).

3. Ullman, "New Machines"; Myron R. Huff, "Drivers Who Finish the 500-Mile Indianapolis Automobile Race on Memorial Day Peril Their Lives Twice in Every Minute of the Grind," *WP*, May 28, 1933, SM2 (quotation).

4. "Takes Edenburn and Rabbit to Make 'Crowd' Story Complete," *IndNews*, May 28, 1932, 15; "Mrs. Rabbit Rears Her Family amid Speedway's Roar," *CT*, May 28, 1933, A4 (quotations).

5. "Fair Speed Demons in Auto Race," *CT*, Sept. 30, 1923, A5; "Woman Driver May Compete at Speedway," *LAT*, May 21, 1931, A12. On Mais, see "'Miss Elfrieda Mais'—Dare Devil and Pioneer Racing Car Driver," *Old Motor*, July 31, 2019, http://theoldmotor.com/?p=176424.

6. "De Paolo Gets Place in Race," *LAT*, May 26, 1930, 13; "50,000,000 Hear Indianapolis Each Minute on Day of Race," *IndyStar*, May 28, 1930, 12 (quotation); "3 Youths Annex Pole Position at Indianapolis," *WP*, May 29, 1930, 17; John Kieran, "Sports of the Times," *NYT*, May 30, 1930, 24; Hal Foust, "Billy Arnold Wins 500 Mile Auto Race," *CT*, May 31, 1930, 19; "Four Children Made Orphans after Fatal Accident at Speedway Race," *IndNews*, May 31, 1930, 2; Charles W. Dunkley, "Race Won by Arnold," *LAT*, May 31, 1930, 1; "Evans, Driving Only Oil Burner in Grind, First to Qualify at Indianapolis Speedway," *NYT*, May 24, 1931, S3; "40 Auto Racers Qualify," *NYT*, May 28, 1931, 36; Hal Foust, "Schneider Wins 500 Mile Auto Derby," *CT*, May 31, 1931, A1; "500-Mile Auto Race Is Won by Schneider," *NYT*, May 31, 1931, S1; Charles Dunkley, "Auto Classic to Schneider; Youth Killed," *WP*, May 31, 1931, M1, M15.

7. Robert S. Lynd and Helen Merrell Lynd, *Middletown in Transition: A Study in Cultural Conflicts* (New York: Harcourt, Brace, 1937), 265 (quotation), 10, 26, 245, 573.

8. Lewis Mumford, *Technics and Civilization* (New York: Harcourt, Brace, 1934), 236–37 (quotations); Mumford, *The Culture of Cities* (New York: Harcourt, Brace, 1938), 331, 488.

9. "Screen Lights and Shadows," *NYT*, Jan. 3, 1932, X4; "Speed Drama with Cagney, Earle's Film," *WP*, Apr. 16, 1932, A1 (quotation); "Twenty Pilots Seen in New Race Picture," *LAT*, May 1, 1932, B12; "Cagney Shown as Race Driver in Latest Film," *LAT*, May 15, 1932, B15; "Speedway Seen in Race Film at Downtown," *LAT*, May 22, 1932, B9.

10. Frank S. Nugent, "The Screen," *NYT*, May 16, 1936, 11; Nugent, "The Screen," *NYT*, July 15, 1939, 14 (quotations); "The Theatre," *WSJ*, July 17, 1939, 8; "Metropolitan," *WP*, Sept. 2, 1939, 11; "Drama of Auto Racing Dishes Out the Thrills," *CT*, Sept. 18, 1939, 15.

11. "De Palma, His Cash $3, Petitions as Bankrupt," *WP*, Aug. 23, 1931, M13; "Forbid Auto Race on Radio," *WSJ*, May 28, 1932, 1; Orrin E. Dunlap Jr., "Listening-In," *NYT*, May 29, 1932, X10; Charles C. Cohan, "Los Angeles Makes Bid for National

Recognition as Automobile Racing Center," *LAT*, Nov. 20, 1932, D5; "Cheaper Seats for Race at Indianapolis," *LAT*, Apr. 7, 1933, A9; "Motor Speedway Purse Cut," *NYT*, Apr. 23, 1933, S4; "Today on the Radio," *NYT*, May 30, 1934, 15; "New Auto Race Track Planned," *LAT*, Jan. 15, 1939, A11.

12. "Forty Drivers Await Gun for 500-Mile Race Today," *WP*, May 30, 1932, 9, 10; Hal Foust, "Frame Wins Auto Derby with Record Speed," *CT*, May 31, 1932, 15; Charles Dunkley, "Frame Wins Speed Classic," *LAT*, May 31, 1932, 1, 11; "Frame, Auto Race Winner, Gets $31,050," *CT*, June 1, 1932, 27.

13. "Indianapolis Race," *NYT*, May 30, 1939, 13.

14. Bill Potts, "Auto Races Sell Short," *LAT*, Dec. 25, 1932, D4; "Expect 135,000 in Indianapolis," *CT*, May 26, 1940, A6 (quotation).

15. Thomas P. Henry, "The American Automobile Association and Its Interest in Racing," 1930 Official Program, Edward V. Rickenbacker collection (unprocessed), IMS, Indianapolis [hereafter, Rickenbacker collection].

16. "Hump May Be Ironed Out on Hoosier Track," *LAT*, Apr. 15, 1933, 8; "Sets Unofficial Mark," *NYT*, May 13, 1933, 9; "Cummings Does 118.52 M.P.H. in Speed-way Trial," *CT*, May 21, 1933, A5; "Hoosier Speeders Crack-Up," *LAT*, May 23, 1933, A9; "Racing Auto Hits Wall," *NYT*, May 26, 1933, 25; "5 Qualify at Indianapolis," *CT*, May 27, 1933, 19.

17. "Meyer Wins Auto Race," *CT*, May 31, 1933, 19; "Lou Meyer Triumphs," *LAT*, May 31, 1933, 1; "3 Killed as Meyer Wins Indianapolis Auto Classic," *NYT*, May 31, 1933, 1, 24; Nelson B. Bell, "About the Show Shops," *WP*, June 5, 1933, 7 (quotation); "Speedway Race in Movie," *NYT*, June 5, 1933, 18.

18. G. Edward White, *Creating the National Pastime: Baseball Transforms Itself, 1903–1953* (Princeton, NJ: Princeton University Press, 1996), 118–21, 167–79; Brad Austin, *Democratic Sports: Men's and Women's College Athletics during the Great Depression* (Fayetteville: University of Arkansas Press, 2015), 173–201.

19. Claude Wolff, "Safety Increases Thrills," 1930 Official Program, Rickenbacker collection; "Speed Test Is Increased," *NYT*, Oct. 23, 1931, 32; E. Y. Watson, "Indianapolis Speed Trials Get under Way with Eight-Cylinder Jobs Predominating," *LAT*, May 21, 1933, D2; "500 Mile Pilots Fret over 6 Gal[lon] Oil Limitation," *CT*, May 24, 1933, 27; E. Y. Watson, "Fuel Limit for Racers," *NYT*, May 13, 1934, XX10; "Petillo Breaks Track Record," *CT*, May 19, 1935, A6; Andy Hamilton, "Speed—Made in Los Angeles," *LAT*, May 24, 1936, I3, I29; "Fuel Restriction at Indianapolis Auto Race Lifted," *CT*, June 27, 1936, 19; "Fuel Limit Race Rule Repealed," *LAT*, June 27, 1936, 14.

20. "Midgets Growing Up," *LAT*, Oct. 1, 1935, A10.

21. Andrew R. Boone, "Racing Midget Autos," *Popular Science Monthly*, May 1934, 26 (quotation); Braven Dyer, "Press Box," *LAT*, Aug. 12, 1934, E3; "New Midget Racing Autos Being Built," *LAT*, Sept. 23, 1934, E4; "Divorce in Auto Racing," *LAT*, Jan. 30, 1936, A10; "Bill Henry Says," *LAT*, July 22, 1937, A9; "Midget Races Keep Boys Fed," *LAT*, May 14, 1940, A10; Bob Smyser, "Bob Swanson Dies after Crash on Ohio Track," *LAT*, June 14, 1940, A13; Todd Gould, *For Gold and*

Glory: Charlie Wiggins and the African-American Racing Car Circuit (Bloomington: Indiana University Press, 2002), 167;

22. E. Y. Watson, "Racing Cars Speedier," *LAT*, May 24, 1931, E2; "Two Racers Killed in Indianapolis Test," *NYT*, May 27, 1931, 7; Hal Foust, "150,000 to See 500 Mile Automobile Race Today," *CT*, May 30, 1931, 11 (quotation).

23. "Benefield's Mechanic Killed in Auto Crash," *NYT*, May 26, 1932, 16; Hal Foust, "Driver Is Killed in Crash on Indianapolis Speedway," *CT*, May 28, 1932, 15; "Auto Driver and Mechanic Die in Speedway Accident," *WP*, May 29, 1933, 9; "Heavy Death Toll Bar to Auto Race," *NYT*, June 4, 1933, E6; "Senator Soaper Says," *LAT*, June 15, 1933, 11; "Two Die as Car Crashes in Speed Test," *CT*, May 26, 1934, 21; Hal Foust, "90,000 to Watch 500 Mile Auto Race Today," *CT*, May 30, 1934, 17 (quotation).

24. Kenneth Crist, "Fame Dies on the Roaring Road," *LAT*, Apr. 8, 1934, G9 (quotations); "Bill Henry Says," *LAT*, May 29, 1934, A9; Reginald M. Cleveland, "Fans from Coast to Coast Swarm to Indianapolis for Automobile Race Today," *NYT*, May 30, 1939, 26.

25. "Victory Prize Is Increased," *LAT*, Oct. 8, 1933, D4. On NRA, see David M. Kennedy, *Freedom from Fear: The American People in Depression and War, 1929–1945* (New York: Oxford University Press, 1999), 177–89.

26. Bill Henry, "Lou Meyer Favored at Indianapolis," *LAT*, May 30, 1934, A7; Paul Gallico, "Speedway Race No Ordinary Sports Event," *WP*, June 1, 1935, 17 (quotation); Harold Harrison, "500-Mile Race Is World's Greatest Democratic Picnic," 1941 Official Program, Rickenbacker collection.

27. "Reveal $3,000,000 Lottery," *NYT*, July 13, 1931, 5; "Auto Speed Kings Will Race Today," *NYT*, May 30, 1934, 23; "50,000 Speedway Lottery Tickets Seized by Police," *CT*, Dec. 17, 1938, 20.

28. "Pass Betting Bill in Indiana House," *NYT*, July 27, 1932, 14; "Indiana Solons Okeh Betting," *LAT*, Feb. 26, 1937, A14; "On the Line with Considine," *WP*, Apr. 13, 1940, X17.

29. William Herschell, "Feel Sorry for the Pessimists of 1909," *IndNews*, May 26, 1934, 9.

30. William Herschell, "Indianapolis Motor Speedway, Warming Up to Its Twenty-Third Sweepstakes," *IndNews*, May 25, 1935, 9. On technology in American culture, see Leo Marx, *The Machine in the Garden: Technology and the Pastoral Ideal in America*, rev. ed. (New York: Oxford University Press, 2000).

31. William Herschell, "Speedway Filled in Early Hours," *IndNews*, May 31, 1937, 22.

32. "Cummings Wins Race," *LAT*, May 31, 1934, 1; Bill Cummings, "Cummings Happy Man," *LAT*, May 31, 1934, A11; Hal Foust, "Cummings Takes 500 Mile Race," *CT*, May 31, 1934, 19; "Cummings Victor in 500-Mile Race," *NYT*, May 31, 1934, 26. Camel ad, *NYT*, June 18, 1934, 12 (quotation). On Wiggins, see Jim Ayello, "Why Aren't There Any Black Drivers in the Indy 500?," *IndyStar*, May 24, 2017, https://

www.indystar.com/story/sports/motor/2017/05/24/why-arent-there-any-black
-drivers-indy-500/340775001/.

33. "Amelia beyond Omaha," *IndNews*, June 1, 1931, 1; "Amelia Earhart Will
Referee Speed Classic," *LAT*, May 20, 1935, 14 (quotations); "50,000 Watch Six
Qualify for Auto Race," *CT*, May 27, 1935, 23; Joseph J. Corn, *The Winged Gospel:
America's Romance with Aviation, 1900–1950* (New York: Oxford University Press,
1983), 122; Edward V. Rickenbacker, *Rickenbacker* (Englewood Cliffs, NJ: Prentice-
Hall, 1967), 189–96, 415–16.

34. William Herschell, "The Driver in the Stands," 1930 Official Program, Rickenbacker collection.

35. "150,000 to See 33 Cars Start 500 Mile Race Today," *CT*, May 30, 1936, 13,
14; "Meyer Wins Classic for Third Time," *LAT*, May 31, 1936, 1, 9, 13 (quotation);
"Young Fan Parks Car 4 Weeks near Track," *NYT*, May 30, 1939, 26; Arch Ward, "In
the Wake of the News," *CT*, Oct. 4, 1939, 27. On women motorists, see Virginia
Scharff, *Taking the Wheel: Women and the Coming of the Motor Age* (Albuquerque:
University of New Mexico Press, 1991).

36. "Three Killed in Race Trials at Indianapolis," *CT*, May 22, 1935, 1; "Three
Auto Racers Killed, One Injured, in Memorial Day Trials at Indianapolis," *NYT*,
May 22, 1935, 1; "Neighbor Asks Court to Ban 500 Mile Race," *CT*, May 26, 1935,
B4 (quotation); "Accelerator Jams; Race Driver Has Narrow Escape," *CT*, May 28,
1935, 25.

37. "Traffic Lights Planned for Indianapolis Race," *WP*, Mar. 7, 1935, 21.

38. Hal Foust, "Petillo Wins Auto Race; One Driver Killed," *CT*, May 31, 1935,
1; "Indianapolis Record Set by Petillo," *LAT*, May 31, 1935, 1; Kelly Petillo, "Petillo
Gives De Paolo Credit for Race Win," *LAT*, May 31, 1935, 10; Frank Finch, "Son of
Banana Peddler Wins Indianapolis Race," *LAT*, May 31, 1935, 10.

39. Paul Gallico, "Speedway a Laboratory, Deaths Not in Vain, Asserts Gallico,"
WP, May 31, 1935, 21 (quotation); "Los Angeles Scores Again," *LAT*, June 1, 1935,
A4.

40. "Standard Has New Auto Oil to Introduce," *LAT*, Dec. 14, 1930, E3; "Test
Tires for Speed," *NYT*, May 28, 1933, XX9; "New Gas Gives Autoists 20% More Mile-
age," *CT*, May 16, 1934, 12; "New 'Heavy' Gasoline of Increased Power Developed
by Standard Oil," *NYT*, May 20, 1934, XX10; "Crosley's New Low Priced Car," *CT*,
Apr. 29, 1939, 23; "New Crosley Auto to Be Sold in Stores," *NYT*, June 14, 1939, 17;
"Motors and Motor Men," *NYT*, July 9, 1939, 130; "1940 Studebaker Champion,"
CT, Oct. 1, 1939, C15.

41. "Speedway Curves May Be Changed to Reduce Crash Peril," *IndNews*, May
30, 1935, 1; "Officials Plan Track Changes," *IndyStar*, May 31, 1935, 13; T. E. Myers
to Fisher, Aug. 8, 1935, 12: 760, Carl Graham Fisher Papers, HistoryMiami Research
Center, Miami, Florida [hereafter, Fisher Papers]; Fisher to T. E. Myers, Aug. 15,
1935, 12: 761–62, Fisher Papers (Fisher quotations); Myers to Fisher, Aug. 23, 1935,
12: 763, Fisher Papers (Myers quotation).

42. Theodore E. (Pop) Myers, "Cites Safety of Speedway," *IndyStar*, May 30, 1936, 32.

43. Rickenbacker to Fisher, Apr. 30, 1937, 15: 1552, Fisher Papers; "Two Race Drivers Hurt," *NYT*, May 16, 1936, 20; "2 Die, 5 Hurt in Accidents on Speedway," *CT*, May 29, 1937, 1; "Speed Race Victim Dies," *NYT*, June 3, 1937, 9; "Veteran Racing Driver Killed at Indianapolis," *WP*, Sept. 21, 1939, 20; "Crash Kills Speed Driver," *NYT*, May 8, 1940, 23; Rickenbacker, *Rickenbacker*, 154 (quotation); James Craig Reinhardt, *The Indianapolis 500: Inside the Greatest Spectacle in Racing* (Bloomington, IN: Red Lightning Books/Indiana University Press, 2019), 19.

44. George Gilman, letter to the editor, *WP*, June 2, 1930, 6.

45. Theodore L. Chase, letter to the editor, *WP*, June 22, 1930, M9.

46. T. Henry, "American Automobile Association."

47. Arch Ward, "Talking It Over," *CT*, May 29, 1936, 21.

48. "Industry Keenly Attuned to Indianapolis Race," *LAT*, May 29, 1938, A6.

49. E. Y. Watson, "Radical Changes in Design of Cars Predicted by Head of National Automobile Organization," *LAT*, June 14, 1931, E4; "See All of Us Driving at 100 Miles an Hour," *NYT*, June 18, 1931, 32.

50. Reginald M. Cleveland, "A Super-highway for America," *NYT*, Nov. 10, 1935, XX1. On bypasses, see "Thru Routes Should Bypass Large Urban Centers, Says Macauley," *Lincoln Highway Forum*, Dec. 1924, 9: 460, Fisher Papers.

51. "The Parkway Passes," *NYT*, June 18, 1937, 20 (quotation); John A. Jakle and Keith A. Sculle, *Motoring: The Highway Experience in America* (Athens: University of Georgia Press, 2008), 152.

52. Fisher to Fred A. Britten, Dec. 31, 1931, 15: 42–43, Fisher Papers; Fisher to Albert Lasker, Mar. 1, 1932, 15: 46, Fisher Papers; Fisher to D. A. Crawford, Dec. 3, 1932, 10: 250, Fisher Papers; Fisher to Sarah Wilford, Dec. 27, 1935, 12: 723–24, Fisher Papers; Mark S. Foster, *Castles in the Sand: The Life and Times of Carl Graham Fisher* (Gainesville: University Press of Florida, 2000), 267–72.

53. "Bill Henry Says," *LAT*, May 25, 1934, A9.

54. "A. C. Newby of Indianapolis Speedway Dies," *CT*, Sept. 12, 1933, 20; "Form Exclusive Club," *LAT*, Apr. 21, 1935, E4; "Four Names Added to '100-Mile-an-Hour Club'," *LAT*, May 26, 1937, A15; "Traf[f]ic Crash Kills Race Pilot Bill Cummings," *CT*, Feb. 9, 1939, 21 (quotation); Paul Zimmerman, "Sport Postscripts," *LAT*, May 28, 1940, A9.

55. "Meyer Is New Iron Man of 500 Mile Race," *CT*, Apr. 18, 1938, 24; "Meyer's 4,385 Miles in Races New Mark on Indianapolis Track," *NYT*, Apr. 18, 1938, 19 (quotation); Andy Hamilton, "'Iron Man' of the Speedway," *LAT*, May 29, 1938, G3.

56. "Race Drivers Last Longer Than Most Sports Notables," *LAT*, May 1, 1938, A12 (quotation); "Shaw's $71,300 Leads Racers at Indianapolis," *CT*, Apr. 14, 1940, B5.

57. Eric Hobsbawm, introduction to *The Invention of Tradition*, ed. Eric Hobsbawm and Terence Ranger (Cambridge: Cambridge University Press, 1983), 1 (quotations), 4–5.

58. "In the Week's Reports," *NYT*, Feb. 23, 1936, XX9; "Borg-Warner $10,000 Trophy," *IndNews*, May 25, 1936, 14; Levi Strauss and Co. ad, *IndyStar*, May 27, 1936, 3 (quotation); "Drivers Attend Pre-race Dinner," *IndNews*, May 29, 1936; "Meyer Is Only Pilot to Win 3 500 Mile Race," *CT*, May 31, 1936, B4; "Meyer Wins Classic for Third Time," *LAT*, May 31, 1936, 1, 9, 13; "Meyer Earns $29,850," *CT*, June 2, 1936, 25. Meyer likely drank traditional buttermilk, which is less viscous than cultured buttermilk.

59. "Wirephotos Sent Direct from Trac[k]," *LAT*, May 31, 1936, 13 (quotation); "Lou Meyer Plans Busy Race Season This Year," *LAT*, June 1, 1936, A9. On Lange, see Linda Gordon, *Dorothea Lange: A Life beyond Limits* (New York: Norton, 2009); *Migrant Mother*, photograph by Dorothea Lange, 1936, in Smithsonian National Museum of American History, https://americanhistory.si.edu/collections/search/object/nmah_1313354.

60. Reinhardt, *Indianapolis 500*, 134.

61. "Legislative Calendar," *IndyStar*, Feb. 27, 1937, 3; "New Buildings, Coupled with Traditions of the Past, Have Stories to Tell Revealing 'The Crossroads of America' as a Center of Progressive Energy," *IndNews*, Feb. 27, 1937, 11 (quotation); James H. Madison, *Indiana through Tradition and Change: A History of the Hoosier State and Its People, 1920–1945* (Indianapolis: Indiana Historical Society, 1982), 208–11.

62. Mary E. Bostwick, "So You're Going to the Speedway," *IndyStar*, May 31, 1937, 41.

63. "Hepburn Close Second in Thrilling Grind," *LAT*, June 1, 1937, A13; Reginald M. Cleveland, "New Indianapolis Auto Record Is Set as Show Triumphs in Thrilling Finish," *NYT*, June 1, 1937, 29; "'We Won!' Checkered Flag Brings Victory Smile," *IndNews*, June 1, 1937, 1; "Wilbur Shaw's Race 'Take' Totals $36,000," *LAT*, June 2, 1937, A13.

64. "Rules Revised for Indianapolis Test," *NYT*, July 22, 1937, 27; "Mirrors to Look Back for Drivers at Indianapolis," *CT*, Apr. 7, 1938, 19; "Hold 1st Trials for Indianapolis Race Saturday," *CT*, May 15, 1938, B10 (quotation); Hal Foust, "Four More Win Right to Start 500 Mile Race," *CT*, May 27, 1938, 27; "Speedway Fans Come from Far Distances," *LAT*, May 31, 1938, A13; "It Takes 364 Days a Year," *IndyStar*, Jan. 28, 1940, 1. On FIFA and the Olympics, see Barbara J. Keys, *Globalizing Sport: National Rivalry and International Community in the 1930s* (Cambridge, MA: Harvard University Press, 2006).

65. "Increase Purse for Indianapolis 500 Mile Race," *CT*, Apr. 3, 1938, B5; "Roberts Sets New Record in Qualifying Run," *CT*, May 22, 1938, B5; W. F. Fox Jr., "Fans from Everywhere in Stands at Speedway Race," *IndNews*, May 30, 1938, 2; Hal Foust, "Roberts Wins Record Auto Race; 1 Killed," *CT*, May 31, 1938, 17; Paul Lowry, "Los Angeles Driver Wins Speed Classic," *LAT*, May 31, 1938, 1; "Roberts Sets Record to Win Indianapolis Auto Classic," *NYT*, May 31, 1938, 24; Cal Whorton, "Dream Nears Fulfillment," *LAT*, May 31, 1938, A13 (quotation); "Roberts Draws $31,950 as Winner of 500 Mile Race," *CT*, June 1, 1938, 24.

66. "Tunney Named Honorary Starter of 500 Mile Race," *CT*, May 11, 1939, 28; "Posters to Aid Race Visitors," *IndyStar*, May 28, 1939, 5; Reginald M. Cleveland, "Fastest 500-Mile Race on Record Presaged by Qualifying Figures," *NYT*, May 29, 1939, 17 (quotation).

67. Hal Foust, "Shaw Wins, Snyder 2nd in Auto Race; 1 Dies," *CT*, May 31, 1939, 17, 20; "Roberts Killed in Big Race; Shaw Victor," *LAT*, May 31, 1939, 1, 19; "Here's How Speed Drivers Finished at Indianapolis," *LAT*, May 31, 1939, 22; Reginald M. Cleveland, "Roberts, 1938 Victor, Dies in Triple Crash as Shaw Takes Indianapolis Race," *NYT*, May 31, 1939, 32; "Wilbur Shaw Wins $27,405," *LAT*, June 1, 1939, A9.

68. "A Big Price for Little," *LAT*, May 31, 1939, A4 (quotation); Reginald M. Cleveland, "Racing Cars Point Way," *NYT*, June 4, 1939, XX8; "Death on the Speedway, from the St. Louis Post-Dispatch," *LAT*, June 8, 1939, A4.

69. "Gehrig, Lewis Contributed to Peak Year," *WP*, Dec. 31, 1939, B5, B7; Daniel J. Simone, "Racing, Region, and the Environment: A History of American Motorsports" (PhD diss., University of Florida, 2009), 74.

70. "Miami Beach Pioneer Dies," *LAT*, July 16, 1939, 2; "Carl G. Fisher Dies; Resort Organizer," *NYT*, July 16, 1939, 33; "'Business before Pleasure,' Discarded by Fisher, Lucky, Versatile Promoter," *IndyStar*, July 16, 1939, 6; "Fisher Noted as Sports Devotee," *IndNews*, July 17, 1939, 13; "Carl G. Fisher, Once Worth 20 Millions, Leaves $40,000," *CT*, July 21, 1939, 12; Benton E. Jacobs, "Miami Beach Talks Honor for Creator," *NYT*, July 23, 1939, E6 (quotation); Foster, *Castles in the Sand*, 297–300, 303; Jerry M. Fisher, *The Pacesetter: The Untold Story of Carl G. Fisher* (Fort Bragg, CA: Lost Coast, 1998), 286–87.

71. "Woman Enters 2 Italian Cars in 500 Mile Race," *CT*, Apr. 25, 1940, 28; Hal Foust, "Shaw Scores 3D Victory in 500 Mile Race," *CT*, May 31, 1940, 19; "Memorial Day Throngs Pack Nation's Stadia," *WP*, May 31, 1940, 25; "'I'll Be Back after No. 4 in 1941'—Shaw," *CT*, May 31, 1940, 23; "Shaw Collects His $31,875 for 3d Race Victory," *CT*, June 1, 1940, 19; "Wilbur Shaw Gets Firestone Air Post," *NYT*, Sept. 1, 1940, 9. On Schell, see Neil Bascomb, *Faster: How a Jewish Driver, an American Heiress, and a Legendary Car Beat Hitler's Best* (Boston: Houghton Mifflin Harcourt, 2020).

Chapter 9. Tradition Never Stops

1. "Carl Fisher Memorial Dedicated in 1941," *Miami History*, accessed Sept. 26, 2021, https://miami-history.com/news/carl-fisher-memorial-dedicated-in-1941/ (first quotation); Fisher to C. B. Floyd, Oct. 9, 1924, 15: 118, Carl Graham Fisher Papers, HistoryMiami Research Center, Miami, Florida (Fisher quotations); Luisa Yanez, "Fisher Island Is a Hot Celebrity Hideout," *South Florida Sun-Sentinel*, Oct. 14, 1996, https://www.sun-sentinel.com/news/fl-xpm-1996–10–14–9610130245-story.html.

2. "G.M. Unit Lets Contract for Plane Engine Plant," *WSJ*, July 23, 1935, 1; "Addition to Engine Plant Starts Soon," *LAT*, Apr. 30, 1939, A18; "Mystery Plant Builds Motors for War Planes," *CT*, Jan. 21, 1940, A5; "More Military Orders Quicken

Factory Work," *CT*, June 20, 1940, 31; "Allison Expanding Steadily to Keep Pace with Orders," *WSJ*, June 20, 1940, 13; Bob Jackson, "Racing to Defense," 1941 Official Program, Edward V. Rickenbacker collection (unprocessed), IMS, Indianapolis [hereafter, Rickenbacker collection].

3. Dick Hyland, "Most Sudden Death," *LAT*, May 26, 1940, 16; Hal Foust, "A Few Theories Are Shot Down by Ace Airman," *CT*, May 30, 1940, 8 (quotation); "Rickenbacker Tells Story of Atlanta Crash," *CT*, Mar. 20, 1941, 10; Bob Considine, "On the Line with Considine," *WP*, Apr. 19, 1941, 15–16; "Rickenbacker Kept in Hospital," *NYT*, May 28, 1941, 3. On German aviation, see Peter Fritzsche, *A Nation of Flyers: German Aviation and the Popular Imagination* (Cambridge, MA: Harvard University Press, 1994).

4. "French Drivers Wait at Lisbon," *LAT*, May 1, 1941, 25; "32 from Europe Arrive on Clipper," *NYT*, May 14, 1941, 12; "Leonard Lyons," *WP*, May 16, 1941, 12; "French Autos Get Chance to Qualify," *NYT*, May 27, 1941, 33; "Litz Gains Place in 500-Mile Race," *NYT*, May 29, 1941, 25; James Craig Reinhardt, *The Indianapolis 500: Inside the Greatest Spectacle in Racing* (Bloomington, IN: Red Lightning Books/Indiana University Press, 2019), 123 (quotations).

5. Hal Foust, "Motorists Look Ahead to May 30 and 3 Day Week-End Outing," *CT*, May 18, 1941, C18, and "Rose Wins Auto Race," *CT*, May 31, 1941, 13–14; "Rose and Davis Team Up to Win Indianapolis Classic," *LAT*, May 31, 1941, 9, 13; "Rose Finishes First in Davis's Car after Shaw Hits Wall at Indianapolis," *NYT*, May 31, 1941, 16; Bob Considine, "Victor Drives Floyd Davis' 'Old Wreck' after 177 Mi[les]," *WP*, May 31, 1941, 15, 17; "On the Line with Considine," *WP*, June 1, 1941, SP1; "Winning Car at Indianapolis Earns $29,985," *CT*, June 1, 1941, B1; "Death Claims Chevrolet, Auto Pioneer," *LAT*, June 7, 1941, 9.

6. Phillips J. Peck, "Why Is a Race Driver?," 1941 Official Program, Rickenbacker collection.

7. "Defense Bond Quiz," *WST*, July 12, 1941, 3; "500-Mile Race Will Go On," *LAT*, July 2, 1941, 17; "Go On with Plans for Indianapolis 500 Mile Event," *CT*, Dec. 28, 1941, A6; "500-Mile Race Off until War Is Won," *NYT*, Dec. 30, 1941, 26 (quotation); W. F. Fox Jr., "No Race Today—the 500-Milers Are Helping Win the War," *IndNews*, May 30, 1942, 4; Al Bloemker, *500 Miles to Go: The Story of the Indianapolis Speedway* (New York: Coward-McCann, 1961), 206.

8. "Sports Prepared to Carry On," *NYT*, Dec. 9, 1941, 49; Jack Guenther, "U.S. Sports May Continue despite the War," *WP*, Dec. 9, 1941, 26; Considine, "On the Line with Considine," *WP*, Jan. 18, 1942, SP2 (his quotation); "Veteran Head of Indianapolis Speedway Quits," *CT*, Jan. 6, 1942, 23; "'Pop' Myers Leaves Post at Speedway," *IndyStar*, Jan. 6, 1942, 1 (Myers quotation), 12.

9. "500 Mile Race Off; May Run Shorter Event," *CT*, Dec. 30, 1941; "Auto Racing Prohibited for Duration," *WP*, July 4, 1942, 16 (quotation).

10. "Indianapolis' Famed Track Silent Today," *WP*, May 30, 1942, 14 (quotation); "By the Way with Bill Henry," *LAT*, Feb. 10, 1943, A1; "DePaolo, Famed Race Driver, Awarded Legion of Merit," *LAT*, May 23, 1945, 8.

11. "Silent, Deserted Speedway Lives in Memory of War Working Racers," *IndyStar*, May 30, 1943, 12 (quotation); "Indianapolis District Golfers Chase Dick McCreary at Speedway," *IndNews*, June 16, 1943, 20; "Speedway Dimout First in County," *IndNews*, Aug. 5, 1942, 1, 4; "County Holds First Blackout in Speedway near Vital War Plants," *IndNews*, Oct. 8, 1942, 10; Joseph J. Corn, *The Winged Gospel: America's Romance with Aviation, 1900–1950* (New York: Oxford University Press, 1983), 123.

12. "Night Driving to Industrial Areas about Chicago Rises 50%," *NYT*, June 14, 1942, 29; "The Week in Business," *WP*, Sept. 20, 1942, R4; Hal Foust, "Alcohol as Auto Fuel before War Ends Is Foreseen," *CT*, Nov. 8, 1942, 18, and "Trib-Buna Tires to Get 500 Mile Workout Today," *CT*, Aug. 28, 1943, 3, and "Trib-Buna Ties Real Rubber in 500-Mile Test," *CT*, Aug. 29, 1943, 1 (quotations); "New Synthetic Rubber Tires Stand Up in Test," *LAT*, Aug. 29, 1943, 17; "Synthetic Auto Tires Stand Up in a Grind," *NYT*, Aug. 29, 1943, 40; "Trib-Buna Tire Test Extended to Use on Road," *CT*, Aug. 31, 1943, 6; Foust, "Trib-Buna Tire Test Shows Life of 27,280 Miles," *CT*, Sept. 5, 1943, 7; Braven Dyer, "The Sports Parade," *LAT*, June 6, 1945, 10. On synthetic rubber, see Daniel Immerwahr, *How to Hide an Empire: A History of the Greater United States* (New York: Farrar, Straus, and Giroux, 2019), 269.

13. Howard F. Wentworth, untitled article, *WP*, Nov. 15, 1940, 25; Christopher W. Wells, *Car Country: An Environmental History* (Seattle: University of Washington Press, 2012), 196–98. On Futurama, see Robert W. Rydell, *World of Fairs: The Century-of-Progress Exhibitions* (Chicago: University of Chicago Press, 1993), 133–35.

14. A. K. Estill, "Express Highways," *WSJ*, Feb. 16, 1944, 1. On the Pennsylvania Turnpike, see John A. Jakle and Keith A. Sculle, *Motoring: The Highway Experience in America* (Athens: University of Georgia Press, 2008), 152–53.

15. "Auto Races Called Test Laboratory," *NYT*, Oct. 26, 1945, 21; Bert Pierce, "Traffic and Parking Snarl Faced by American Cities," *NYT*, Dec. 31, 1945, 1, 8; Coleman ad, *IndyStar*, Jan. 21, 1945, 29 (quotation); "Auto Route to Schloss Home Place Described," *IndyStar*, June 9, 1940, 36. On GI Bill and FHA, see Glenn C. Altschuler and Stuart M. Blumin, *The GI Bill: The New Deal for Veterans* (New York: Oxford University Press, 2009), 198–202; Richard Rothstein, *The Color of Law: A Forgotten History of How Our Government Segregated America* (New York: Liveright, 2017), 70–75.

16. "Speedway Ghostly for 2d Straight Memorial Day," *WP*, May 28, 1944, M6; "Legion Group Takes Option on Auto Speedway," *CT*, Aug. 18, 1944, 19; "June 2 Likely Date of Kentucky Derby," *NYT*, May 10, 1945, 26; Arthur Daley, "Sports of the Times," *NYT*, May 30, 1945, 22; Robert Shaplen, "Hoosier Pied Piper, Part I," *Sports Illustrated*, May 25, 1958, 75 (quotation).

17. Bert Pierce, "New Auto Devices to Be Tested in '46," *NYT*, June 3, 1945, 30 (quotation); Bob Deindorfer, "Science Comes to Sports," *LAT*, Oct. 21, 1945, E10.

18. "Predicts New Era in Racing by Autos," *NYT*, Aug. 19, 1945, S7.

19. "War Air Aces Seen as New Speedway Stars," *WP*, Aug. 25, 1945, 6.

20. "O.D.T. Lifts Ban on Sports Travel," *LAT*, Aug. 17, 1945, A7; "Lifting of Sports Curbs Opens Way for All Big Fall and Winter Events," *NYT*, Aug. 18, 1945, 14; "Indianapolis Auto Track Sold by Rickenbacker for $750,000," *NYT*, Nov. 15, 1945, 22 (quotations); "Indianapolis 500 Mile Auto Speedway Sold," *CT*, Nov. 15, 1945, 37; Sigur E. Whitaker, *Tony Hulman: The Man Who Saved the Indianapolis Motor Speedway* (Jefferson, NC: McFarland, 2014), 5–6.

21. Wilbur Shaw, *Gentlemen, Start Your Engines* (New York: Coward-McCann, 1955), 274–76 (quotations), 279–81; Robert Shaplen, "Hoosier Pied Piper, Part II," *Sports Illustrated*, June 2, 1958, 61–62.

22. "Speedway Improvements Will Require $250,000," *NYT*, Feb. 27, 1946, 36; "Bardowski, Corregidor Veteran, Sparks Trials for Auto Classic," *NYT*, May 20, 1946, 17; "Rocket Speeds Car 130 M.P.H.," *CT*, May 22, 1946, 29; "The Speedway Gets a Facial," *IndNews*, May 29, 1946, 20; "Raytheon to Test Its Radio Phone at Speedway Race," *WSJ*, May 29, 1946, 5; Whitaker, *Tony Hulman*, 16.

23. Gene Dawson, "Flyboys Swarm to Race," *IndNews*, May 29, 1946, 10 (quotation); "Airports Crowded as 'Fly to Race' Fan Numbers Grow," *IndNews*, May 30, 1946, 1.

24. "Hold Your Hats, It's Doin' 6 Per!" *IndNews*, May 29, 1946, 26; Bert Pierce, "Auto Classic Won by George Robson," *NYT*, May 31, 1946, 18; Mary E. Bostwick, "Festive Crowds Greet Return of Race Classic," *IndStar*, May 31, 1946, 1 (quotation), 3; "Two Auto Racing Drivers Killed; One Won the Indianapolis Classic," *NYT*, Sept. 3, 1946, 1, 20.

25. Domenica Bongiovanni, "Indy 500: The Surprising History of '(Back Home Again in) Indiana' and Everyone Who Sang It," *IndyStar*, May 16, 2019, https://www.indystar.com/story/entertainment/indy-500/2019/05/16/everyone-who-sang-back-home-again-indiana-indy-500-jim-nabors-neighbors-indianapolis-motor-speedway/1154040001/; Reinhardt, *Indianapolis 500*, 118.

26. "Jack Johnson Loses Life in Auto Crash," *CT*, June 11, 1946, 25; "Jack Johnson Dies in Auto Crash," *NYT*, June 11, 1946, 1.

27. Avery Yang, "Wendell Scott Faced Discrimination from NASCAR, but Kept Winning Anyway," *Sports Illustrated*, Feb. 5, 2020, https://www.si.com/racing/2020/02/05/black-history-month-wendell-scott. On baseball's color line, see Ryan A. Swanson, *When Baseball Went White: Reconstruction, Reconciliation, and Dreams of a National Pastime* (Lincoln: University of Nebraska Press, 2014).

28. Jim Murray, "Ribbs Is Built for Speed," *LAT*, May 23, 1991, OCC1 (quotations); Jim Ayello, "Why Aren't There Any Black Drivers in the Indy 500?," *IndyStar*, May 24, 2017: https://www.indystar.com/story/sports/motor/2017/05/24/why-arent-there-any-black-drivers-indy-500/340775001/. On scientific racism, see Jaime Schultz, "Racialized Osteology and Athletic Aptitude, or 'Black' Bones as Red Herrings," *Journal of Sport History* 46, no. 3 (Fall 2019): 325–46.

29. Shaplen, "Hoosier Pied Piper, Part I," 69–70, 75–77. On Camp, see Roger R. Tamte, *Walter Camp and the Creation of American Football* (Urbana: University of Illinois Press, 2018).

30. Shaplen, "Hoosier Pied Piper, Part II," 60–62.

31. Ibid., 63–64.

32. Early usages include Socony Mobil ad, *LAT*, June 1, 1959, A11; "Green Flag for Ruttman in Indy '500'," *LAT*, Jan. 17, 1960, C9; Chicago Auto Racing ad, *CT*, June 4, 1960, A3; "At Indy," *Austin Statesman*, May 30, 1963; "Sports' New Faces Put on Dandy Show," *WP*, Dec. 27, 1963, A19. By 1962, it was common enough to be used in a newsletter at Guantanamo Bay naval base: George Thomson, "Sports," *Sunday Supplement*, May 27, 1962, 4. The first usage found in the *New York Times* is Robert A. Wright, "The Indianapolis 500—It's a 3½-Hour Commercial," *NYT*, May 28, 1967, 11. The term may have originated in midget car racing.

33. Shaplen, "Hoosier Pied Piper, Part I," 70 (quotation), 72–74, 77–78.

34. John Kieran, "Sports of the Times," *NYT*, Apr. 30, 1939, 86; Arthur J. Dailey, "Academy of Sports Previewed at Fair," *NYT*, June 14, 1939, 34 (quotation). On nostalgia at the 1939 fair, see Marco Duranti, "Utopia, Nostalgia and World War at the 1939–40 New York World's Fair," *Journal of Contemporary History* 41, no. 4 (Oct. 2006): 663–83.

35. Kenneth J. Bindas, *Modernity and the Great Depression: The Transformation of American Society, 1930–1941* (Lawrence: University Press of Kansas, 2017), 117 (quotation), 162; Steven Watts, *The People's Tycoon: Henry Ford and the American Century* (New York: Vintage, 2005), 403–15.

36. Donald Davidson, Ellen Bireley, and Don A. Armbruster, *Indianapolis Motor Speedway Hall of Fame Museum* (Lawrenceburg, IN: Creative Company, 2005), 4; Whitaker, *Tony Hulman*, 151–52; "Wilbur Shaw Museum Planned," *NYT*, May 5, 1955, 48; "*Speedway* Museum for Shaw Is Set," *IndyStar*, May 30, 1955, 34; "Hard to Break," *IndNews*, July 26, 1955, 13; "500's Great Moments Relived in New Speedway Museum," *IndyStar*, May 30, 1956, 29 (quotation); W. F. Fox Jr., "The Yarnin' Basket," *IndNews*, Sept. 29, 1956, 15.

37. "Speedway Getting to Be a Showplace," *IndNews*, May 29, 1956, 26; "Speedway Boasts 'New Look' Offices, Museum," *IndyStar*, May 30, 1956, 36 (quotations).

38. Jonathan Levy, *Ages of American Capitalism: A History of the United States* (New York: Random House, 2021), xiv.

39. "Wilbur Shaw Dies in Air Crash, Won Top Auto Race Three Times," *NYT*, Oct. 31, 1954, 1; Gilbert Millstein, "Why They Race," *NYT*, May 24, 1959, SM23; Mark Chandler, "Here's a Museum for Dad and the Boys: Racing Cars!," *CT*, May 20, 1962, F5 (quotations); Ray Sons, "'500' Roadsters Now Are Museum Pieces," *WP*, May 23, 1965, C4; Whitaker, *Tony Hulman*, 152–55.

40. Ginny Ade, "Indianapolis: More Than '500'," *CT*, May 2, 1976, C10–11; "Speedway Museum," *IndNews*, May 10, 1976, 18; "Popular Place," *IndNews*, May 20, 1976, 31; Whitaker, *Tony Hulman*, 155. On the Bicentennial, see Tammy S. Gordon, *The Spirit of 1976: Commerce, Community, and the Politics of Commemoration* (Amherst: University of Massachusetts Press, 2012).

41. Martin Luther King Jr., "Letter from a Birmingham Jail," Apr. 16, 1963 (quotation), *African Studies Center, University of Pennsylvania*, https://www.africa.upenn.edu/Articles_Gen/Letter_Birmingham.html. On interstates, family vacations, and Black automobility, see Mark H. Rose and Raymond A. Mohl, *Interstate: Highway Politics and Policy since 1939*, 3rd ed. (Knoxville: University of Tennessee Press, 2012); Susan Sessions Rugh, *Are We There Yet? The Golden Age of American Family Vacations* (Lawrence: University Press of Kansas, 2008); Gretchen Sorkin, *Driving While Black: African American Travel and the Road to Civil Rights* (New York: Liveright, 2020); Mia Bay, *Traveling Black: A Story of Race and Resistance* (Cambridge, MA: Belknap, 2021), 107–50. On housing inequality, see Keeanga-Yamahtta Taylor, *Race for Profit: How Banks and the Real Estate Industry Undermined Black Homeownership* (Chapel Hill: University of North Carolina Press, 2019).

42. Lewis Mumford, *The Highway and the City* (New York: Harcourt, Brace, and World, 1963), 234–37.

43. Jeremiah B. C. Axelrod, *Inventing Autopia: Dreams and Visions of the Modern Metropolis in Jazz Age Los Angeles* (Berkeley: University of California Press, 2009), 252–59, 297–304.

44. "It Takes 364 Days a Year," *IndyStar*, Jan. 28, 1940, 1; Joseph J. Cripe, "Why Not a 'Speedway Week'?" *IndNews*, May 29, 1946, 15 (quotation).

45. Corbin Patrick, "City Could Improve Its Tourist Appeal," *IndyStar*, Mar. 4, 1956, 23.

46. Richard Wager, "Auto Racing Year Round Lure to Indianapolis," *CT*, Nov. 27, 1963, G3. On Miami Beach's influence, see Hal Rothman, *Devil's Bargains: Tourism in the Twentieth-Century American West* (Lawrence: University Press of Kansas, 1998), 296, 299.

47. Jesse Berrett, *Pigskin Nation: How the NFL Remade American Politics* (Urbana: University of Illinois Press, 2018), 18 (quotation); Benjamin G. Rader, *Baseball: A History of America's Game*, 3rd ed. (Urbana: University of Illinois Press, 2008), 94.

48. Wray Vamplew, "Facts and Artefacts: Sports Historians and Sports Museums," *Journal of Sport History* 25, no. 2 (Summer 1998): 270 (quotation); *Representing the Sporting Past in Museums and Halls of Fame*, ed. Murray G. Phillips (London: Routledge, 2012).

49. Pierre Nora, "Between Memory and History: *Les Lieux de Mémoire*," *Representations* 26 (Spring 1989): 7–24. On sport memory, see Rita Liberti and Maureen M. Smith, *(Re)Presenting Wilma Rudolph* (Syracuse, NY: Syracuse University Press, 2015).

50. Author visit to Indianapolis Motor Speedway Museum, June 8, 2021.

51. Richard Lugar, "Indianapolis Motor Speedway and the Indianapolis 500," *Congressional Record—Senate*, Apr. 25, 1996, S4252 (quotations); see also André Carson, "Indianapolis Motor Speedway," *Congressional Record—House*, May 26, 2011, H3686, and *Congressional Record—House*, May 17, 2016, H2436.

52. André Carson, et al., H. Res. 608, 111th Cong., 1st Sess., July 7, 2009, 1–4; Evan Bayh and Richard Lugar, S. Res. 207, 111th Cong., 1st Sess., July 6, 2009, 1–4.

53. Leonard Wiener, "Selling Business on a Locale—Extolling Positives," *CT*, Dec. 30, 1974, C7 (quotation); William Blomquist and Roger B. Parks, "Fiscal, Service, and Political Impacts of Indianapolis-Marion County's Unigov," *Publius* 25, no. 4 (Autumn 1995): 48, 53; Neil deMause and Joanna Cagan, *Field of Schemes: How the Great Stadium Swindle Turns Public Money into Private Profit*, rev. ed. (Lincoln: University of Nebraska Press, 2008), 4–5; Whitaker, *Tony Hulman*, 128.

54. Jeffrey Tenuth, *Indianapolis: A Circle City History* (Charleston, SC: Arcadia, 2004), 140; Daniel Rosensweig, *Retro Ball Parks: Instant History, Baseball, and the New American City* (Knoxville: University of Tennessee Press, 2005); Benjamin D. Lisle, *Modern Coliseum: Stadiums and American Culture* (Philadelphia: University of Pennsylvania Press, 2017), 255–59 ("urbanoid"); Zach Osterman, Gregg Doyel, and Dana Hunsinger Benbow, "It's Official: 2021 NCAA Tournament to Be Played Entirely in Central Indiana," *IndyStar*, Jan. 4, 2021, https://www.indystar.com/story/sports/college/2021/01/04/2021-march-madness-played-entirely-indianapolis-central-indiana/4124594001/.

55. Annie Gilbert Coleman, "Making Time and Place at the Indy 500," *Environmental History* 16 (Apr. 2011): 330.

56. Philip O'Kane, "A History of the 'Triple Crown' of Motor Racing: The Indianapolis 500, the Le Mans 24 Hours and the Monaco Grand Prix," *International Journal of the History of Sport* 28, no. 2 (Feb. 2011): 282, 284.

57. Fredric Jameson, *Postmodernism; or, The Cultural Logic of Late Capitalism* (Durham, NC: Duke University Press, 1991).

58. Jane Fisher, *Fabulous Hoosier: A Story of American Achievement* (New York: Robert M. McBride, 1947), 241.

59. S. Paul O'Hara, *Gary, The Most American of All American Cities* (Bloomington: Indiana University Press, 2011), 158–63; Andrew R. Highsmith, *Demolition Means Progress: Flint, Michigan, and the Fate of the American Metropolis* (Chicago: University of Chicago Press, 2015), 258–61; Sherry Lee Linkon, *Steeltown U.S.A.: Work and Memory in Youngstown* (Lawrence: University Press of Kansas, 2002); Gabriel Winant, *The Next Shift: The Fall of Industry and the Rise of Health Care in Rust Belt America* (Cambridge, MA: Harvard University Press, 2021).

60. Deborah B. Markisohn, "Slogans and Nicknames," in *Encyclopedia of Indianapolis*, ed. David J. Bodenhamer and Robert G. Barrows (Bloomington: Indiana University Press, 1994), 1267 (quotation). On Detroit, see Thomas J. Sugrue, *The Origins of the Urban Crisis: Race and Inequality in Postwar Detroit*, updated ed. (Princeton, NJ: Princeton University Press, 2013). On the historical relationship between the Rust Belt and the Sunbelt, see Brian M. Ingrassia, "Rust Belt Problems, Sunbelt Solutions: St. Louis, Dallas-Fort Worth, and the Migratory History of the 'Metroplex' Concept," *Southwestern Historical Quarterly* 126, no. 3 (Jan. 2023): 305–31.

61. Author visit to Indianapolis Motor Speedway, June 9, 2021.

INDEX

BRIAN M. INGRASSIA is an associate professor of history at West Texas A&M University and the author of *The Rise of Gridiron University: Higher Education's Uneasy Alliance with Big-Time Football*.

Pigskin Nation: How the NFL Remade American Politics   *Jesse Berrett*

Hockey: A Global History   *Stephen Hardy and Andrew C. Holman*

Baseball: A History of America's Game   *Benjamin G. Rader*

Kansas City vs. Oakland: The Bitter Sports Rivalry That Defined an Era
    Matthew C. Ehrlich

The Gold in the Rings: The People and Events That Transformed the Olympic Games
    Stephen R. Wenn and Robert K. Barney

Before March Madness: The Wars for the Soul of College Basketball
    Kurt Edward Kemper

The Sport Marriage: Women Who Make It Work   *Steven M. Ortiz*

NFL Football: A History of America's New National Pastime, NFL Centennial
    Edition   *Richard C. Crepeau*

Passing the Baton: Black Women Track Stars and American Identity   *Cat M. Ariail*

Degrees of Difficulty: How Women's Gymnastics Rose to Prominence and Fell
    from Grace   *Georgia Cervin*

From Football to Soccer: The Early History of the Beautiful Game in the
    United States   *Brian D. Bunk*

Tennis: A History from American Amateurs to Global Professionals   *Greg Ruth*

Surf and Rescue: George Freeth and the Birth of California Beach Culture
    Patrick Moser

Dyed in Crimson: Football, Faith, and Remaking Harvard's America   *Zev Eleff*

Beyond the Black Power Salute: Athlete Activism in an Era of Change
    Gregory J. Kaliss

Speed Capital: Indianapolis Auto Racing and the Making of Modern America
    Brian M. Ingrassia

REPRINT EDITIONS

The Nazi Olympics   *Richard D. Mandell*

Sports in the Western World (2nd ed.)   *William J. Baker*

Jesse Owens: An American Life   *William J. Baker*

The University of Illinois Press
is a founding member of the
Association of University Presses.

———————————————————————

University of Illinois Press
1325 South Oak Street
Champaign, IL 61820–6903
www.press.uillinois.edu